Classics in Graph Theory

Recollections from my teaching

Franz Rothe

Word Art Publishing
9350 Wilshire Blvd
Suite 203, Beverly Hills, CA 90212
www.wordartpublishing.com
Phone: 1 (888) 614 - 1370

© 2021 Franz Rothe. All rights reserved.

No part of this book may be reproduced, stored in a retrieval system, or transmitted by any means without the written permission of the author.

Published by Word Art Publishing

ISBN:	Paperback	978-1-955070-04-1
	Hardback	978-1-955070-07-2
	Ebook	978-1-955070-05-8

Because of the dynamic nature of the Internet, any web addresses or links contained in this book may have changed since publication and may no longer be valid. The opinions expressed in this manuscript are solely the opinions of the author and do not represent the opinions or thoughts of the publisher and the publisher hereby disclaims any responsibility for them. The author has represented and warranted full ownership and/or legal right to publish all the materials in this book.

Introduction

The *front cover* shows a 3-regular, 3-connected, 3-edge-colorable graph which is neither Hamiltonian, nor bipartite, nor planar. See figure on page 230. The exact logical relations of these different properties for graphs are treated starting page 193.

The *back cover* shows an electrical network and how is to be labelled for the calculation of the voltages and currents. See the figure on page 132.

Preface

Charlotte, January 11, 2021

This book has been growing during the last year exploiting many resources: my unfinished notes, recollecting material taught and not taught my time at the University of North Carolina at Charlotte, some of my online notes from these courses, some internet searches, some new ideas during writing,—to make it short out of an unfinished career that was unexpectedly interrupted by my eye problems.

After being forced to retire about four years ago, I did continue to occupy myself with several topics from mathematics. Too, I finally took the time and effort to learn mathematica and use it to support my work. Because of the diversity and amount of topics, and to be able to present a book of handy size, I have divided the material into two volumes. The book in hand in just the first half, and the second half is to follow.

Some material is much more concrete and computationally oriented than a math course at a university, other sections heavily depend on proofs worked out in all details, more carefully than possible in a short lecture. For most of the problems, but not all, solutions are included. In spite of all this, I want to remind the reader that this book cannot be read like a novel. The reader should not be disappointed while slowing down. Indeed paper and pencil at hand are advisable.

Here is a paragraph by Hermann Weyl fitting nicely to the intention of the present book.

> Important though the general concepts and propositions may be with which the modern and industrious passion for axiomatizing and generalizing has presented us, in algebra perhaps more than everywhere else, nevertheless I am convinced that the special problems in all their complexity constitute the stock and core of mathematics, and that to master their difficulties requires on the whole the harder labor.

classification: 05C10 05C30 68R10 68Wxx
keywords: Instructional exposition, Graph theory (including graph drawing), Algorithms, Planar graphs, geometric and topological aspects of graph theory, Enumeration in graph theory

Contents

I Classical Topics   3

- I.1 First Encounter with Graphs 5
  - I.1.1 The definition 5
  - I.1.2 Names and notation for the basic graphs 8
  - I.1.3 The handshaking lemma 10
  - I.1.4 Walk, trail, path and circuit and cycle 12
  - I.1.5 Connected and disconnected graphs 14
  - I.1.6 Clique, independence and complement 16
  - I.1.7 Isomorphism 18
  - I.1.8 Automorphism group 26
  - I.1.9 Bipartite graphs 30
  - I.1.10 Matching and covering 33
  - I.1.11 Subsets and multisubsets 36
  - I.1.12 Counting labelled and unlabelled graphs 36
  - I.1.13 Cartesian products 38
  - I.1.14 Series of special graphs 38
  - I.1.15 The degree sequence 43
  - I.1.16 About nonexistence of triangles 46
  - I.1.17 Instant insanity 48
- I.2 Eulerian Graphs 53
  - I.2.1 Existence of cycles 60
  - I.2.2 More about Eulerian properties 63
  - I.2.3 More Cartesian products 66
- I.3 Hamiltonian Graphs 67
  - I.3.1 Necessary for Hamiltonian properties 72
  - I.3.2 Sufficient assumptions insuring Hamiltonian properties 81
  - I.3.3 Eulerian and Hamiltonian properties 91
- I.4 Matrix representations of graphs 92
- I.5 The line graph 94
- I.6 Trees 99
  - I.6.1 Rooted trees 103
  - I.6.2 Labeled trees 105
  - I.6.3 Braced frames 107

		I.6.4 Spanning trees	109

- I.7 Algorithms ... 111
  - I.7.1 Heuristic methods for the traveling salesman problem ... 114
  - I.7.2 Dijstra's algorithm ... 119
  - I.7.3 Maximal flow ... 122
  - I.7.4 The Hungarian Algorithm ... 125
- I.8 Electrical Networks ... 128
  - I.8.1 Justification of the electrical network calculation ... 136
- I.9 The Matrix-Tree Theorem ... 139
  - I.9.1 Once more electrical networks ... 144
- I.10 Connectivity ... 145
  - I.10.1 Block-cutvertex decomposition ... 148
- I.11 Menger's Theorem ... 149
- I.12 Planar Graphs ... 153
  - I.12.1 The two handshaking lemmas and Euler's formula ... 153
  - I.12.2 Euler's formula and Hamiltonian cycles ... 155
  - I.12.3 Book-keeping the lengths of faces ... 164
  - I.12.4 Other planarity considerations ... 170
  - I.12.5 Planarity Testing ... 171
  - I.12.6 Some mixed Problems ... 178
- I.13 Coloring ... 184
  - I.13.1 Vertex coloring ... 184
  - I.13.2 Planar and Eulerian graphs ... 191
  - I.13.3 Planar, three-regular and bipartite graphs ... 192
  - I.13.4 Edge coloring ... 193
- I.14 More about 3-regular graphs ... 199
  - I.14.1 Tait's conjecture and counterexamples ... 199
  - I.14.2 Face and edge coloring ... 203
  - I.14.3 Tutte's conjecture and counterexamples ... 206
  - I.14.4 Barnette's conjectures ... 214
  - I.14.5 Snarks ... 215
  - I.14.6 The landscape of 3-regular graphs ... 225
  - I.14.7 Questions ... 235
- I.15 An independent proof of the Four-Color Theorem ... 238

Part I

Classical Topics

I.1 First Encounter with Graphs

I.1.1 The definition

Definition 1 (Graph). A graph consists of a finite set of vertices and a finite set of edges. Each edge has two *ends* or *end-vertices*, which may be equal or distinct.

For the graph G we denote the set of vertices by $V(G)$ and the set of edges by $E(G)$. The number of vertices is usually denoted by letter n or v and is called the *order* of the graph. The number of edges is usually denoted by letter m or e. Some authors call the graph with only one vertex and no edges the trivial graph. [1]

Definition 2 (Simple graph and general graph). A *loop* is an edge for which both ends are equal. A graph is called *loopless* iff each edge has two distinct ends. Two or more edges with the same ends a called multiple edges. A graph with neither loops nor multiple edges is called *simple*.

It is common usage, also followed in this book, to restrict attention to simple graphs without explicit notice. On the contrary, when we want to stress that the graph in question need not to be simple, we talk about a *general graph*.

Definition 3 (Adjacencies). Two vertices are called *adjacent* iff they are the ends of the same edge. Two edges are called adjacent iff they have one or two common ends. An edge and a vertex are called adjacent iff the vertex is an end of the edge.

Basically there are four different ways to specify a graph. This situation is a bid similar to the four ways a function may be defined in calculus.

- A graph may be specified by drawing a figure. The edges are depicted as any segments, which are allowed by be both straight or curved. The vertices are given by dots at the ends of these segments. It must be allowed that the segments for different edges have additional crossings that are not considered to be vertices. Therefore, it is necessary to depict the vertices clearly, for example by making them a bid larger dots.

- Directly as defined, a graph may be given by listing its vertices, listing its edges, and stating their adjacencies. The order of these listings are arbitrary and have to be disregarded.

- One may fix an arbitrary order for the above listings, and give the adjacenies of vertices as the *adjacency matrix*, and the adjacencies between vertices and edges as the *incidence matrix*. Both matrices gets entries 0 meaning nonadjacent and 1 for adjacent. Entry 2 occurs in the incidence matrix at a loop.

---

[1] The word trivial is often abused in mathematics,—here especially seriously. Indeed one can introduce an empty graph and call it trivial, too. But the graph with one single vertex is not empty!

- A graph may be defined while working with any other more abstract structure. In that context, it needs to be explained *how* this underlying structure is used to define the vertices, how to define the edges, and state how it has to be decided whether a vertex and an edge are adjacent. One needs to check *inside the underlying structure* that these explanations produce a graph. It really needs a proof to justify the definition of a graph from the underlying structure. Only after such a proof has been achieved, we may say that the graph is *well defined*.

Graphs appear naturally in many applications from mathematics, natural and social sciences. To mention a few, there are the three- and higher dimensional polyhedra and polytopes in geometry, the electrical networks, chemical compounds, and social networks. In the applications, the vertices and edges usually get additional properties like weights, colors and other individual properties. Such graphs are commonly called *networks*.

Problem 1. *We give in figure 6 a graph with vertices $A, \ldots, M$ that shows the various routes one can take when tracing the labyrinth shown to the left. Use the graph to list all the routes from center A to exit M that do not retrace edges. Add to the graph extra vertices, and post some more signs in the labyrinth to produce a more reliable guide for less experienced visitors.*

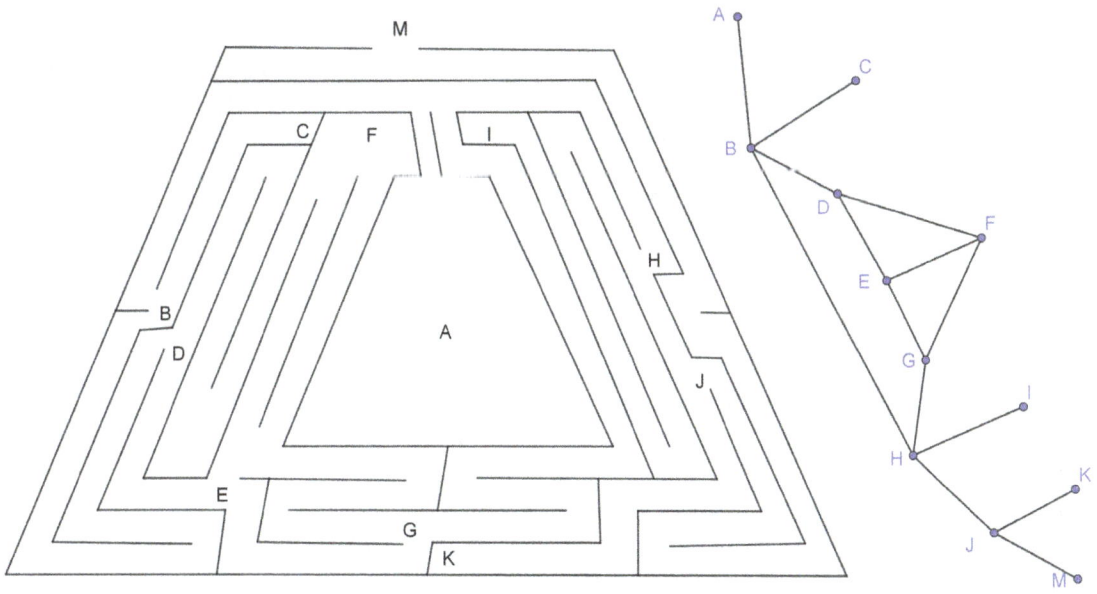

Figure 1: A labyrinth and a guiding graph.

Problem 2. *There are six people at a party. We claim: one can always find either three people who all know each other, or three people none of whom knows neither of the other two. Prove this statement. You can begin:*

We use the graph with the six people as vertices, and an edge between any two people who know each other. Take any person A.

At first, we suppose that person A knows at least three other guests B, C and D. ...

Now we suppose the contrary that person A has at most two friends among the guests. Hence there are three persons U, V or W, which A does not know. ...

Answer. We use the graph with the six people as vertices, and an edge between any two people who know each other. Take any person A.

At first, we suppose that person A knows at least three other guests B, C and D.

If all three guests B, C and D do not know the other two among B, C, D, we are ready. Otherwise two of them know each other, and both know A. Hence we have found there people which all know each other.

Now we suppose the contrary that person A has at most two friends among the guests. Hence there are three persons U, V or W, which A does not know.

If all three guests U, V and W know the other two, we are ready. Otherwise two of them do not know each other, and both do not know A. Hence we have found there people which all do not know each other.

Problem 3. *A youth club organizer wishes to arrange outings to a zoo for the nine children: Andrew, Bob, Catherine, Deirdre, Edward, Fiona, Gina, Harry and Iris. Unfortunately, Catherine refuses to go on an outing with any of the boys; Andrew will not go if there are any girls except Deirdre; Edward and Harry must not be allowed to go together since they will cause havoc; Fiona cannot stand Bob or Gina; and Bob and Edward both dislike Iris.*

(i) *Put the kids in big circle. Express the information given above by a graph with the dislikes as edges.*

(ii) *How many edges has the dislike graph?*

(iii) *How many edges has its complement, the like-graph?*

(iv) *Convince yourself that three outings or more are needed, explain why.*

(v) *Find a solution how to go with three outings. Color red the kids for the outing where Andrew goes;— green the kids where Catherine goes; finally blue the kids of the third group.*

Answer. **(i)** Put the kids in big circle. Express the information given above by a graph with the dislikes as edges.

(ii) The dislike graph has 12 edges.

(iii) The complete graph with 9 vertices has $9 \cdot 8 / 2 = 36$ edges. Hence the complement like-graph has $36 - 12 = 24$ edges.

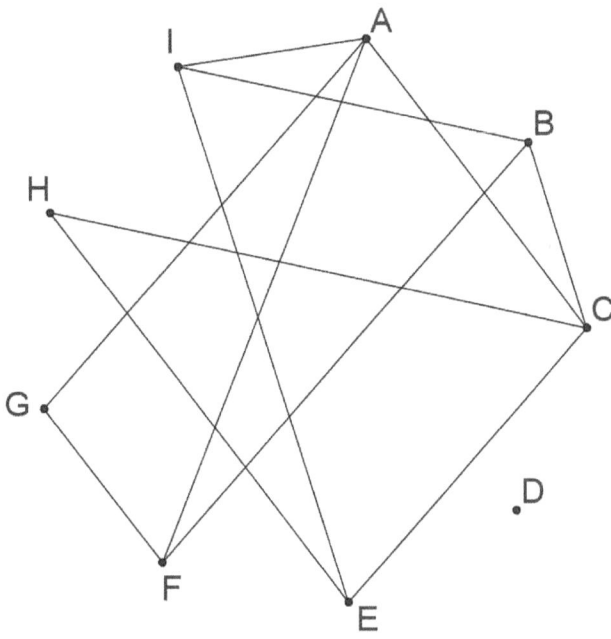

Figure 2: Nine kids go to the zoo.

(iv) Since triangles exist as subgraph, one needs three outings or more.

(v) Find a solution how to go with three outings. Color red the kids for the outing where Andrew goes;— green the kids where Catherine goes; finally blue the kids of the third group.

I.1.2 Names and notation for the basic graphs

Any graph with no edges at all is called a *null graph*. There exists the null graph N_n for each natural number $n \geq 1$. The complement of the null graph is the *complete graph* K_n. Again, the subscript gives the number of vertices. The graph K_n is simple and has exactly one edge between any two distinct vertices, thus altogether $\frac{n(n-1)}{2}$ edges. For any pair (a,b) of natural numbers, there exists the *complete bipartite graph* denoted by $K_{a,b}$. This graph has $n = a + b$ vertices which now are separated into two group of a respectively b vertices. Again, this is a simple graph. There exists exactly one edge between any vertex in the a-group and the b-group, altogether $m = a \cdot b$ edges. In the figure on page 10 the vertices from the two distinct groups are colored blue and red.

We need to define the *cycle graph* C_n which has n vertices and n edges. The *path graph* P_n has n vertices but only $n - 1$ edges. One sees that the subscript gives the number of vertices. All definitions in this subsection define unlabelled graphs. No order of the vertices nor edges is

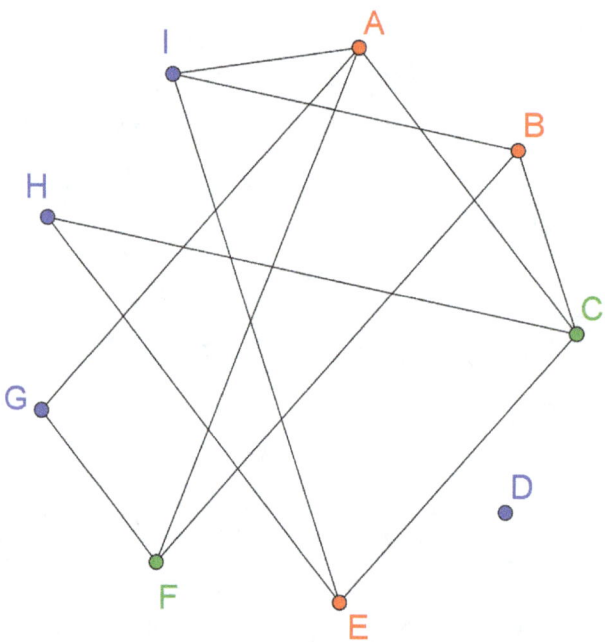

Figure 3: Nine kids go to the zoo in three groups.

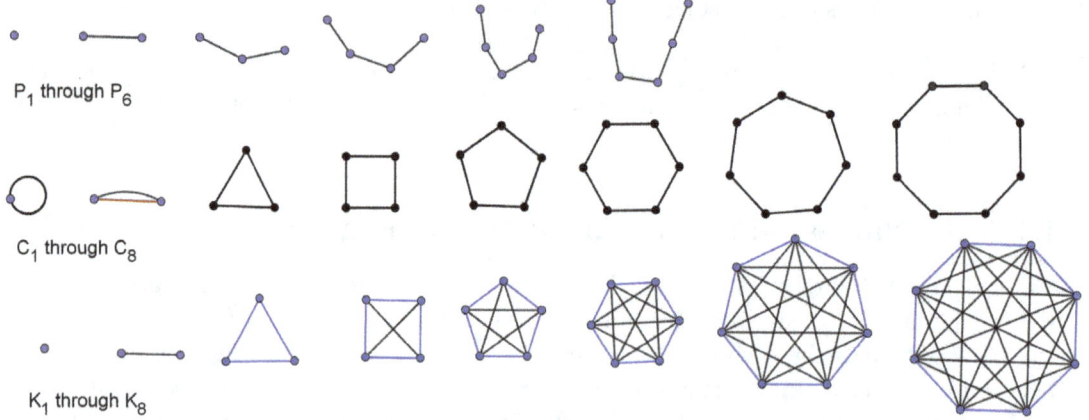

Figure 4: Path graphs, cycles graphs and complete graphs.

implied. The are some easy coincidences:

$$N_1 = K_1 = P_1 \,,\, K_2 = P_2 = K_{1,1} \,,\, P_3 = K_{1,2} \,,\, K_3 = C_3 \,,\, C_4 = K_{2,2}$$

From ancient times and the last book from Euclid's Elements, one knows the Platonic bodies:

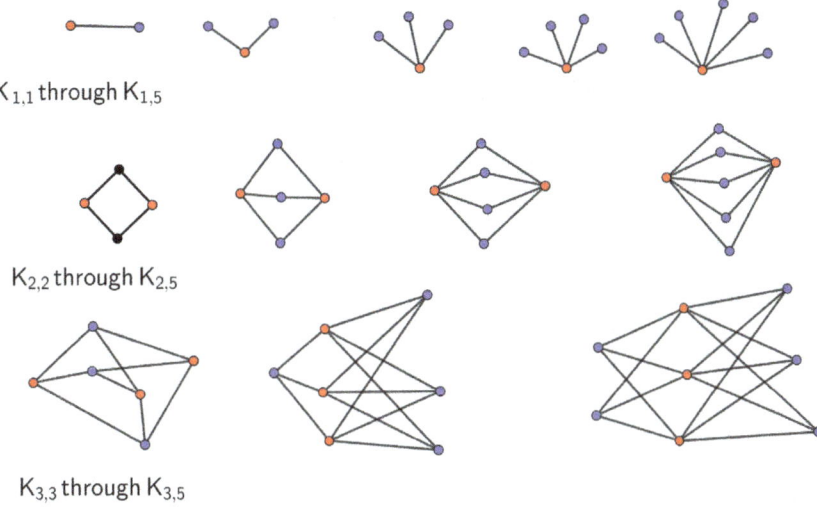

Figure 5: Complete bipartite graphs.

the tetrahedron, cube, octahedron, dodecahedron and icosahedron. We denote the first three by K_4, Q_3 and Oct_3. For the cube and octahedron exist the corresponding polyhedra for all dimensions. Here the subscript denotes the dimension.

Of the other graphs that shall occur below repeatedly, I mention only the $a \times b$-grid $P_a \times P_b$, *Petersen graph*, the rhombic dodecahedron and the 6-cage.

From any given graphs, one may build new ones by several *graph operations*. There exist constructive and destructive operations. For any simple graph there exists the complement. For any general graph there exists its line graph. For any two graphs there exist their set union, their disjoint union, join and Cartesian product. The exact definitions are given below. Concerning destruction, one may from any graph pull out any number of edges. As well one may pull out any number of vertices, where it is understood that all edges having them as an end are pulled out, too.

I.1.3 The handshaking lemma

Definition 4 (degree). The number of vertices which are adjacent to any given vertex v is called the *degree* of this vertex and denoted by $\deg v$.

As usual, we denote the minimum degree by δ and the maximum degree by Δ.

Proposition 1 (Handshaking lemma). *For any (simple or general) graph, the sum of the degrees of all vertices equals twice the number of edges.*

$$\sum_v \deg_G(v) = 2m$$

Proof the handshake lemma by induction. We proceed by induction on the number m of edges. The statement is true for a null graph, with any number of vertices, since the degrees of all vertices are zero. For the induction step, we assume the statement to be true for all graphs with less than m edges, and check it for any graph G with m edges. Let $e = vw$ be any edge of G.

$$\sum_v \deg_{G \setminus e}(v) = 2(m-1)$$

holds by the induction assumption. But for the graph G, the degrees of vertices v and w have been increased by one, and all other degrees remain as for $G \setminus e$. Hence

$$\sum_v \deg_G(v) = 2 + \sum_v \deg_{G \setminus e}(v) = 2m$$

as to be checked. □

A graph is called *regular* if all vertices have the same degree. Here are some simple consequences of the handshake lemma:

- the sum of the degrees is always even;
- the number of odd vertices is always even;
- for a r-regular graph $n \cdot r = 2m$;
- for a regular graph with odd degrees, the number of vertices is even.

An explanation.   • The sum of the degrees equals $2m$ which is always even.

- The sum of the degrees of the even vertices is even, as is the sum of the degrees of all vertices. Hence the sum of the degrees of the odd vertices is even, too. But a sum of odd integers is only even for an even number of terms. Hence the number of odd vertices is even.

- For a r-regular graph $n \cdot r = 2m$ since this is the sum of the degrees of all vertices.

- For a regular graph, the product $n \cdot r$ is even. Hence at least one of the factors is even. If the degree r is odd, the number n of vertices is even.

□

Proposition 2 (Handshake lemma for digraphs). *For any digraph, the sum of the out-degrees, as well as the sum of the in-degrees of all vertices equals the number of arcs.*

Proof. We proceed by induction on the number m of arcs. The statement is true for a null graph, with any number of vertices. For the induction step, we assume the statement to be true for all digraphs with less than m arcs, and check it for any digraph G with m arcs. Let $a = \vec{vw}$ be any arc of digraph G.

$$\sum \text{out-degrees of vertices of } G \setminus a = \sum \text{in-degrees of vertices of } G \setminus a = m - 1$$

holds by the induction assumption. But for the digraph G, the out-degree of vertex v, and the in-degree of vertex w have been increased by one, and all other degrees remain as for $G \setminus a$. Hence

$$\sum \text{out-degrees of vertices of } G = \sum \text{out-degrees of vertices of } G \setminus a + 1 = m$$
$$\sum \text{in-degrees of vertices of } G = \sum \text{in-degrees of vertices of } G \setminus a + 1 = m$$

as to be checked. □

I.1.4 Walk, trail, path and circuit and cycle

Definition 5 (**Walk**). A *walk* is a succession of any number k of edges of the given graph, where each one among these edges has to be adjacent to the next one. The *length* of the walk is the number of its edges. A walk is called *closed* if its first and last edge are the same. Otherwise the walk is called *open*.

Remark 1. No other restriction than being adjacent is imposed on the successive edges. Therefore the notion of walk appears quite often in the context of *random walk*. A walk of length zero consists just of one vertex.

Remark 2. The definition of walk specifies the names of the vertices respectively edges which are parsed. Therefore a walk may also be given by a finite sequence of edges

$$e_1, e_1, \ldots, e_k$$

(I.1.1) or for a simple graph with vertices v_i and $e_i = v_{i-1}v_i$ by

$$v_0v_1, v_1v_2, \ldots, v_{k-1}v_k$$

We give definitions for several common types of special walks by imposing less or more restrictions.

Definition 6 (**Trail and circuit**). A *trail* is a walk for which no edges are repeated. A closed trail is also called a *circuit*.

Definition 7 (**Path and cycle**). A *path* is a walk for which no vertices are repeated, with the exception that the last vertex may equal the first one. A closed path is also called a *cycle*. A path for which the first and the last vertex are different is called an *open* path. The length of a path is given by the number its edges, not its vertices. A cycle of length three is also called a *triangle*.

We see that every path is a trail, and every trail is walk, but the converses are not true. Every cycle is a circuit, and every circuit is a closed walk, but the converses are not true.

Remark 3. In all these definition it is understood that the names of the vertices respectively edges which are parsed are *specified*. Only for that reason a walk may also be given by a finite sequence, as in the formulas (I.1.1).

The latter remark is not as selfevident as the reader may expect. Indeed, neither graphs nor their subgraphs are considered to be labelled by default, whereas the walks, paths and cycles are labelled by default.

In other words, a subgraph specifies only *subsets* of vertices and edges, but the walks, paths and cycles specify *lists* of them. In the same token, when as subgraph is given by a walk, path or cycle, the names of its vertices and edges are disregarded.

The distinction between path or cycle and the subgraph with the same vertices becomes important in the context of uniqueness and counting. If we want disregard the general convention and instead consider a path or cycle or triangle to be a subgraph, we speak of *unlabelled* or *unmarked* path, cycle or triangle. For example, the graph from figure 13 contains exactly one *unlabelled* 4-cycle. But from here one gets eight labelled 4-cycles, depending on which vertex to choose as start and which direction to move through the object. In general, to one unlabelled k-cycle correspond $2k$ cycles, and to one unlabelled path correspond 2 different paths.

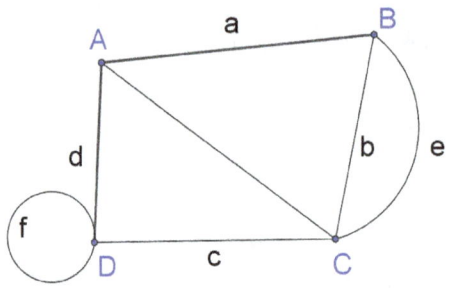

Figure 6: An example graph.

Problem 4. *For the graph on figure 13 find an open walk that is not a trail, and an open trail that is not a path, each of length four.*

Problem 5. *For the graph on figure 13 find a closed walk that is not a circuit, and a circuit that is not a cycle, each ones of length four.*

Problem 6. *For the graph on figure 13 find all unnamed cycles of length three and of length four. Which ones of these objects are unique.*

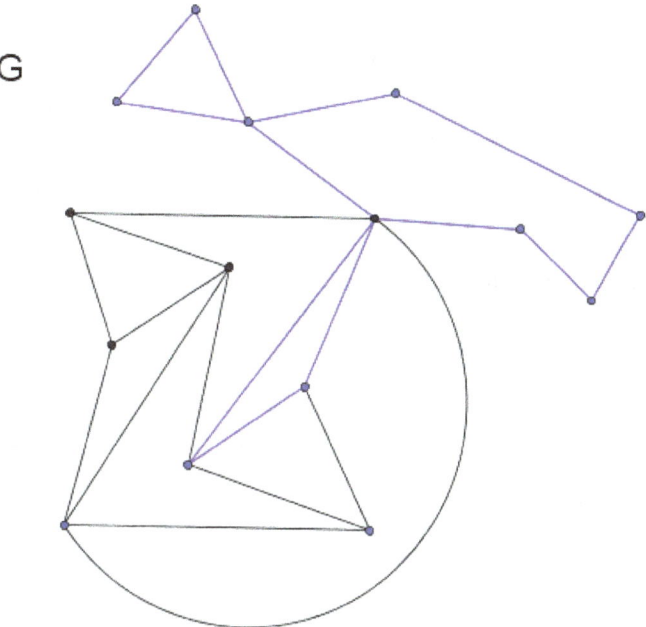

Figure 7: Any graph.

Problem 7. *Into the graph in figure on page 14, draw in blue a closed trail that is not a cycle—not too short, please. State its length, and how many vertices your trail visits.*

Answer. The closed trail I have drawn consist of the three cycles of length $3, 3$ and 6. It has length 12 and visits 10 vertices.

I.1.5 Connected and disconnected graphs

Definition 8 (Connected graph). A graph is called *connected* if and only if for any two vertices u and v, there exists a path from u to v.

Proposition 3. *For any graph G, the following three statements are equivalent:*

(a) *for any two vertices u and v, there exists a path from u to v;*

(b) *for any two vertices u and v, there exists a walk from u to v;*

(c) *the graph G is not the vertex-disjoint union of two subgraphs.*

Reason. (a) $\Rightarrow$ (b) is obvious since every path is a walk.

To show that not (c) ⇒ not (b), we assume that the graph is the vertex-disjoint union $G = A + B$. For two vertices u in A and v in B, there exists no walk from u to v.

To show that not (a) ⇒ not (c), we assume no path exists from vertex u to vertex v. Let A be the set of all vertices that can be reached with a path starting at u, and $B = V_G \setminus A$ be the set of the remaining vertices. The vertex v is contained in B. The graph is the vertex-disjoint union $G = A + B$, negating statement (c). □

Definition 9 (Components of a graph). A graph has the components $C_1, C_2, \ldots, C_h$ if and only if the following two conditions hold:

- Each component C_i is connected.

- Any two components C_i and C_j are vertex disjoint.

Remark. Obviously, the sum $G + H$ of any two vertex-disjoint graphs is not connected. The components of any graph are the subgraphs characterized by the two properties:

- they are connected;

- they are *maximal* subgraphs which are connected.

One immediately sees that these subgraphs are vertex disjoint and hence yield the components. □

Problem 8. *Find a simple graph of order $n = 6$ and size $m = 10$ that is not connected. Explain your example in the standard notation (using K_n, N_n, C_n, P_n, their unions, joins, and so on) and give a drawing.*

Answer. Since the graph is not connected, it is the disjoint sum of at least two components: Write $6 = a + b$ as sum of positive integers a and b, and take as both components complete graphs K_a and K_b. Thus one gets the following graphs:

$$6 = 3+3: \quad m(K_3 + K_3) = 3+3 = 6$$
$$6 = 2+4: \quad m(K_2 + K_4) = 1+6 = 7$$
$$6 = 1+5: \quad m(K_1 + K_5) = 0+10 = 10$$

Only in the last example, we get ten edges as required. Hence the solution is $K_1 + K_5$.

Proposition 4. *A disconnected simple graph with n vertices satisfying*

(Ore n-2) $\qquad\qquad\qquad$ *If* $u \nsim v$ $\quad$ *then* $\quad \deg u + \deg v \geq n - 2$

is the disjoint union of two complete graphs. Especially, the degree sum for any two nonadjacent vertices u and v is $\deg u + \deg v = n - 2$.
A simple graph with n vertices satisfying (Ore n-2), with the proper inequality holding in at least one case is connected.

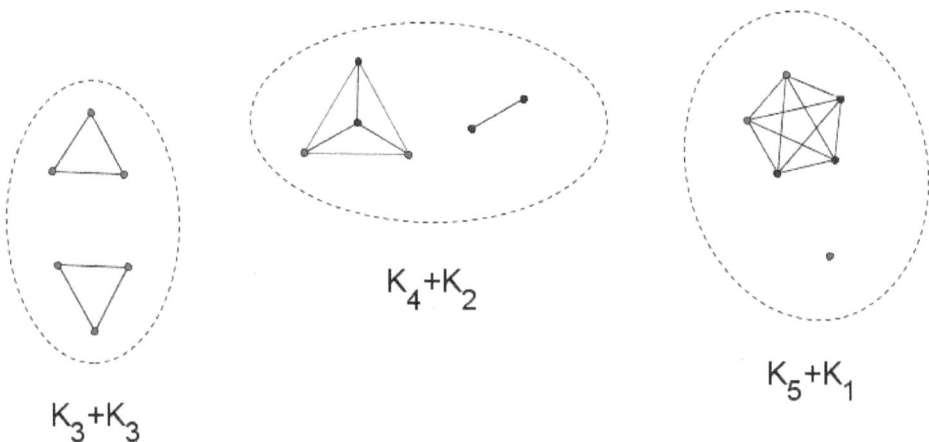

Figure 8: Some graphs with six vertices and two components.

Proof. We assume (Ore n-2) to hold for a disconnected graph G. Hence the vertices $V_G = A + B$ are the disjoint union of sets A and B with no edges connecting them. Take a vertex u in A and a vertex v in B. Since the graph is assumed to be simple

$$\deg u \leq |A| - 1$$
$$\deg v \leq |B| - 1$$

Adding both inequalities yields

$$\deg u + \deg v \leq |A| + |B| - 2 = n - 2$$

The assumption (Ore n-2) yields the reversed inequality. Hence

$$n - 2 \leq \deg u + \deg v \leq |A| + |B| - 2 = n - 2$$

holds with equality everywhere. We conclude $\deg u = |A| - 1$ for all vertices u in A, and $\deg v = |B| - 1$ for all vertices u in B. Hence the graph G is the union of two components which both are complete graphs: $G = K_a + K_b$.

Assume that (Ore n-2) holds, and furthermore, there exist two vertices x and y such that $\deg x + \deg y \geq n-1$. The argument above ruled out the case that the graph is the vertex-disjoint union of two subgraphs. Hence the only possibility left turns out to be that G is connected. □

I.1.6 Clique, independence and complement

Definition 10 (Clique and clique number). A complete subgraph $K_c \subseteq G$ of any graph G is called a *clique* of the graph. The maximum number of vertices which are all adjacent to each other is called the *clique number* of a graph. It is denoted by $\omega(G)$.

Definition 11 (Independent set and independence number). An *independent* or *stable* set in a graph is a set of pairwise nonadjacent vertices. The *independence number* is the maximum number of pairwise nonadjacent vertices. It is denoted by $\alpha(G)$.

Definition 12 (Induced subgraph). Given a graph G and a subset $S \subseteq V_G$ of its vertices, the *induced subgraph* $G[S]$ has the vertices in the subset S, and *all* the edges vw of the original graph for which both end-vertices v and w are in the set S.

Definition 13 (Complement of a simple graph). The *complement* $\overline{G}$ of a simple graph G has the same vertices as G. The edges of *complement* $\overline{G}$ are drawn between the vertices that are not adjacent in G. Hence

$$V(\overline{G}) = V(G) \quad \text{and} \quad E(\overline{G}) = E(K_n) \setminus E(G)$$

Problem 9. *Convince yourself that the clique number and independence number of the complement are*

$$\alpha(\overline{G}) = \omega(G) \quad \text{and} \quad \omega(\overline{G}) = \alpha(G)$$

Proposition 5 (Connectedness of the complement). *Either the (simple) graph G or its complement $\overline{G}$ is connected.*

Problem 10. *How can the complement of a disconnected graph be expressed as a wedge? Which subgraph does this graph always have? Prove Proposition 5.*

Answer. Assume that G is not connected. Then it is the disjoint union $G = A + B$ of two graphs A and B, with no edges joining them. The complement is the wedge

$$\overline{A+B} = \overline{A} \vee \overline{B}$$

and hence contains the complete bipartite graph $K_{A,B}$ as a subgraph. Too, these edges provide a path between any two vertices, no matter whether lying in either A or B. Hence the complement $\overline{G}$ is connected.

A simple graph G that is isomorphic to its complement is called *self-complementary*.

Problem 11. *How many edges has a self-complementary graph with n vertices? Prove that self-complementary graph has $n = 4k$ or $n = 4k+1$ vertices.*

Answer. Since for every graph, $m(\overline{G}) = m(K_n) - m(G)$, and the complete graph K_n has $m = \dfrac{n(n-1)}{2}$ edges.

$$m(\overline{G}) = \frac{n(n-1)}{2} - m(G)$$

Since we assume that G is isomorphic to its complement $\overline{G}$, both have the same number of edges: $m(G) = m(\overline{G})$.

$$m(G) = \frac{n(n-1)}{2} - m(G)$$
$$m(G) = \frac{n(n-1)}{4}$$

Since m is an integer, the formula (*) implies that $n(n-1)$ is divisible by 4. Hence either n or $n-1$ is divisible by 4. In the first case, one gets $n = 4k$ and $m = k(4k-1)$. In the second case, one gets $n = 4k+1$ and $m = k(4k+1)$.

Problem 12. *How many edges has a self-complementary graph with $n = 4$. Find and draw all (non-isomorphic) self-complementary graphs of order 4.*

Answer. The problem above yields $m = \frac{n(n-1)}{4} = \frac{4(4-1)}{4} = 3$. Too, we have seen that a self-complementary graph is always connected. Hence we have a tree.

There are two trees with four vertices: The path graph P_4 is self-complementary. The other tree $K_{1,3}$ is not, since $\overline{K_{1,3}} = K_1 + K_3$ is disconnected.

Problem 13. *How many edges has a self-complementary graph with $n = 5$. Find and draw all (non-isomorphic) self-complementary graphs of order 5.*

Answer. The problems above tell $m = \frac{n(n-1)}{4} = \frac{5(5-1)}{4} = 5$. A self-complementary graph is always connected. As you can see from the list in the book, there are five non isomorphic connected graphs of order $n - 5$ with 5 edges. Two of them turn out to be self-complementary, the cycle C_5, and the triangle with two extra edges attached at two different vertices.

Definition 14 (Antiautomorphism). An *antiautomorphism* of a self-complementary graph G is a bijection $\phi : V_G \mapsto V_G$ such that for any two vertices $v \cong w$ if and only if $\phi(v) \not\cong \phi(w)$.

I.1.7 Isomorphism

Definition 15 (Isomorphism). Let G and H be any simple graphs. A mapping $\phi : V_G \mapsto V_H$ is called a *isomorphism* if and only if

- the mapping ϕ is a bijection,

- the vertices v and w are adjacent in the original graph G if and only if their images $\phi(v)$ and $\phi(w)$ are adjacent in H.

For a pair of general graphs to be isomorphic, we require that the number of edges connecting two vertices $\phi(v)$ and $\phi(w)$ of $\phi(G)$ equals the number of edges connecting the vertices v and w in graph G.

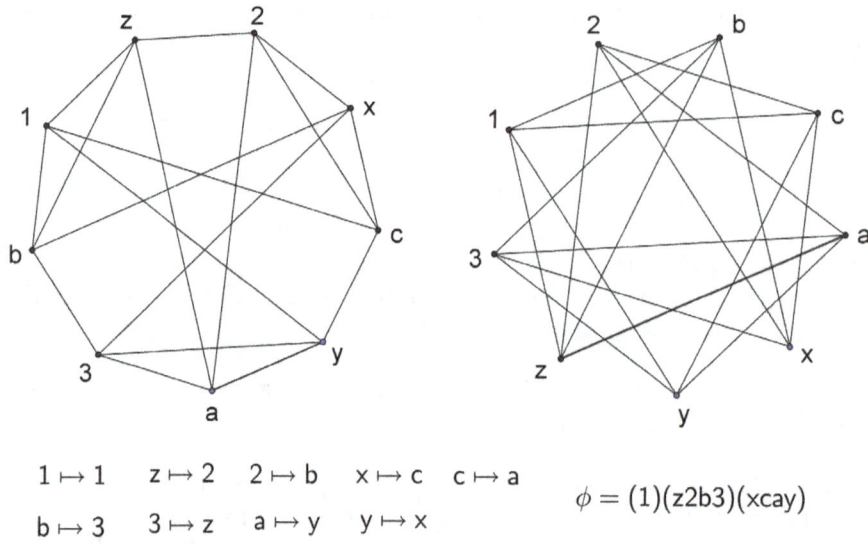

Figure 9: The antiautomorphism of a 9 vertex self-complementary graph.

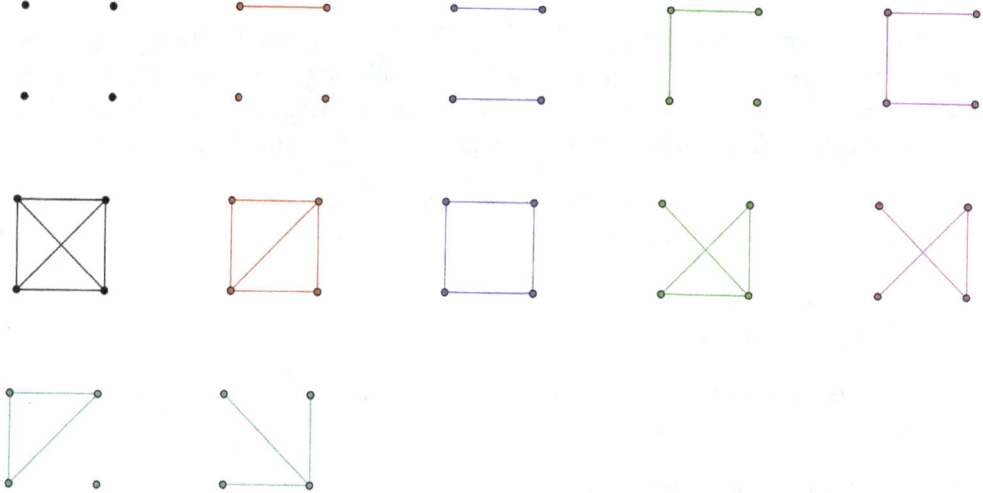

Figure 10: Eleven graphs with four vertices. The self-complementary one is shown twice.

Problem 14. *Draw all eleven non-isomorphic simple graphs with $n = 4$ vertices. Indicate pairs of complementary graphs with the same color. Which graph turns out to be self-complementary?*

Answer.

Problem 15. *There are six different non-isomorphic graphs with five vertices and five edges. One of them is disconnected. Draw these six different graphs.*

Problem 16. *Draw two non-isomorphic regular graphs with $n = 8$ and $m = 12$.*

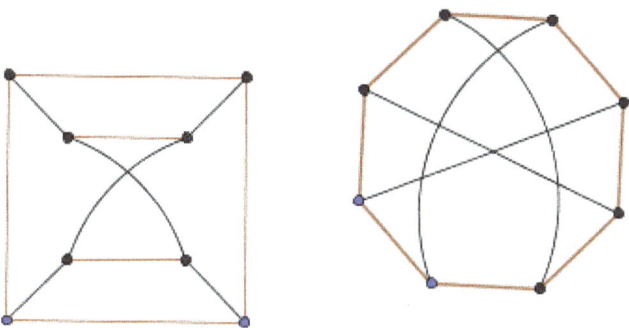

Figure 11: Are these two graphs isomorphic?

Problem 17. *Show that the two graphs in the figure on page 20 are isomorphic. To this end, number the vertices in both graphs in a way that yields an isomorphism.*

Answer. An isomorphism is indicated in the figure on page 21. It can be found by cycling through a sequence of four squares, of which any two successive have one edge in common. Such a sequence is

$$5126,\ 2673,\ 7348,\ 4815$$

and then back to the fist square. Gluing these squares together just along their respective common edge yields a Moebius strip.

Problem 18. *Convince yourself that the two graphs in the figure on page 21 are isomorphic. To this end, color some vertices, or edges in a way to make the isomorphism obvious.*

Answer.

Problem 19. *By suitably labelling the vertices and color some edges, show that the two graphs in the figure on page 22 are isomorphic.*

The symbol D_n denotes the group of rotations and reflections of a regular n-gon. It has $2n$ elements and is called the *dihedral group*.

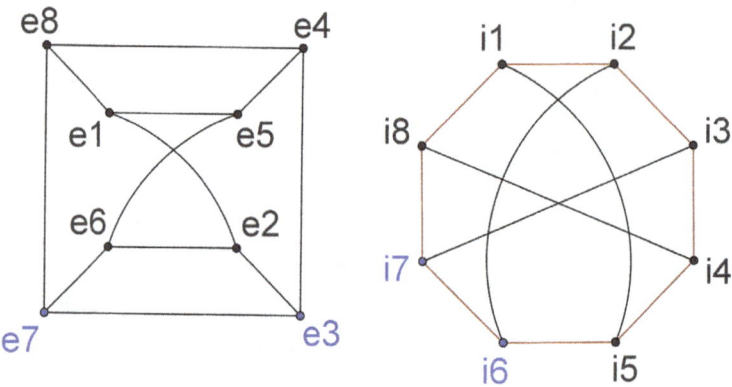

Figure 12: The isomorphism is shown by the numbering.

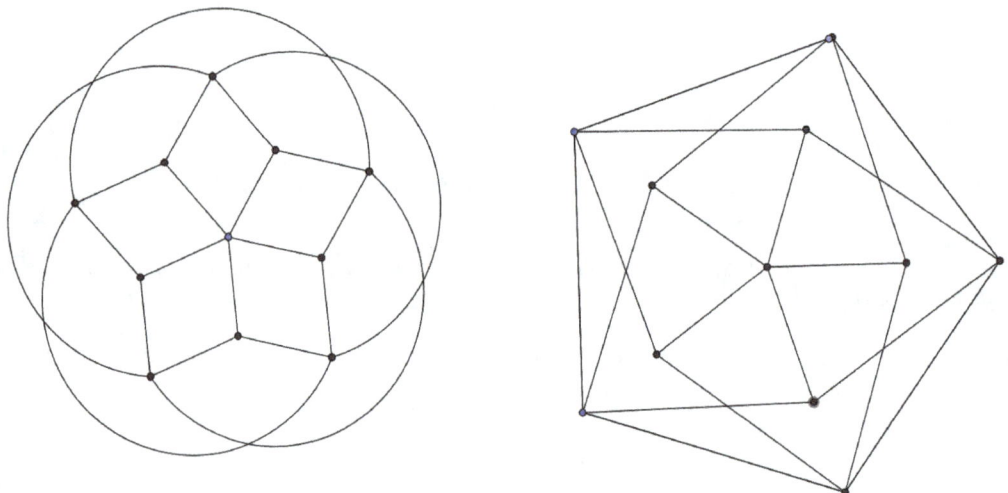

Figure 13: Who is Mr. Groetzsch?

Remark 4. As shown in the figure on page 23, one can draw the Petersen graph with the edges along either a 5-cycle, a 6-cycle, an 8-cycle or a 9-cycle. In these four drawing, it is easy to arrange the remaining vertices and edges in a way to confirm the symmetry groups D_5 (rotations and reflections of a regular 5-gon), D_3, D_4 or once more D_3.

For the automorphism group of the Peterson graph, this implies $D_5 \subset \mathrm{Aut}(Petersen)$, $D_3 \subset \mathrm{Aut}(Petersen)$, and $D_4 \subset \mathrm{Aut}(Petersen)$, respectively. Hence 10, 6 and 8 are divisors of the order $|\mathrm{Aut}(Petersen)|$. Hence the automorphism group of the Petersen graph has at least 120 elements.

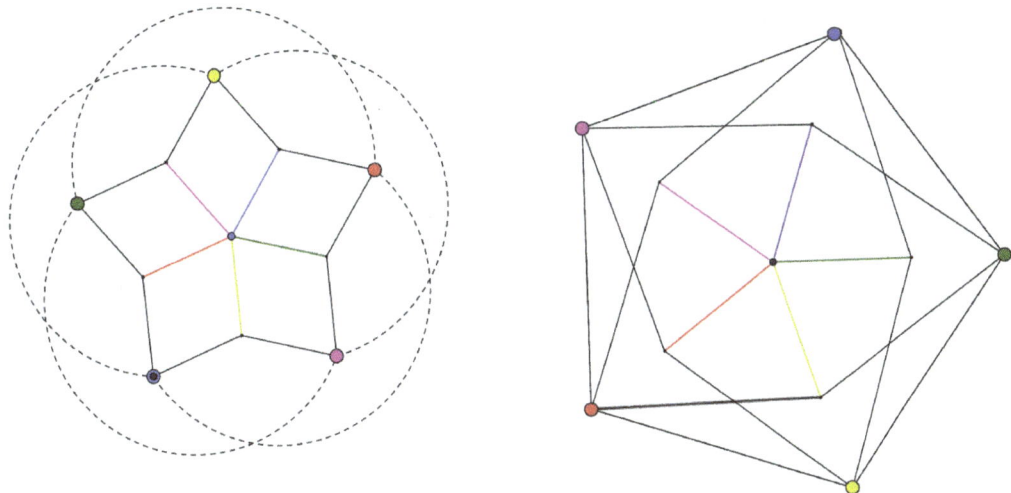

Figure 14: Mr. and Mrs. Groetzsch

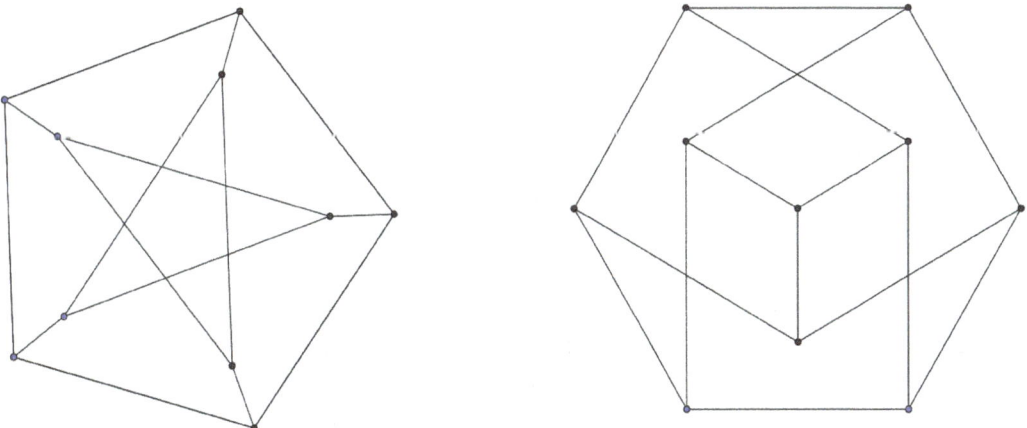

Figure 15: Who is Mr. Petersen?

Problem 20. *Give a reason why the two graphs G and H in the figure on page 24 are not isomorphic.*

Answer (Reason 1). Both graphs have exactly four vertices of degree four. In both graphs, these vertices are a cycle. In graph G, two opposite edges of this cycle both occur in <u>one</u> triangle only. In graph H, two opposite edges of this cycle both occur in <u>two</u> triangles. Hence the two graphs are not isomorphic.

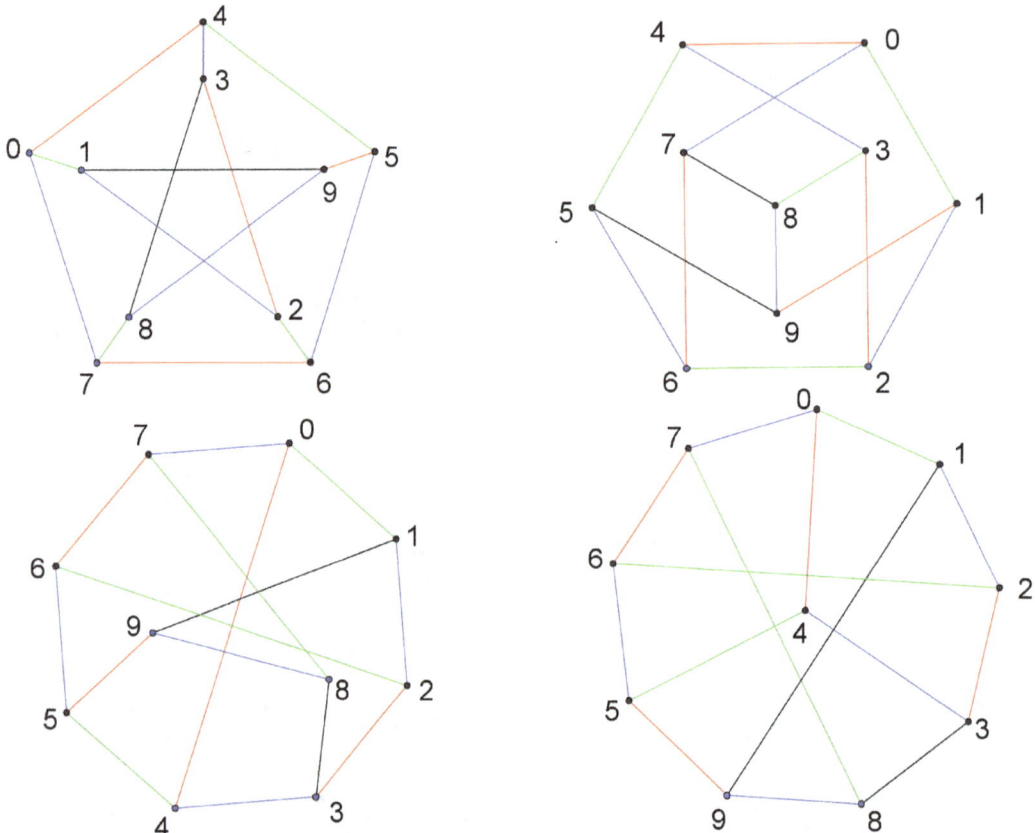

Figure 16: Four ways to draw the Petersen graph.

Answer (Reason 2). Both graphs have exactly two pairs of triangles with a common edge. In graph G, the vertices at the end of the common edge have degree four and degree three. In graph H, two vertices of degree four are the ends of the common edge.

Answer (Reason 3). In graph G, there exists an 8-cycle, in which vertices of degree three and degree four alternate. Such a cycle does not exist in graph H, only 4-cycles have vertices alternating between degree three and four.

Answer (Reason 4). In graph G, there exists a 4-cycle with three vertices of degree three and the fourth one of degree four. Such a cycle does not exist in graph H, only 4-cycles with four vertices of degree four, or with two vertices of degree four and two vertices of degree three are present.

Problem 21. *Match the 3-regular graphs from the picture on page 25 with the descriptions.*

containing exactly one triangle and two 4-cycles

the cube graph Q_3

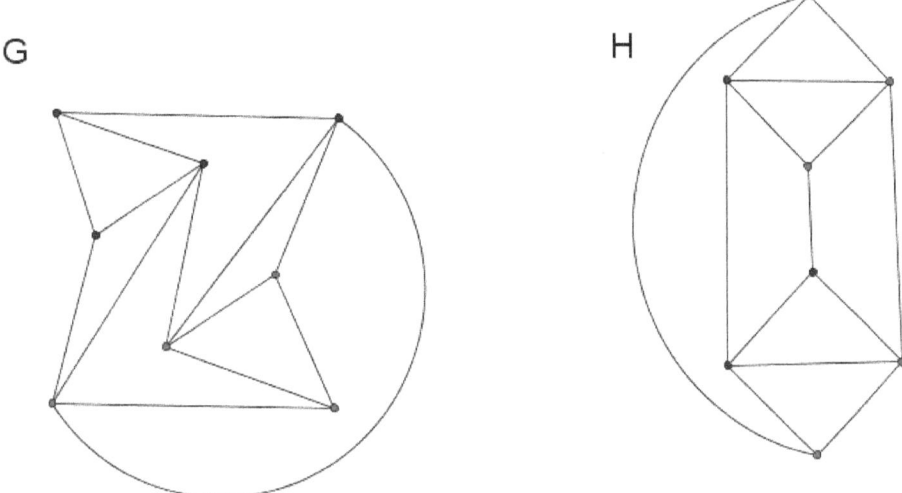

Figure 17: Are these two graphs isomorphic?

planar connected graph containing exactly two triangles

planar $\kappa = 2$-connected graph containing four triangles

the disconnected graph $K_4 + K_4$

non-planar graph containing no triangle and four 4-cycles

Answer. In the order given in the picture, these are properties characterizing the graph uniquely:

upper row, left: the cube graph Q_3

upper row, second from left: the disconnected graph $K_4 + K_4$

upper row, right: planar connected graph containing exactly two triangles

lower row, left: planar $\kappa = 2$-connected graph containing four triangles

lower row, second from left: containing only one triangle and two 4-cycles

lower row, second from right: non-planar graph containing no triangle, four 4-cycles, and eight 5 cycles, which can be obtained from a cube by altering two edges

lower row, right: is isomorphic with lower row, second from right.

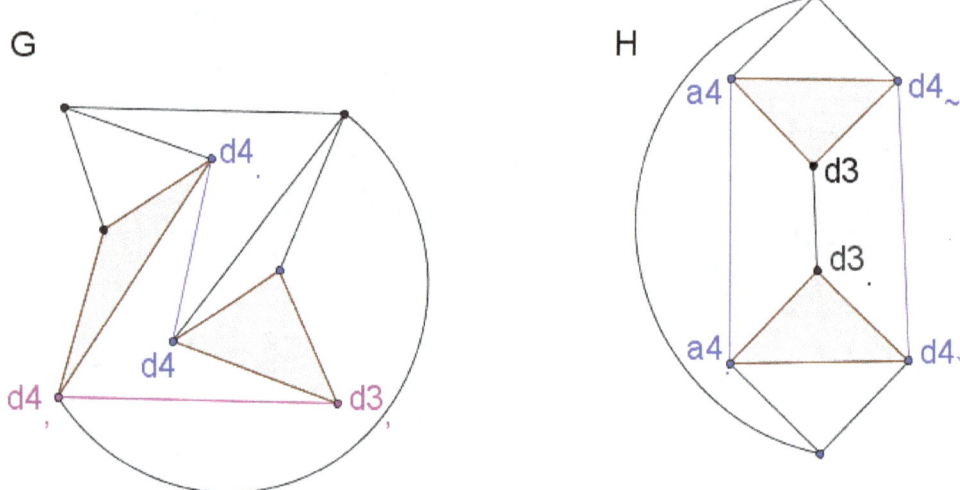

Figure 18: These two graphs are not isomorphic.

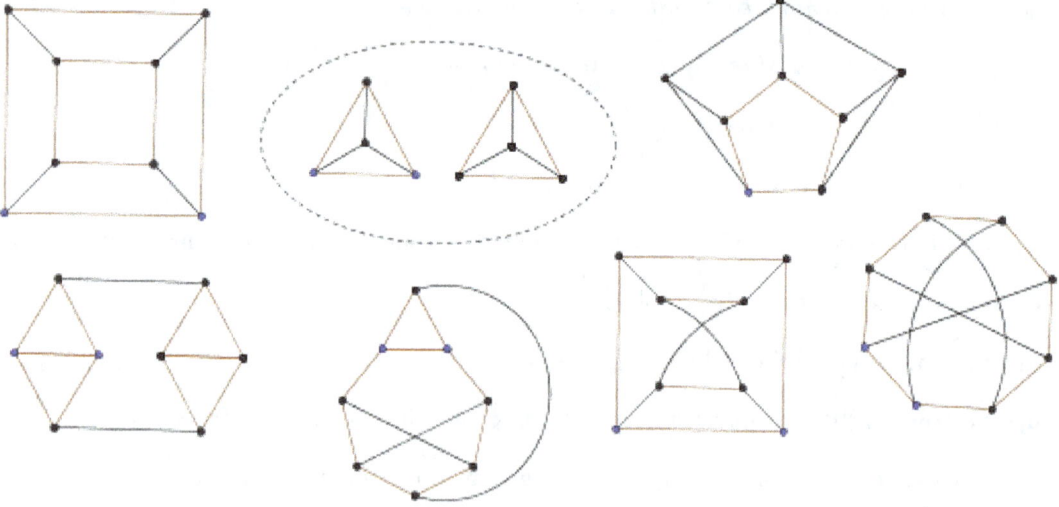

Figure 19: There are at least six pairwise non-isomorphic three-regular simple graphs with eight vertices.

Definition 16 (Image of a graph). Let G be any graph, Y be any set and $\phi : V_G \mapsto Y$ be any mapping. The *image graph* $\phi(G)$ has as set of its vertices the range $\phi(V_G)$. An edge connects two vertices $\phi(v)$ and $\phi(w)$ of $\phi(G)$ if and only if the vertices v and w are adjacent in the original graph G.

For a general graph, we require that the number of edges connecting two vertices $\phi(v)$ and $\phi(w)$ of $\phi(G)$ equals the number of edges connecting the vertices v and w in graph G.

Definition 17 (Homomorphism). Let G and H be simple graphs. A mapping $\phi : V_G \mapsto V_H$ is called a *homomorphism* means:

Two vertices h and k are adjacent in H if and only if

- $h = \phi(v), k = \phi(w)$—they are in the range of ϕ,
- the vertices v and w are adjacent in the original graph G.

I.1.8 Automorphism group

Definition 18. The *automorphism group* $\mathrm{Aut}(G)$ of a graph consists of all isomorphisms of the graph to itself. The *group orbit* of a vertex v of the graph is the set of all images gv of that vertex, where the automorphism g takes as values all group elements.

Remark 5. The automorphism group for a multiple graph, like for example the r-thick path, depends on the exact definition of this group. I prefer to count switches of multiple edges, with vertices fixed, as extra elements of the group.

Usually there are several group orbits. They are always disjoint. The number of items in a group orbit is always a divisor of the order of the group.

Problem 22. *The figure on page 27 give all* 21 *simple connected graphs which have* $n = 6$ *vertices and* $m = 7$ *edges.*

Give the orders of the automorphism group for each one of these graphs.

Color the group orbits containing several vertices in different color. Please use the follow colors:

Mark the group orbits with two vertices in blue. If there are several, use blue crosses, blue circles, etc. to distinguish the group orbits.

Use green color for group orbits of three vertices,

and red for group orbits of four vertices.

Leave the fixed elements black as is.

Answer.

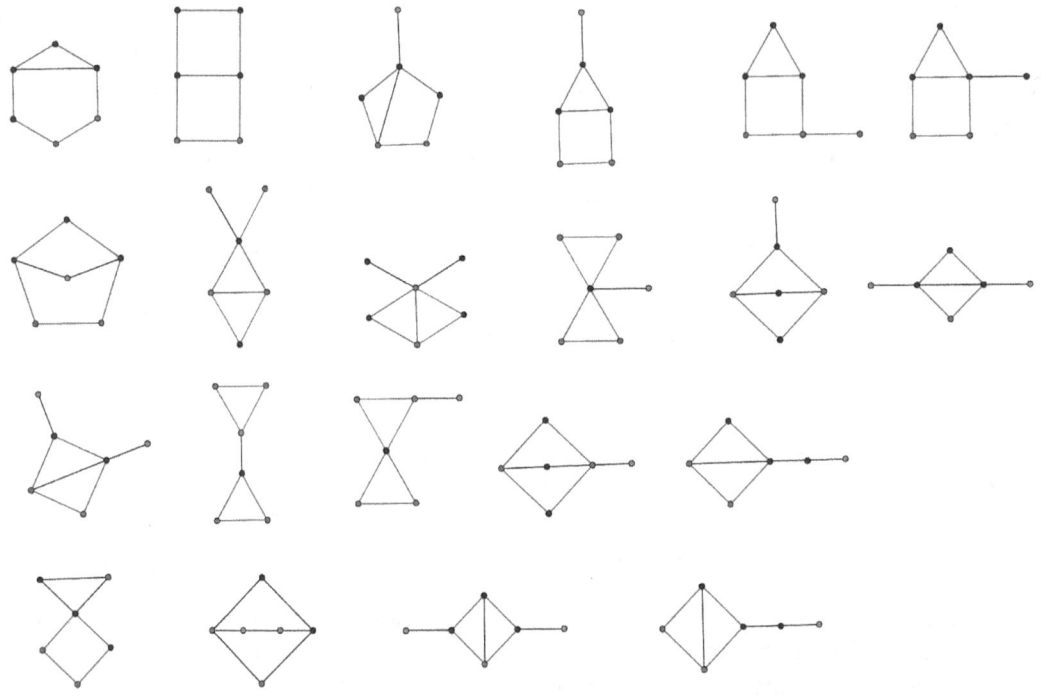

Figure 20: 21 simple connected graphs with 6 vertices and 7 edges.

Problem 23. *Find the automorphism group for the two graphs shown in the figure on page 29. Color the group orbits with different colors.*

Answer. The two graphs shown in the figure on page 29 have different automorphism groups.

For the graph G shown on the left-hand side, the automorphism group is generated by the permutations
$$a = (12), \; b = (34), \; c = (56), \; d = (13)(24)$$
and has 16 elements. There is one group orbit of four elements shown in blue, one of two elements. shown in red.

For the graph H shown on the right-hand side, the automorphism group is generated by the permutations
$$x = (14)(23), \; y = (23)(56)$$
and has 4 elements. There are three group orbit of two elements each one, shown in different shades of red.

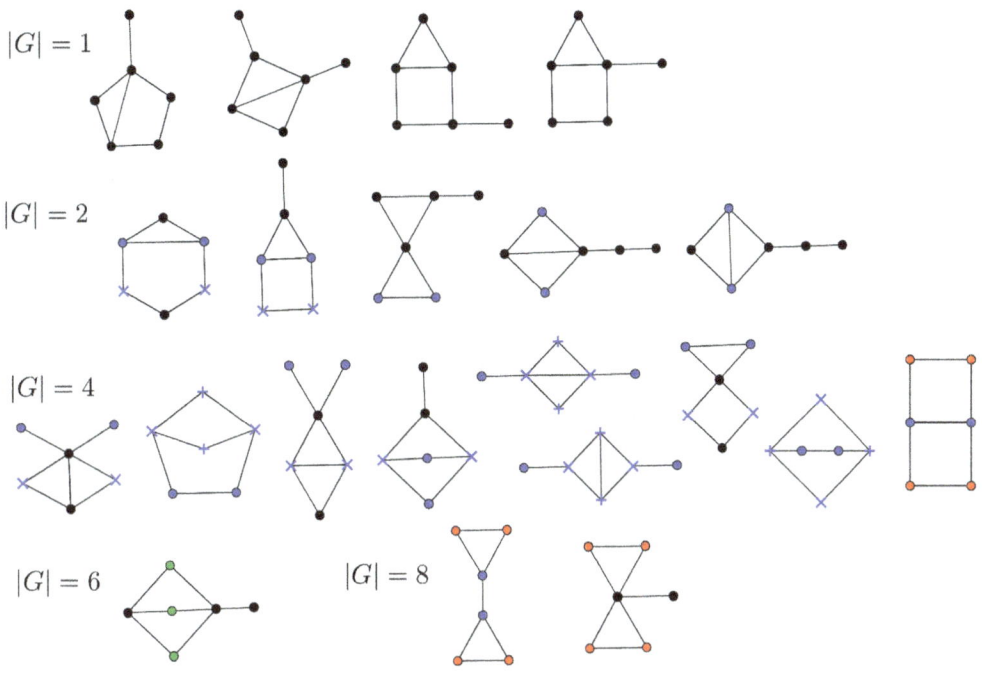

Figure 21: Automorphism group orders and orbits.

Problem 24. *What is the automorphism group for the pseudo-rhomb-cuboctahedron from the figure on page 30. Find the three group orbits of the vertices and mark them with different colors.*

Answer. The automorphism group is the semidirect product $D_4 \times_s S_2$, which has the order 16. There are 24 vertices, and the number of vertices in a group orbit is a divisor of the order of the group. We see from this information that several group orbits have to occur. Actually, there are three orbits of 8 vertices, marked red white and black in the figure on page 31.

Problem 25. *Find a smallest simple graph with at least two vertices, for which the identity is the only automorphism. ("All vertices look differently from inside the graph.") There are indeed several solutions. How many can you find?*

Answer. I find two solutions as shown in the figure on page 32: A tree T with $n = 7$ vertices and $m = 6$ edges, and graph G with $n = 6$ and $m = 6$. The graph H has automorphism group $\text{Aut}(H) = S_2$.

Remark 6. For a graph where the identity is the only automorphism, one may say "all vertices look differently from inside the graph." For a graph where its automorphism group acts transitively on the vertices, one may say "all vertices look the same from inside the graph."

graph G

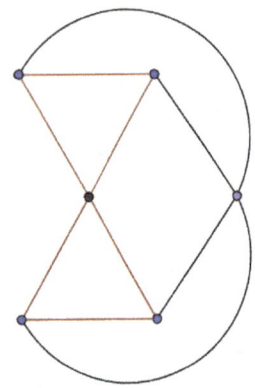

graph H

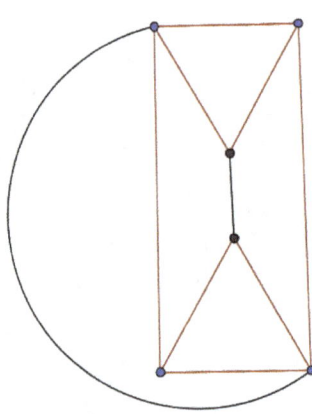

Figure 22: What are the automorphism groups?

graph G

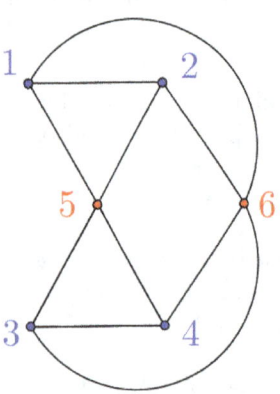

graph H

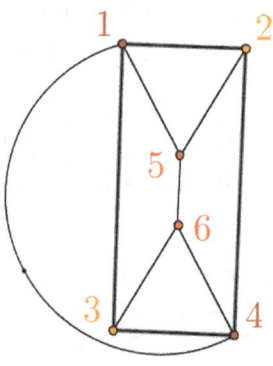

Figure 23: The two graphs have different automorphism groups.

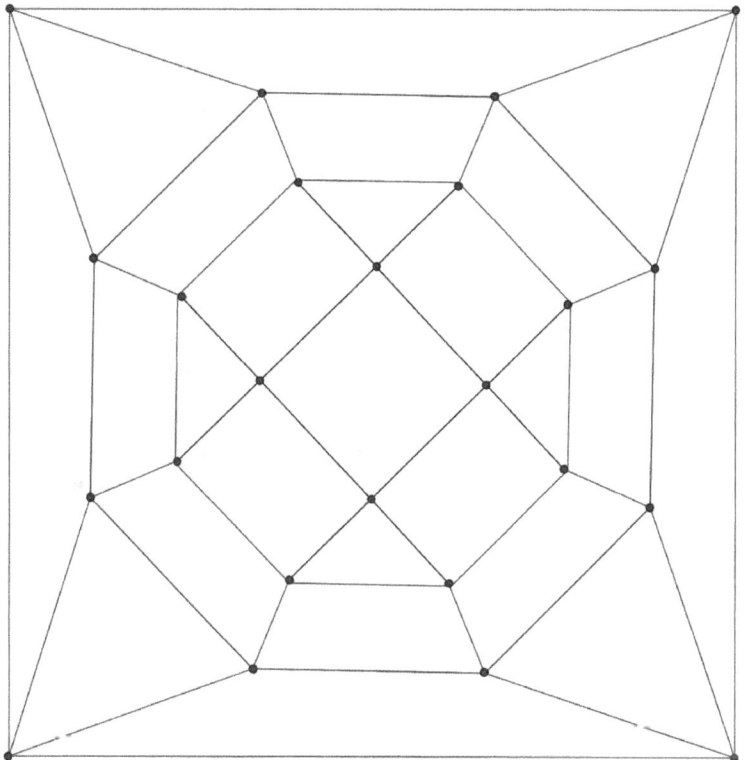

Figure 24: The pseudo-rhomb-cuboctahedron.

I.1.9 Bipartite graphs

Definition 19 (Bipartite graph). A graph is called *bipartite* if and only if its vertices can be partitioned into two disjoint sets such that there are only edges connecting vertices of these two sets R and S. We shall use the notation (R, S) or (R, S, E) for a bipartite graph with edges between vertices in the sets R and S, and the set of edges E.

Proposition 6 (Characterizations of a bipartite graph). *Equivalent are*

(a) *The vertices of graph G are partitioned into two disjoint sets $V_G = R + S$, and any edge of G is adjacent to one vertex in R and one vertex in S.*

(b) *The vertices of the graph G are properly two-colorable.*

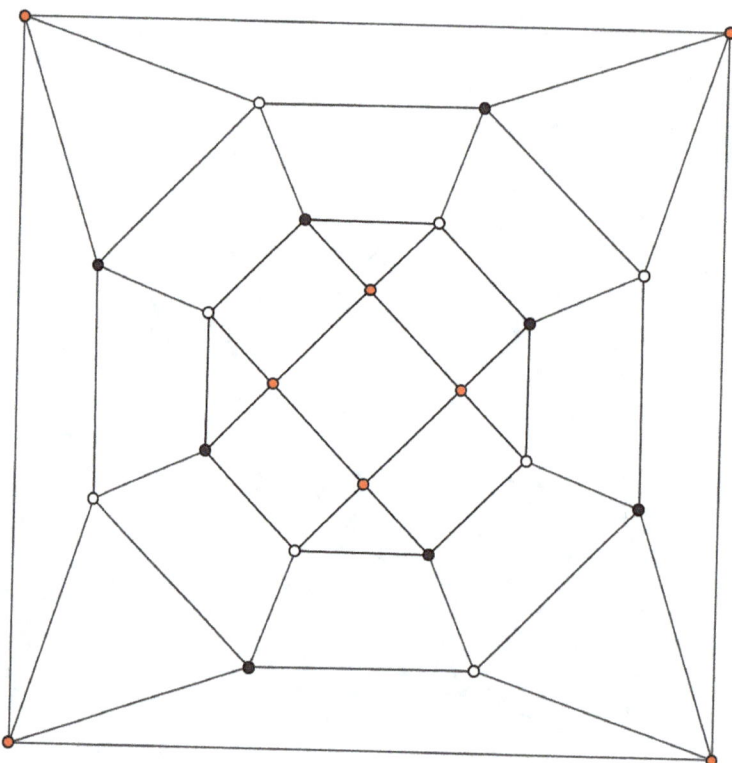

Figure 25: There are three group orbits for the pseudo-rhomb-cuboctahedron.

(c) *Each cycle in the graph G has even length.*

"(a) *equivalent* (b)": We color the vertices of R black and of S white and obtain a proper two-coloring, since the edges of G only connect vertices of the two different sets R and S. Conversely the two colors define the partitioning of the vertices into the disjoint sets R and S and any edge of G is adjacent to one vertex in R and one vertex in S. □

"(b) *implies* (c)": If the graph is two-colored, each cycle is two-colored and hence even—since odd cycles need three colors for a proper coloring. □

"(c) *implies* (a)": Assume each cycle in the graph G has even length. We start with any vertex v and put it into the set S. Let the set S contain all vertices which can be connected with v

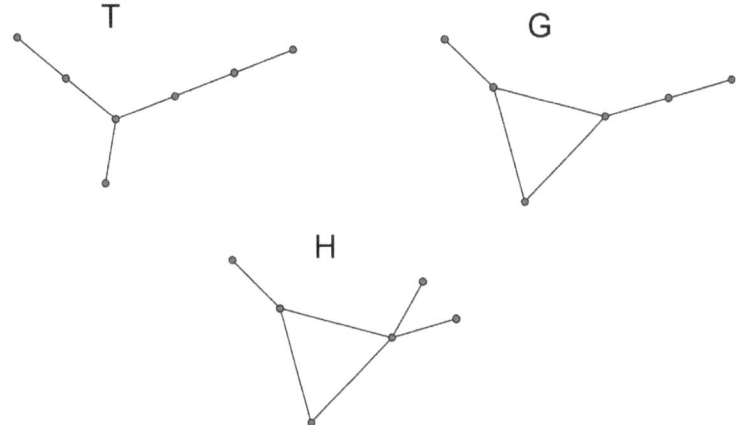

Figure 26: Only the tree T and the graph G have the trivial automorphism group S_1.

by a path of even length, and R all vertices which can be connected with v by a path of odd length. These two sets are disjoint, for otherwise there would exist a cycle of odd length.

We have obtained a proper two-coloring of the component of G containing vertex v. In case the graph is not connected, we choose another vertex not already colored and repeat the procedure, until all vertices have been colored. □

Remark 7. A simple graph with n vertices is bipartite if and only if it is a subgraph of the complete bipartite graph $G \subseteq K_{r,s}$ for some $r, s \geq 1$ with sum $r + s = n$.

Proposition 7 (Handshake lemma for bipartite graphs). *For any (simple or general) bipartite graph (A, B), the sum of the degrees of all black vertices in A, and the sum of the degrees of all white vertices in B are both equal to the number of edges.*

(I.1.2) $$\sum_{v \in A} \deg_G(v) = \sum_{v \in B} \deg_G(v) = m$$

Problem 26. *Convince yourself that a regular bipartite, non-null graph always has the same number of black and white vertices.*

Problem 27. *The complete __tripartite__ graph $T_{r,s,t}$ consists of three sets of vertices, with r, s and t elements, respectively, and an edge joining two vertices if and only if they lie in two different sets.*

(a) *Draw the graph $T_{2,2,2}$.*

(b) *How many vertices and how many edges does $T_{2,2,2}$ have.*

(c) *How many triangles are there in $T_{2,2,2}$.*

(d) *Draw the complement $\overline{T_{2,2,2}}$.*

(e) *Give the complement in standard notation (e.g. $P_3 + C_3$, $P_2 \vee N_3$, $K_4 \times N_2$ etc.).*

Problem 28. *Which parts of the characterizations of a bipartite graph in proposition 6 hold similarly for tripartite graphs?*

Definition 20 (Join of two graphs). The *join* $A \vee B$ of any two graphs A and B is constructed from the disjoint union $A + B$ by drawing extra edges joining each vertex of A to each vertex of B.

The join $N_1 \vee G$ of a graph with the null graph is the *pyramid* over the graph G.

Problem 29. *What is the join of two null graphs N_a and N_b. Explain why the number of vertices and edges of the join of any two graphs are*

$$n(A \vee B) = n(A) + n(B)$$
$$m(A \vee B) = m(A) + m(B) + n(A)n(B)$$

Answer. The number of vertices of the two given graphs A and B are added to get the number of vertices of the disjoint union or the join.

The join $N_a \vee N_b$ of two null graphs N_a and N_b is the complete bipartite graph $K_{a,b}$. The edges of the join are the edges of the two graphs A and B, and the edges of the complete bipartite graph $K_{a,b}$. Thus one gets the sum formula $m(A \vee B) = m(A) + m(B) + n(A)n(B)$.

I.1.10 Matching and covering

Definition 21 (Matching). A *matching* in a graph is a subset $M \subseteq E_G$ of its edges having no common end-vertices. A matching is *non-extendable* or *maximal* if and only if it is not a proper subset of a larger matching. A matching is *maximum* if and only if it is a matching having the maximally possible number of edges.

Definition 22 (Vertex cover). A *vertex cover* in a graph is a subset $Q \subseteq V_G$ of its vertices that contains at least one endpoint of each vertex. A vertex cover is *non-restrictable* or *minimal* if and only if none of its proper subsets is a smaller vertex cover. A vertex cover is *minimum* if and only if it is a vertex cover having the minimally possible number of vertices.

Lemma 1. *For any graph, a matching contains at most so many edges as any vertex cover contains vertices. Hence $\alpha'(G) \leq \beta(G)$ holds for any graph.*

Proof. Given are the matching $M \subseteq E_G$ and the vertex cover $Q \subseteq V_G$. Each edge $e \in M$ has at least one end-vertex from the cover $v(e) \in Q$. To different edges $e \neq f \in M$ are assigned different vertices $v(e) \neq v(f)$. In other words, the mapping v is injective. Hence $|M| \leq |Q|$. □

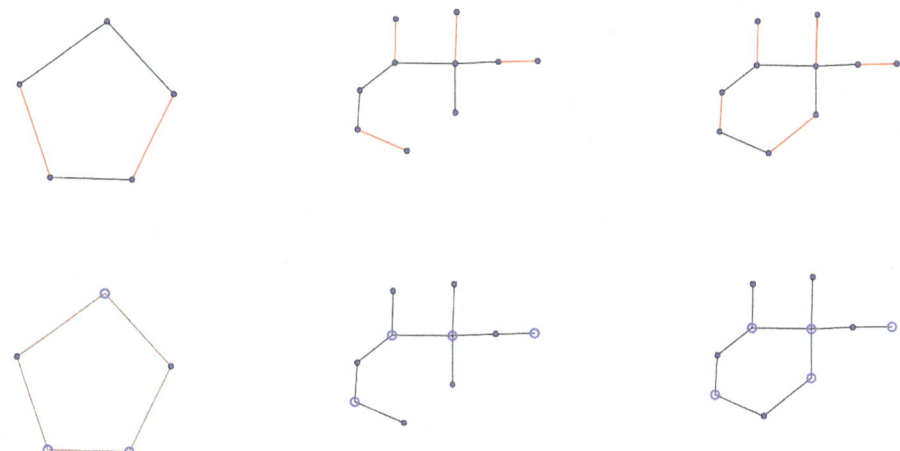

Figure 27: Maximum matching and minimum cover.

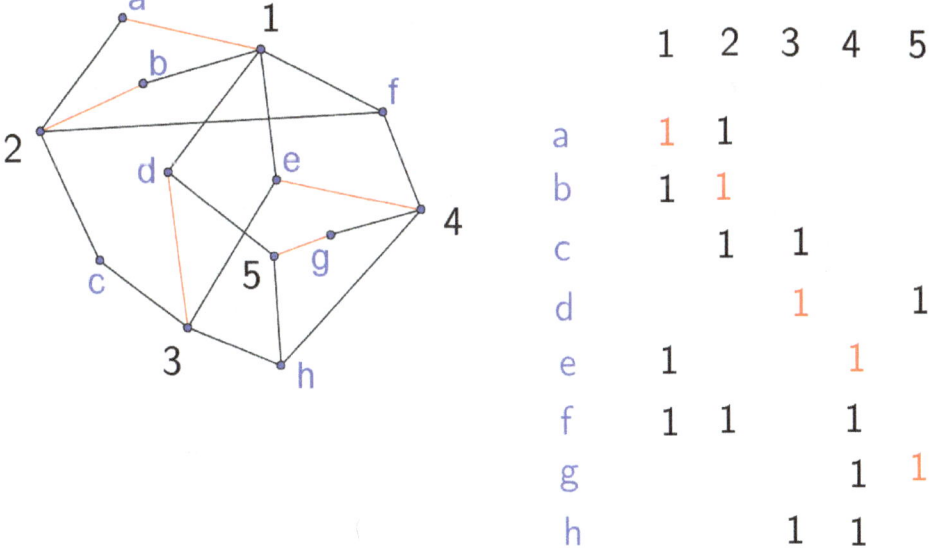

Figure 28: Maximum matching and its matrix representation.

Problem 30. *Find a maximum matching and a minimum vertex cover for each one of the three graphs in the figure on page 34.*

Theorem 1 (König-Egervary Theorem (1931)). *For a bipartite simple graph, the maximum size of a matching equals the minimum size of a vertex cover.*

Menger's Theorem in the vertex form implies the König-Egervary Theorem. The given bipartite graph G is extended to graph $G \cup \{s,t\}$ by connecting all black vertices of G to the source s, and all white vertices of G to the terminal t. Any matching in G corresponds one-to-one to a set of internally vertex disjoint paths in the extended graph $G \cup \{s,t\}$. Any vertex cover of G corresponds one-to-one to a vertex cut in the extended graph $G \cup \{s,t\}$.

By Menger's Theorem in the vertex form 13, the maximal number of internally vertex disjoint paths in the extended graph $G \cup \{s,t\}$ equals the minimal number of a vertex cut, again for the extended graph $G \cup \{s,t\}$. Hence the maximal matching in G has the same size as the minimal vertex cover of G. □

Independent proof of the König-Egervary Theorem. The theorem is obviously true for all bipartite graphs with $n \leq 4$ vertices since any odd cycles have been excluded. As induction assumption, we assume the statement of the theorem to hold for all bipartite graphs with less than n vertices, and for all bipartite graphs with n vertices but less than m edges.

Given is a bipartite graph G with n vertices and m edges. If all degrees of G have degree at most two, the graph is a disjoint union of cycles and paths, in which case the statement is easy to check, the odd cycles being excluded. Hence we may assume there exists a vertex u of degree at least 3 and neighbors $v \sim u, v_1 \sim u$ and $v_2 \sim u$. Let W be a vertex cover of $G \setminus v$ of maximum size $|W| = \beta(G \setminus v)$. Since $V_G \cup \{v\}$ is a vertex cover of G, the induction assumption implies

$$|W| + 1 = \beta(G) = \beta(G \setminus v) + 1 = \alpha'(G \setminus v) + 1$$

In the case that $\alpha'(G \setminus v) < \alpha(G)$, we conclude from Lemma 1 that $\beta(G) \leq \alpha'(G) \leq \beta(G)$, and get the assertion $\beta(G) = \alpha'(G)$ as claimed.

Hence we are left with the case that $\alpha'(G \setminus v) = \alpha'(G)$. Let M be a maximum matching of $G \setminus v$. It is a maximum matching of G, too, and no edge of M is adjacent to v.

Either $uv_1 \notin M$ or $uv_2 \notin M$, and we may assume $e := uv_2 \notin M$. Let Q be a minimum vertex cover of $G \setminus e$. No edge of M is adjacent to v. Each edge of M has at least one end in Q. Hence $v \notin Q$. Since uv is an edge of $G \setminus e$, we conclude that $u \in Q$.

Since $u \in Q$ and $e = uv_2$, the vertex cover Q covers the graph G, too. Hence $|Q| = \beta(G \setminus e) = \beta(G)$.

$$\begin{aligned}
|M| &= \alpha'(G \setminus v) & &\text{since } M \text{ is a minimum vertex cover of } G \setminus v; \\
\alpha'(G \setminus e) &= \alpha'(G) & &\text{since } e \notin M; \\
\alpha'(G \setminus e) &= \beta(G \setminus e) & &\text{by induction assumption;} \\
\alpha'(G \setminus v) &= \alpha'(G) & &\text{from case above;} \\
\beta(G \setminus e) &= |Q| & &\text{since } Q \text{ is a minimum vertex cover of } G \setminus e. \\
|Q| &= \beta(G) & &\text{from above.} \\
|M| &= \alpha'(G) = \beta(G) = |Q|
\end{aligned}$$

We have obtained for G a matching and of vertex cover of the same size. Each edge of M has exactly one end in Q. □

Remark 8. A much simpler reasoning is based on König's color theorem 18. This reasoning works for the special case of regular bipartite graphs, among others. See the proposition 65 about regular bipartite graphs below.

I.1.11   Subsets and multisubsets

Remark 9. Objects can be chosen from a supply with n different kinds. One puts k objects into a bag, the order does not matter. If repetition is not allowed, there are

$$\binom{n}{k} = \frac{n(n-1)(n-2)\cdots(n-k+1)}{1\cdot 2 \cdot 3 \cdots k}$$

ways to chose *subsets* of size k from n objects.
But if every object is available in as many copies as wanted, there are

$$\binom{n+k-1}{k} = \frac{n(n+1)(n+2)\cdots(n+k-1)}{1\cdot 2 \cdot 3 \cdots k}$$

ways to chose *multisubsets* of size k from n objects..

Both formulas have k factors—as many as objects are chosen—up and down. But in the case of repetitions allowed the sequence up is increasing.

I.1.12   Counting labelled and unlabelled graphs

We put the n vertices of the respective graph at fixed coordinates, and assign to these points in the plane the labels $1, 2, 3, \ldots, n$. Two labelled graphs are isomorphic iff they have the same number of edges between any two of these points. Two unlabelled graphs are isomorphic if and only if they are isomorphic graphs, as explained in Definition 15.

These agreements are substantial for counting labelled and unlabelled graphs, possibly with some additional properties. One gets much larger numbers when counting labelled graphs. But in terms of the mathematical ideas involved, it turns out to be much easier to count labelled graphs than the unlabelled ones.

Proposition 8. (a) *The number of labelled simple graphs with n vertices is* $2^{\frac{n(n-1)}{2}}$.

(b) *The number of labelled simple graphs with n vertices and m edges is* $\binom{\frac{n(n-1)}{2}}{m}$.

(c) *The number of labelled general loopless graphs with n vertices and m edges is*

$$\binom{m-1+\frac{n(n-1)}{2}}{m}$$

(d) *The number of labelled general graphs with n vertices and m edges is*

$$\binom{m - 1 + \frac{n(n+1)}{2}}{m}$$

Proof. **(a)** There are $\frac{n(n-1)}{2}$ places where one may or may not put an edge. For each place the decision gives a factor two for the number of possibilities.

(b) Among the $\frac{n(n-1)}{2}$ places where to possibly put an edge, one has to choose m ones.

(c) From the $M := \frac{n(n-1)}{2}$ places where to possibly put one or several edges, one has to choose m ones, allowing for repetitions. There are

$$\frac{M \cdot (M+1) \cdot (M+2) \cdots (M+m-1)}{m} = \binom{M+m-1}{m}$$

possibilities.

(d) From the $L := \frac{n(n-1)}{2} + n = \frac{n(n+1)}{2}$ places where to possibly put one or several edges or loops, one has to choose m ones, allowing for repetitions. There are

$$\frac{L \cdot (L+1) \cdot (L+2) \cdots (L+m-1)}{m} = \binom{L+m-1}{m}$$

possibilities.

□

By Cayley's Theorem 29, there are n^{n-2} different labeled trees with n vertices. Indeed, the labeled trees are in bijective correspondence to their Prüfer codes. The code for a tree is a list of length $n-2$, the entries of which are integers in the range $1, 2, \ldots, n$. The following table assembles some counting results for small graphs.

n	$\frac{n(n-1)}{2}$	labelled simple graphs	unlabelled simple graphs	labelled trees	unlabelled trees
1	0	1	1	1	1
2	1	2	2	1	1
3	3	8	4	3	1
4	6	64	11	16	2
5	10	1 024	34	125	3
6	15	32 768	156	1 296	6
7	21	2 097 152	1 044	16 807	11
8	28	268 435 456	12 346	262 144	23
9	36			4 782 969	47

I.1.13 Cartesian products

Definition 23 (Cartesian product of two graphs). The Cartesian product $G \times H$ of two graphs G and H

- has as set of vertices the product $V_G \times V_H = \{(g,h) : g \in V_G, h \in V_H\}$;
- as set of edges those joining vertices (g,h) and (g',h') were either $g \overset{G}{\sim} g'$, $h = h'$ or $g = g'$, $h \overset{H}{\sim} h'$.

Problem 31. *Draw the following Cartesian products.*
(a) $P_2 \times P_2$ (b) $P_2 \times C_3$ (c) $P_3 \times C_3$
(d) $P_3 \times P_2$ (e) $P_2 \times K_4$ (f) $P_2 \times K_{1,3}$

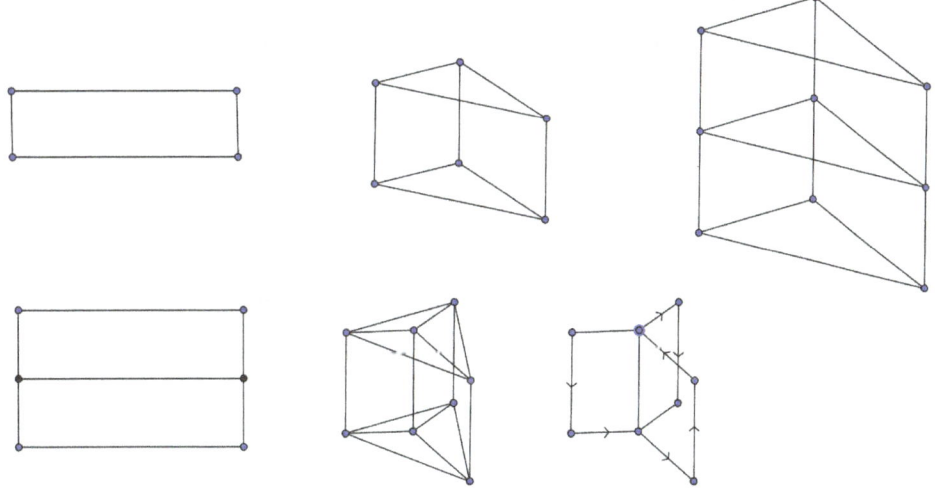

Figure 29: Cartesian products.

Proposition 9. *The Cartesian product of two graphs is connected if and only if both graphs are connected.*

Problem 32. *Prove Proposition 9.*

I.1.14 Series of special graphs

Definition 24 (The cube in any dimension). The d-dimensional cube Q_d is defined recursively by setting
$$Q_1 := P_2, \quad Q_{d+1} := Q_d \times P_2.$$
Here P_2 is the *path graph* with two vertices.

Problem 33 (Counting vertices and edges). *We see the cubes are defined in any dimension d.*

(a) *Draw the examples for dimension $d = 1, 2, 3$.*

(b) *Start a table to list the number of vertices n_d and the number of edges m_d for $d = 1 \ldots 7$ dimensions.*

(c) *Find recursive formulas to determine n_{d+1} and m_{d+1} from given n_d and m_d.*

(d) *Guess closed formulas for n_d and m_d.*

(e) *Prove the closed formula for m_d by induction.*

Answer. (a) The cube Q_d for dimension $d = 1, 2, 3$.

(b) Here is a table listing the number of vertices n_d and the number of edges m_d for $d = 1, 2, 3, 4, 5$:

d	n_d	m_d
1	2	1
2	4	4
3	8	12
4	16	$8 + 2 \cdot 12 = 32$
5	32	$16 + 2 \cdot 32 = 80$
6	64	$32 + 2 \cdot 80 = 192$
7	128	$64 + 2 \cdot 192 = 448$

(c) The recursive formulas for n_d and m_d follow from the the recursive definition of the cubes. The number of vertices is doubled in each step. Hence $n_{d+1} = 2n_d$. The two copies of Q_d which make up Q_{d+1} bring $2m_d$ edges. Additionally, we need n_d edges joining the two copies. Hence $m_{d+1} = 2m_d + n_d$.

(d) It is easy to guess that $n_d = 2^d$. We use the recursion formula $m_{d+1} = 2m_d + n_d$ to get the number of edges for d up to seven. To guess a general formula for m_d, I divide $\frac{m_d}{d}$ and see that one gets 2^{d-1}, at least for the examples. Thus one conjectures that $m_d = d(2^{d-1})$.

(e) We now prove the formula for m_d by induction. We have already seen that the formula holds for $d = 1, 2, 3$. Here is the induction step from d to $d+1$:

$$m_{d+1} = 2m_d + n_d \qquad \text{by the recursive formula}$$
$$= d(2^{d-1}) + 2 \cdot 2^d \qquad \text{by the induction assumption}$$
$$= (d+1)2^d \qquad \text{which is the corresponding formula for } d+1.$$

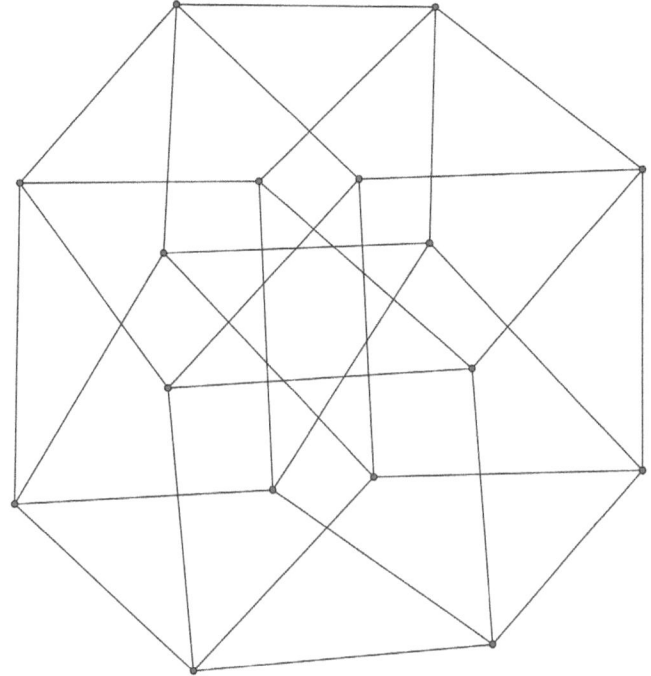

Figure 30: The four-dimensional cube Q_4.

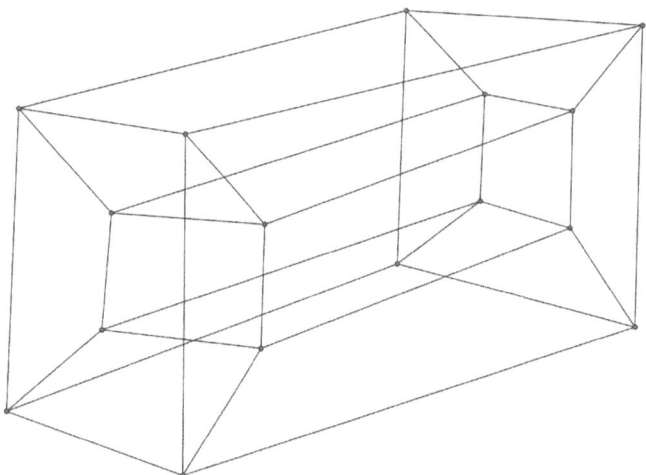

Figure 31: Another representation of Q_4.

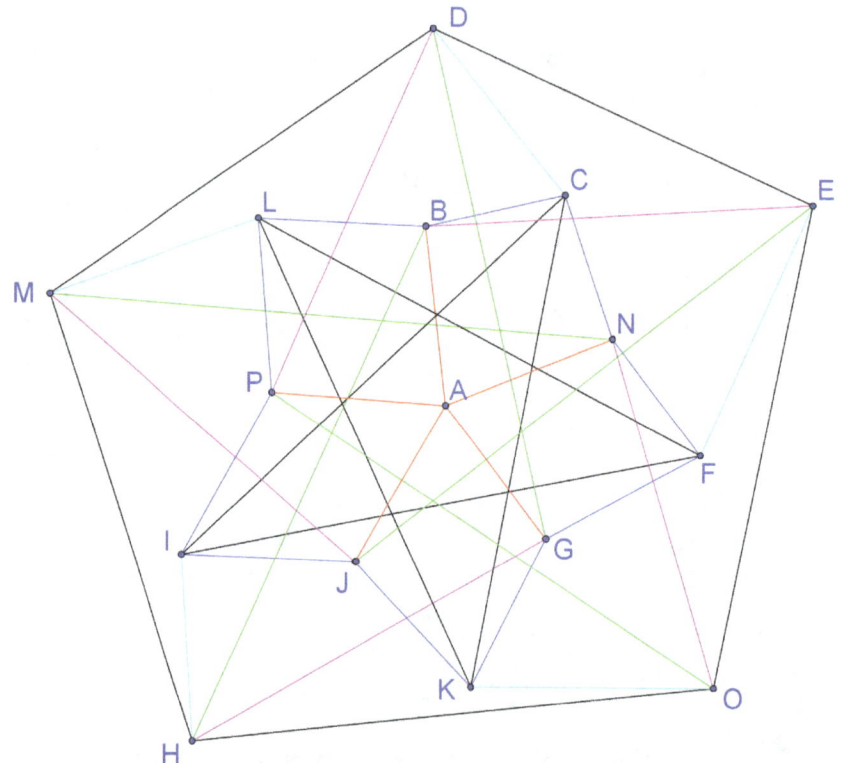

Figure 32: The four-dimensional cube Q_4 with antipodes joint.

Definition 25 (The octahedron in any dimension). The d-dimensional octahedron Oct_d is defined recursively by setting

$$\text{Oct}_1 := N_2\,,\quad \text{Oct}_{d+1} := \text{Oct}_d \vee N_2$$

Here $A \vee B$ denotes the *join* of two graphs A and B, and N_2 is the null graph with two vertices.

Problem 34. *Determination of the number of vertices and edges.*

(a) *Draw Oct_d for $d = 1, 2, 3$*

(b) *Start a table to list the number of vertices n_d and the number of edges m_d for the d-dimensional octahedron Oct_d for $d = 1, 2, 3, 4, 5$.*

(c) *Give recursive formulas for n_d and m_d.*

(d) *Guess closed formulas for n_d and m_d.*

(e) *Prove the formula for the number of edges m_d by induction.*

Answer. (a) The octahedron Oct_d for dimension $d = 1, 2, 3$.

(b) Here is a table listing the number of vertices n_d and the number of edges m_d for $d = 1, 2, 3, 4, 5$:

d	n_d	m_d
1	2	0
2	4	4
3	6	12
4	8	$12 + 2 \cdot 6 = 24$
5	10	$24 + 32 \cdot 8 = 40$

(c) To get recursive formulas for n_d and m_d, we use the recursive definition of the octahedrons. The number of vertices and edges of the join of any two graphs is

$$n(A \vee B) = n(A) + n(B)$$
$$m(A \vee B) = m(A) + m(B) + n(A)n(B)$$

Hence recursive definition of the octahedrons yield

$$n_{d+1} = n_d + 2$$
$$m_{d+1} = m_d + 2n_d$$

(d) It is easy to guess that $n_d = 2d$. We use the recursion formula $m_{d+1} = m_d + 2n_d$ to get the number of edges for d up to five. To guess a general formula for m_d, I divide $\frac{m_d}{d}$ and see that one gets $2(d-1)$, at least for d up to 5. Thus one conjectures that

$$n_d = 2d$$
$$m_d = 2d(d-1)$$

Problem 35. *Prove the formula for the number of edges m_d by induction.*

Answer. We now prove the formula for m_d by induction. We have already seen that the formula holds for $d = 1, 2, 3$. Here is the induction step from d to $d+1$:

$$\begin{aligned} m_{d+1} &= m_d + 2n_d & \text{by the recursive formula} \\ &= 2d(d-1) + 2d & \text{by the induction assumption} \\ &= 2(d+1)d & \text{which is the corresponding formula for } d+1. \end{aligned}$$

Problem 36. *Count the edges of the complement $\overline{\text{Oct}_d}$ and give a description of it.*

Answer. The complement $\overline{\text{Oct}_d}$ has $2d$ vertices and d edges. One can see this by the subtraction

$$m(\overline{\text{Oct}_d}) = m(K_{2d}) - m(\text{Oct}_d) = \frac{2d(2d-1)}{2} - 2d(d-1) = d$$

It is 1-regular, and hence a complete matching.

I.1.15 The degree sequence

The vertices of a simple graph are ordered in any way to obtain a monotone sequence

$$d_1 = \deg(v_1) \geq d_2 = \deg(v_2) \geq \cdots \geq d_n = \deg(v_n)$$

for the degrees—which is simply called *degree sequence*. [2]

Problem 37. *Two isomorphic graphs have the same degree sequence, but two graphs with the same degree sequence need not be isomorphic. Draw an example of two non-isomorphic simple graphs with the same degree sequence.*

There exists an easy algorithm to decide whether a given sequence is the degree sequence of a simple graph. If yes, the algorithm allows one to construct such a graph. If such a graph does not exist, the algorithm proves non-existence. The algorithm is based on the following:

Proposition 10. *In the simple graph G are chosen a vertex v of highest degree $\deg(v) = \Delta$, and any Δ vertices which have the next highest degrees. From the given graph G, one can construct a graph H with the same degree sequence and additionally the following property (P):*

(P) *The highest degree vertex v is adjacent to the chosen $\deg(v)$ vertices with the next highest degrees.*

Next we state the reduction algorithm, and in the end go on to prove it by means of the above proposition 10.

Algorithm 1 (Reduction algorithm). *For any given degree sequence, either a simple graph is constructed, or nonexistence of such a graph proved. To this end, we put the degree sequence $d_1 \geq d_2 \geq \cdots \geq d_n$ into the first row of a matrix, the columns of which give the labeled vertices.*

Iteration step producing the $i+1$-th row from the i-th row: In the i-th row, any one of the vertices of highest degree d_i is deleted—which we mark by scratching through this number. There are chosen any d_i vertices of the next highest degrees—and marked by a box. To produce the $i+1$-th row, the column for the deleted vertex is left blank, and the degrees marked by a box are lowered by one.

The process is repeated until

- *either an I-th row of only zeros results;*

- *or there do not exist the required number d_i of boxed vertices of next highest degrees; or even if the required number d_i of boxed vertices exists, in the row below some negative degree would occur,—-produced from a boxed isolated vertex.*

---
[2] Sometimes, one uses the increasing order, too.

In the first case, a simple graph H with the given degree sequence exists, and is constructed as follows: The labeled vertices of the graph H to be constructed, correspond to the columns of the matrix. They are marked at arbitrarily—but conveniently chosen—points in the drawing plane. By backtracking the rows, for each row of the matrix, there are drawn edges between the vertex to be deleted and the boxed vertices.

In the second case, a simple graph with the given degree sequence does not exist, and the algorithm proves non-existence.

Proof Proposition 10: The transformation from graph G to the graph H with the same degree sequence and the required property (P) is done by means of sequence of square switches. A *square switch* alters the edges between four vertices v, w, x, y from the pattern to the right to that on the left:

(square-switch)

$$
\begin{array}{ccc}
v \sim w & & v \not\sim w \\
\not\sim \quad \not\sim & \longrightarrow & \sim \quad \sim \\
x \sim y & & x \not\sim y
\end{array}
$$

It does not matter whether there are edges along the diagonals of the square. Obviously, a square switch leaves the degree sequence invariant.

We assume property (P) has not been accomplished, and find the square switch. There exist vertices w and x such that

$$v \sim w, \; v \not\sim x \quad \text{and} \quad \deg w \leq \deg x$$

In case that $\deg w = \deg x$, we need a square switch only if vertex x, but not vertex w has been chosen as a neighbor of v. Among the vertices $V_G \setminus \{x, v, w\}$, the vertex x has actually more neighbors than w. This is clear since $\deg x \geq \deg w$, and x is not adjacent to v, but w is adjacent to v. Hence there exists a forth vertex y such that $y \sim x$ and $y \not\sim w$. Thus the situation as in the left square of the operation (square-switch) occurs.

By performing the square switch, we get $v \sim x$ and $v \not\sim w$ as required. Too, the sum

$$S(v) := \sum_{n \sim v} \deg n$$

of the degrees of neighbors of v is increased by one.

Now the entire procedure can be repeated until $S(v)$ is maximal. For maximum value of $S(v)$, the above procedure cannot be done. Hence the required property (P) does hold, as to be shown. □

Validity of the algorithm. Assume the algorithm stops with a sequence of zeros. in the last row I of the matrix. Hence this row corresponds to a null graph N_s for some $s \geq 1$.

Each row $i = 1 \ldots I$ of the algorithm corresponds to a graph H_i. The degree sequence of H_{i+1} is obtained from that of H_i by deleting the vertex v_i of maximum degree chosen in row i to be deleted, and lowering the degrees of the d_i boxed vertices each by one. Hence $H_{i+1} = H_i - v_i$ and $H_i = H_{i+1} \vee v_i$. From the null graph $H_I = N_s$, we reconstruct $H_{i-1} = H_i \vee v_{i-1}$ for all rows $i = I \ldots 2$ until we get back to H_1 which has the required degree sequence.

Conversely, if a graph G exists for the given degree sequence, the algorithm stops with a row of zeros. The formal reasoning proceeds by the induction on the number of vertices. The assertion holds degree sequence of length one and two. Assume the assertion is check for all degree sequences of lengths less than I.

We have given a an graph G with degree sequence of length I. Let v_1 be the vertex of highest degree chosen to be deleted. By Proposition 10, we construct a graph H with the same degree sequence as G and property (P). The graph $H - v_1$ has the degree sequence in the second row of the matrix. By induction assumption, the continuation of the algorithm terminates with a row of zeros. Hence the algorithm for graph G terminates with a row of zeros, too.

As the contrapositive, we see that an algorithm stopping with another alternative proves non-existence of a graph with the given degree sequence.

$\square$

Corollary 1. *Two simple graphs have the same degree sequence if and only if there exists a finite sequence of square-switches transforming one graph to the other one.*

Problem 38. (a) *How many edges would a graph with the degree sequence $5, 5, 4, 3, 3, 2$ have.*

(b) *Apply the reduction algorithm to the list $5, 5, 4, 3, 3, 2$*

(c) *To show that the list S gives the degrees of the vertices of some simple graph G, construct such a graph going backwards through the list from the reduction procedure. Check the number of edges.*

(d) *Draw a plane representation.*

Answer. (a) By the handshaking lemma, $2m = 5 + 5 + 4 + 3 + 3 + 2 = 22$. Hence the graph has $m = 11$ edges, presupposing its existence.

(b)

$$\begin{array}{cccccc} \boxed{5} & \boxed{5} & \boxed{4} & \boxed{3} & \boxed{3} & \boxed{2} \\ & \boxed{4} & \boxed{3} & \boxed{2} & \boxed{2} & \boxed{1} \\ & & \boxed{2} & \boxed{1} & \boxed{1} & 0 \\ & & & 0 & 0 & 0 \end{array}$$

Since the reduction algorithm ends with a list of zeros, which means a null graph, there exists a graph with the given degree sequence.

(c) To show that the list S gives the degrees of the vertices of some simple graph G, we construct such a graph going backwards through the list from the reduction procedure. Check the number of edges.

(d) The figure on page 46 gives a plane representation.

I find the following example more instructive.

Problem 39. *Apply the reduction algorithm to the degree sequence* $(4,4,3,3,3,3)$. *Draw a simple graph with that degree sequence, with as few crossing among edges as possible. Check whether it is planar.*

Answer. The graph has 10 edges. The reduction algorithm yields

$$
\begin{array}{cccccc}
\cancel{4} & 4 & 3 & 3 & 3 & 3 \\
\cancel{3} & 2 & 2 & 2 & 2 & 3 \\
  & 1 & 1 & 2 & 2 & \cancel{2} \\
\cancel{1} & 0 & 1 & & & \\
  & 0 & 0 & & & \\
\end{array}
$$

Since the reduction algorithm ends with a list of zeros, which means a null graph, there exists a graph with the given degree sequence.

The reconstruction of a graph from the list of degrees yields a graph as shown,—in a plane representation.

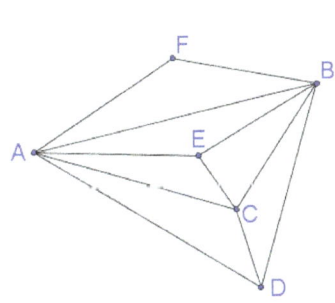 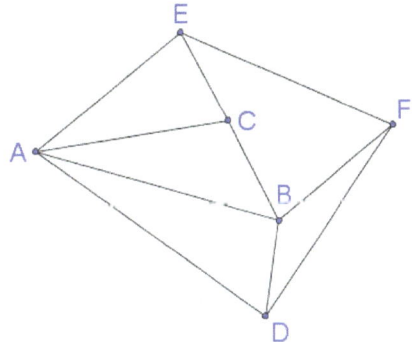

Figure 33: Reconstructed graphs.

I.1.16 About nonexistence of triangles

Proposition 11 (Proposition of Turan). *A simple graph with $n \geq 3$ vertices and no triangles has at most $m \leq \frac{n^2}{4}$ edges.*

Proof. To begin the induction, we check the assertion for $n = 3$ and $n = 4$. Indeed, a graph with 3 vertices and no triangles has at most 2 edges, and $2 \leq \frac{9}{4}$. A graph with 4 vertices and no triangles has at most 4 edges, and $4 \leq \frac{16}{4}$.

For the induction step, I assume the assertion holds for graphs with less than n vertices. Given is a graph G with $n \geq 5$ vertices, and no triangles. For the null graph the assertion is true. Otherwise, we choose any two adjacent vertices $u \sim v$, and let $H = G \setminus \{u, v\}$ be the induced subgraph, obtained pulling out vertices u and v. Because of our assumption that G has no triangles, clearly H has no triangles neither. Hence the induction assumptions tells that $m(H) \leq \frac{(n-2)^2}{4}$. Because G has no triangles, he two vertices u and v cannot have a common neighbor in H, and hence the sum of their degrees is at most $\deg u + \deg v \leq n - 2 + 1 + 1 = n$. Now the number of edges of G is bounded by

$$m(G) = m(H) + \deg u + \deg v - 1 \leq \frac{(n-2)^2}{4} + n - 1 = \frac{n^2}{4}$$

with the term -1 to avoid counting the edge from u to v twice. Hence we have confirmed G has at most $\frac{n^2}{4}$ edges, as to be shown. □

Proposition 12 (Turan's estimate). *[About a graph with no triangles] The degrees of a simple graph with $n \geq 3$ vertices and no triangles satisfies*

(I.1.3) $$\sum_{\text{vertices } v} \deg v^2 \leq m \cdot n$$

Proof. Rearranging of the sum yields

$$\sum \{ \deg u + \deg v : \text{vertices } u, v \text{ with } u \neq v \text{ and } u \sim v \}$$
$$= 2 \sum \{ \deg u : \text{vertices } u, v \text{ with } u \neq v \text{ and } u \sim v \}$$
$$= 2 \sum_{\text{vertices } u} \left[\sum \{ \deg u : \text{vertices } v \text{ with } v \neq u \text{ and } v \sim u \} \right]$$
$$= 2 \sum_{\text{vertices } u} \deg u^2$$

Because the graph has no triangles, any two vertices u and v cannot have a common neighbor, and hence the sum of their degrees is at most $\deg u + \deg v \leq n - 2 + 2 = n$ and hence

$$2 \sum_{\text{vertices } u} \deg u^2 = \sum \{ \deg u + \deg v : \text{vertices } u, v \text{ with } u \neq v \text{ and } u \sim v \}$$
$$\leq \sum \{ n : \text{vertices } u, v \text{ with } u \neq v \text{ and } u \sim v \} = 2n \cdot m$$

The sums over the pairs of vertices (u, v) with $u \neq v$ all count every edge twice. □

Problem 40. *Prove that the estimate (I.1.3) implies Turan's estimate $m \leq \frac{n^2}{4}$.*

Solution. To see that estimate (I.1.3) implies Turan's estimate, we use the handshaking lemma and the Cauchy-Schwarz inequality:

$$4m^2 = \left[\sum_{\text{vertices } u} \deg u \cdot 1 \right]^2 \leq \left[\sum_{\text{vertices } u} \deg u^2 \right] \cdot \left[\sum_{\text{vertices } u} 1^2 \right]$$
$$= \left[\sum_{\text{vertices } u} \deg u^2 \right] \cdot n \leq m \cdot n^2$$

and hence $m \leq \frac{n^2}{4}$ as stated in Turan's Theorem. □

Problem 41. *Prove that for any bipartite graph holds $m \leq \frac{n^2}{2}$.*

Solution. Any bipartite graph G with n vertices is a subgraph of $K_{a,b}$ with $n = a + b$. The number of vertices of the complete bipartite graph $K_{a,b}$ equals ab. Hence for the number of edges of G holds
$$4m \leq 4ab \leq (a+b)^2 = n^2$$
which confirms the assertion, which is Turan's estimate. □

Problem 42. *Prove that for the complete bipartite graph $K_{a,b}$ holds even the estimate (I.1.3).*

Proof. For the complete bipartite graph $K_{a,b}$ holds $n = a + b, m = a \cdot b$
$$\sum_{\text{vertices } v} \deg v^2 = a^2b + b^2a = abn = m \cdot n$$
□

We have obtained some remarkable relations between the different properties above. We may summarize them in the following diagram:

(I.1.4)

$$
\begin{array}{ccc}
G = K_{a,b} \text{ is complete bipartite} & \xrightarrow{\text{clear}} & G \text{ is bipartite} \\
\downarrow \text{problem 42} & & \downarrow \text{problem 41} \\
\sum_{\text{vertices } v} \deg v^2 \leq m \cdot n & \xrightarrow{\text{problem 40}} & \text{Turan's } m \leq \frac{n^2}{4} \\
\downarrow \text{problem 40} & & \downarrow \text{proposition 12} \\
\text{Turan's } m \leq \frac{n^2}{4} & \xrightarrow{\text{proposition 12}} & G \text{ has no triangles}
\end{array}
$$

Open problem 1. *Does the estimate (I.1.3) hold for all simple bipartite graphs.*

Open problem 2. *For which ones of the implications from figure (I.1.4) does the converse hold.*

I.1.17 Instant insanity

For the recreational game *instant insanity* are needed four cubes, the faces of which are colored in red, blue, green and yellow. We depict the cubes in their flattened out form. The goal of the game is to pile the cubes of top of each other so that all four colors appear on each sides of the resulting stack. A trial and error approach is inadvisable. Below is explained a solution in which each one of the four cubes is represented by a general graph.

Problem 43. *Solve the instant insanity game for the four cubes below.*

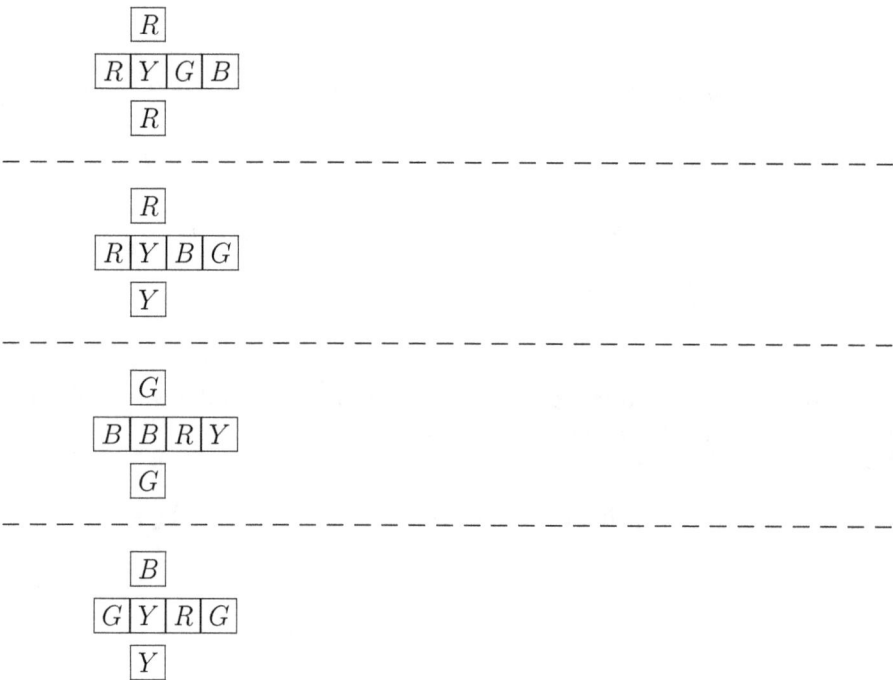

Draw your stack of cube—with all four colors on top of each other, seen from left and right; and from front and back.

Problem 44. *Solve the instant insanity game for the four cubes below.*

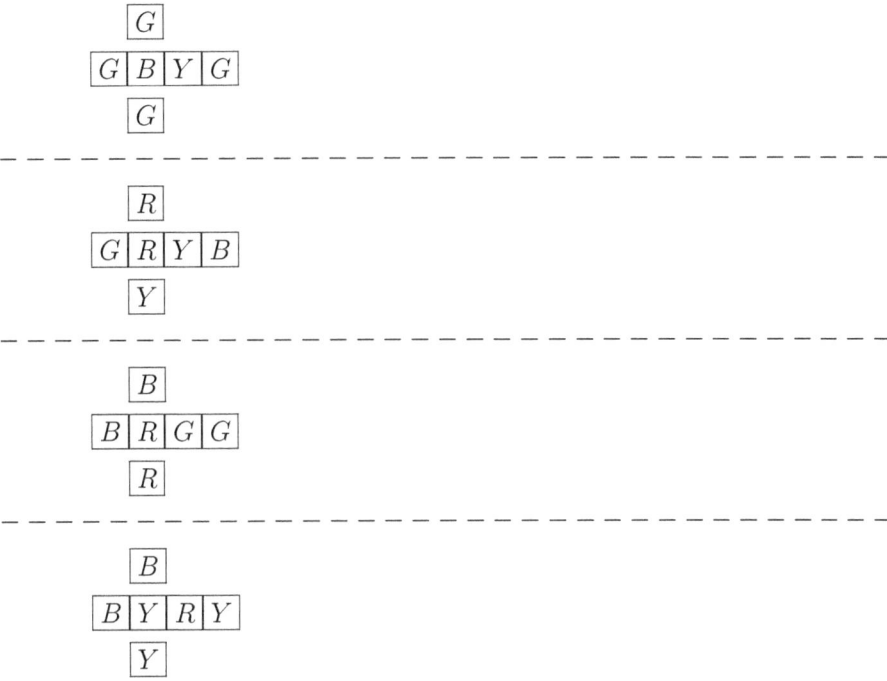

Draw your stack of cube—with all four colors on top of each other, seen from left and right; and from front and back.

Answer. From the nets of the four cubes, we get four graphs. Each has four vertices, labeled by the colors red, blue, green and yellow, and three labeled edges. An edge connects the colors of opposite faces of the respective cube. From these four graphs, we construct two graphs which describe a solution: graph H_1, which describes the coloring of front and back, and H_2 for the coloring of the left and right faces of the stacked cubes.

The graphs H_i have the following three properties:

(1) Each graph H_i has four edges, one from each cube.

(2) There are no common edges of the two graphs H_1 and H_2.

(3) All vertices of each graph H_i have degree two.

We give the cycles of the graph H_1 some arbitrarily chosen directions. As we parse the edges of a cycle, at first the color of the front face, and after that the color of the back face of the corresponding cube occurs.

Similarly, we assign some direction to the cycles of H_2. Parsing the edges of any cycle, at first the color of the left, and after that the color of the right face of the corresponding cube occurs. In the figures on page 51, two solutions are obtained for the cubes of problem 44.

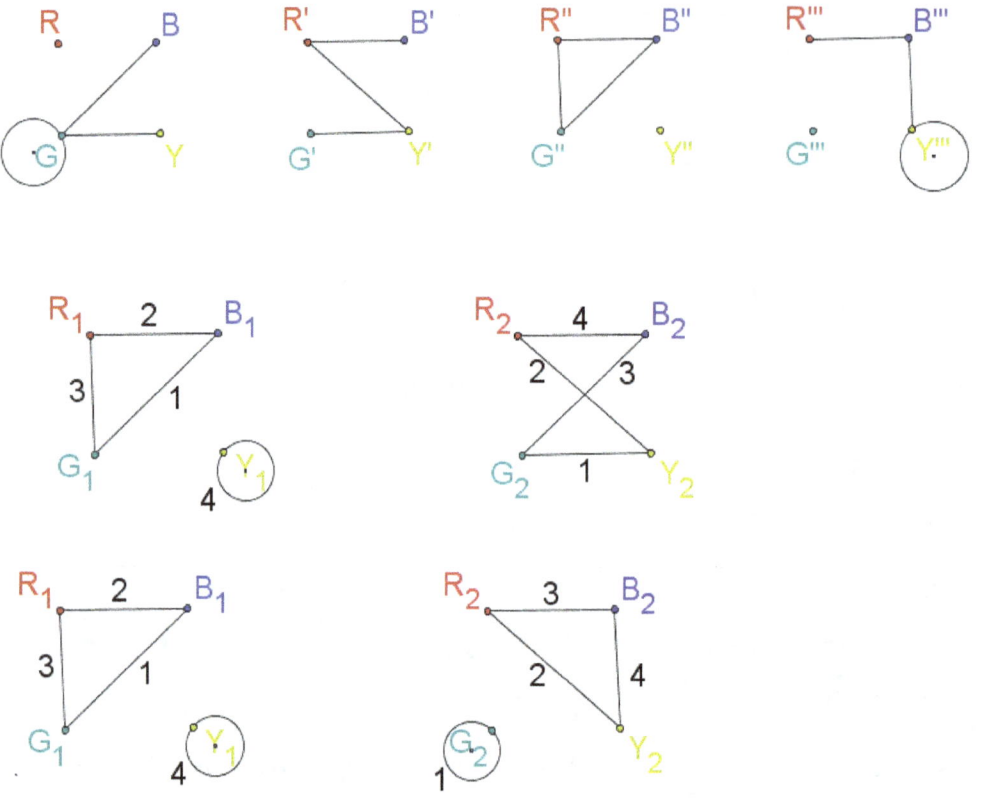

Figure 34: Two solutions of Problem 44.

Remark 10. Here is convenient labeling of all 24 edges: For $k = 1, 2, 3, 4$, the edges from the k-th cube are numbered $k, k+4, k+8$. Each one of the two graphs H_1 and H_2 has edges with numbers $1, 2, 3, 4 \mod 4$. The four remaining edges are discarted.

Problem 45. *Solve the instant insanity game for the four cubes below. Draw your stack of cube—with all four colors on top of each other, seen from left and right; and from front and* *back.*

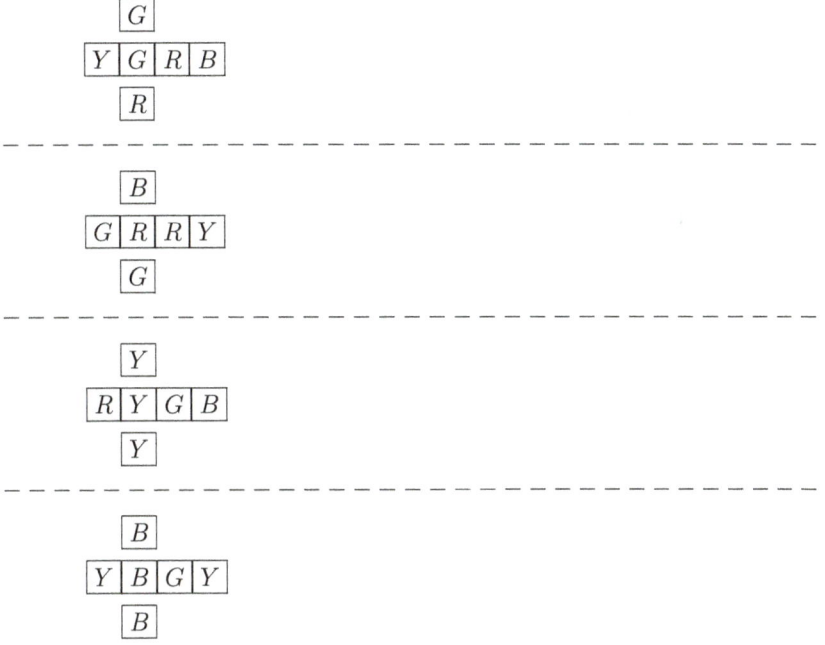

Answer. Solutions are given in the figures on page 52 and 53.

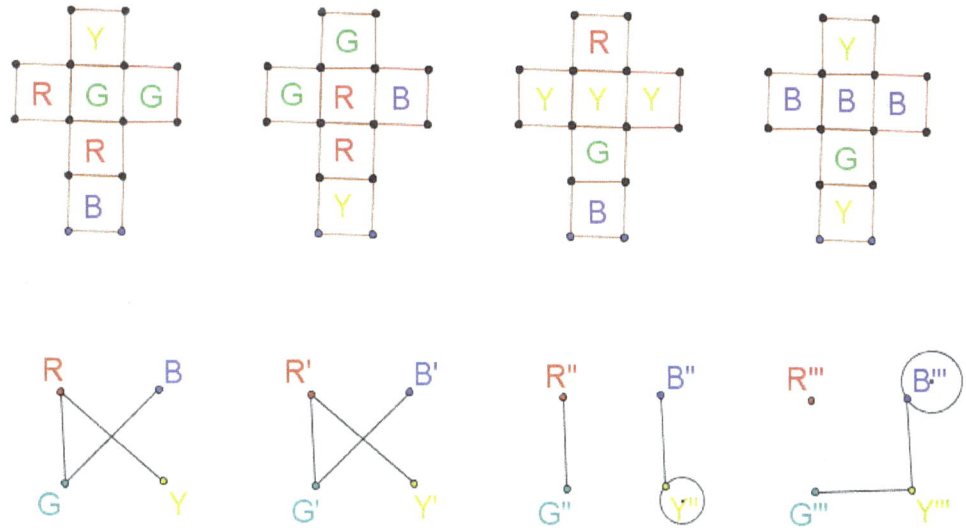

Figure 35: How to get the graphs for the four cubes.

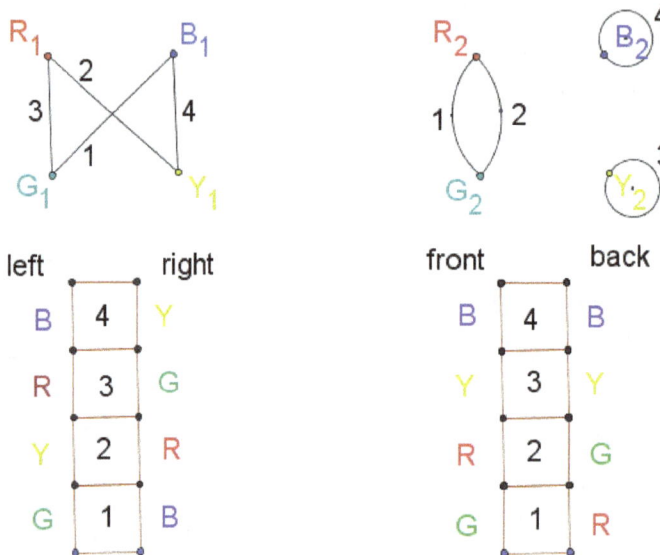

Figure 36: How to stack the four colored cubes.

I.2 Eulerian Graphs

Definition 26 (Eulerian trail and Eulerian graph). A closed trail that includes every edge exactly once is called an *closed Eulerian trail* or *Eulerian circuit*. [3] A graph with an Eulerian trail is called *Eulerian*.

Definition 27 (semi-Eulerian graph). I call a graph *semi-Eulerian* if and only if there exists an open trail—but not a closed trail—which visits each edge exactly once.

Definition 28 (non-Eulerian graph). I call a graph *non-Eulerian* if and only if it is neither Eulerian nor semi-Eulerian.

Definition 29. A vertex with degree zero is called *isolated* or a *trivial component*. A vertex is *even* if its degree is even. A graph with vertex degrees all even is called an *even graph*

Theorem 2 (Euler). *A graph has a closed trail that visits every edge exactly once if and only if*

(a) *each vertex has even degree.*

(b) *all edges lie in a single nontrivial component of the graph.*

Especially, a graph without isolated vertices is Eulerian if and only if it is even and connected.

---
[3]Note that it is a rare exception that the Eulerian trail becomes a cycle.

Corollary 2. *A connected graph has an* open *Eulerian trail if and only if exactly two vertices have odd degree.*

Proof the Corollary. If there exists an *open* Eulerian trail starting at vertex v and ending at vertex w, these two vertices have odd degree and all other vertices are even. Conversely, assume that G is a connected graph with the two vertices v and w odd, and all other vertices even. Let H be the graph obtained from G by adjoining an additional edge vw. Euler's Theorem 2 shows that H has a closed Eulerian trail. By removing the extra edge vw, we obtain an open Eulerian trial in the original graph G. □

Plan of proof for Euler's theorem. At first we show that existence of the Eulerian trail implies the assumptions that the graph is connected and even. Thus we confirm that these assumptions are *necessary*.[4] In a second step we prove that these two assumptions really imply existence of the Eulerian trail. Hence they are called *sufficient* conditions.[5] □

Proof necessity. Given any Eulerian graph, we need to check that any vertex v is even. We imagine to pass through the closed trail in a given direction. Each time the vertex v is hit, it is approached and left along two different edges. Let the Eulerian trail contain the vertex s times. Thus altogether $2s$ different edges adjacent to v are covered by the Eulerian trail. Since all edges are covered, the degree of v is $2s$ and hence even.

To check that the graph is connected, take any two vertices v and w. The closed trail contains edges adjacent to both. Hence a part of the Eulerian trail is a path from v to w. □

Lemma 2 (Return lemma). *A cycle exists in any graph all vertices of which have degree at least two.*

Proof. One may continue a path until it is maximal. Let u be its end vertex. Because the degree of u is at least two, it has another neighbor w besides its predecessor in the path. Since the path is assumed to be maximal, this neighbor w must be an earlier vertex of the path. Thus we have completed a cycle. □

Proposition 13. *The edges of an even graph can be split (partitioned) into cycles, no two of which have an edge in common.*

Proof the Proposition. We use induction on the number m of edges. The result is true for $m \leq 3$. For the induction step, we assume the result has been shown for all graphs with less than m edges. Now let G be an even graph with m edges. By the return Lemma, there exists a cycle C. We delete the edges of this cycle to obtain a graph G' with less than m edges. By the induction assumption, this smaller graph can be split into edge disjoint cycles. Adjoining the cycle C, we get a partition of the original graph G into edge-disjoint cycles. □

---

[4]It is somewhat awkward to speak about a necessary "condition" because we are really looking for a more or less handy <u>consequence</u> of the desired result.

[5]Douglas B. West calls this general plan of proof TONCAS: "The obvious necessary conditions are also sufficient".

Problem 46. *Illustrate the above proposition by use of different colors for your cycles. Does it matter whether the graph is connected or not?*

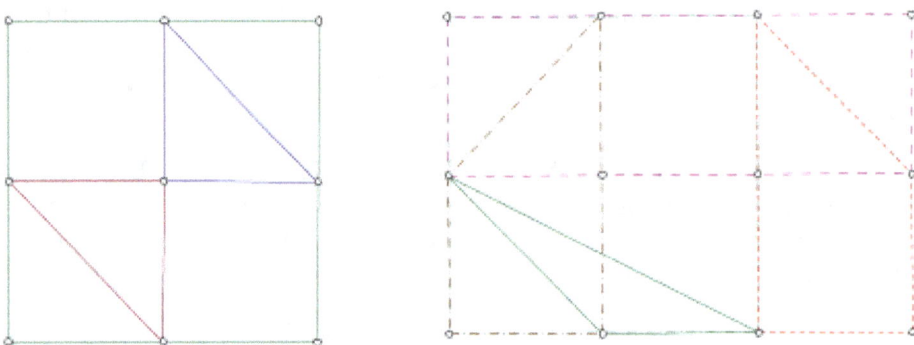

Figure 37: An even graph can be split into edge disjoint cycles.

Answer.

Lemma 3. *Any two closed trails with a vertex, but no edge in common, can be joint to one closed trail.*

Lemma 4. *Assume the graph G is connected, and its edges are partitioned into the of edge-disjoint cycles set $C_1, C_2 \ldots C_r$, such that $E_G = \cup_{i=1}^{r} C_i$. Then there exists a closed trail containing all edges of graph G exactly once.*

Proof the Lemma 4. We use induction on the number m of edges. The result is true for $m = 0$ or $m = 1$. For the induction step, we assume the assertion to be true for all graphs with less than m edges. Now let G graph have m edges, and assume its edges are partitioned into the edge-disjoint cycles $E_G = \cup_{i=1}^{r} C_i$.

Take the cycle $C := C_1$. If all vertices on this cycle have degree two, then $G = C$ since the graph is assumed to be connected. Hence we are ready.

Otherwise there exists a vertex v in cycle C with $\deg_G(v) \geq 3$. From graph G, we delete the edges of cycle C. Thus we obtain a graph $G' = G \setminus E_C$. Let $G_1, \ldots G_p$ be the components of G' which are not isolated vertices. For each $i = 1 \ldots p$, let v_i be the vertex in $G_i \cap C$ to which one comes first as one goes around the circle C, starting from v, say in clockwise direction. Each one of the graphs G_i is connected and has only even vertices. Since these graphs have less than m edges, we conclude from the induction assumption that the graph G_i has a closed Eulerian trail T_i, starting from v_i.

We can now obtain a closed Eulerian trial of the original graph G graph. We start at vertex v and follow the cycle C clockwise. At each vertex v_i, we interrupt and follow the closed trail

T_i. After coming back to vertex v_i, we go on to follow the cycle C clockwise until we arrive at the vertex v_{i+1}. In this way, one comes back to the starting vertex v and has obtained a closed Eulerian trail for the given graph G. □

End of the proof sufficiency. We assume the graph G is connected and all its vertices have even degree. By Proposition 13, the edges can be partitioned into edge-disjoint cycles.

$$E_G = \cup_{i=1}^r C_i$$

Since the graph G is assumed to be connected, by Lemma 4, there exists a closed trail containing all edges exactly once. In other words, the graph is Eulerian. □

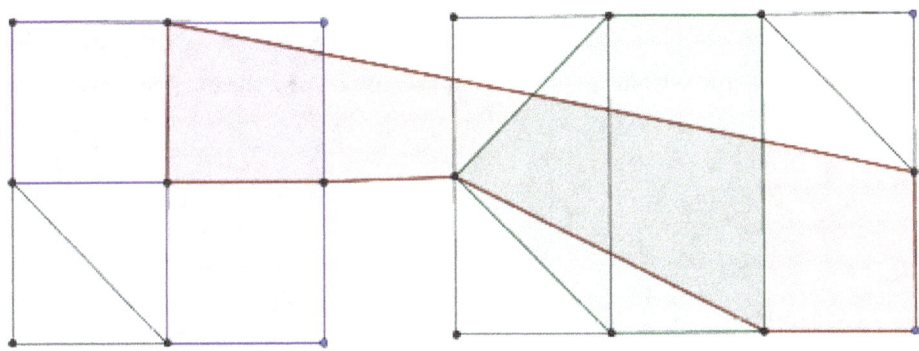

Figure 38: Trails can be joint.

Problem 47. *Illustrate the above lemma by a numbering of edges of your long trail obtained from the cycles surrounding the three colored regions.*

Problem 48. *Illustrate the above proposition for the graph from the figure on page 57. Use different colors for your cycles. Draw all different partitions into cycles. How many are there?*

Answer.

Problem 49. *The four-dimensional cube is drawn in the figure on page ??. At first color edge-disjoint cycles using different colors for their edges. From these cycles, get an Eulerian closed trail in the four-dimensional cube.*

Answer.

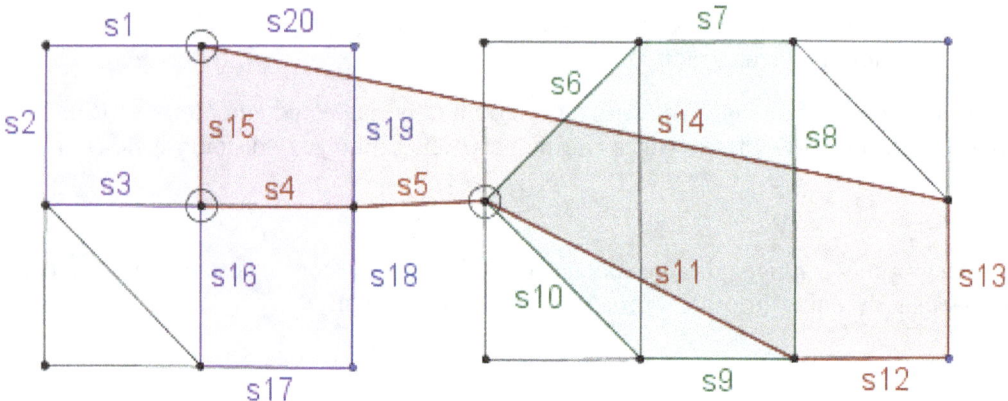

Figure 39: Here three trails have been joint. Trails are switched at the circled vertices.

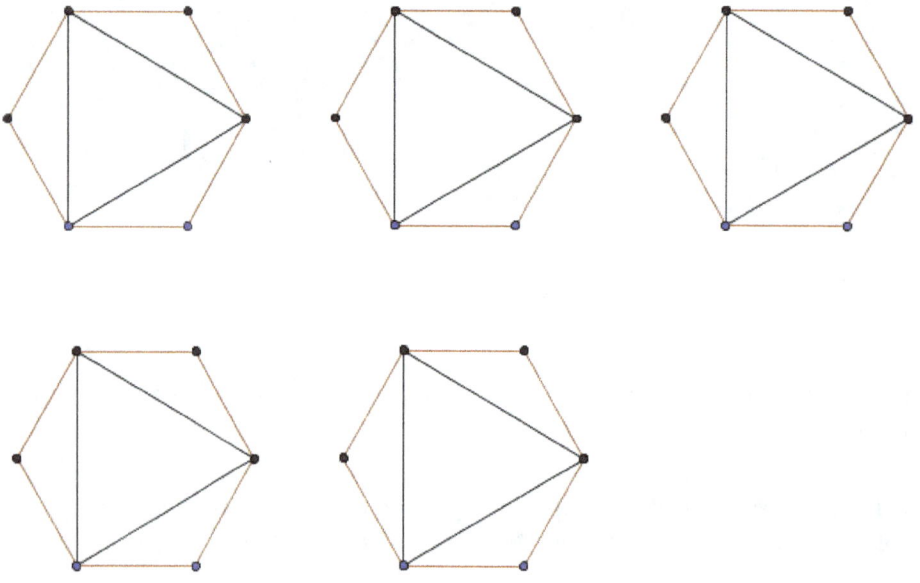

Figure 40: Split this graph into edge disjoint cycles.

Problem 50. *Draw the complete bipartite graph $K_{2,5}$ and show by another color a path of maximal length. How many edges does such a path have?*

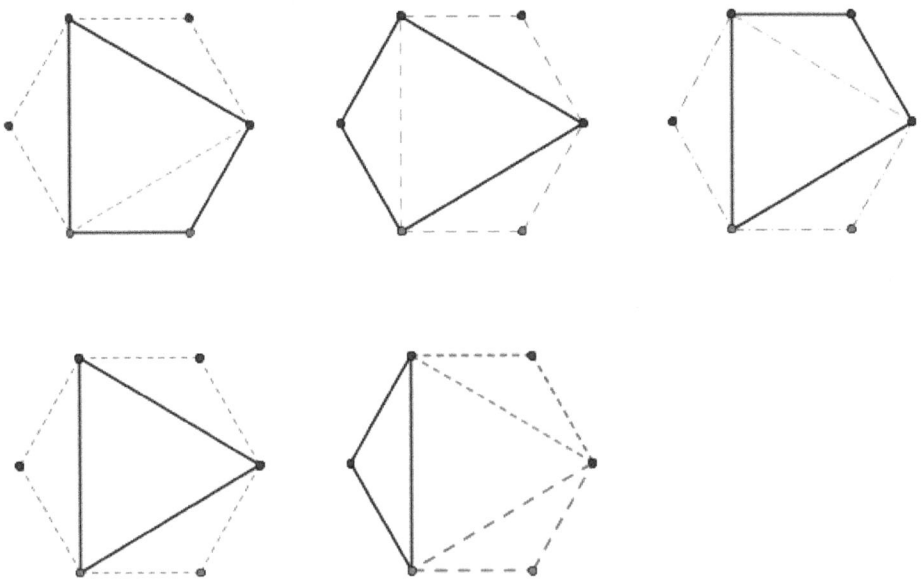

Figure 41: This graph has five different partitions into edge-disjoint cycles.

Problem 51. *Under which conditions for the numbers a and b is the complete bipartite graph $K_{a,b}$ Eulerian?*

Answer. There are a vertices of degree b and b vertices of degree a. Hence the complete bipartite graph $K_{a,b}$ is Eulerian if and only if a and b are both even.

Problem 52. *For which values of number n is the complete graph K_n Eulerian?*

Answer. All vertices have degree $n-1$. The complete graph K_n is Eulerian if and only if n is odd.

Problem 53. *The graphs $K_{1,1}$ and $K_{1,2}$ turn out to be semi-Eulerian. For which cases is the complete bipartite graph $K_{a,b}$ semi-Eulerian?*

Answer. The complete bipartite graph $K_{a,b}$ is semi-Eulerian if and only if $a = b = 1$, or $a = 2$ and b odd, or $b = 2$ and a odd.

Proposition 14. *The edges of a connected graph G with $2p$ odd vertices can be partitioned into p edge-disjoint open trials. Each open trial starts and ends at a different odd vertex. Thus one has obtained a two-to-one mapping from the odd vertices to these open trials. Indeed, this mapping may be prescribed in advance, before constructing the trials that partition the edges.*

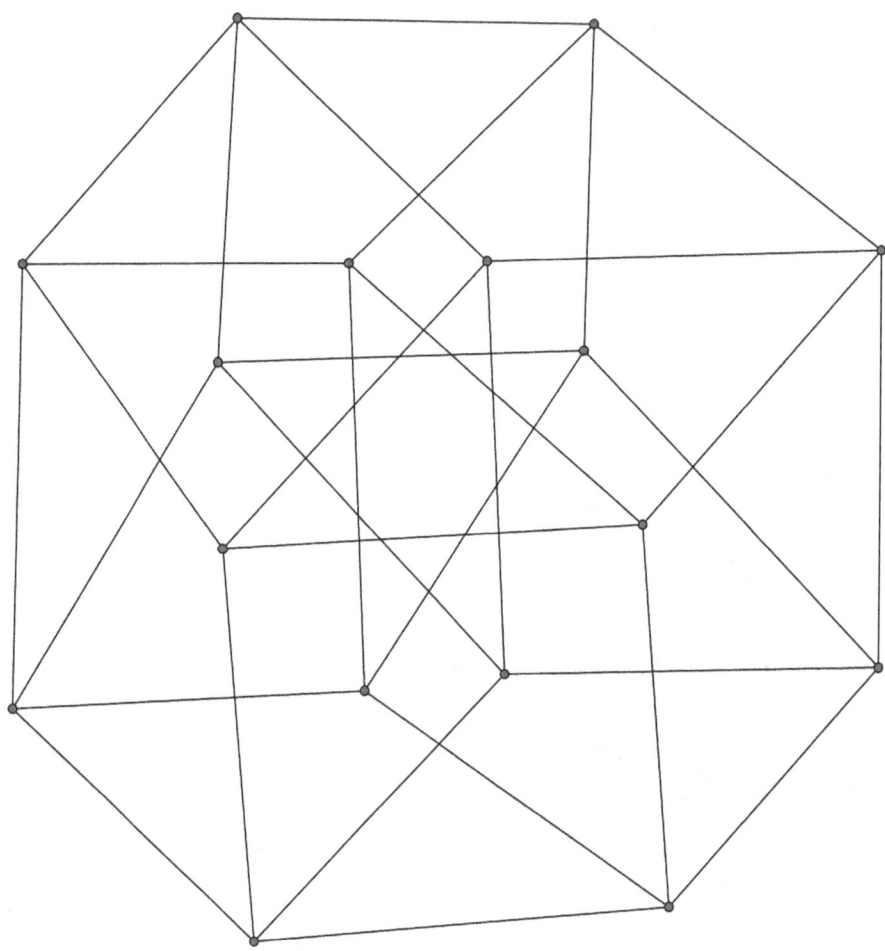

Figure 42: The four-dimensional cube is Eulerian.

Proof. Let H be the graph obtained from G by connecting each pair of odd vertices, which are assigned to one open trial, by an extra edge. Thus we obtain an Eulerian graph. Euler's Theorem 2 shows that H has a closed Eulerian trail. By removing the p extra edges, we obtain p edge-disjoint open trials in the original graph G, which together cover every edge of G exactly once. □

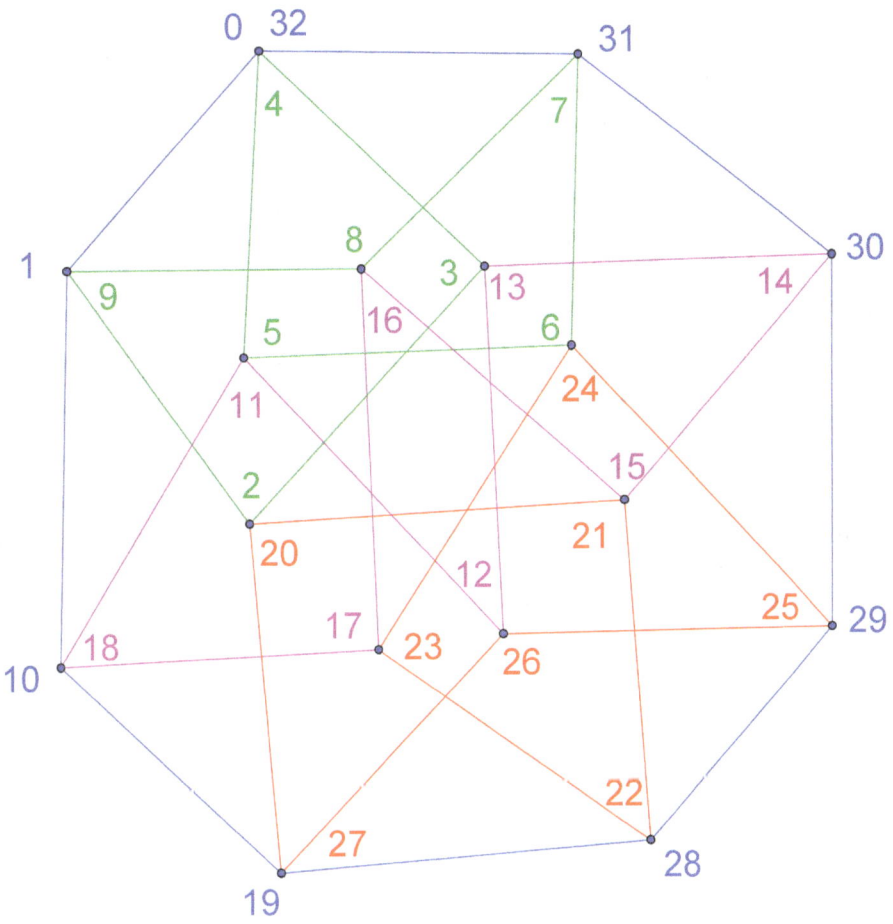

Figure 43: The four-dimensional cube is Eulerian.

I.2.1 Existence of cycles

Problem 54 (Existence of a cycle). *If all vertices of a simple graph have degree at least $\delta \geq 2$, there exists a cycle of length at least $1 + \delta$. Give examples where the length of the longest cycle is equal to $1 + \delta$.*

Answer. Starting at any vertex v_1, one can continue a path $v_1, v_2, \ldots, v_i$ until the only neighbors of v_i are among the vertices $v_1, v_2, \ldots, v_{i-1}$.

This can only happen for $i - 1 \geq \delta$, because of the minimal degree δ. But, on the other hand, since there are only finitely many vertices, one eventually gets to a vertex v_k adjacent to an earlier vertex w in the path. Hence one gets a cycle.

We still need to confirms its minimal length. To this end, we continue the path until we get to a vertex v_k that is adjacent <u>only</u> to earlier vertices of the path.

Indeed vertex v_k has a neighbor w among $v_1, v_2, \ldots, v_{k-\delta}$. Notice that it is impossible that $v_{k-\delta+1}, \ldots, v_{k-1}$ are the only neighbors of v_k, since v_k has at least δ neighbors.

Thus one gets a cycle through the vertices w and v_k, of length at least $1 + \delta$. Note that this is not necessarily a cycle through the vertex v_1, where one has started the path.

Eight conjectures about existence of cycles. Which ones of the following conjectures are true for a simple graph, which are false. Give a counterexample for the false conjectures, and a simple reason for the true ones as for example: "continue a path until till a vertex gets adjacent to an earlier vertex", or use some important theorem.

(1) "If all vertices have degrees at least two, a cycle exists."
(2) "If all vertices have degrees at least two, a cycle exists through any given vertex."
(3) "If all vertices have even degrees at least two, a cycle exists through any given vertex."
(4) "If all vertices have even degrees at least two, a cycle exists through any two given vertices."
(5) "If no cutvertex exists, a cycle exists through any two given vertices."
(6) "In a bridgeless connected graph with at least three vertices, a cycle exists through any given vertex."
(7) "In a bridgeless connected graph, a cycle exists through any two given vertices."
(8) "In an Eulerian graph, a cycle exists through any two given vertices."

Problem 55. *Is it true or not?*
(1) "If all vertices have degrees at least two, a cycle exists."

Answer. True, with all degrees at least being two, one can continue a path until one gets to a vertex adjacent to an earlier vertex w in the path. Thus one gets a cycle through this vertex w—although not necessarily a cycle through the vertex, where one has started the path.

Problem 56. *Is it true or not?*
(2) "If all vertices have degrees at least two, a cycle exists through any given vertex."

Answer. The conjecture is false, as the example below shows.
A vertex of degree two can be in a long bridge, and no cycle through it exists.

Problem 57. *Is it true or not?*
(3) "If all vertices have even degrees at least two, a cycle exists through any given vertex."

Answer. True, Euler's theorem implies that such a graph is the union of edge disjoint cycles—no matter whether it is connected or not. One of these cycles passes through the given vertex.

Problem 58. *Is it true or not?*
(4) *"If all vertices have even degrees at least two, a cycle exists through any two given vertices."*

Answer. The conjecture is false because of the possible existence of a cut-vertex—even in an Eulerian graph.

If all vertices have even degrees at least two, still two given vertices can lie in different components once a cut-vertex is pulled from the graph.

Problem 59. *Is it true or not?*
(5) *"If no cut-vertex exists, a cycle exists through any two given vertices."*

Answer. —*True by Menger's theorem.* With no cut-vertex, the connectivity is $\kappa \geq 2$, and hence the connectivity between any two vertices $\kappa(s,t) \geq 2$. Hence at least two vertex-disjoint paths exist between the vertices s and t, from which one gets a cycle through s and t.

Answer. —*Independent proof.* Let x be any vertex, and take any second vertex y. Nonexistence of a cut vertex implies nonexistence of a bridge. Hence there exists a cycle C through vertex x—as actually explained in item (6) below.

If $y \in C$, we are ready. Otherwise, we construct a cycle through vertex x that gets closer to vertex y than the cycle C. Let z be a vertex in C with minimal distance from y. Let P_1 and P_2 be the two disjoint paths from x to z making the cycle $C = P_1 \cup P_2$. Let P_0 be a shortest path from z to y. All vertices of $P_0 - z$ have smaller distance to y than z.

Because there exists no cut vertex, the graph $G \setminus z$ is connected. Hence there exists a path Q from x to y in $G \setminus z$. Draw a figure containing the items introduced so far.

Let $b \in Q$ be the vertex nearest to x lying in the path P_0, too. Let $a \in \overline{xb} \cap Q$ be the vertex lying in the cycle C, too, and farthest from x. We may assume that $a \in P_1$. Now a cycle through the vertices x and b is obtained by concatination the two disjoint paths $R := (P_1 \cap \overline{xa}) \cup (Q \cap \overline{ab})$ and $S := P_2 \cup (P_0 \cap \overline{zb})$. Indicate the new cycle $R \cup S$ in your figure.

The cycle $R \cup S$ contains vertex b, which is closer to y than z. By using this construction repetitively, we finally get a cycle through any two given vertices x and y.

Problem 60. *Is it true or not?*
(6) *"In a bridgeless connected graph with at least three vertices, a cycle exists through any given vertex."*

Answer. True—the awkward case K_1 is excluded by assuming $n \geq 3$. Here is the reason: take any vertex s and a neighbor t. Since the edge st is not a bridge, there exists a path from s to t in the graph $G \setminus st$. Together with the edge st, we get a cycle through the vertex s.

Problem 61. *Is it true or not?*
(7) *"In a bridgeless connected graph, a cycle exists through any two given vertices."*

Answer. The conjecture is false, because the two given vertices can lie in different components, once a cut-vertex is pulled from the graph. See the example below:

Problem 62. *Is it true or not?*
(8) *"In an Eulerian graph, a cycle exists through any two given vertices."*

Answer. The conjecture is false for the same reason as conjecture (7):
the two given vertices can lie in different components once a cut-vertex is pulled from the graph.

I.2.2   More about Eulerian properties

Proposition 15. *The edges of a connected graph with k odd vertices can be partitioned into $\frac{k}{2}$ edge-disjoint trails. Hence such a graph can be drawn with $\frac{k}{2}$ pen-strokes.*

Proof. The handshaking lemma implies that the number k of odd vertices is even. From the given graph G we construct a larger graph $\widehat{G}$, by adding $\frac{k}{2}$ edges to join the odd vertices in pairs. We get a connected and even graph—and hence Eulerian—graph. From the closed Eulerian trail in $\widehat{G}$, we now delete the extra edges. In this way, the trail is partitioned into $\frac{k}{2}$ edge-disjoint trails. Together they cover each edge of the original graph G exactly once. □

Problem 63 (Bridges and Eulerian graphs). *Can an Eulerian graph have a bridge. Why or why not?*

Answer. No, an Eulerian graph cannot contain a bridge. A closed walk containing all edges would need to cross the bridge twice. Hence no closed trail can contain all edges exactly once—but this is required for an Eulerian graph.

Problem 64 (Bridges in a semi-Eulerian graph). *Can a semi-Eulerian graph have a bridge. Why or why not? Give examples for different possible cases.*

Answer. An semi-Eulerian graph may have any number of bridges, even no bridge at all. The two odd vertices lie at the ends of an open trail, which passes through all edges once—and crosses all the bridges.

Problem 65. *Draw a semi-Eulerian graph with three nonadjacent bridges.*

Problem 66. *Draw a 3-regular graph with a bridge.*

Lemma 5. *For a connected graph with a bridge, there exist an odd number of odd vertices on both sides of a bridge.*

Proof. Let $e = ab$ be the bridge and let $G - e = A + B$ be the decomposition into components. Let A be the component containing vertex a and B be the component containing vertex b. After having removed the bridge, there is an even number of odd vertices in A, regarded as vertices of component A. Similarly, as seen from the component B, there is an even number of odd vertices in B. Now we put the bridge back. Both vertices a and b switch their even/odd parity,—either from even to odd, or from odd to even.

After putting the bridge back, there is an odd number of odd vertices among the vertices A, and an odd number number of odd vertices among the vertices of B,—now as seen from the original graph G. □

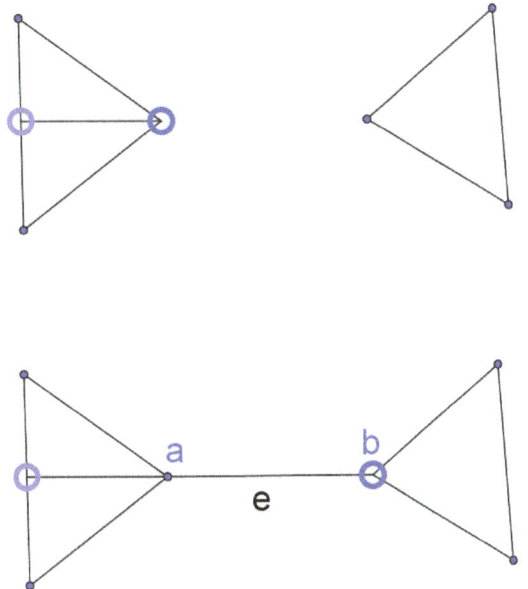

Figure 44: There exist odd vertices on both sides of a bridge.

Problem 67. *A regular graph of any odd degree may have a bridge. The drawing shows a three-regular graph with a bridge, and a 5-regular graph one.*

(a) *How many vertices, and how many edges does the three-regular graph drawn in the figure on page 65 have.*

(b) *How many vertices, and how many edges does the 5-regular graph drawn in the figure on page 65 have.*

(c) *By the Corollary to Euler's theorem, the edges of the graph can be partitioned into seven disjoint trails. As one of them, we choose the path of length 13 as drawn. On each side of the bridge, one needs still three other trails. They can be chosen to be symmetric for both sides.*

(d) *Use three different colors to indicate the remaining trails.*

Answer. (a) The three-regular graph drawn in the figure on page 65 has 10 vertices and 15 edges.

(b) The 5-regular graph drawn in the figure on page 65 has 14 vertices and 35 edges.

(c) By the Corollary to Euler's theorem, the edges of the 5-regular graph can be partitioned into seven disjoint trails. As one of them, we choose the path of length 13 as drawn. On each side of the bridge, one needs still three other trails. They can be chosen to be

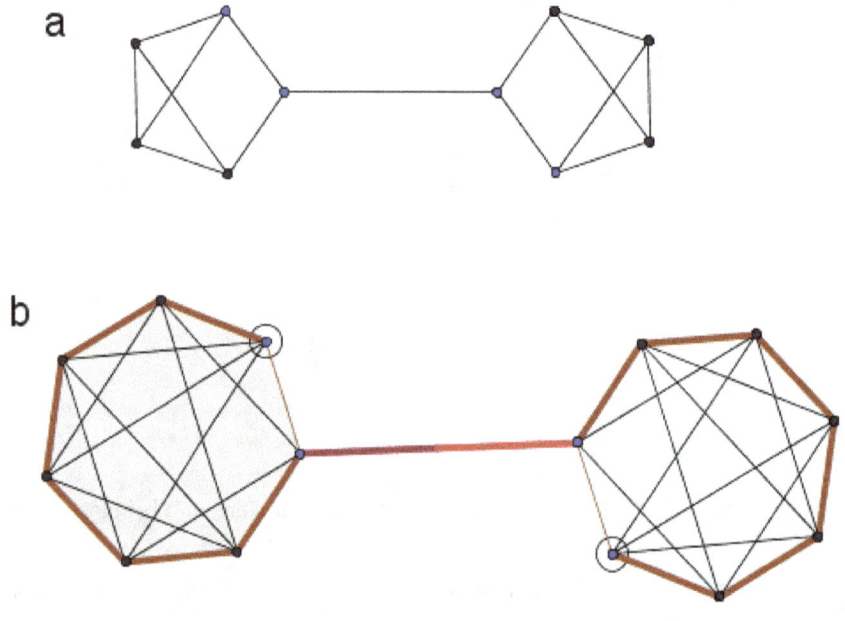

Figure 45: A three-regular and a 5-regular graph with a bridge.

symmetric for both sides. The total length of the three remaining trails on one side is eleven edges. An illustrative coloring is done below.

This is the idea of Fleury's Algorithm to construct an Eulerian trail for an Eulerian graph. We start at any vertex a, and traverse the edges. We imagine to erase the edges and isolated vertices already covered. To traverse this remaining graph, any bridge is avoided as the next edge, unless there is no other edge left.

Algorithm 2 (Fleury's Algorithm). *Construct an Eulerian trail for the Eulerian graph G.*

start: *We choose any vertex a as start vertex. Let $b := a$ be the current vertex, and $H := G$ be the current graph.*

step: *If vertex b has degree one, we make its unique neighbor c the next current vertex, and $H := H - b$ the next current graph.*

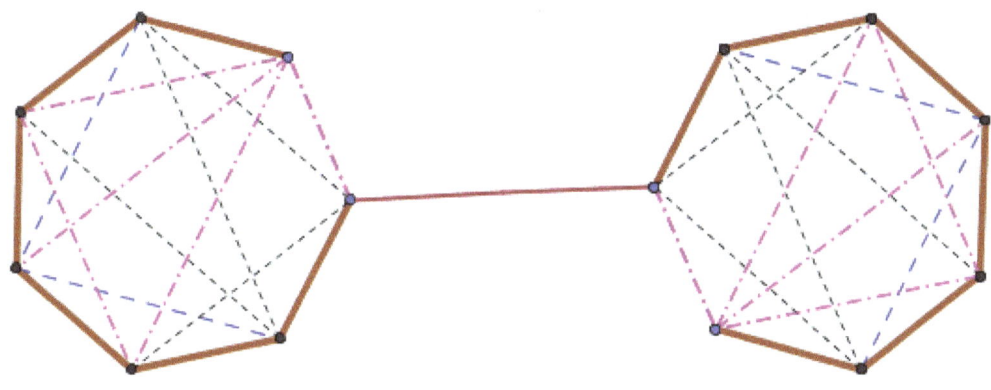

Figure 46: A partition of the edges into seven trails.

Otherwise, we successively check the edges adjacent to the current vertex b, until we find an edge bc which is not a bridge of the current graph H. We make c the current vertex and $H := H - bc$ the current graph.

The algorithm stops when the current graph has no more edges.

Remark 11. In the first step, and sometimes even for some later steps, it happens the current vertex $b = a$. Then the remaining graph is Eulerian, and we may choose any edge adjacent to a as the next one.

For the steps where the current vertex $b \neq a$, the remaining graph is semi-Eulerian. This graph can have many bridges, but at most one bridge adjacent to vertex b. Once one has found a bridge, one is allowed to traverse any other edge as the next one.

Problem 68. *Use Fleury's algorithm to draw some given graphs in one pen-stroke, returning at the end to the starting point.*

Problem 69. *Draw an example for a semi-Eulerian graph with three bridges $u_i v_i$, which have six different u_i and v_i for $i = 1, 2, 3$.*

I.2.3 More Cartesian products

Proposition 16 (About an Eulerian Cartesian product). *Assume that the Cartesian product $G \times H$ of two connected graphs G and H is Eulerian. Then either case (a) or (b) holds.*

(a) *All vertices of both graphs G and H have odd degrees. Both graphs have even orders.*

(b) *Both graphs G and H are Eulerian.*

Conversely in both cases (a) *and* (b), *the Cartesian product is Eulerian.*

Proof. We start by distinguishing the cases

(a): There exists a vertex u_0 of G with odd degree $\deg_G(u_0)$.

(b): All vertices u of the graph G have even degrees $\deg_G(u)$.

In case (a), let vertex u_0 of G have odd degree $\deg_G(u_0)$. In the Cartesian product $G \times H$ of two graphs G and H, the degree of a vertex (u,v) is

$$(*) \qquad \deg_{G \times H}(u,v) = \deg_G(u) + \deg_H(v)$$

This sum is even, since the Cartesian product is assumed to be Eulerian. For any vertex v of H, formula (*) implies that $\deg_H(v)$ is odd, since it is the difference of an even an an odd number, and hence odd. Hence all vertices v of the graph H have odd degrees. Finally, we see in a similar way that all vertices of graph G have odd degrees.

The handshaking lemma implies that the sum of degree is even. Hence the number of odd vertices is even. Both G and H have only odd vertices, and hence they both have an even number of vertices.

In case (b), the graph G is Eulerian. The sum formula (*) now implies that H is Eulerian, too.

The proof the converse is even easier. □

I.3 Hamiltonian Graphs

Definition 30 (Hamiltonian graph). A graph is called *Hamiltonian* if and only if there exists a cycle which visits each <u>vertex</u> exactly once.

Definition 31 (semi-Hamiltonian graph). I call a graph *semi-Hamiltonian* if and only if there exists an *open path*—but not an cycle—which visits each <u>vertex</u> exactly once.

Definition 32 (non-Hamiltonian graph). I call a graph *non-Hamiltonian* if and only if it is neither Hamiltonian nor semi-Hamiltonian.

Problem 70. *Draw the graph of an icosahedron and find a Hamiltonian cycle.*

Problem 71. *Under which conditions for the numbers a and b is the complete bipartite graph $K_{a,b}$ Hamiltonian?*

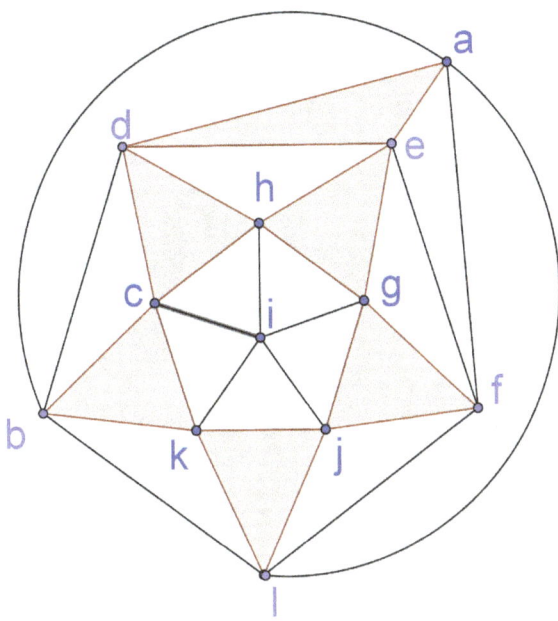

Figure 47: The icosahedron graph is Hamiltonian.

Answer. The complete bipartite graph $K_{a,b}$ is Hamiltonian if and only if $a = b \geq 2$.

Problem 72. *The graphs $K_{1,1}$ and $K_{1,2}$ turn out to be semi-Hamiltonian. For which cases is the complete bipartite graph $K_{a,b}$ semi-Hamiltonian?*

Answer. The complete bipartite graph $K_{a,b}$ is semi-Hamiltonian if and only if $a = b = 1$ or $|a - b| = 1$.

Problem 73. *Draw a plane representation of the icosahedron graph. Give a numbering of the vertices that indicates a Hamiltonian cycle.*

Problem 74. *Find and indicate a Hamiltonian cycle in the Grötzsch graph.*

Problem 75. *Draw the Petersen graph and use numbering of vertices to indicate a Hamiltonian path.*

Problem 76. *Under which condition for the numbers m and n are the grids $P_m \times P_n$ Hamiltonian. Give complete reason for your answer.*

Answer. After a bid of experimentation, one can conjecture:

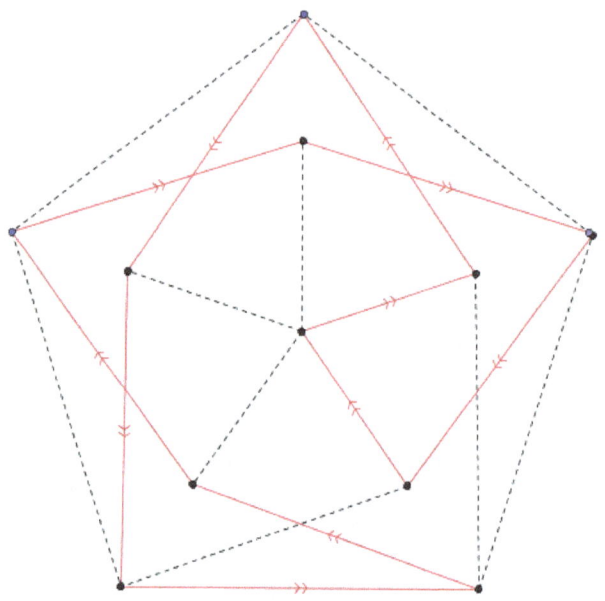

Figure 48: The Grötzsch graph is Hamiltonian.

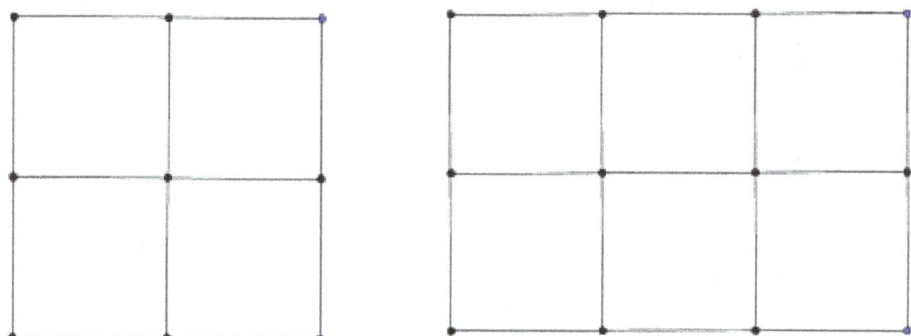

Figure 49: Two grids $P_m \times P_n$ with $m = 3$ and $n = 3, 4$.

(a) If mn is odd (or equivalently $\min[m,n] = 1$), the grid $P_m \times P_n$ is not Hamiltonian, but still semi-Hamiltonian.

(b) If mn is even and either $m \geq 2$ or $n \geq 2$, the grid $P_m \times P_n$ is Hamiltonian.

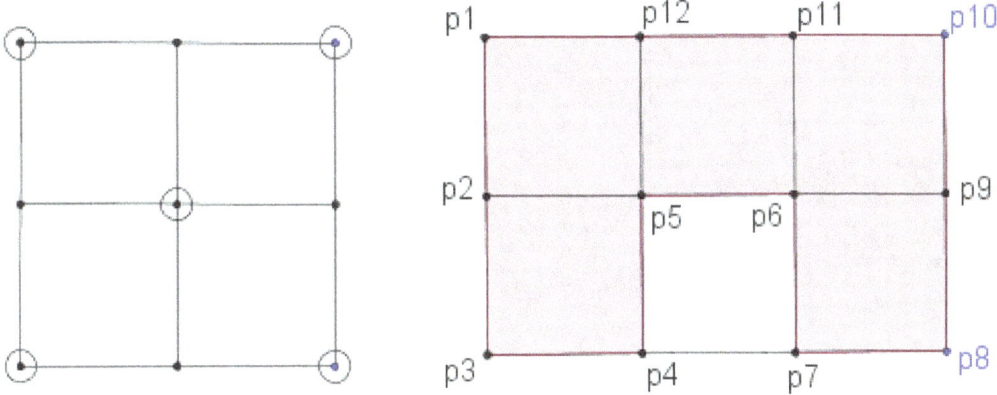

Figure 50: The grids $P_m \times P_n$ are Hamiltonian for mn even, but not for mn odd.

Here is the reason: All the grids can be properly two-colored in a checker board manner. Hence all cycles are even. Now mn is the number of vertices of the grid. If this is odd—but all cycles are even, there cannot exist a Hamiltonian cycle.

The second statement is checked by giving a closed cycle for mn even. Since $\min m, n \geq 2$, one can meander in one coordinate, and close the cycle in the other coordinate, as shown in the drawing.

Problem 77. *Provide a drawing of the graphs $P_2 \times C_3$, $P_2 \times K_4$, and $C_3 \times C_3$, and indicate a Hamiltonian cycle.*

Answer.

Definition 33 (demi-Hamiltonian graph). I call a graph *demi-Hamiltonian* if and only if it is either semi-Hamiltonian or Hamiltonian.

Problem 78. *Given any two graphs G and H. Prove or disprove:*

1. *If G and H are demi-Hamiltonian, then $G \times H$ is demi-Hamiltonian.*

2. *If G and H are demi-Hamiltonian, and one of them has an even number of vertices, then $G \times H$ is Hamiltonian.*

3. *If G is demi-Hamiltonian and H is Hamiltonian, then $G \times H$ is Hamiltonian.*

Answer. Assume G and H have m and n vertices, respectively.

1. Assume G and H are demi-Hamiltonian. Hence they have subgraphs $P_m \subseteq G$ and $P_n \subseteq H$, and $P_m \times P_n \subseteq G \times H$. We know that $P_m \times P_n$ is demi-Hamiltonian. Hence $G \times H$ is demi-Hamiltonian.

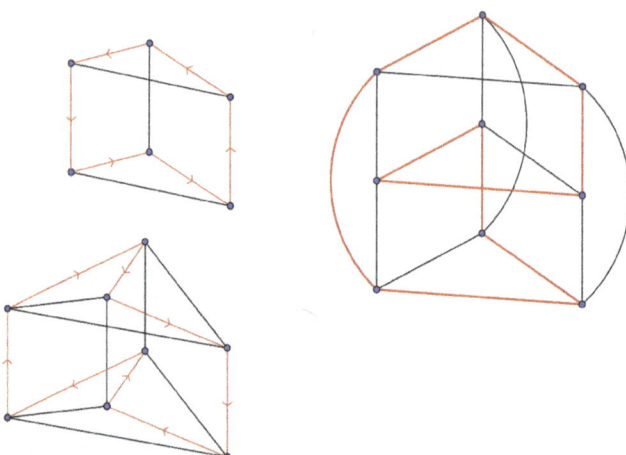

Figure 51: Hamiltonian cycles exist in $P_2 \times C_3$, $P_2 \times K_4$, and $C_3 \times C_3$.

2. If nm is even, then $P_m \times P_n$ is Hamiltonian. Hence $G \times H$ is Hamiltonian.

3. Assume G demi-Hamiltonian, and H is Hamiltonian. Hence $P_m \subseteq G$ and $C_n \subseteq H$ are subgraphs. Hence $P_m \times C_n \subseteq G \times H$. We know that $P_m \times C_n$ is Hamiltonian. Hence $G \times H$ is Hamiltonian.

Problem 79. *Let $n \geq 3$ and $m \geq 3$ be odd. Find a semi-Hamiltonian graph G of order n such that $G \times P_m$ is Hamiltonian.*

Problem 80. *Draw the graph $P_2 \times K_{2,4}$ and find a Hamiltonian cycle.*

A nice way to use the Hamiltonian property of a graph is to draw the Hamiltonian cycle on the outer boundary. As an example, I take the graph $\overline{L(K_6)}$, also known as 6-*cage*. I show the graph at first in figure 72 as it happens to arise in an initial attempt. Secondly one sees in figure 73 the same graph now with the Hamiltonian cycle on the outer boundary. The realization of these two figures was facilitated for me by the circumstance that the 6-cage is Eulerian, too.

Problem 81. *Find a Hamiltonian cycle in the $(7,2)$-quasi Petersen graph from the figure on page 74. You may prefer to find at first a three coloring of the edges.*

Answer. There are essentially four ways for 3-coloring of a 7-cycle:

$$1,2,1,2,1,2,3 \text{ or } 1,2,3,1,2,3,2 \text{ or } 1,2,3,1,2,1,3 \text{ or } 1,2,3,1,3,1,2 \text{ or }$$

One checks that only coloring the inner 7-cycle in the last manner leads to a proper 3-edge coloring of the entire graph. Moreover, the colors 2 and 3 then give a Hamiltonian cycle.

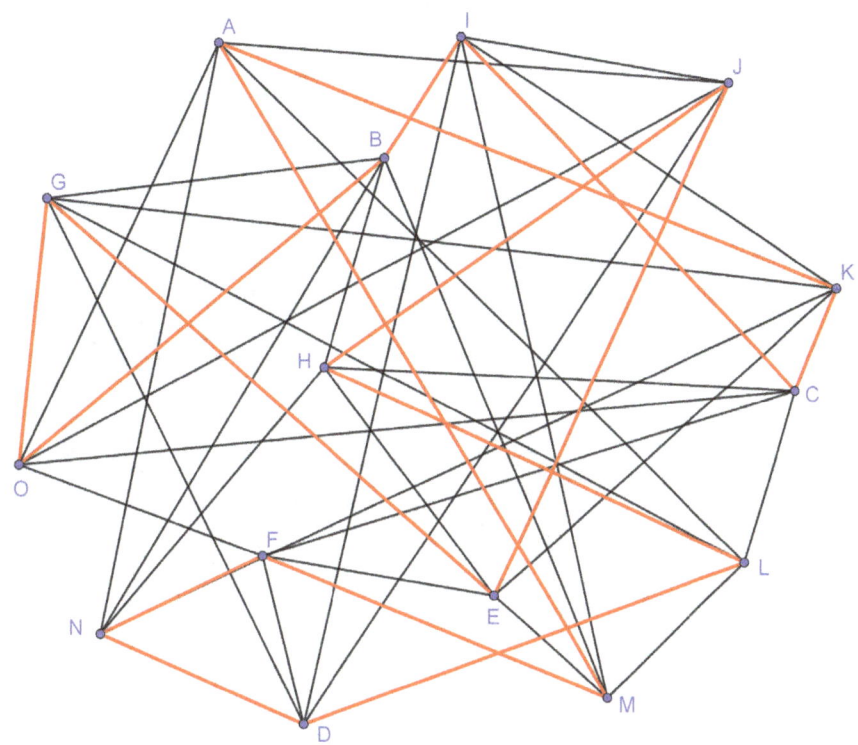

Figure 52: The 6-cage with a Hamiltonian cycle in red.

Problem 82. *Find a Hamiltonian cycle in the $(10,3)$-quasi Petersen graph from the figure on page 76. You may prefer to find at first a three coloring of the edges.*

Answer.

I.3.1 Necessary for Hamiltonian properties

Proposition 17. *In a two-colorable graph with r black and s white vertices, the length of any cycle is at most $2\min[r,s]$ The*

$$\text{path length} \leq \begin{cases} n-1 & \text{for } |r-s| \leq 1 \\ n-|r-s| & \text{for } |r-s| \geq 1 \end{cases}$$

In other terms, the length of any path is at most $\min[2r, 2s, r+s-1]$.

If a two-colorable graph is Hamiltonian, then $r = s$. If a two-colorable graph is semi-Hamiltonian, then $|r-s| \leq 1$. Hence a two-colorable graph with $|r-s| \geq 2$ is non-Hamiltonian.

Problem 83. *Give examples of a two-colorable graph which is*

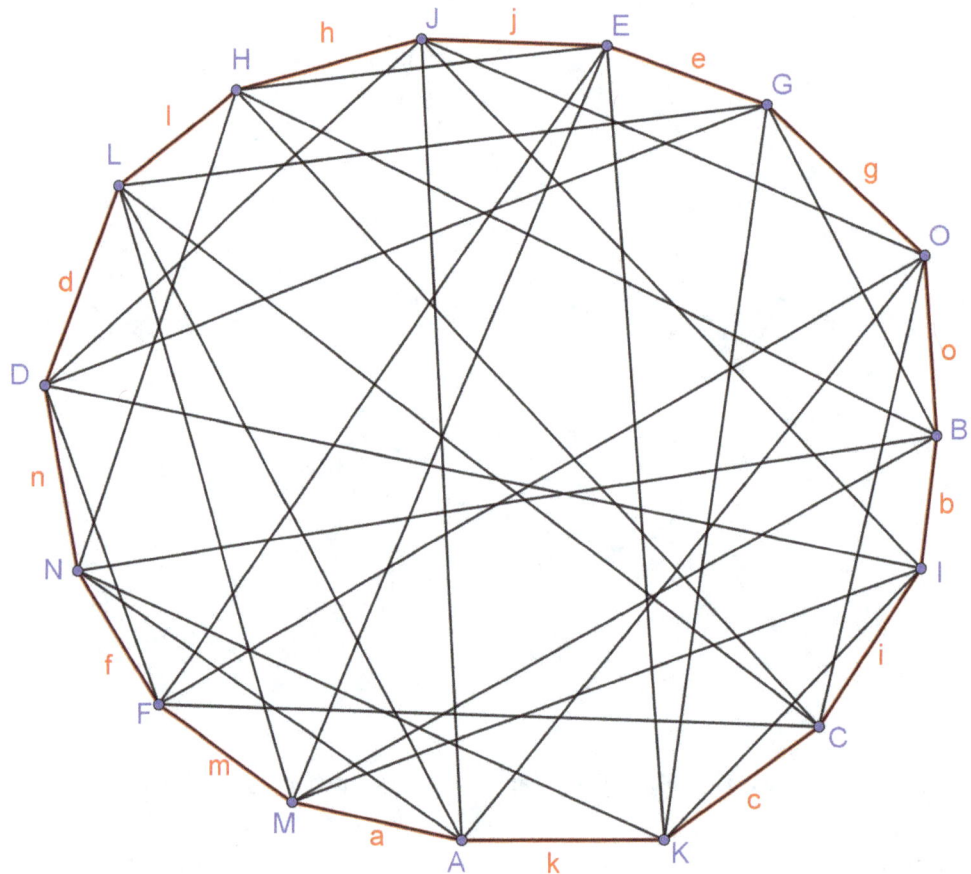

Figure 53: The 6-cage with the same Hamiltonian cycle as outer boundary.

(a) *Hamiltonian and the numbers of the black and the white vertices are equal,*

(b) *semi-Hamiltonian and the numbers of the black and the white vertices are equal,*

(c) *non-Hamiltonian and the numbers of the black and the white vertices are equal,*

(d) *semi-Hamiltonian and the numbers of the black and the white vertices differ by one,*

(e) *non-Hamiltonian and the numbers of the black and the white vertices differ by one.*

Theorem 3 (Pulling-out Theorem). *If a graph is Hamiltonian, pulling out any s of its vertices leaves a graph $G \setminus S$ with at most s components.*

If a graph is semi-Hamiltonian, pulling out any s of its vertices leaves a graph $G \setminus S$ with at most $s+1$ components.

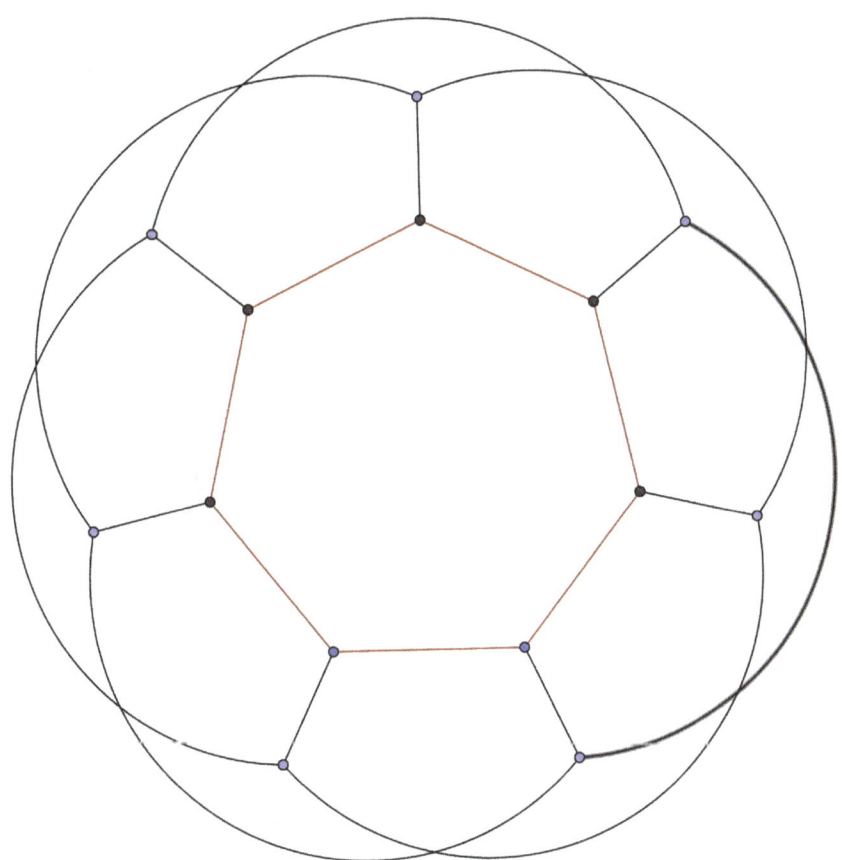

Figure 54: The $(7,2)$ quasi-Petersen graph is Hamiltonian.

Problem 84. *Show that the graph in the figure on page 79 is not Hamiltonian. You can use the Pulling-out Theorem. Find an open Hamiltonian path.*

Answer.

Problem 85. *Assume $2i < n$, and let the graph G be obtained by joining K_i on the one hand with N_i, on the other hand with K_{n-2i}: No edges are put between N_i and K_{n-2i}. Hence*

$$G = (N_i + K_{n-2i}) \vee K_i$$

One could symbolically write $N_i \overleftarrow{\vee} K_i \overrightarrow{\vee} K_{n-2i}$.

(a) *Drawn the graph G for $i = 2$ and $n = 7$.*

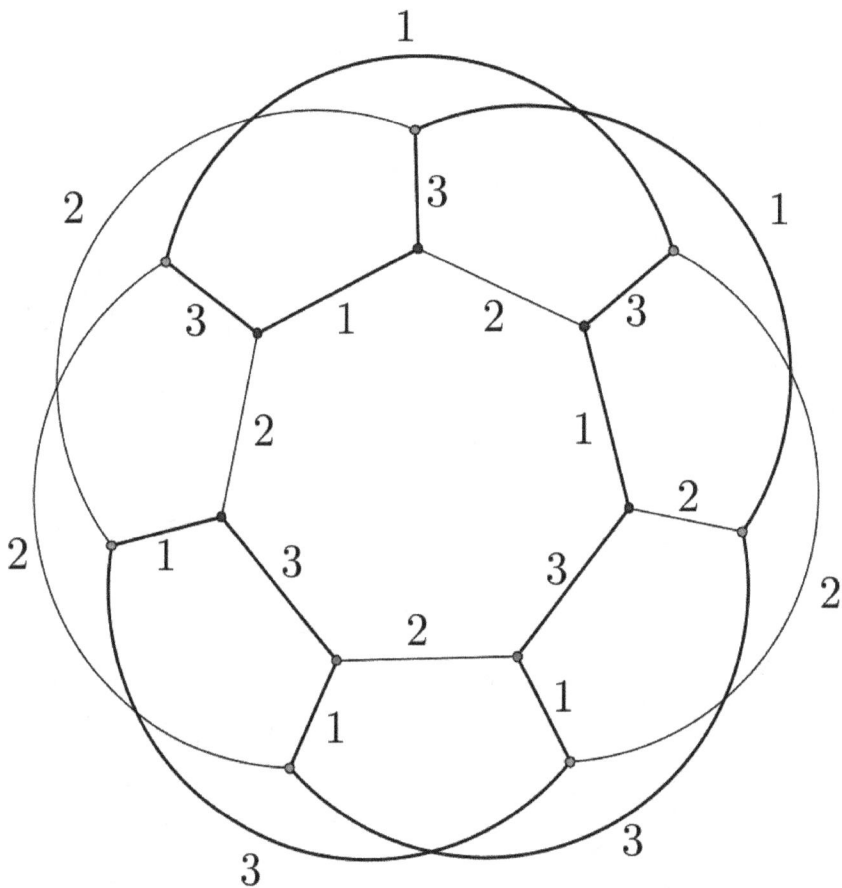

Figure 55: The $(7, 2)$ quasi-Petersen graph is Hamiltonian.

(b) Find the degree sequence of this graph, in increasing order.

(c) Use the pulling-out Theorem to show the graph is not Hamiltonian for $i = 2$ and $n = 7$.

(d) Find the degree sequence of for any n and $i < \frac{n}{2}$.

(e) Use the Pulling-out Theorem and prove the graph is not Hamiltonian for any n and $i < \frac{n}{2}$.

Problem 86. The graph G drawn above has no Hamiltonian cycle. One can check this fact by going through all possible cases how to built a maximal cycle through the vertex at the center. Nevertheless, deleting any s vertices, <u>always</u> separates the graph into at most s components.

(a) Draw the graph $G \setminus \{A, O\}$, and describe it. How many components does it have?

(b) Draw the graph $G \setminus \{A, U, V\}$ and describe it. How many components does it have?

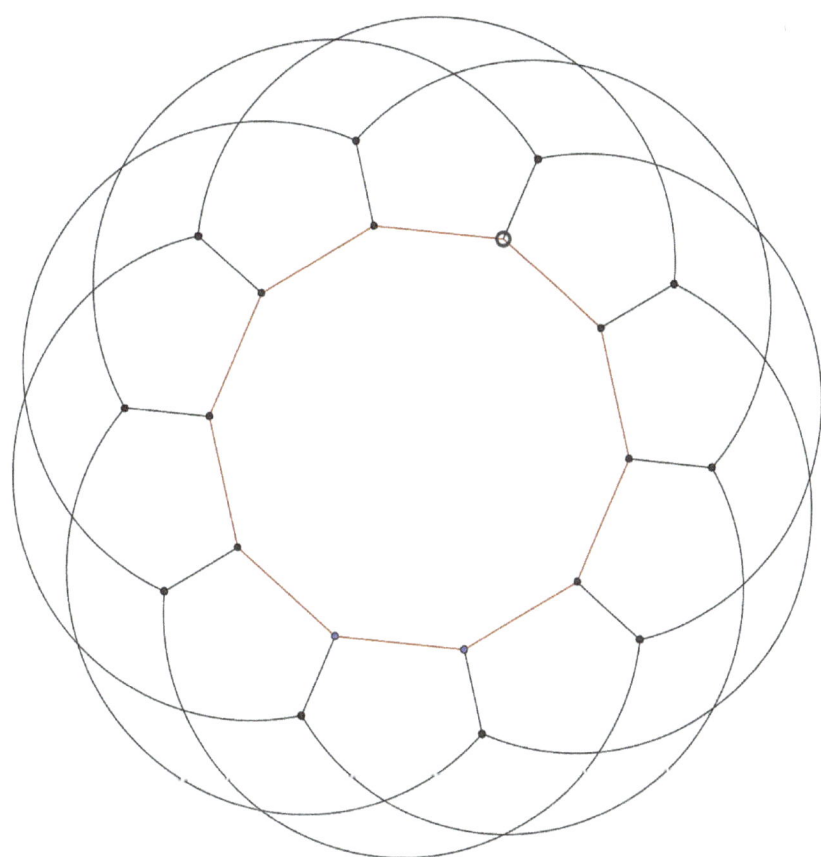

Figure 56: The $(10, 3)$ quasi-Petersen graph.

(c) *Draw the graph $G \setminus \{A, B, O\}$ and describe it. How many components does it have?*

Answer. (a) $G \setminus \{A, O\}$ has two components, the isolated vertex U and the path graph $WCBV$.

(b) $G \setminus \{A, U, V\}$ is connected and consists of two triangles with the common edge OC.

(c) $G \setminus \{A, B, O\}$ has three components. It consists of the isolated vertices U and V and the edge CW.

Problem 87. *Draw the graph $P_2 \times K_{1,3}$. Give a reason why it is non-Hamiltonian, semi-Hamiltonian, or Hamiltonian.*

Does there exist a Hamiltonian path? Does there exist a Hamiltonian cycle? If not, how can we exclude a any Hamiltonian cycle?

Answer. The graph $P_2 \times K_{1,3}$ is semi Hamiltonian. Indeed, a Hamiltonian path exists, as indicated.

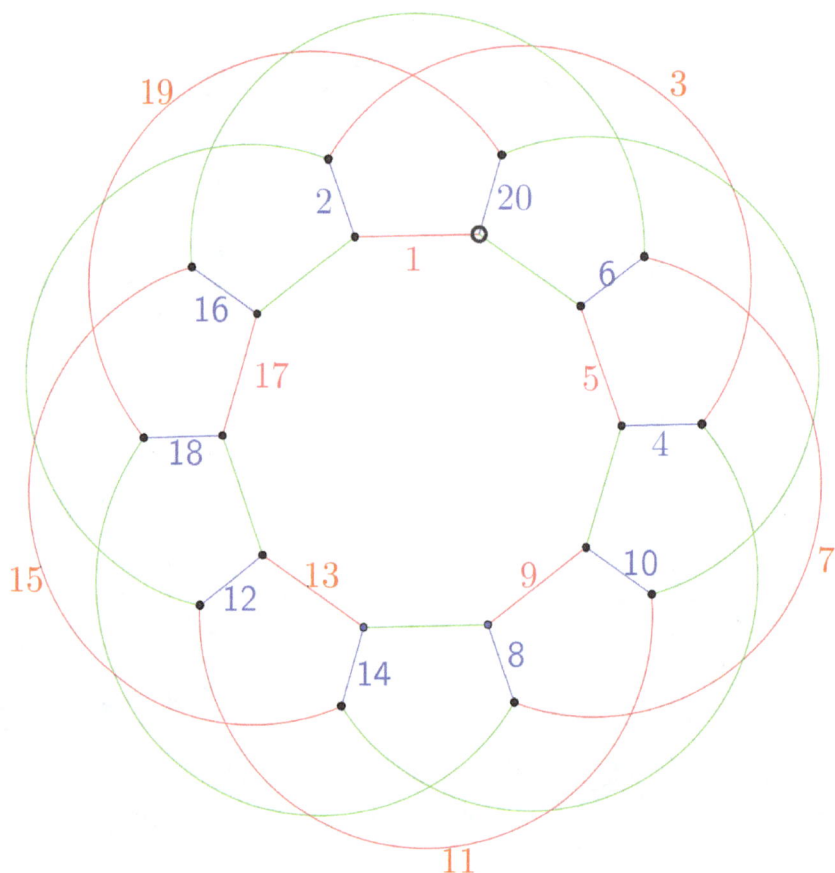

Figure 57: The $(10, 3)$ quasi-Petersen graph is Hamiltonian.

To see that the graph has no Hamiltonian cycle, we use the pulling-out theorem 3. Indeed $P_2 \times K_{1,3} - \{a, b\}$ has three components. Hence the graph $P_2 \times K_{1,3}$ cannot be Hamiltonian.

Proposition 18 (Bipartite Hamiltonian graphs). *Assume the given graph is bipartite, with r black and s white vertices. If the graph is Hamiltonian, the number of black and white vertices are equal.*

If the graph is semi-Hamiltonian, the number of black and white vertices can differ at most by one.

Problem 88. *Decide whether the graph $P_2 \times K_{1,3}$ can be semi-Hamiltonian, or Hamiltonian, by means of this proposition.*

Answer. The graph $P_3 \times K_{1,3}$ has no Hamiltonian cycle. Without going through a complicated analysis of cases, one can see this by use of a proper two coloring of G.

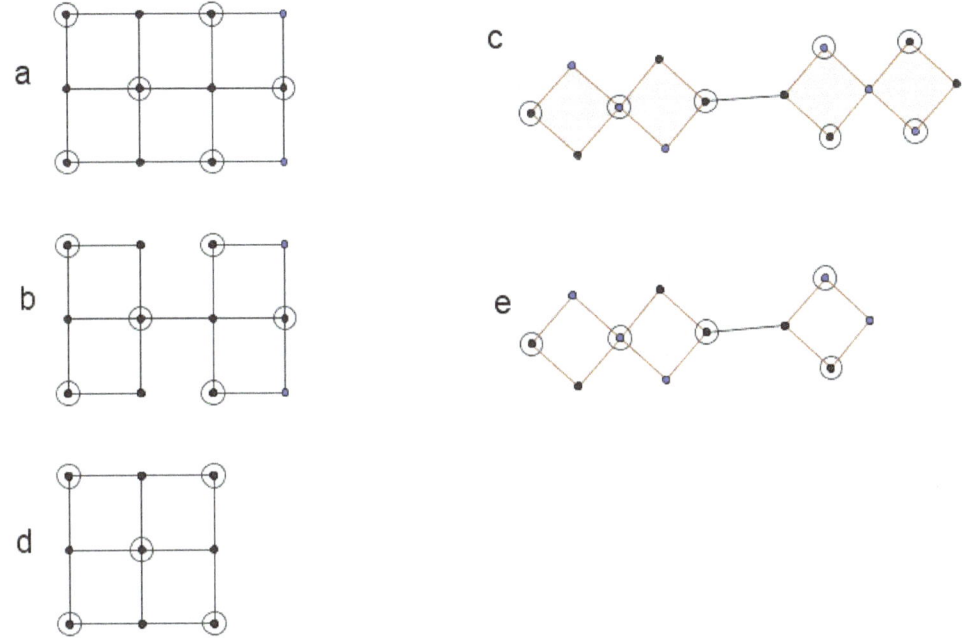

Figure 58: Two colorable Hamiltonian, semi-Hamiltonian, and non-Hamiltonian graphs with $|s - t| = 0, 1$.

If I color the vertex of degree 5 in the middle black, I get 5 black and 7 white vertices. Every cycle contains the same number of black and white vertices. Hence the maximal length of a cycle is at most 10. But the graph has 12 vertices. Hence no Hamiltonian cycle exists.

An open path contains one more vertex of one kind than the other kind. A maximal path with all 5 white and 6 black vertices has length 11. A path of length 11 does exist, as indicated. But a Hamiltonian path would have length 12. Such a path cannot exist.

An open Hamiltonian path does exist, nevertheless, as one has to check directly.

Problem 89. *Draw the dodecahedron graph and find a proper three-coloring of the edges.*

Explain the procedure you use. Explain how the edges of the dodecahedron can be partitioned into three disjoint sets of equal size such that the edges of each set are a perfect matching.

Answer. The dodecahedron is a three-regular Hamiltonian graph. At first one finds Hamiltonian cycle. This cycle has even length, and hence can be colored with two colors. The third color is used for the remaining edges not in the cycle.

In this way, the edges can be properly colored with three colors. Take any of the three colors. Two edges of this color are never adjacent to each other. But for any vertex v, there is exactly one edge of the color chosen adjacent to the vertex v. Hence the edges of the chosen color are a complete matching.

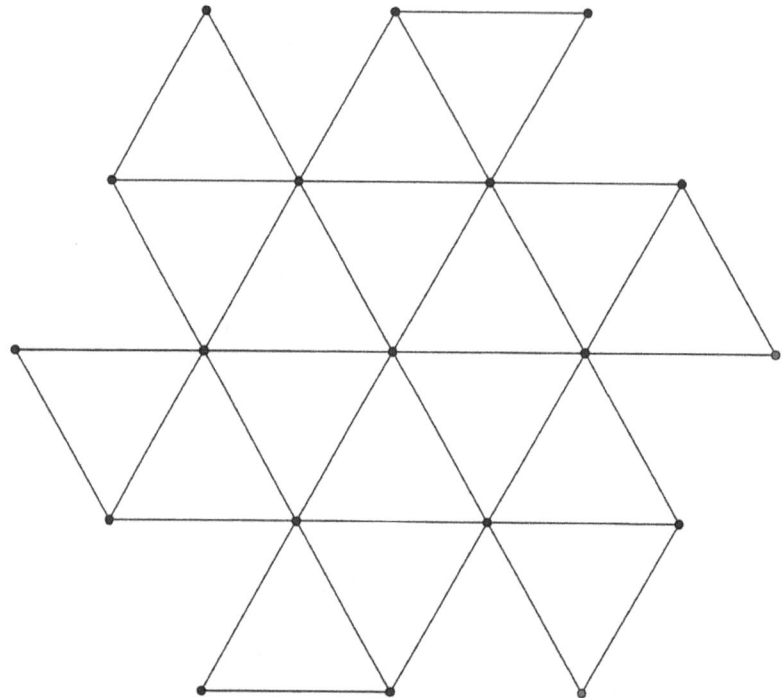

Figure 59: Pulling out suitable vertices shows the graph is not Hamiltonian.

Problem 90. *Draw the graph $P_2 \times K_{2,4}$ and find a Hamiltonian cycle.*

Answer.

Problem 91. *Give a reason why the graph from figure on page 82 is not Hamiltonian. Determine the maximum length C for cycles, and the maximum length L for open paths.*

Answer. The graph is bipartite, with 7 white and 7 black vertices. But a Hamiltonian cycle is not ruled out, since there are equal numbers of black and white vertices. By means of the pulling-out theorem, a Hamiltonian cycle is ruled out. Indeed removal of the two vertices a, b to the left, and the two vertices e, f to the right leaves five components, each one of which is a copy of P_2.

Since all cycles are even, we conclude $C \leq 12$. Existence of a cycle of 12 follows from the previous problem. Indeed, the subgraph $H = G \setminus \{c, d\} = P_2 \times K_{2,4}$ is Hamiltonian. Hence $C = 12$.

To determine the maximum path length, one may remove one edge from H and attach at one of its end vertices a path leading to vertices c and d. Hence $L = 13$.

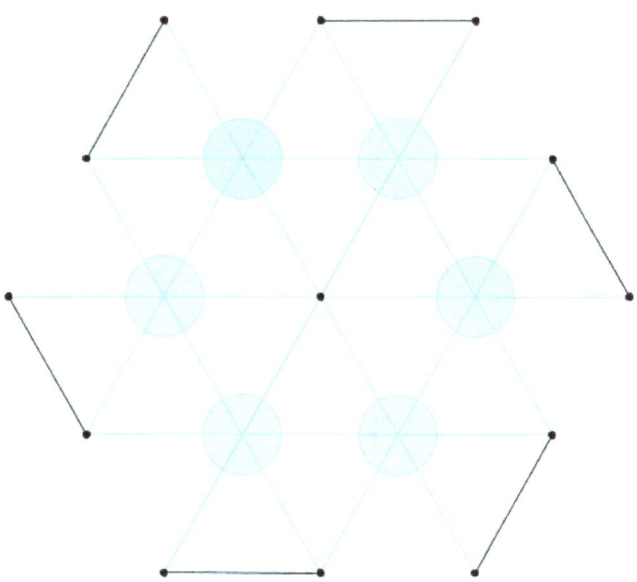

Figure 60: Pulling out the six vertices of the middle hexagon leaves a disconnected graph with seven components.

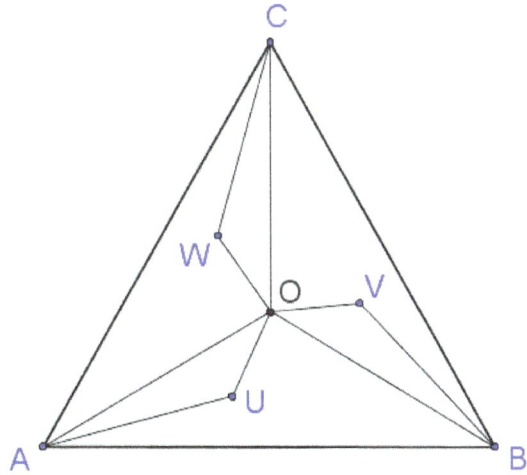

Figure 61: Stubbornly not Hamiltonian.

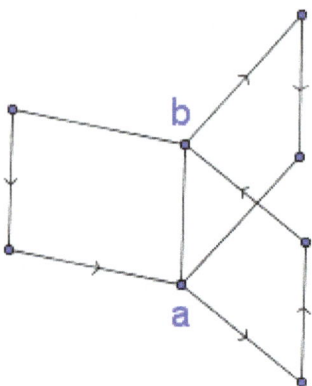

Figure 62: $P_2 \times K_{1,3}$ has a Hamiltonian path, but no Hamiltonian cycle.

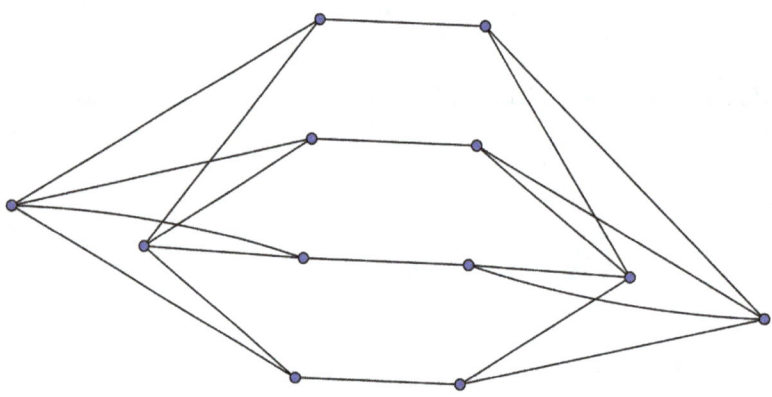

Figure 63: The graph $P_2 \times K_{2,4}$.

I.3.2 Sufficient assumptions insuring Hamiltonian properties

Theorem 4 (Ore's Theorem). *Assume that G is a simple graph with $n \geq 3$ vertices and Ore's assumption*

(Ore) $\qquad\qquad\qquad$ *If* $\quad u \not\sim v \quad$ *then* $\quad \deg u + \deg v \geq n$

holds. Then the graph is Hamiltonian.

Corollary 3 (Ore's Theorem). *Assume that G is a simple graph with $n \geq 3$ vertices and*

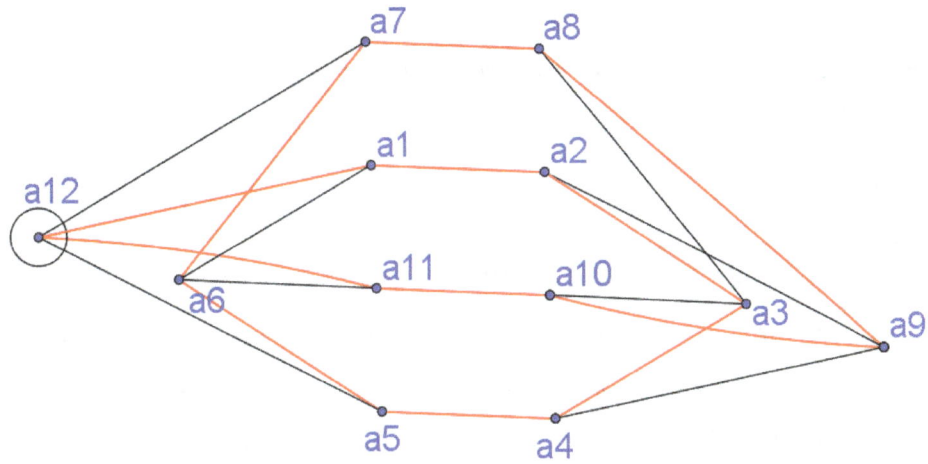

Figure 64: The graph $P_2 \times K_{2,4}$ is Hamiltonian.

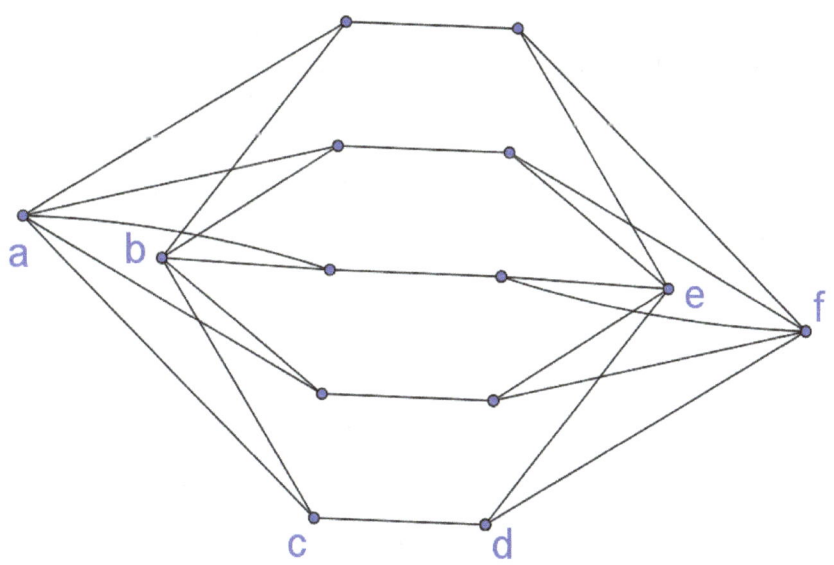

Figure 65: Why is this graph not Hamiltonian?

Ore's assumption

(Ore n-1)   If $\;u \not\sim v\;$ then $\;\deg u + \deg v \geq n - 1$

holds. Then the graph is semi-Hamiltonian, or Hamiltonian.

Corollary 4 (Dirac's Theorem). *A graph with minimal degree $\delta \geq \frac{n}{2}$ and at least 3 vertices is Hamiltonian.*

Remark 12.
$$\kappa \leq \lambda \leq \delta < \frac{n}{2}$$
hold for any graph which has at least 3 vertices and is not Hamiltonian.

Lemma 6. *The graph G is demi-Hamiltonian if and only if graph $G \vee K_1$ is Hamiltonian.*

Problem 92. *Use this lemma to derive the corollary from Ore's theorem.*

Problem 93. *Let G be a graph with n vertices and m edges, and assume*
$$m \geq \frac{(n-2)(n-1)}{2} + 2$$
Use Ore's Theorem to prove that G is Hamiltonian.

A cleaned-up version. We check that a graph with at least $\frac{(n-2)(n-1)}{2} + 2$ edges satisfies Ore's assumption. Given any two vertices u and v that are not adjacent in G, let $G' := G \setminus \{u, v\}$. The graph G' is simple, has $n - 2$ vertices and $m' = m - \deg u - \deg v$ edges. For this number, we get
$$m' = m - \deg u - \deg v \geq \frac{(n-2)(n-1)}{2} + 2 - \deg u - \deg v$$
On the other hand m' is less equal the number of edges of a complete graph and hence
$$m' \leq \frac{(n-2)(n-3)}{2}$$
Hence
$$\deg u + \deg v \geq \frac{(n-2)(n-1)}{2} + 2 - \frac{(n-2)(n-3)}{2} = n$$
confirming Ore's assumption. Hence, by Ore's Theorem, the graph is indeed Hamiltonian. □

Answer. In terms of edges of the complement graph $\overline{G}$, the assumption of the problem means
$$\overline{m} = \frac{n(n-1)}{2} - m \leq \frac{n(n-1)}{2} - \frac{(n-2)(n-1)}{2} - 2 = \frac{n^2 - n - n^2 + 3n - 2 - 4}{2} = n - 3$$

We can now check the assumption (Ore) of Ore's Theorem: If the vertices u and v are not adjacent in G, they are adjacent in the complement. For the complement graph the sum of their degrees is rather small. If all its edges are adjacent to either u or v, we get $\deg_{\overline{G}} u + \deg_{\overline{G}} v = \overline{m} + 1$, since the edge between u and v is counted doubly.

If not all edges are adjacent to either u or v, this sum of degrees is even smaller. Hence we conclude
$$\deg_{\overline{G}} u + \deg_{\overline{G}} v \leq \overline{m} + 1 \leq n - 2$$
Back to the original graph, we can now check that the sum in the assumption (Ore) is large enough. Since $\deg_{\overline{G}} u + \deg_G u = n - 1$,
$$\deg_G u + \deg_G v = 2n - 2 - (\deg_{\overline{G}} u + \deg_{\overline{G}} v) \geq 2n - 2 - (n - 2) = n$$
as we need to have to be able to use assumption (Ore). Hence, by Ore's Theorem, the graph is indeed Hamiltonian.

Problem 94. *Give an example for a simple connected graph with n vertices which is not Hamiltonian, but has $m = \frac{(n-2)(n-1)}{2} + 1$ edges.*

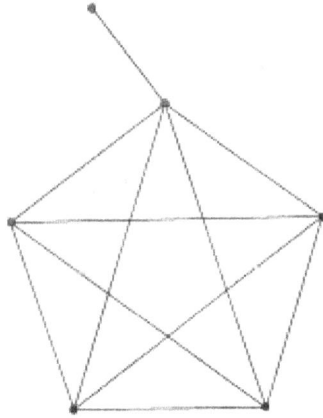

Figure 66: A graph with n vertices and as many as $m = \frac{(n-2)(n-1)}{2} + 1$ edges, which is not Hamiltonian. Drawn is the example $n = 6, m = 11$.

Answer. The expression $\frac{(n-2)(n-1)}{2}$ is the number of edges of the complete graph with $n - 1$ vertices. We take this graph K_{n-1}, and add to it an additional vertex v and connect it to *only one* vertex of K_{n-1}.

The resulting graph has numbers of vertices n and edges m as required. Because of its vertex v of degree one, this graph cannot be Hamiltonian.

Proposition 19 (Sufficient number of edges to enforce a Hamiltonian cycle). *A simple graph with $n \geq 3$ vertices and at least $\frac{(n-2)(n-1)}{2} + 2$ edges is Hamiltonian.*

Independent proof. To begin the induction, we check the assertion for $n = 3$. Indeed, a graph with 3 vertices and at least 3 edges is a triangle—which is Hamiltonian.

For the induction step, I assume the assertion holds for graphs with less than n vertices. Given is a graph G with $n \geq 4$ vertices and

(*) $$m \geq \frac{(n-2)(n-1)}{2} + 2$$

edges. At first, we check that there exists a vertex of degree $n-2$ or $n-1$. Indeed, if this would be false, the handshaking lemma would bound the number of edges by
$2m = \sum \deg u \leq n(n-3) = (n-2)(n-1) - 2 < (n-2)(n-1) + 4$ contradicting assumption (*). Now we choose such a vertex of degree either

case (a): $\deg v = n-2$ or

case (b): $\deg v = n-1$,

and let $H = G - \{v\}$.

In the case (a), the graph H has

$$m(H) = m(G) - \deg v \geq \frac{(n-1)(n-2)}{2} + 2 - (n-2) = \frac{(n-3)(n-2)}{2} + 2$$

vertices. Hence the induction assumption tells that H is Hamiltonian. Since $n - 2 > \frac{n-1}{2}$, two neighbors $h_1 \sim h_2$ in the Hamiltonian cycle of H are adjacent to v. Replacing the edge $h_1 h_2$ by the two edges $h_1 v$ and $v h_2$ yields a Hamiltonian cycle in G.

In case (b), the graph H has

$$m(H) = m(G) - \deg v \geq \frac{(n-1)(n-2)}{2} + 2 - (n-1) = \frac{(n-3)(n-2)}{2} + 1$$

vertices, which can be one edge less. If H is Hamiltonian, we argue as above. Now assume that H is not Hamiltonian. Because addition of any edge yields a Hamiltonian graph, H is semi-Hamiltonian. If the open Hamiltonian path in H leads from vertex h_1 to vertex h_2, adding the two edges $h_1 v$ and $v h_2$ yields a Hamiltonian cycle in G. □

We now give a detailed proof Ore's theorem. Indeed, we shall prove the following more general theorem 5.

Theorem 5. *Assume that G is a simple graph with $n \geq 3$ vertices.*

(a) *If the graph is connected and Ore's assumption*

(Ore p)   If $u \nsim v$ then $\deg u + \deg v \geq p$

holds for some $1 \leq p \leq n-2$, then there exists an open path of length at least p. In other words $L \geq \min[n-1, p]$.

(b) *In the cases $p \geq n-1$, the graph is connected and semi-Hamiltonian or Hamiltonian.*

(c) In the cases $p \geq n$, the graph is Hamiltonian, and especially connected.

Lemma 7. *Assume $v_0, v_1, v_2, \ldots, v_p$ is am open Hamiltonian path of the simple graph G. If the sum of the degrees of its end-vertices satisfies*

(I.3.1) $$\deg v_0 + \deg v_p \geq p + 1$$

then the graph is Hamiltonian.

Proof. We use the inclusion-exclusion principle for the two sets

$$A = \{i : 1 \leq i \leq p \text{ and } v_0 \sim v_i\}$$
$$B = \{i : 1 \leq i \leq p \text{ and } v_{i-1} \sim v_p\}$$

Since $|A| = \deg v_0$ and $|B| = \deg v_p$, assumption (I.3.1) yields

$$|A \cap B| = |A| + |B| - |A \cup B| \geq \deg v_0 + \deg v_p - p \geq 1$$

Hence $A \cap B \neq \emptyset$ and there exists an index such that $1 \leq i \leq p$ for which both $v_0 \sim v_i$ and $v_{i-1} \sim v_p$ hold. In the cases $i = 1$ or $i = p$ we see $v_0 \sim v_p$ holds, and the graph has the Hamiltonian cycle $v_0, v_1, \ldots, v_p$ back to v_0. In the remaining cases $2 \leq i \leq p-1$, the graph has the Hamiltonian cycle

$$v_0, v_1, \ldots, v_{i-1}, v_p, v_{p-1}, \ldots, v_i \text{ back to } v_0$$

$\square$

Lemma 8. *Let $u_0, u_1, \ldots, u_p$ be a non-extendible path in a simple graph G. If either $u_p \sim u_0$ or $\deg u_0 + \deg u_p \geq p+1$, there exists a cycle of length $p+1$.*

If there exists no cycle of length $p+1$, then $u_p \nsim u_0$ and $\deg u_0 + \deg u_p \leq p$.

Proof. The second assertion is the contrapositive of the first one, and thus equivalent. We need onoly to prove the first assertion. The case $u_p \sim u_0$ is obvious, so we may assume $u_p \nsim u_0$. Since the path is assumed to be non-extendible, the only neighbors of its end-vertices u_0 and u_p can be the vertices $u_0, u_1, \ldots u_p$ of the path. We delete from the graph all vertices not in this path, and obtain an induced subgraph H with the vertices $u_0, u_1, \ldots u_p$. Since

$$\deg_H u_0 + \deg_H u_p = \deg_G u_0 + \deg_G u_p \geq p + 1$$

by assumption, lemma 7 implies that the subgraph H is Hamiltonian. In other words, the original graph G has a cycle of length $p+1$. $\square$

In the following, I use the letter L to denote the maximum length (number of edges) of an open path, and the letter C to denote the maximum length (number of edges) of a cycle.

Lemma 9. *If the simple connected graph G is not Hamiltonian, then $C \leq L$.*

Proof. Indeed, assume the graph not to be Hamiltonian, and take a cycle of maximum length C. There exists a vertex w not in this cycle, and since the graph is connected, there exists a path of length l from w to some vertex v in the cycle. We delete from the cycle one of the two edges adjacent to vertex v and adjoin the path. Thus one obtains a path of length $C + l - 1$. Hence $L \geq C + l - 1 \geq C$ as claimed. □

We see that for any simple connected graph G, there are these three cases.

- The graph is Hamiltonian, and $L = n - 1$ and $C = n$;
- the graph is semi-Hamiltonian, and $L = n - 1$ and $C \leq L$;
- the graph is non-Hamiltonian, and $L \leq n - 2$ and $C \leq L$.

Lemma 10. *Let $u_0, u_1, \ldots u_L$ be a path of maximum length in a simple connected G, and assume the graph is not Hamiltonian. Then $u_0 \not\sim u_L$ and $\deg u_0 + \deg u_L \leq L$.*

Proof. Since the path $u_0, u_1, \ldots u_L$ has maximum length, it is non-extendible. Since the graph is not Hamiltonian, lemma 9 yields $C \leq L \leq n - 1$. Hence exists no cycle of length $L + 1$. We now use lemma 8. Thus one concludes $u_0 \not\sim u_L$ and $\deg u_0 + \deg u_L \leq L$. □

Lemma 11. *In a simple connected graph satisfying Ore's assumption*

(Ore p) $\qquad\qquad\qquad$ *If* $u \not\sim v$ *then* $\deg u + \deg v \geq p$

the maximum path length is $L \geq \min[n - 1, p]$.

Proof. In the case $L = n - 1$, we are ready, so we may assume $L \leq n - 2$ and thus the graph is non-Hamiltonian. Let $u_0, u_1, \ldots u_L$ be a path of maximum length. By lemma 10, one gets $u_0 \not\sim u_L$. Hence Ore's assumption (Ore p) and lemma 10 yield

$$p \leq \deg u_0 + \deg u_L \leq L$$

as to be shown. □

Lemma 12. *A simple graph satisfying (Ore n-1) is connected.*

Proof. We assume (Ore n-1) holds. But suppose towards a contradiction, the graph is not connected. Clearly the assumption (Ore n-1) implies the weaker condition (Ore n-2). By proposition 4, a disconnected simple graph satisfying (Ore n-2) is the disjoint union of two complete graphs, and the degree sum for any two nonadjacent vertices $u \not\sim v$ is $\deg u + \deg v = n - 2$, violating assumption (Ore n-1). This contradiction shows the graph is connected.

Hence the assumption (Ore n-1) implies the graph is connected. □

Lemma 13. *Ore's assumption*

(Ore n-1) $\qquad\qquad\qquad$ *If* $u \not\sim v$ *then* $\deg u + \deg v \geq n - 1$

implies the graph to be semi-Hamiltonian or Hamiltonian.

Proof. We may assume that the graph is not Hamiltonian, otherwise we are ready anyway. By lemma 12, the assumption (Ore n-1) implies that the graph is connected. Let $u_0, u_1, \ldots u_L$ be a path of maximum length. Now lemma 10 yields $u_0 \not\sim u_L$ and $\deg u_0 + \deg u_L \leq L$. Together with Ore's assumption (Ore n-1) one gets

$$n - 1 \leq \deg u_0 + \deg u_L \leq L$$

and thus the graph is semi-Hamiltonian. $\square$

Lemma 14. *Ore's assumption*

(Ore n) $\qquad\qquad$ If $\quad u \not\sim v \quad$ then $\quad \deg u + \deg v \geq n$

implies the graph is Hamiltonian.

Proof. By lemma 13, there exists a Hamiltonian path $v_0, v_1, v_2, \ldots, v_{n-1}$. In case $v_0 \sim v_{n-1}$, we get a Hamiltonian cycle and are ready. So we may assume $v_0 \not\sim v_{n-1}$. Hence Ore's assumption implies $\deg v_0 + \deg v_{n-1} \geq n$. Now lemma 7 tells the graph is Hamiltonian. $\square$

Proposition 20. *Assume a simple connected graph with $n \geq 4$ satisfies Ore's assumption (Ore p) for some $3 \leq p \leq n-1$. The path graphs P_2 and P_3 being excluded, there exists a cycle. Of course, $C = n$ and $L = n - 1$ hold for a Hamiltonian graph. In case the graph is not Hamiltonian, the maximum length C of cycles and L for open path satisfy the inequalities*

$$\frac{p+2}{2} \leq C \leq L$$

Proof. Assume the graph is not Hamiltonian, and not P_2. Let $u_0, u_1, \ldots u_L$ be a path of maximum length. By Lemma 10, we know that $u_0 \not\sim u_L$ and $\deg u_0 + \deg u_L \leq L$. Because of $u_0 \not\sim u_L$, and hence assumption (Ore p) yields $\deg u_0 + \deg u_L \geq p$. Hence $p \leq L \leq n-1$, in agreement with Lemma 11.

Let i be the maximal index with $u_0 \sim u_i$, and j be the maximal index with $u_{L-j} \sim u_L$. Possibly reversing the numbering of the path allows us to assume $j \leq i$. Moreover $\deg u_0 \leq i$ and $\deg u_L \leq j$ since neighbors of u_0 and u_L can only be among the vertices of the <u>maximum</u> path. Hence we conclude

$$p \leq \deg u_0 + \deg u_L \leq i + j \leq 2i$$

The maximum cycle has length $C \geq i+1$ since we get the $i+1$-cycle $u_0, \ldots u_i$ back to u_0. Hence

$$\frac{p+2}{2} \leq i+1 \leq C \leq L$$

holds for the not Hamiltonian case. Moreover $p \geq 3$ implies $C \geq 3$ and existence of a cycle. $\square$

Remark 13. The proposition cannot easily be sharpened. One see this from the following example Let $n \geq 4$ and let graph G be the disjoint union of the complete graphs $K\lfloor n/2 \rfloor$ and $K\lceil n/2 \rceil$ with an extra edge between two vertices of these graphs. Ore's assumption holds with $p = \lfloor n/2 \rfloor - 1 + \lceil n/2 \rceil - 1 = n - 2$, but not any larger p. The maximum cycle length is $C = \lceil n/2 \rceil = \lceil p+2/2 \rceil$.

Theorem 6 (Theorem of Chvátal (1972)). *A simple graph with $n \geq 3$ vertices is Hamiltonian if its degree sequence $d_1 \leq d_2 \leq \cdots \leq d_n$ satisfies the condition*

$$d_i > i \text{ or } d_{n-i} \geq n - i \quad \text{for } 1 \leq i < n/2$$

Proposition 21. *A simple graph with $n \geq 3$ vertices is semi-Hamiltonian or Hamiltonian if its degree sequence $d_1 \leq d_2 \leq \cdots \leq d_n$ satisfies the condition*

$$d_i \geq i \text{ or } d_{n+1-i} \geq n - i \quad \text{for } 1 \leq i < (n+1)/2$$

Theorem 7 (Theorem of Chvátal-Erdös (1972)). *A simple graph with $n \geq 3$ vertices and connectivity κ larger or equal the independence number α is Hamiltonian. In other words:*

> *Suppose that one needs to pull out at least as many vertices to disconnect the graph—as there are mutually nonadjacent vertices. Then the graph has a Hamiltonian cycle.*

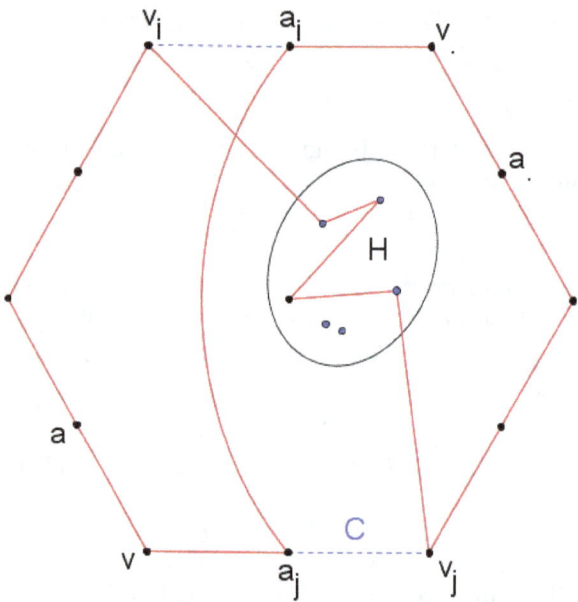

Figure 67: For a non-Hamiltonian graph, the independence number is greater than the connectivity: $\alpha > \kappa$.

The Theorem of Chvátal-Erdös is the contrapositive of the following proposition:

Proposition 22. *Suppose a simple graph with $n \geq 3$ vertices is not Hamiltonian. Let c be the maximum length of cycles and C be a cycle of maximum length. Let H be any component of the complement $\tilde{H} = G - C$. Let l be the number of vertices of the cycle C which are adjacent to H. Then the following holds:*

(a) $2\kappa \leq 2l \leq c < n$.

(b) $l < \alpha$.

(c) $\kappa < \alpha$, *even if no cycles exist.*

Proof Proposition 22. If no cycle exists at all, then G is a forest and hence $\kappa = 1$ and $n \geq 3$ implies $\alpha \geq 2$. Hence assertion (c) holds. We may now assume that a cycle exists. If the independence number $\alpha = 1$, the graph is complete, and K_n is Hamiltonian since $n \geq 3$ is assumed. Hence we see that $\alpha \geq 2$ and $G \neq K_n$.

Let c be the maximum length of cycles and C be a cycle of maximum length. Since the graph is not Hamiltonian, the complement $\tilde{H} = G - C$ is not empty. Let H be any component of $\tilde{H}$.

(a) Let $v_1, v_2, \ldots, v_l$ be the vertices of the cycle C which are adjacent to H, ordered in the way as they occur going around C clockwise. None of these vertices are adjacent in C, because otherwise one gets a longer cycle by introducing vertices of H into the cycle C, contradicting maximality. The graph $G - \{v_1, v_2, \ldots, v_l\}$ is disconnected, and hence $l \geq \kappa$ by the definition of connectivity. Hence we have obtained $2\kappa \leq 2l \leq c < n$, confirming part (a).

(b) Let $a_1, a_2, \ldots, a_l$ be the vertices of the cycle C following $v_1, v_2, \ldots, v_l$ as one goes around C clockwise. We claim that none of the vertices a_i and a_j can be adjacent to each other. Indeed, if a_i and a_j would be adjacent, one could construct a longer cycle

$$a_j, \ldots \overrightarrow{C} \ldots v_i \, H \, v_j, \ldots \overleftarrow{C} \ldots a_i a_j$$

from C. This longer cycle is obtained by deletion of the edges $u_i a_i$ and $u_j a_j$ from C, and using a detour $v_i \, H \, v_j$ through H to go from u_i to u_j. The first part $\overrightarrow{C}$ of the cycle is passed clockwise, the second part $\overleftarrow{C}$ is passed counterclockwise. Consequently we obtain an independent set $\{a_1, a_2, \ldots, a_l, h\}$ where $h \in H$ is any vertex. Thus we have shown that $\alpha \geq l + \alpha(H) > l$.

(c) Together, the arguments in (a) and (b) yield $\kappa < \alpha$.

$\square$

Easy consequence. For any graph the length c of the longest cycle satisfies

$$c \geq \min[n, 2\kappa]$$

Especially, a graph with $n \leq 2\kappa$ is Hamiltonian.

Since $\kappa \leq \delta$, the last statement is a bid weaker than Dirac's Theorem 4

Proposition 23 (An easy generalization of Erdös' theorem). *Assume that for the graph G, the independence number α less than connectivity κ plus one: $\alpha \leq \kappa + 1$. Then the graph is demi-Hamiltonian.*

Proof. Adjoin an extra vertex v to the given graph G. The wedged graph $H := G \vee v$ has the same independence number $\alpha(H) = \alpha(G)$. But the connectivity has been increased by one. Indeed, $\kappa(H) \geq \kappa(G) + 1$, because one needs to pull out vertex v to disconnect H.

Now the assumption $\alpha \leq \kappa + 1$ for graph G implies $\alpha(H) \leq \kappa(H)$. By Erdös' theorem, one concludes that the wedged-up graph H is Hamiltonian.

After having pulled out v, a Hamiltonian cycle in H leaves an open semi-Hamiltonian path in the original graph $G = H - v$. □

I.3.3 Eulerian and Hamiltonian properties

Problem 95. *Given an example of a graph with 10 vertices and 13 edges that is Eulerian and non-Hamiltonian.*

Answer (First idea). A graph with two or more cut-vertices is non-Hamiltonian. Merging each of two vertices of a square with a vertex of a second and third square gives an Eulerian but non-Hamiltonian graph with $n = 10$ and $m = 12$.

One can—of course—just adjoin another edge as a loop. A more natural solution is obtained by subdividing the loop with two vertices, and canceling two vertices of degree two.

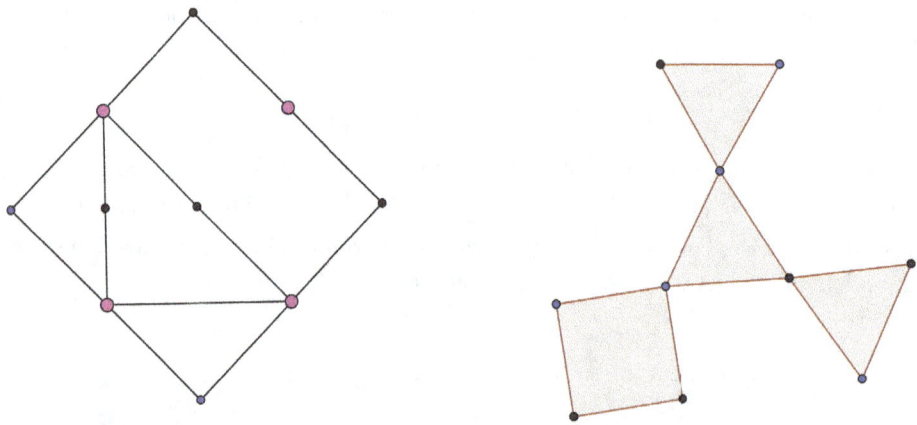

Figure 68: Two graph which are Eulerian and non-Hamiltonian.

Answer (Second idea). A bipartite graph with four black and six white vertices is non-Hamiltonian. I begin with a cycle of four black and four white vertices—and finally get a graph which is not bipartite, but the pulling out theorem shows that it is non-Hamiltonian. Indeed pulling out the four white vertices leaves all six black vertices isolated.

Problem 96. *Explain why a bipartite Eulerian graph has an even number of edges. Does it always have an even number of vertices, too?*

Answer. By Proposition 13, the edges of an even graph can be split into cycles, no two of which have an edge in common.

The cycles of a bipartite graph are all even (see Proposition 6). Since they are edge-disjoint, the total number of edges is even, too.

It is easy to find a bipartite Eulerian graph with an odd number of vertices. Two 4-cycles hanging together at a cut-vertex give an example with $n = 7$. Only $n = 1, 3, 5$ are excluded.

I.4 Matrix representations of graphs

Definition 34 (The adjacency matrix). For a general graph with n vertices and m edges, the *adjacency matrix*, denoted by A, is an $n \times n$-matrix. For $i \neq j$, the matrix element a_{ij} gives the number of edges joining the vertices i and j. For $i = j$, the diagonal element a_{ii} equals *twice* the number of loops at vertex i.

Definition 35 (The incidence matrix). For a general graph with n vertices and m edges, the *incidence matrix* is an $n \times m$-matrix J. The element Inc_{ij} counts the number of ends that occurs at vertex i because of the edge j. The element $Inc_{ij} = 1$ means that vertex i is one end of edge j. The element $Inc_{ij} = 2$ means that vertex i has the loop-edge j attached.

Furthermore, let D be the diagonal matrix with d_{ii} the degree of vertex i. Again, a loop at vertex i adds *two* to the degree of i. Let e denote the vector with all components equal to 1. The superscript ^{t} indicates transposition, converting column and row vectors.

Problem 97. *Give the matrices A, D, Inc for the graph from the figure below.*

Answer.

$$A = \begin{bmatrix} 0 & 0 & 0 & 1 \\ 0 & 0 & 0 & 2 \\ 0 & 0 & 2 & 1 \\ 1 & 2 & 1 & 0 \end{bmatrix}, \quad D = \begin{bmatrix} 1 & 0 & 0 & 0 \\ 0 & 2 & 0 & 0 \\ 0 & 0 & 3 & 0 \\ 0 & 0 & 0 & 4 \end{bmatrix}, \quad Inc = \begin{bmatrix} 0 & 1 & 0 & 0 & 0 \\ 0 & 0 & 1 & 1 & 0 \\ 2 & 0 & 0 & 0 & 1 \\ 0 & 1 & 1 & 1 & 1 \end{bmatrix}$$

Let $e_j \in \mathbf{Z}^j$ be the column-vector with all components 1. Let $deg \in \mathbf{Z}^n$ be the column-vector the entries of which are the degrees for all vertices.

Obviously hold $Inc \cdot e_m = deg$ and $e_n^t \cdot Inc = 2e_m^t$.

Problem 98. *Use this remark to prove the* hand shaking lemma, *telling that the sum of the degrees equals twice the number of edges.*

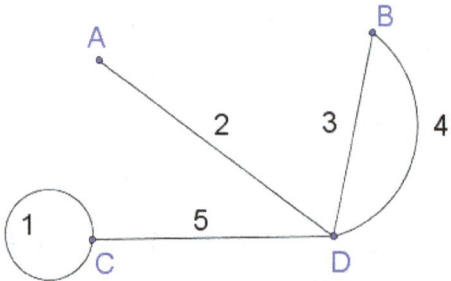

Figure 69: An example graph.

Proof of handshaking lemma.

$$\sum degrees = e_n^t \cdot deg = e_n^t \cdot Inc \cdot e_m = 2e_m^t \cdot e_m = 2m$$

Hence the sum of the degrees equals twice the number of edges. □

Lemma 15. *The adjacency matrix A and incidence matrix Inc of any (even general) graph satisfy*

(I.4.1) $$Inc \cdot Inc^t = A + \text{Diag}(deg)$$

where $D := \text{Diag}(deg)$ is the diagonal matrix with the degrees.

Proof. Take any two columns c_k and c_l of the incidence matrix. Assume $k \neq l$. For any nonadjacent vertices k and l the columns c_k and c_l have no entry 1 at the same vertex. Hence $\langle c_k, c_l \rangle = 0$ We see that the vertices $k \neq l$ are adjacent if and only if the columns c_k and c_l have one entry 1 at the same vertex. This in turn happens if and only $\langle c_k, c_l \rangle = 1$.

In the case $k = l$, the vertex k and k itself are adjacent to as many edges as the degree $\deg(k)$ tells. Hence holds $\langle c_k, c_k \rangle = \deg(k)$.

Put together one gets the matrix equation (I.4.1). □

Simple facts. **(a)** The matrix A is symmetric: $A = A^t$.
(b) With $e \in \mathbb{R}^n$, both $Ae = De = deg \in \mathbb{R}^n$ is the vector of the vertex degrees.
(c) $e^t A e = e^t D e = \sum deg$ equals the sum of the degrees of all vertices.
(d) Let $e_m \in \mathbb{R}^m$ be once more a vector of all entries equal to one.
Then $Inc\, e_m = d \in \mathbb{R}^n$ is the vector of the vertex degrees.
(e) With $e \in \mathbb{R}^n$, the left product is $e^t Inc = 2e_m^t \in \mathbb{R}^m$.
(f) Finally

(J) $$Inc \cdot Inc^t = A + D$$

Problem 99. *As an easy consequence of* (J), *we get another proof the handshaking lemma. Too, confirm that*
$$e^t A e = e^t D e = 2m$$
with $e \in \mathbb{R}^n$

Answer. With $e \in \mathbb{R}^n$ and $e_m \in \mathbb{R}^m$, the remarks above yield:
$$e^t Inc\, Inc^t e = 2e_m^t 2e_m = 4m$$
$$e^t A e = e^t D e = e^t \deg = \sum_{\text{vertices } v} \deg v$$

Now formula (J) implies
$$4m = 2 \sum_{\text{vertices } v} \deg v$$
Division by two yields the handshaking lemma.

I.5 The line graph

Definition 36 (The line graph). For a general graph G, the *line graph* $L(G)$, is defined as follows:

- The "vertices" of the line graph $L(G)$ are the edges of the original graph G.
- Two vertices of the line graph are "adjacent" if they are adjacent edges of the original graph.

Problem 100. (a) *Draw C_3 and $K_{1,3}$ and their line graphs.*

(b) *Convince yourself that the line graph of a cycle is a cycle:* $L(C_n) \cong C_n$.

(c) *Give a reason why the line graph $L(K_n)$ has $n(n-1)/2$ vertices and is $2n-4$-regular.*

(d) *Find the line graph of K_4. Draw K_4 and its line graph, and convince yourself that $L(K_4) \cong Oct_3$.*

(e) *Find the number of vertices, and the degree for the complement of the line graph of K_5.*

(f) *Draw K_5 with its edges named $1, 2, 3, 4, 5$ and a, b, c, d, e where $1 \parallel a$, $2 \parallel b$, $3 \parallel c$, $4 \parallel d$, $5 \parallel e$. Convince yourself that the complement $\overline{L(K_5)}$ is isomorphic to the Petersen graph,—which one can here see in the "flower style".*

It is indeed rather easy to get the line graph from the drawing of any small graph. Just use a new color, not used for any vertices or edges of the given graph. Using this color, put a new vertex at the midpoint of each edge of the given graph. Finally draw the new edges of the line graph, in the new color, too, at all places where any two edges of the given graph are adjacent.

Remark 14. One can now prove (with some care in the $\sim$ step) that

$$\text{Aut}(Petersen) = \text{Aut}(L(K_5)) \sim \text{Aut}(K_5) = \mathcal{S}_5$$

The automorphism group of the Petersen graph is the symmetric group permutating five elements.

Answer. As shown in figure 95, the tetrahedron K_4 has as line graph the octahedron: $L(K_4) = Oct_3$. As shown in figure 96, the complement of the line graph of K_5 is the Petersen graph: $\overline{L(K_5)} = Petersen$.

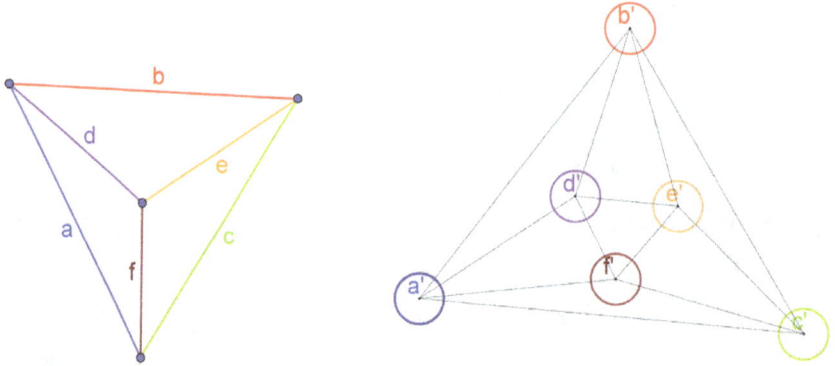

Figure 70: The tetrahedron K_4 has as line graph the octahedron.

Lemma 16. *The adjacency matrix $A[L(G)]$ of the line graph and incidence matrix $Inc[G]$ of any (even general) graph G satisfy*

(I.5.1) $$Inc^t \cdot Inc = A[L(G)] + 2Id_m$$

Proof. Take any two rows r_k and r_l of the incidence matrix. Assume $k \neq l$ at first. For any nonadjacent edges k and l the rows r_k and r_l have no entry 1 at the same vertex. Hence $\langle r_k, r_l \rangle = 0$ We see that the edges $k \neq l$ are adjacent if and only if the rows r_k and r_l have one entry 1 at the same vertex. This in turn happens if and only $\langle r_k, r_l \rangle = 1$.

In the case $k = l$, the edge k and k itself have both end-vertices in common. Hence holds $\langle r_k, r_k \rangle = 2$.

Put together one gets the matrix equation (I.5.1). □

Problem 101. *Take the graph with the list of edges*
$(1,2), (1,3), (1,4), (2,3), (2,4), (3,5)$. *Calculate the adjacency matrix and the incidence matrix. Check lemma 15 and lemma 16.*

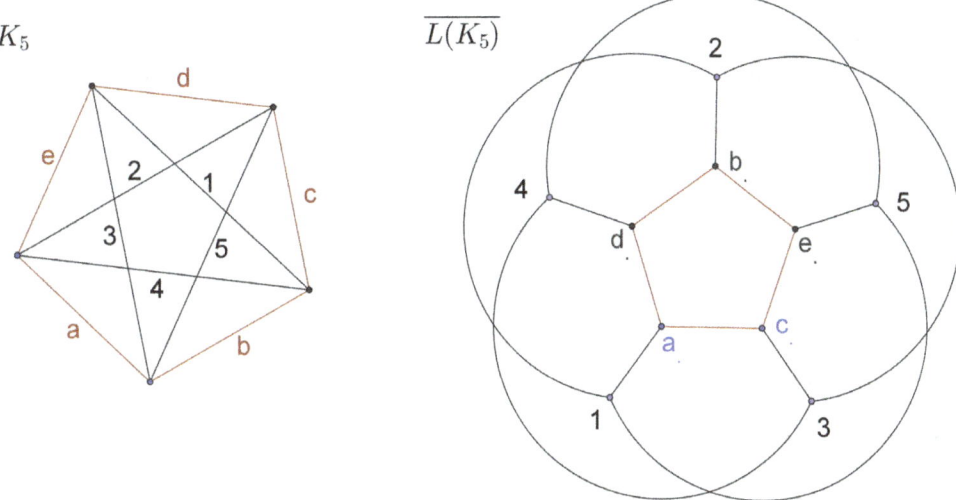

Figure 71: The complement of the line graph of K_5 is the Petersen graph.

Solution.

$$A = \begin{bmatrix} 0 & 1 & 1 & 1 & 0 \\ 1 & 0 & 1 & 1 & 0 \\ 1 & 1 & 0 & 0 & 1 \\ 1 & 1 & 0 & 0 & 0 \\ 0 & 0 & 1 & 0 & 0 \end{bmatrix} \quad Inc = \begin{bmatrix} 1 & 1 & 1 & 0 & 0 & 0 \\ 1 & 0 & 0 & 1 & 1 & 0 \\ 0 & 1 & 0 & 1 & 0 & 1 \\ 0 & 0 & 1 & 0 & 1 & 0 \\ 0 & 0 & 0 & 0 & 0 & 1 \end{bmatrix}$$

and the products are

$$Inc \cdot Inc^t = \begin{bmatrix} 3 & 1 & 1 & 1 & 0 \\ 1 & 3 & 1 & 1 & 0 \\ 1 & 1 & 3 & 0 & 1 \\ 1 & 1 & 0 & 2 & 0 \\ 0 & 0 & 1 & 0 & 1 \end{bmatrix} \quad Inc^t \cdot Inc = \begin{bmatrix} 2 & 1 & 1 & 1 & 1 & 0 \\ 1 & 2 & 1 & 1 & 0 & 1 \\ 1 & 1 & 2 & 0 & 1 & 0 \\ 1 & 1 & 0 & 2 & 1 & 1 \\ 1 & 0 & 1 & 1 & 2 & 0 \\ 0 & 1 & 0 & 1 & 0 & 2 \end{bmatrix}$$

$\square$

Here a possible solution with mathematica. For lack of space I give only the input.

```
myedges = {1 \[UndirectedEdge] 2, 2 \[UndirectedEdge] 3,
   3 \[UndirectedEdge] 1, 1 \[UndirectedEdge] 4, 2 \[UndirectedEdge] 4,
   3 <-> 5}
mygraph =
 Graph[myedges, VertexLabels -> Placed[Automatic, Center],
  VertexSize -> .3, ImageSize -> 200]
```

```
Adj = AdjacencyMatrix[mygraph]; mygraph1 =
AdjacencyGraph[Adj, VertexLabels -> Placed[Automatic, Center],
 VertexSize -> .3, ImageSize -> 200]

EdgeList[mygraph1]

Adj1 = AdjacencyMatrix[mygraph1];

Adj1 // MatrixForm

Inc1 = IncidenceMatrix[mygraph1];

Inc1 // MatrixForm

Inc1.Transpose[Inc1] // MatrixForm

Transpose[Inc1].Inc1 // MatrixForm

AdjacencyMatrix[LineGraph[mygraph1]] // MatrixForm
```

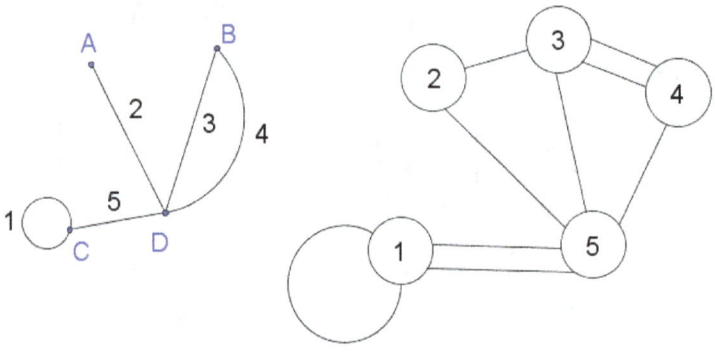

Figure 72: A graph G and its line graph $L(G)$.

Problem 102. *Draw the line graph for the graph in the figure I.4.*

Answer. The line graph for the graph in the figure I.4: is given by the figure on page 97.

Problem 103. *Find the adjacency matrix B for the line graph from problem 102. Calculate Be.*

Answer.
$$B = \begin{bmatrix} 2 & 0 & 0 & 0 & 2 \\ 0 & 0 & 1 & 1 & 1 \\ 0 & 1 & 0 & 2 & 1 \\ 0 & 1 & 2 & 0 & 1 \\ 1 & 1 & 1 & 1 & 0 \end{bmatrix}, \quad Be = \begin{bmatrix} 4 \\ 3 \\ 4 \\ 4 \\ 4 \end{bmatrix}$$

Problem 104. *Calculate the matrix product $Inc^t \cdot Inc$ with J the incidence matrix from problem 102.*

Answer.
$$Inc^t \cdot Inc = \begin{bmatrix} 4 & 0 & 0 & 0 & 2 \\ 0 & 2 & 1 & 1 & 1 \\ 0 & 1 & 2 & 2 & 1 \\ 0 & 1 & 2 & 2 & 1 \\ 2 & 1 & 1 & 1 & 2 \end{bmatrix}$$

Problem 105. *Use result (I.5.1) to derive the formula*

(mL) $$\sum_{\text{vertices } v \text{ of } G} \deg v^2 = 2m_{L(G)} + 2m_G$$

Answer. Let $e_m \in \mathbb{R}^m$ be the vector with all entries equal to one. Formula (I.5.1) implies

(JLe) $$e_m^t Inc_G^t Inc_G e_m^t = e_m^t [A_{L(G)} + 2I_m] e_m$$

We check that $Inc\, e_m = \deg \in \mathbb{R}^n$ is the vector of the degrees. Hence the left hand side of (JLe) is

$$e_m^t Inc_G^t Inc_G e_m^t = \deg^t \cdot \deg = \sum_{\text{vertices } v \text{ of } G} \deg v^2$$

Now we use problem 99 for the line graph and conclude that

$$e_m^t A_{L(G)} e_m = 2m_{L(G)} \quad \text{and} \quad e_m^t [A_{L(G)} + 2Id_m] e_m = 2m_{L(G)} + 2m_G$$

Now formula (JLe) implies the assertion (mL).

Problem 106. *Check formula (mL) derived in a problem above for the example from problem 102.*

Answer. For graph G, the sum of vertex degrees squared is

$$\sum_{\text{vertices } v \text{ of } G} \deg v^2 = 1^2 + 2^2 + 3^2 + 4^2 = 30$$

and the left hand side of formula (mL) is $2m_{L(G)} + 2m_G = 2 \cdot 10 + 2 \cdot 5 = 30$ which confirms (mL) for this example.

Problem 107. *Is it true or not? The line graph of every Eulerian graph is Hamiltonian.*

Problem 108. *Show that the line graph $L(G)$ is a tree if and only if G is a path graph.*

Problem 109. *Show that the line graph $L(G)$ is a cycle if and only if G is either a cycle graph of $K_{1,3}$.*

Problem 110. *Do there exist any other pairs of nonisomorphic simple and connected graphs G and H besides K_3 and $K_{1,3}$ for which the line graphs $L(G) \sim L(H)$ are isomorphic?*

Clearly there exist nonconnected examples: Take any direct sum of the graphs K_3 and $K_{1,3}$ with any number r of summands, and one gets as line graph the sum of r copies of K_3.

I.6 Trees

Definition 37 (acyclic graph). A simple graph without cycles is called *acyclic* or a *forest*.

Definition 38 (Tree). A simple connected acyclic graph is called a *tree*.

Proposition 24. *For any simple graph G, the following three properties are equivalent:*

(i) *G is a tree.*

(ii) *For any two vertices v, w exists a unique path connecting v to w.*

(iii) *G is connected and every edge in G is a bridge.*

Problem 111. *To prove Proposition 24, convince yourself that (i) implies (ii), (ii) implies (iii), and (iii) implies (i).*

"(i) *implies* (ii)": Assume G is a tree and let v and w be any two vertices. Since G is connected, there exists a path from v to w. Since G is acyclic, the path is unique. Conversely, from any two different paths from v to w, one could construct a cycle, contradicting the assumption that G is acyclic. □

"(ii) *implies* (iii)": Existence of a path between any two vertices v and w tells the graph G is connected. For any edge $e = ab$, the graph $G - e$ is disconnected. Conversely, if $G - e$ would be connected, there would exist a second path from a to b—besides the path consisting of the single edge e—in contradiction to the assumed uniqueness. Hence deleting any edge leaves a disconnected graph $G - e$, and thus e is a bridge. □

"(iii) *implies* (i)": The graph G is connected by assumption. No edge of a cycle is a bridge. Since each edge of G is assumed to be a bridge, there cannot exist any cycle in G. □

Theorem 8 (Two basic properties of a tree imply the third one). *For any simple graph G, two of the following properties imply the third one:*

(a) *G is connected.*

(b) *G is acyclic.*

(c) *The number of edges of G is one less than the number of vertices.*

Lemma 17. *The number of edges of a tree is one less than the number of vertices.*

Proof. We use induction on the number n of vertices. The lemma is true for the (trivial) tree K_1 with one vertex, and the tree P_2 with two vertices. For the induction step, we use the "divide and conquer approach". Assume that the statement holds for all trees with less than n vertices. We check the statement for a tree T with n vertices. Deleting any edge e from T leave the disjoint sum of two smaller trees: $T - e = A + B$.

For the smaller trees, the assertion about the number of edges holds by the induction assumption. Hence
$$m_T = m_A + m_B + 1 = (n_A - 1) + (n_B - 1) + 1 = n_T - 1$$
as to be shown. □

"(a) and (b) imply (c)": We have just seen that an connected, acyclic graph has $m = n - 1$ edges. □

Lemma 18. *The number of edges m of an acyclic graph with n edges and k components is $m = n - k$.*

Proof. The acyclic graph is a direct sum of k trees: $G = T_1 + T_2 + \ldots T_k$. Adding all their edges yields
$$m_G = m_1 + m_2 + \cdots + m_k = (n_1 - 1) + (n_2 - 1) + \cdots + (n_k - 1) = n - k$$
□

"(b) and (c) imply (a)": The number of components of an acyclic graph is $k = n - m$. Hence $m = n - 1$ implies $k = 1$, which tells the graph is connected. □

Lemma 19. *Given is a connected graph G. Suppose that p is the least number of edges deletion of which leaves a tree. Then the number of edges of the original graph is $m = n - 1 + p$.*

Proof. That is true for $p = 0$, since a tree is already given, and we know it has $m = n - 1$ edges. Now the statement can be checked by induction on p. □

Definition 39 (Cycle rank). The *cycle rank* γ of a simple graph is the minimal number of edges, deletion of which leaves an acyclic graph.

Problem 112. *Convince yourself that $\gamma \geq 0$ holds for all graphs.*

Proposition 25. *A simple graph G with n vertices, m edges, and k components, has the cycle rank*
$$\gamma(G) = m - n + k$$
This is minimal number of edges, deletion of which leaves an acyclic graph. Hence $\gamma \geq 0$ and $\gamma = 0$ if and only if the graph is acyclic.

Proof. For a connected graph, $k = 1$, Lemma 19 tells $m = n - 1 + p$, and $p = m - n + 1 = \gamma$ is the cycle rank.

Given any simple graph G with k components $G = G_1 + G_2 + \ldots G_k$, we sum over the number of vertices, edges, and the cycle rank to obtain

$$\gamma_G = \gamma_1 + \gamma_2 + \cdots + \gamma_k = (m_1 - n_1 + 1) + (m_2 - n_2 + 1) + \cdots + (m_k - n_k + 1) = m - n + k$$

as the minimal number of edges, deletion of which leaves an acyclic graph. □

"(a) and (c) imply (b)": A connected graph with n vertices, $m = n - 1$ edges and $k = 1$ components has cycle rank $\gamma = 0$ and hence is acyclic. □

Problem 113. *Find a tree that has only end-vertices and vertices of degree 6. The number of vertices is $n = 102$. Calculate the number n_1 of ends, and the number n_6 of branching vertices. Explain your reasoning.*

Answer. Simply count vertices, use the handshaking lemma, and $m = n - 1$ for trees. One gets two equations for the two unknown n_1 and n_6:

$$n_1 + n_6 = n = 102$$
$$n_1 + 6n_6 = 2m = 2n - 2 = 202$$

Subtracting the two equations yields $5\,n_6 = 100$. Hence $n_6 = 20$ and $n_1 = 82$.

Definition 40. *The vertex of degree one of a tree is called end-vertex or leaf.*

Proposition 26. *Every tree has at least two leaves.*

Problem 114 (Counting the leaves of a tree). *For $d = 1, 2, 3, \ldots$ let n_i count the vertices of a tree of degree d. Use the handshaking lemma to derive that*

$$n_1 = 2 + \sum_{d \geq 3}(d-2)n_d$$

Derive that every tree has at least two leaves.

Answer. We use the handshaking lemma in the form

$$2m = \sum_{d \geq 1} dn_d$$

the fact that a tree has $m = n - 1$ edges, and the obvious count

$$n = \sum_{d \geq 1} n_d$$

Hence

$$2 = 2n - 2m = \sum_{d \geq 1}(2-d)n_d = n_1 - \sum_{d \geq 3}(d-2)n_d$$

which implies $n_1 \geq 2$ for the number of leaves.

Second proof. Let $P = v_1, v_2 \ldots v_k$ be a maximal path in the given tree T. The vertex v_1 cannot have any other neighbor except v_2 among the vertices of the path, because T has no cycles. Too, the vertex v_1 cannot have any neighbor among the remaining vertices of $T \setminus P$, since the path is maximal. Hence v_2 is the only neighbor of v_1 and $\deg(v_1) = 1$. Similar we see that $\deg(v_k) = 1$ for the vertex v_k at the other end of the maximal path.

Hence both end-vertices of any maximal path have degree one. Especially, in a tree there exist at least two vertices of degree one. □

Problem 115. *How many trees exist with $n = 8$ vertices, provided all vertices have degree either $1, 2$ or 4.*

(a) *Set up the two linear equations for the numbers n_1, n_2, n_4 of vertices with degree $1, 2, 4$.*

(b) *Solve this system with n_4 as free variable. Write down the triplets (n_1, n_2, n_4) of non-negatives integer solutions.*

(c) *For each of these triplets draw the trees. (Altogether, I get five non-isomorphic solutions.)*

Answer. **(a)** From the handshake lemma and $m = n - 1$, we get

$$n_1 + n_2 + n_4 = 8$$
$$n_1 + 2n_2 + 4n_4 = 14$$

(b) $n_1 = 2 + 2n_4$, $n_2 = 6 - 3n_4$. The non-negatives integer solutions are

$$(n_1, n_2, n_4) = (6, 0, 2), (4, 3, 1), (2, 6, 0)$$

(c) For $(n_1, n_2, n_4) = (6, 0, 2)$ there is one solution. For $(n_1, n_2, n_4) = (4, 3, 1)$ one gets three solutions. For $(n_1, n_2, n_4) = (2, 6, 0)$ there is one solution: the path P_8.

Problem 116 (An example of a large tree). *Assume that a tree has 1000 vertices, maximal degree three, and at most 2 vertices of degree 2. Find n_1, n_2, n_3 for all possible solutions. How many leaves can the tree have?*

Answer. $1000 = n_1 + n_2 + n_3$ and $2m = 1998 = n_1 + 2n_2 + 3n_3$ imply $n_1 = 2 + n_3$. Hence $1000 = 2n_1 - 2 + n_2$. Thus n_2 has to be even. We get two solutions:

(I.6.1) $$n_1 = 501, \ n_2 = 0, \ n_3 = 499$$

(I.6.2) $$n_1 = 500, \ n_2 = 2, \ n_3 = 498$$

I.6.1 Rooted trees

Definition 41 (Rooted tree, leaf). A *rooted tree* is an (unlabelled) tree, with one vertex marked as root. The vertices of degree one that are different from the root, are called the *leaves* of the rooted tree.

Definition 42 (Partial order of vertices). For two vertices v and w of a rooted tree, we say that "`w is a decendent of` v" or "v `is an ancestor of` w" if and only if the unique path from the root r to w contains the vertex v. In this case, we also write $v \preceq w$.

The tree T_v is the induced graph containing as vertices the decendent of v, and vertex v as root.

For two vertices v and w, we say that "`w is a child of` v" or "v `is the parent of` w" if and only if $v \preceq w$ and $v \cong w$ are adjacent.

Remark 15. The point not intuitive is the fact that a child always has only <u>one</u> parent. The parent is hence unique!

Proposition 27. *Equivalent statements are $v \preceq w \Leftrightarrow w \in T_v \Leftrightarrow T_v \supseteq T_w$. Clearly T_v is a rooted tree. For all vertices v, w, x*

(i) $v \preceq v$

(ii) *If $v \preceq w$ and $w \preceq v$ then $v = w$*

(iii) *If $v \preceq w$ and $w \preceq x$ then $v \preceq x$*

Hence the relation $\preceq$ is a partial order.

Often, especially in computer science, the rooted tree is drawn with the root at the top, and the decendents appear in rows. In this way, the tree represents a hierarchical structure.

Too, one can use such a tree to conveniently visualize a *nested multi-set*. If in addition the edges are ordered left to right, one gets a *nested list*.

Instead of taking the content of the list or set empty, I prefer to introduce *primary elements* (the "Urelemente" of Zermelo). All primary elements are different by definition, they are logical constants. With the help of the primary elements, the correspondence of nested list to rooted tree becomes more easy to understand.

Proposition 28. *There is a one-to-one correspondence between nested lists (multi-sets) and rooted trees. Given the rooted tree, the list (multi-set) is constructed as follows.*

- *At each leave is put a primary element of one's choice. Repetition is allowed.*

- *Assume the different items $l, m \ldots p$ have been assigned to the children of vertex v. In case the edges are ordered left to right, the list $[l, m \ldots p]$ is assigned to the vertex v. In case without order of edges, the multi-set $\{l, m \ldots p\}$ is assigned to the vertex v.*

- *In the last step, one obtains the entire nested list or set at the root of the tree.*

Remark 16. It is possible to avoid the primary elements and instead, to assign in the beginning to each leaf the empty list $[\,]$ or empty set $\{\,\}$.

Problem 117. *Draw the rooted ordered tree with the same structure as the following nested list of lists:*

$$[[[[\ ]\ ]]\quad [[[\quad\ ]]\quad [[[\ ]]]]\quad [\ ]]$$

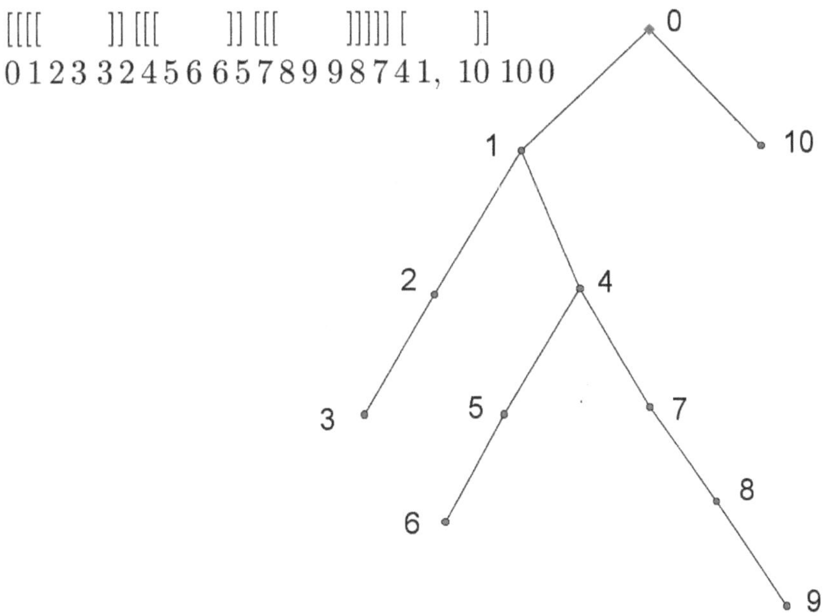

Figure 73: Parsing to convert a list to a rooted tree.

Answer. Give the most left bracket the number 0. Parsing the list from left to right, I number the next opening bracket by the next available integer, the next closing parenthesis by the highest already occurring number.

The rooted tree is obtained starting from the root 0. If there follows in the list an opening parenthesis, a downward edge to the child (if possible right child) is drawn. The child is denoted by the number of this parenthesis.

If there follows in the list a closing parenthesis, one goes back to the parent. This backtracking goes on until there occurs again an opening parenthesis,— for which a downward edge and a new child-vertex on the left is drawn.

For an equilibrated system of parenthesis, one has to arrive back at the root.

$$[[[[\quad\quad]][[[\quad\quad]][[[\quad\quad\quad]]]][\quad\quad]]$$
$$0\,1\,2\,3\quad 3\,2\,4\,5\,6\quad 6\,5\,7\,8\,9\quad 9\,8\,7\,4\,1,10\quad 10\,0$$

I.6.2 Labeled trees

Proposition 29 (Cayley's Theorem—counting labeled trees). *There are n^{n-2} different labeled trees with n vertices.*

Corollary 5 (Spanning trees of the complete graph). *The complete graph K_n has n^{n-2} different spanning trees.*

For the proof we construct a bijection between the labeled trees and their *Prüfer codes*. Each Prüfer code is a list of length $n-2$ with integers $1\ldots n$ as entries.

Construction of the Prüfer code for a given labeled tree. Find the end-vertex (leaf) of the tree with the lowest label. Put the label of its neighbor as next item into the Prüfer code. Pull out the end-vertex—which is best indicated by deleting its label, and repeat the process until only two vertices are left. □

Construction of the labeled tree from a given Prüfer code. We write down three lines underneath each other. The second line is the list $[1, 2, \ldots, n]$. The third line is the given Prüfer code. Into the first line, we successively put the adjacencies we are going to find for the labeled vertices.

Find the lowest label in the remaining list which is not in the remaining Prüfer code. Delete this label from the list. Delete the first item from the remaining Prüfer code and take it up into the first line directly above the item of the list that has just been deleted. Indicate the new adjacency. The above steps are repeated until a list of two labels and an empty Prüfer code is left over. These two remaining labels are adjacent to each other.

Finally one can produce a figure of the labeled tree using the adjacencies between labeled vertices in the first and the second line underneath each other. □

Problem 118. *Reconstruct and draw the labeled tree with the Prüfer code $(1, 1, 3, 5, 5)$.*

Answer. We begin the reconstruction with the three lines:

$$\begin{aligned}&Adjacencies &&:\\ &\quad List &&:\quad 1\ \ 2\ \ 3\ \ 4\ \ 5\ \ 6\ \ 7\\ &\quad Code &&:\quad 1\ \ 1\ \ 3\ \ 5\ \ 5\end{aligned}$$

and get by successive deletion of the lowest term from $List \setminus Code$:

$$
\begin{array}{rcllllllll}
Adjacencies & : & & 1 & & & & & & \\
List & : & 1 & \not{2} & 3 & 4 & 5 & 6 & 7 & \\
Code & : & \not{1} & 1 & 3 & 5 & 5 & & &
\end{array}
\qquad
\begin{array}{rcllllllll}
Adjacencies & : & & 1 & & 1 & & & & \\
List & : & 1 & \not{2} & 3 & \not{4} & 5 & 6 & 7 & \\
Code & : & \not{1} & \not{1} & 3 & 5 & 5 & & &
\end{array}
$$

$$
\begin{array}{rcllllllll}
Adjacencies & : & 3 & 1 & & 1 & & & & \\
List & : & \not{1} & \not{2} & 3 & \not{4} & 5 & 6 & 7 & \\
Code & : & \not{1} & \not{1} & \not{3} & 5 & 5 & & &
\end{array}
\qquad
\begin{array}{rcllllllll}
Adjacencies & : & 3 & 1 & 5 & 1 & & & & \\
List & : & \not{1} & \not{2} & \not{3} & \not{4} & 5 & 6 & 7 & \\
Code & : & \not{1} & \not{1} & \not{3} & \not{5} & 5 & & &
\end{array}
$$

$$
\begin{array}{rcllllllll}
Adjacencies & : & 3 & 1 & 5 & 1 & & 5 & & \\
List & : & \not{1} & \not{2} & \not{3} & \not{4} & \underline{5} & \not{6} & \underline{7} & \\
Code & : & \not{1} & \not{1} & \not{3} & \not{5} & \not{5} & & &
\end{array}
$$

Now we draw the labeled tree, which is done in the figure on page 106.

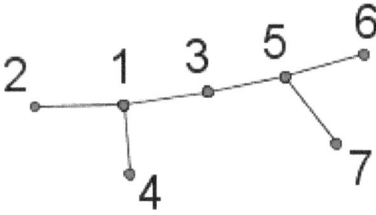

Figure 74: Reconstruction of a tree.

Figure 75: What are the Prüfer codes for the two trees?

Problem 119. *Find the Prüfer codes for the two labeled tree from the figure on page 106.*

This is an example for two non-isomorphic trees, the Prüfer codes of which are permutations of each other.

Answer. The Prüfer codes for the two labeled tree from the figure on page 106 are:

$$(3, 2, 1, 1) \quad \text{and} \quad (3, 1, 1, 2)$$

I.6.3 Braced frames

Problem 120. *Which one of the braced frameworks depicted below is rigid. Which one has a minimal bracing.*

Draw the relevant bipartite graphs and explain what you need to check about them.

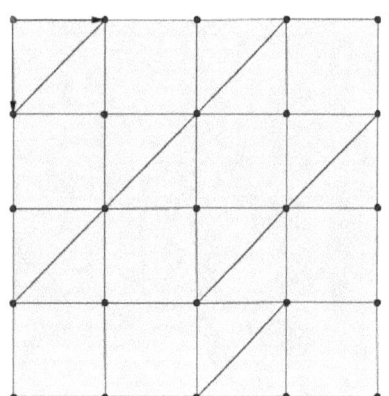 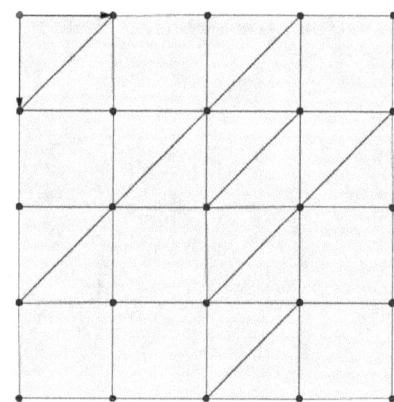

Figure 76: Two frames. Which one is rigid, which is minimal.

Answer. The relevant bipartite graph has vertices corresponding to the vertical- and horizontal sides of the frame. A vertical and horizontal side gets connected by an edge if and only if the corresponding rectangle has a brace.

Assume that just one point of the grid is fixed. Each component of the bipartite graph corresponds to a part of the network the rods of which can be turned independently.

The number of degrees of freedom for the rotation of the rods is the number of angles needed to determine the direction of all rods. The number of degrees of freedom for the rotation of the rods is equal to the number of components of the bipartite graph.

The frame is rigid if and only if its bipartite graph is connected.

Reason. In this case, there is just one component, and the only degree of freedom is rotation of the entire frame. □

The frame is minimal if and only if its bipartite graph is acyclic.

reason. Taking out an edge of the bipartite graph that closes a cycle does not change number of its components. Hence the number of degrees of freedom of motion of the frame is not changed either. □

Remark 17. A cycle of the bipartite graph corresponds to *loop of braces*. One can cycle through a loop by moving between braces alternatingly along rows and columns of the frame. Taking out the brace in a loop does not change the number of degrees of freedom.

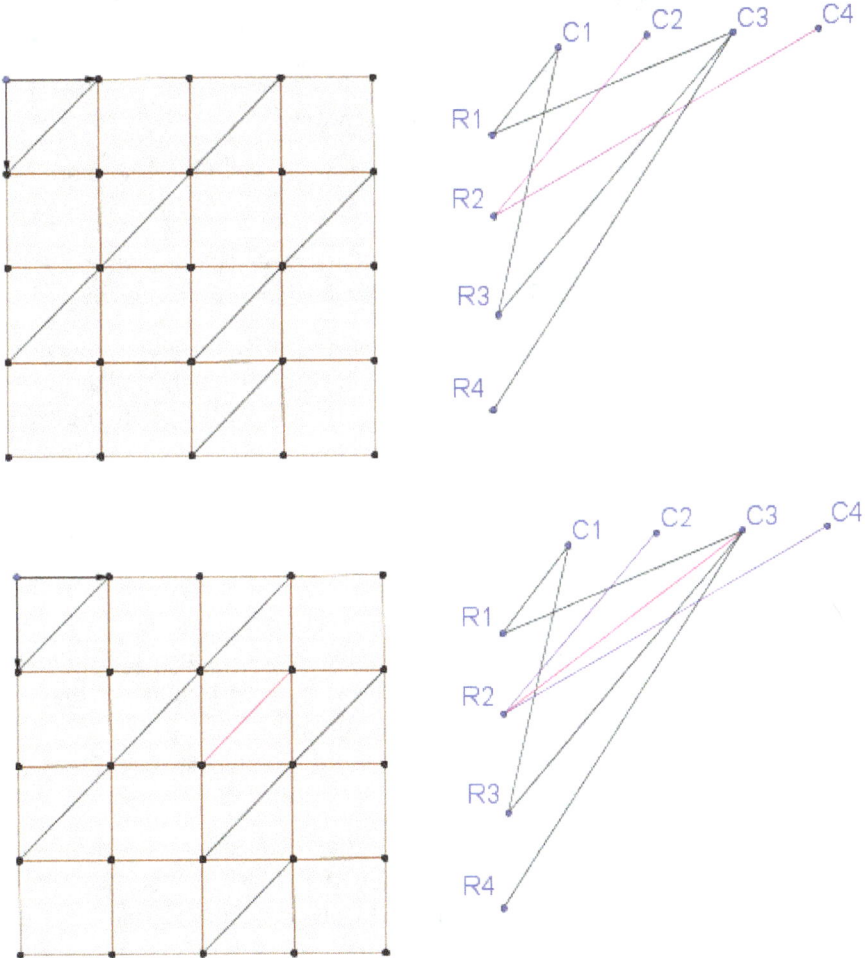

Figure 77: The bipartite graphs for the two frames.

The bipartite graphs for the two given frames are included in the figure on page 108.

The first one has two components and hence it is not connected. Too, there is a cycle. Hence the frame is not rigid. The bracing is not minimal.

The second bipartite graph is connected, and has a cycle. Hence the frame is rigid, but the bracing is not minimal.

I.6.4 Spanning trees

Definition 43 (Spanning graph). A *spanning graph* for any graph G is a pair (G, H) where $H \subseteq G$ is a subgraph with the same set of vertices as the given graph G.

Definition 44 (Spanning forest, spanning tree). A *spanning forest* for any graph G is a forest F which is a subgraph with the same set of vertices as the given graph. If the given graph is connected, one gets a *spanning tree*. The edges in $E_G \setminus E_T$ are called *back-edges*.

A spanning forest can be produced essentially in two different ways:

- either by deleting edges of the given graph in order to interrupt cycles until no more cycles exist;
- or by growing subtrees starting from a root. Thus one increases the number of vertices and edges for a sequence of subtrees until all vertices of the given graph are covered.

The second approach can be nicknamed "joining the club". Starting with a root v_0, the vertices of the given connected graph are enumerated in a way such that for all $i = 1 \ldots n$ the vertices $v_0, v_1 \ldots v_i$ and the i edges chosen between them are a tree T_i. Finally T_n is a spanning tree for the given connected graph.

Lemma 20. *Given is any rooted tree. For any two vertices v and w, there exists a unique path P connecting v to w. On this path, there exists a unique vertex y, which is an ancestor of both vertices v and w.*

Proof. The uniqueness of y is obvious. Let the path have the vertices $v = v_0, v_1, \ldots v_p = w$. If v is an ancestor of w, then $y = v$ and we are ready. Otherwise, we start at v and follow the vertices of the path as long as v_i is the parent of v_{i-1}. We let $y := v_k$ be the last vertex where this happens. If $y = w$, then w is an ancestor of v and we are ready.

Otherwise $1 < k < p$ and v_k is the parent of both v_{k-1} and v_{k+1}, and hence an ancestor of both v and w, and we are ready. $\square$

The process gets more interesting when some restricting rule for electing new members to the club is stipulated. The *seniority rule* stipulates that only the oldest member for whom it is possible, is allowed to hire a new member of the club. In other words, the new vertex v_i and edge $v_j v_i$ taken in the i-th step are chosen such that the number $j < i$ is minimal possible. A spanning tree grown by "joining the club according to the seniority rule" is a *first-breadth spanning tree*.

Remark 18. Given is any connected graph and a first-breadth tree.

- For any vertex v, the subtree T_v is a first-breadth spanning tree for the induced subgraph $G[T_v]$.

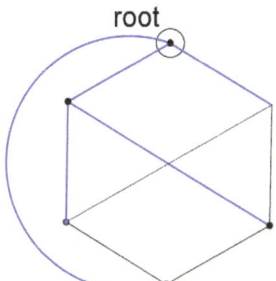 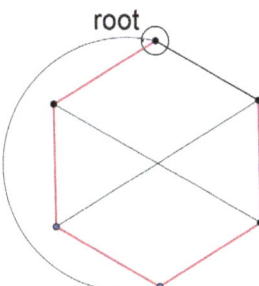

Figure 78: A first-breadth and a first-depth spanning tree.

- If all edges have the same cost, the first-breadth spanning tree is a shortest-path spanning tree.

The *juniority rule* stipulates that only the youngest member for whom this is possible, is allowed to hire a new member of the club. In other words, the new vertex v_i and edge $v_j v_i$ chosen in the i-th step are such that the number $j < i$ is maximal possible. A spanning tree grown by "joining the club according to the juniority rule" is a *first-depth spanning tree*.

Remark 19. Given is any connected graph and a *first-depth spanning tree*. For any vertex v, the subtree T_v is a first-depth spanning tree for the induced subgraph $G[T_v]$.

Proposition 30. *Given is a graph G and a first-depth spanning tree T. Assume that the vertices v and w are neighbors in the graph G, but not in the spanning tree. In other words, it is assumed that neither v is the parent of w, nor w the parent of v.*

If T is a first-depth spanning tree, then either v is an ancestor of w, or w is an ancestor of v:

$$v \cong_G w \text{ and } v \not\cong_T w \quad \text{imply} \quad v \preceq w \text{ or } w \preceq v$$

Proof. As the first-depth spanning tree is grown from the root $r = v_0$, the vertices are numbered. We may suppose $v = v_i$ and $w = v_k$ with $i < k$ are the numbers of the vertices "joining the club". Because of the assumption of the proposition, the vertices v and w are not neighbors in the tree, and hence $v_{i+1} \neq w$ and $i \leq k - 2$.

As in the lemma, let P be the unique path in the tree from v to w, and let y be the unique vertex on the path, which is an ancestor of both vertices v and w. In the case that $y \neq v$, the vertices on the path $P_1 = y \ldots v$ have first joined the club, afterwards the vertices on the path $P_2 = y \ldots w$ get their turn to join the club.

Under the assumption that $v \cong_G w$, it cannot happen that $y \neq v$. Indeed the juniority rule enforces that the path P_1 has still to be extended and one may not go back to ancestor y. It is just forbidden to built the path P_2. Hence $v \cong_G w$ implies $y = v$ and v is an ancestor of w as claimed. □

Proposition 31. *Given is a graph G and a first-breadth spanning tree T. Assume that the vertices v and w are neighbors in the graph G, but not in the spanning tree. Let y be the common ancestor of v and w. The paths $P_1 = y \ldots v$ and $P_2 = y \ldots w$ have lengths differing by at most one.*

For any two different spanning trees S and T of the same graph, one constructs an interpolating sequence of (spanning) trees. Going from tree S to tree T, one has still the choice to at first adjoin an edge of the new tree, or first delete an edge of the old tree.

Proposition 32 (Metamorphosis of trees). *Given are two spanning trees S and T of a connected graph G with n vertices.*

(a) *For each edge $e \in E_T \setminus E_S$, there exists an edge $d \in E_S \setminus E_T$ such that adjoining the edge e to S, and deleting the edge d, yields a tree $S' := S \cup e - d$.*

(b) *For each edge $\hat{d} \in E_S \setminus E_T$, there exists an edge $\hat{e} \in E_T \setminus E_S$ such that deleting the edge $\hat{d}$ from S, and adjoining the edge $\hat{e}$ yields a tree $S_1 := (S - \hat{d}) \cup \hat{e}$.*

(c) *Hence there exists a sequence of spanning trees*

$$S = S^{(0)}, \ S', \ S'' \ \ldots \ S^{(p)} = T$$

beginning with S and ending with T such that for all steps $i = 1 \ldots p$, the successive trees $S^{(i-1)}$ and $S^{(i)}$ have $n - 2$ edges in common.

Proof. Let S and T be two different spanning trees of the same graph G with n vertices.

(a) To the tree S, we adjoin the chosen edge $e \in E_T \setminus E_S$. In tree S, there exists a unique path between the ends of e. The graph $S \cup e$ has a cycle. Since T is a tree, too, and $e \in E_T$, this cycle contains a second edge $d \notin E_T$. Hence $d \in E_S \setminus E_T$. This is the edge to be deleted. Since $S' := S \cup e - d$ is acyclic and has $n - 1$ edges, it is a tree.

(b) From tree S, we delete the chosen edge $\hat{d} \in E_S \setminus E_T$. Let $\hat{d} = st$. Since T is a tree, too, there exists in T a unique path from s to t. This path contains an edge $\hat{e} \notin E_S$, since the graph S is acyclic. Hence $\hat{e} \in E_T \setminus E_S$. The graph $(S - \hat{d}) \cup \hat{e}$ is connected and has $n - 1$ edges, and hence it is a tree.

The proof item (c) is left to the reader. □

Problem 121. *Give a short explanation for item (c).*

I.7 Algorithms

Algorithm 3 (Prime's algorithm). *In a given graph G with weighted edges, a spanning tree of minimal total cost is constructed. Following Prime's algorithm, the tree is grown from a given root as an increasing sequence of trees*

$$T_0 \subset T_1 \subset \cdots \subset T_{k-1} \subset T_k \subset \cdots \subset T_{n-1}$$

start: T_0 is the given root.

first step: T_1 takes any one of the cheapest edges from the root and connects the root to a second vertex.

step $T_{k-1} \to T_k$: As next edge e_k, we take any one of the cheapest edges with only one end in $V(T_{k-1})$. Let $T_k := T_{k-1} \cup e_k$.

The algorithm stops when $n-1$ edges have been chosen. The tree $T := T_{n-1}$ is a spanning tree of minimal total cost.

Validity of Prime's algorithm. We have to compare the total cost of the tree T with the cost of any other spanning tree S for the given edge-weighted graph G. To this end, we change tree S in a stepwise process,

$$(7) \qquad S = S^{(0)}, \; S', \; S'' \; \ldots \; S^{(p)} = T$$

into trees more and more similar to Prime's tree T.

Assume that the trees S and T are different. Let $k \geq 1$ be the first step in which the two trees differ, hence

$$e_1 \ldots e_{k-1} \in E_T \cap E_S \quad \text{but} \quad e_k \in E_T \setminus E_S$$

Let $e_k = xy$ and let x be the end of e_k first reached by Prime's algorithm. Hence $x \in V(T_{k-1})$ but $y \notin V(T_{k-1})$. In the tree S, there exists a unique path from vertex x to vertex y. Starting

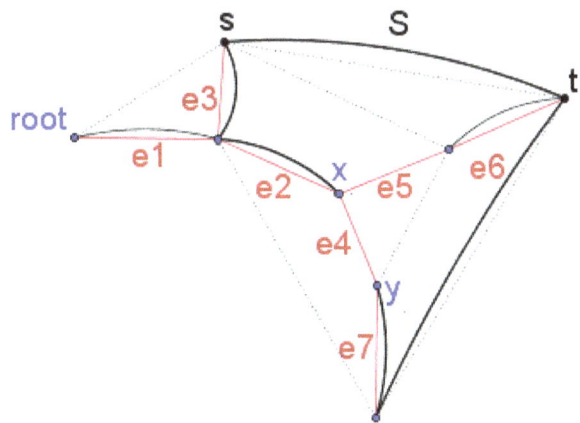

Figure 79: At step $k = 4$ the growing Prime's tree compares costs of edges xy and st.

at vertex x, we follow this path until we arrive at the first edge st not in T_{k-1}. Hence the path taken from x to s is contained in T_{k-1}, and $s \in V(T_{k-1})$, but $t \notin V(T_{k-1})$.

At the k-th step of Prime's algorithm, one has the choice to take either xy or st as the next edge. Since $e_k = xy$, but edge st is not taken, we know that e_k is at least as cost effective an edge as st. We define a tree S' by adjoining e_k and deleting st. Hence

$$S' := S \cup e_k - st$$
$$\text{cost}(e_k) \leq \text{cost}(st)$$
$$\text{cost}(S') \leq \text{cost}(S)$$

Too, the trees S' and T differ at a later step than S and T. Hence by repetition of the process, we get a sequence (7) of trees more and more similar to Prime's tree, and ending with $S^{(p)} = T$. Furthermore

$$\text{cost}(T) \leq \cdots \leq \text{cost}(S') \leq \text{cost}(S)$$

$\square$

Algorithm 4 (Kruskal's algorithm). *In a given graph G with weighted edges, a spanning tree of minimal total cost is constructed.*

preparation: *Obtained a list of the edges sorted by increasing cost.*

growing a forest: *One adjoins in each step the cheapest edge available. The only restriction is to avoid any cycles.*

The algorithm stops when $n-1$ edges have been chosen. In this step one obtains a spanning tree of minimal total cost.

Since in Kruskal's algorithm, there are less restrictions how to choose the most cost effective edges than in Prime's algorithm and we have already confirmed the validity of Prime's algorithm, we get as an immediate consequence:

Corollary 6. *Kruskal's algorithm yields a minimal spanning tree, too.*

Corollary 7. *If there exists two minimal spanning trees S and T, then there exists a sequence of minimal spanning trees*

$$S = S^{(0)}, \; S', \; S'' \; \ldots \; S^{(p)} = T$$

were successive trees $S^{(i-1)}$ and $S^{(i)}$ have $n-2$ edges in common.

Corollary 8. *If the costs of all edges are different, the minimal spanning tree is unique.*

Reason. Indeed, the reasoning above shows that for any tree S different from Prime's tree T, we get strictly more cost, since

$$S' := S \cup e_k - st$$
$$\text{cost}(e_k) < \text{cost}(st)$$
$$\text{cost}(T) < \cdots < \text{cost}(S') < \text{cost}(S)$$

$\square$

Problem 122. *Use Kruskal's algorithm to find a minimum spanning tree for the weighted graph on the opposite page.*

I.7.1 Heuristic methods for the traveling salesman problem

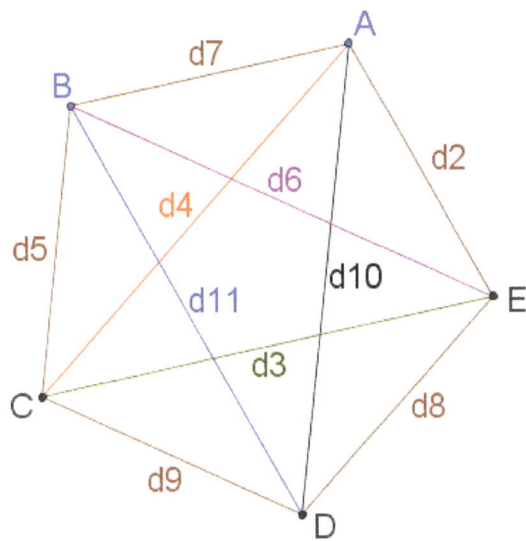

Figure 80: Find the shortest round trip.

Problem 123. *A zoo-keeper visiting the antelopes wishes to visit the bears, camels, dingos and elephants at their locations A, B, C, D, E. The distances of the locations are shown in the diagram on page 114. Using trial and error, find a route for a round trip of shortest total distance.*

Answer. The shortest round trip is $A \mapsto C \mapsto B \mapsto D \mapsto E \mapsto A$ and has the total length of 30 units.

Algorithm 5 (Nearest neighbor method). *The nearest neighbor algorithm is a heuristic method to get an upper bound for the shortest round trip. Successively, a list of directed cycles $C_1, C_2, \ldots, C_n$ is constructed.*

start: *We start with any vertex y_1. We look for the nearest neighbor y_2 and get the two-cycle $C_2 = y_1 y_2$, going back to y_1.*

step: *We find two vertices y_k in C_k and z_k not in C_k, which have the shortest distance for any two vertices lying in C_k and not in C_k. To obtain the cycle C_{k+1} from C_k, the new vertex z_k is inserted into the cycle C_k directly before y_k.*

Theorem 9. *Assume the distance function $d(v_i, v_k)$ between edges is*

symmetric: $d(v_i, v_k) = d(v_k, v_i)$,

the triangle inequality holds: $d(v_i, v_k) \le d(v_i, v_j) + d(v_j, v_k)$,

Then the round trip obtained by the nearest neighbor method costs less than double the minimal cost of a round trip.

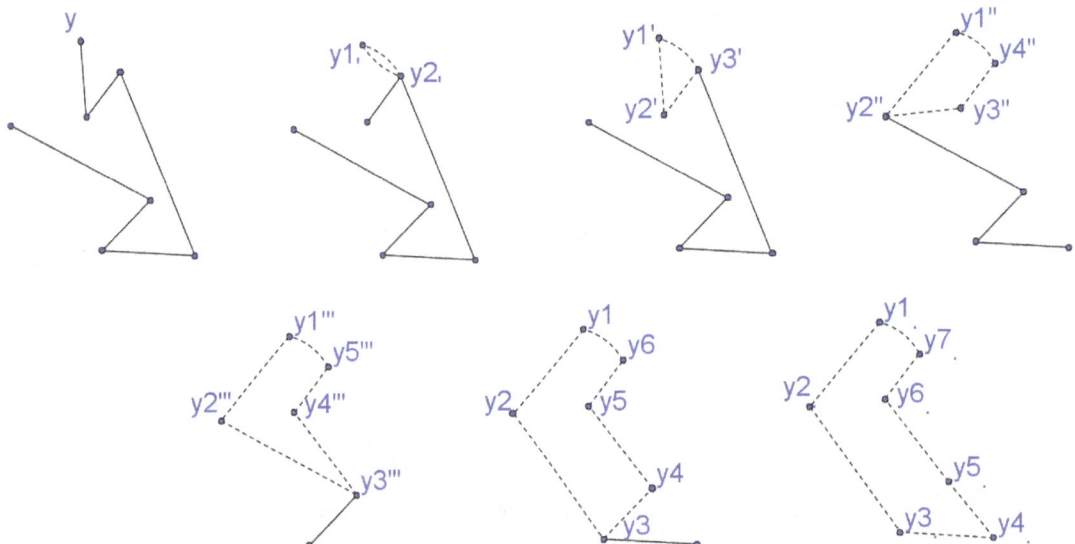

Figure 81: The round trip in the figure bottom left is at most double as long as the Hamiltonian path in the figure top right.

Proof. We show that the nearest neighbor method yields a round trip which has at most double the cost of any round trip C^*, and hence of the minimal round trip, too.

Inductively, we define the set of edges S_k and the edges t_k for $k = 1, 2, 3, \ldots, n-1$. This is done in the following way, along with the construction of the circuits C_k of the nearest-neighbor algorithm:

start: We start with any vertex y_1. We look for the nearest neighbor y_2 and get the two-cycle $C_2 = y_1 y_2$, going back to y_1. Let e^* be any edge adjacent to vertex y_1. Let S_1 be the set of edges of $C^* - e^*$, which is a Hamiltonian path.

step: We find two vertices y_k in C_k and z_k not in C_k, which have the shortest distance for any two vertices lying in C_k and not in C_k. To obtain the cycle C_{k+1} from C_k, the new vertex z_k is inserted into the cycle C_k directly before y_k.

Let t_k be an edge in S_k which connects a vertex in C_k to a vertex not in C_k. Such an edge exists because $S_1 = C^* - e^*$ is a Hamiltonian path. Let $S_{k+1} = S_k \setminus t_k$.

stop: The cycle C_k has k edges, and the set S_k has $n - k$ edges. Hence C_n is a Hamiltonian cycle and S_n is empty. The algorithm stops for $k = n$.

We now check that
$$\operatorname{cost}(C_{k+1}) \leq \operatorname{cost}(C_k) + 2\operatorname{cost}(t_k)$$
for all $k = 1, 2, \ldots, n-1$. We use the triangle inequality and the fact that $y_k z_k$ is the cheapest edge between vertices in C_k and not in C_k, and hence cheaper than the edge t_k.

$$\begin{aligned}\operatorname{cost}(C_{k+1}) &= \operatorname{cost}(C_k) + \operatorname{cost}(y_{k-1}z_k) + \operatorname{cost}(z_k y_k) - \operatorname{cost}(y_{k-1}y_k) \\ &\leq \operatorname{cost}(C_k) + \operatorname{cost}(y_{k-1}y_k) + \operatorname{cost}(y_k z_k) + \operatorname{cost}(z_k y_k) - \operatorname{cost}(y_{k-1}y_k) \\ &= \operatorname{cost}(C_k) + 2\operatorname{cost}(y_k z_k) \leq \operatorname{cost}(C_k) + 2\operatorname{cost}(t_k)\end{aligned}$$

Adding the inequalities for $k = 1, 2, \ldots, n-1$ yields

$$\operatorname{cost}(C_n) \leq \operatorname{cost}(C_1) + 2 \sum_{k=1}^{n-1} \operatorname{cost}(t_k) = 0 + 2\operatorname{cost}(C^* - e^*) < 2\operatorname{cost}(C^*)$$

as to be shown. The example shown in the figure on page 115 has $n = 7$. The part top right shows the start vertex y_1 and the Hamiltonian path S_1, the following parts correspond to $k = 2$ through 7. The round trip is obtained in the figure bottom left. Its cost is at most double that of the Hamiltonian path in the figure top right. □

Corollary 9. *We use the nearest neighbor method starting from a vertex adjacent to the most costly edge e^*. Then we obtain a round trip which costs at most double the cost of any Hamiltonian path avoiding e^*. Equality is achieved for all vertices lying on a straight segment.*

Algorithm 6 (Sorted edges method). *The sorted edges method is an even rougher heuristic method to get an upper bound for the shortest round trip.*

preparation: *Obtained a list of the edges sorted by increasing cost.*

growing paths: *One or several paths are grown by adjoining in each step the cheapest edge available. There are two restrictions:*

- *Avoid branching of the set of paths.*
- *Avoid any cycle.*

The algorithm stops when n edges have been chosen. One obtains only a rough upper bound for the cheapest round trip.

Algorithm 7 (Lower bound for a round trip). *Choose any vertex v and find the two cheapest edges e and f from and to v. Construct a minimal spanning tree T in the remaining graph $G \setminus v$. We obtain a lower bound for the cost of any round trip C^*:*

$$\operatorname{cost}(T) + \operatorname{cost}(e) + \operatorname{cost}(f) \leq \operatorname{cost}(C^*)$$

Problem 124. *A salesman has to do a round trip through cities A, B, C, D, E, F. Use the nearest-neighbor method with the costs from the table to get a fair suggestion.*

	A	B	C	D	E	F
A	-	3	3	2	7	3
B	3	-	3	4	5	5
C	3	3	-	1	4	4
D	2	4	1	-	5	5
E	7	5	4	5	-	4
F	3	5	4	5	4	-

Answer. I chose at starting point A, and get the list of cycles

$$C_2 : A - D$$
$$C_3 : A - C - D$$
$$C_4 : A - C - D - F$$
$$C_5 : A - C - D - F - B$$
$$C_6 : A - E - C - D - F - B(-A)$$
$$\text{cost}(C_6) = 7 + 4 + 1 + 5 + 5 + 3 = 25$$

There are ties, and other choices turn out to be better!

	Edmonton	London	Montreal	Ottava	Regina	Toronto
Edmonton	-	2144	2301	2173	482	2107
London	2144	-	425	357	1696	122
Montreal	2301	425	-	127	1853	344
Ottava	2173	357	127	-	1725	248
Regina	482	1696	1853	1725	-	1659
Toronto	2107	122	344	248	1659	-

Problem 125. *You want to do a round trip through the listed six cities of Canada, and minimize the total distance traveled. Compare your results.*

(a) *Use the heuristic nearest-neighbor method to find an* upper *bound for the shortest trip.*

(b) *Use the heuristic sorted edges method to find an* upper *bound for the shortest trip.*

(c) *Use a minimal connector in the graph with one city removed to get a* lower *bound for any round trip.*

Answer. **(a) upper bound by nearest-neighbor method:** I chose Toronto as starting point and get the list of cycles

$$C_2 : T - L$$
$$C_3 : O - T - L$$
$$C_4 : M - O - T - L$$
$$C_5 : M - O - R - T - L$$
$$C_6 : M - O - E - R - T - L(-M)$$
$$\text{cost}(C_6) = 127 + 2173 + 482 + 1659 + 122 + 425 = 4988$$

(b) **upper bound by the sorted edges method:** Here is a list of the edges, and its sorted version:

Edmonton-London	2144	London-Toronto	122
Edmonton-Montreal	2301	Montreal-Ottava	127
Edmonton-Ottava	2173	Ottava-Toronto	248
Edmonton-Regina	482	Montreal-Toronto	344
Edmonton-Toronto	2107	London-Ottava	357
London-Montreal	425	London-Montreal	425
London-Ottava	357	Edmonton-Regina	482
London-Regina	1696	Regina-Toronto	1659
London-Toronto	122	London-Regina	1696
Montreal-Ottava	127	Ottava-Regina	1725
Montreal-Regina	1853	Montreal-Regina	1853
Montreal-Toronto	344	Edmonton-Toronto	2107
Ottava-Regina	1725	Edmonton-London	2144
Ottava-Toronto	248	Edmonton-Ottava	2173
Regina-Toronto	1659	Edmonton-Montreal	2301

Growing paths are produced by choosing

T - L,   O - M,   E - R,   T - R,

and need E - M to be closed to a cycle. The total cost is

$$\text{cost}(C_b) = 122 + 127 + 357 + 482 + 1659 + 2301 = 5048$$

(c) **lower bound by minimal connector:** I start at Edmonton and look for the two cheapest edges from there. They have costs $482 + 2107$. It may be of advantage to start at a vertex for which the sum of the two cheapest edges is nevertheless expensive.

A minimal connector in the remaining graph with Edmonton removed is obtained, using Kruskal's algorithm. The edges adjoint in the order

T - L, O - M, T - M, T - R

The lower bound of cost is $122 + 127 + 344 + 1659 + 482 + 2107 = 4841$.

I.7.2 Dijstra's algorithm

Algorithm 8 (Dijstra's algorithm). *In a given graph G with weighted edges and a root given, a spanning tree is constructed for which the paths from the root have minimal lengths.*

To this end, a tree is grown from the root s by adding one edge in each step of the algorithm. We use temporary and permanent markers for the vertices. The permanent markers are also called potential $V(x)$ and they are put into a box in the examples. The markers are noted down into a table.

start: *We assign the permanent label $V(r) = 0$ to the root.*

step: *Let v be the vertex v which got the permanent label in the previous step. The vertices w adjacent to the vertex v get the temporary label $V(v) + cost(vw)$. The temporary labels are noted down into the row of the table for v.*

One looks through the table to find the minimal temporary label, which is not yet permanent. The corresponding vertex w is marked permanently and gets the potential

$$V(w) = \min[V(v) + cost(vw)]$$

The vertex w and its potential $V(w)$ are entered into the next row of the table. The edge vw is marked permanently and adjoined to the growing tree.

The algorithm stops when all vertices are marked permanently.

Remark 20. At the time vertex w is marked permanently with potential $V(w)$, one can delete all the temporary labels in column of w, but not in different columns.

Remark 21. As an alternative, one can delete all the temporary labels in column of w which are strictly smaller than $V(w)$, and mark the temporary labels which are equal to $V(w)$ of any v in column of w with a different color. Mark the corresponding edges vw with a different color. Thus one obtains a subgraph which contains all paths of minimal cost from the root to any given vertex.

Problem 126. *Use Dijstra's algorithm to find the shortest paths from the root at the far left.*

Answer. The tree of shortest paths from the root in given in the figure on page 120. The algorithm is calculated in the following table.

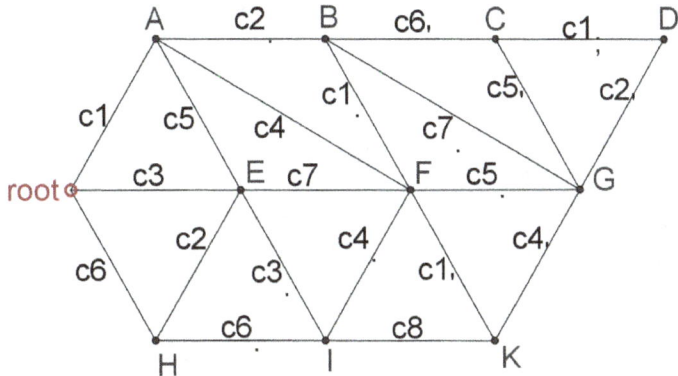

Figure 82: Find all shortest paths from the root.

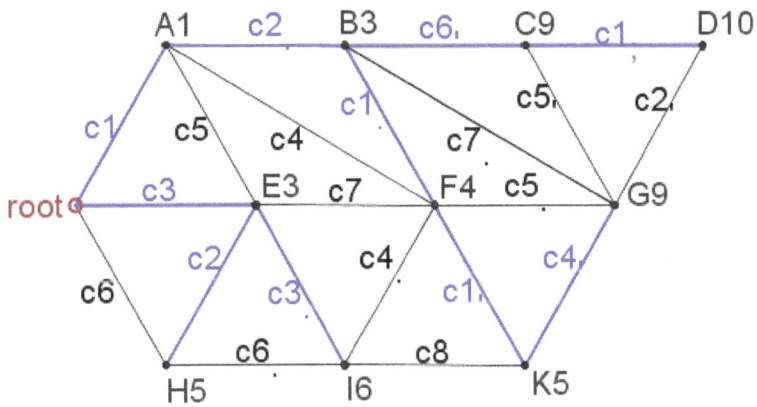

Figure 83: The tree of shortest paths from the root.

vertex	potential	A	B	C	D	E	F	G	H	I	K
root	0	1				3			6		
A	1		3			6	5				
B	3			9			4				
E	3						10		5	6	
F	4									8	5
H	5									11	
K	5							9		13	
I	6										
G	9				11						
C	9				10						
D	10										

Problem 127. *Find the shortest paths from root S to T, and each of the other vertices in the weighted directed graph on page 121.*

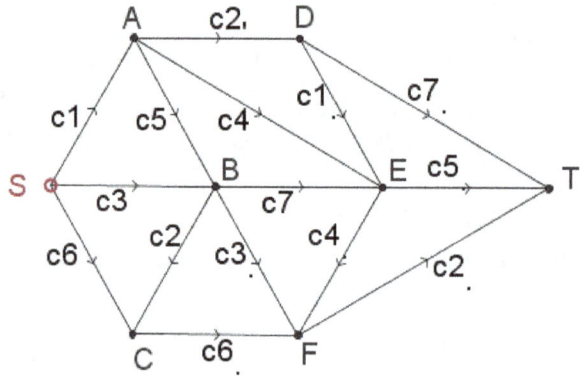

Figure 84: Find all shortest paths from the root.

Answer. The tree of shortest paths from the root in given in the figure on page 121. The

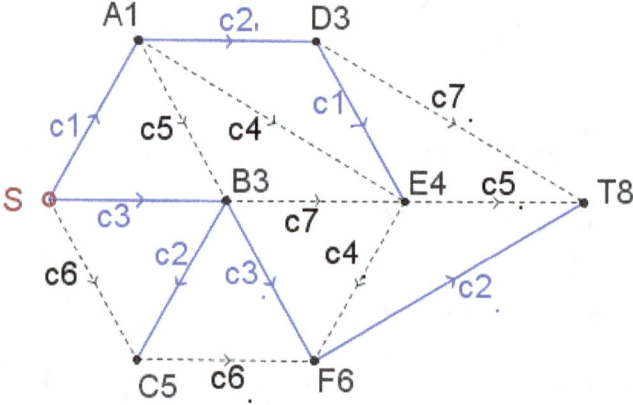

Figure 85: The tree of shortest paths from the root.

algorithm is calculated in the following table.

vertex	potential	A	B	C	D	E	F	T
root	0	1	3	6				
A	1		6		3	5		
B	3			5		10	6	
D	3					4		10
E	4						8	9
C	5						11	
F	6							8
T	8							

I.7.3 Maximal flow

Problem 128. *Suppose a group of tourists wants to go from the entrance E of the park to the mount top T. There is available a system of trails of different sizes, as indicated in the figure 122. How many tourists can simultaneously walk form EO to T.*

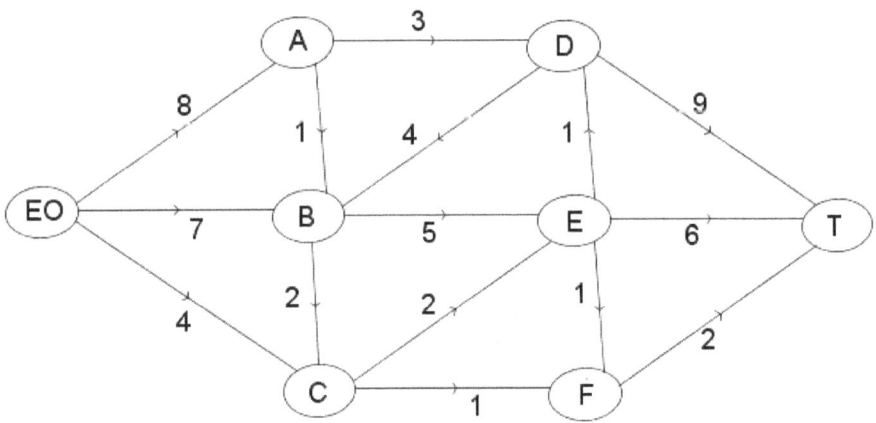

Figure 86: How many tourists can walk from the entrance to the restaurant?

Given is a directed graph G with each arc of known flow capacity, and two vertices are marked as as source and terminal. At all vertices except the source and terminal, it is assumed that the inflow equals the outflow. A flow pattern with maximal net flow from the source to the terminal is to be constructed.

In each step, the Ford-Fulkerson algorithm increases the flow by means of a flow-augmenting path. Each arc of the augmenting path either points in the direction of the flow and its actual flow is less the maximally possible flow;— or it points in the opposite direction and its actual flow is nonzero. During performance of the algorithm, an actual nonzero flow through any arc is noted as a number in parentheses next to the maximal flow capacity.

Algorithm 9 (The Ford-Fulkerson algorithm).

start: We start with the zero flow.

step: We apply the Edmonds-Carp step to find either an augmenting path or an edge cut. In the first case, the flow is increased by the minimum of the possible increases in each arc of the augmenting path. In the second case, we go to the coda.

coda: Check that the outflow at the source, the inflow to the terminal, and the flow across the flow across the edge cut are all three equal, and write down this maximal flow. The edge cut is a direct confirmation that we have obtained the maximum flow.

The algorithm stops when an edge cut has been obtained.

Algorithm 10 (The Edmond-Carp step). *For a given actual flow pattern, the Edmonds-Carp step is used to decide whether an augmenting path still exists. To this end, we produce a list of labeled vertices.*

start: Label the source by label $(\emptyset, a)$. Set the counter $i := 1$.

step: We check the arcs from and to the vertex v just labeled. If the arc points from the vertex v to another vertex w, and the actual flow is less the maximally possible flow and vertex w is unlabeled, vertex w gets the label (v, w). Similarly, if the arc points towards the vertex v from another vertex w, and the actual flow is nonzero, the unlabeled vertex w gets the label (v, w).

If a new vertex has been labeled, the counter i is increased by one. The algorithm stops when no more vertices can be labeled.

coda: If the terminal has been labeled, we have obtained an augmenting path. We can find the path by backtracking. We start at the terminal, and use the label of each vertex to get its predecessor along the augmenting path. Actually, we thus obtain an flow-augmenting path of minimum length.

If the terminal has not been labeled, we have obtained an edge cut. In this case, the maximal counter is less than n, which provides a check. The edge cut consists of all edges which have one end labeled but the other one not labeled. We can find the edge-cut by backtracking, too. We start at the vertex z that has been marked as the last one, and note down the arcs between z and any unmarked neighbors. Next use the label of the current vertex to get its predecessor v, and check in this step for the arcs between the marked vertex v and unmarked neighbors. When we arrive at the source, we have gathered all arcs of the edge-cut.

Remark 22. For simple examples, where one can overlook the entire graph, one can treat the Edmonds-Carp step informally. For each step, one notes down the augmenting path obtained, and the amount by which the flow can be augmented. In the end, if one is sure no such path exists, one colors the labeled vertices and marks the edge cut.

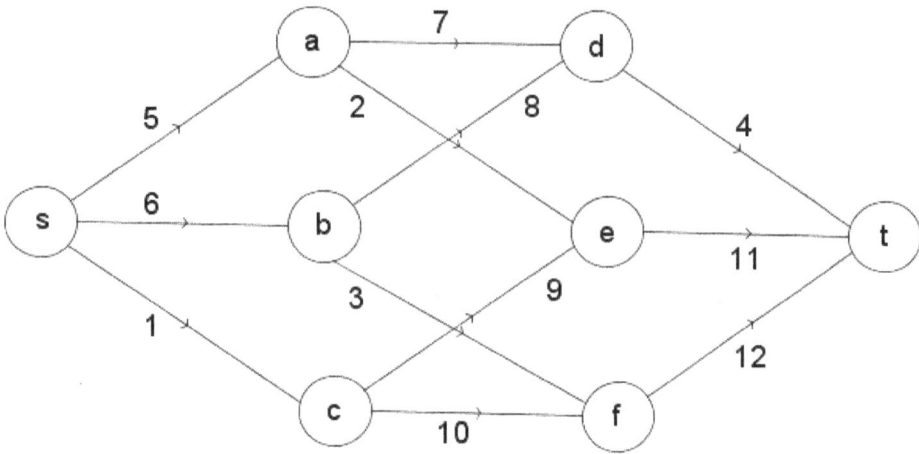

Figure 87: How much traffic can flow from the source to the terminal?

Problem 129. *Use the Ford-Fulkerson algorithm to find a maximal flow and a minimal edge-cut for the network shown on page 124.*

Answer. Rather obvious flow-augmenting paths are

$$s \mapsto a \mapsto d \mapsto t \quad \text{with capacity } 4$$
$$s \mapsto a \mapsto e \mapsto t \quad \text{with capacity } 1$$
$$s \mapsto b \mapsto f \mapsto t \quad \text{with capacity } 3$$
$$s \mapsto c \mapsto e \mapsto t \quad \text{with capacity } 1$$

But there exists still a further flow-augmenting path

$$s \mapsto b \mapsto d \mapsfrom a \mapsto e \mapsto t \quad \text{with capacity } 1$$

with the arc $d \mapsfrom a$ which points in the opposite direction and has actual flow nonzero.

Thus one gets a saturated flow, for which we find an edge-cut. The marked edges are s, a, b, d. The flow across the edge-cut is $1 + 3 + 2 + 4 = 10$ is maximal. This equals the number 10 of cars started at the entrance, as well as of those arrived at the terminal.

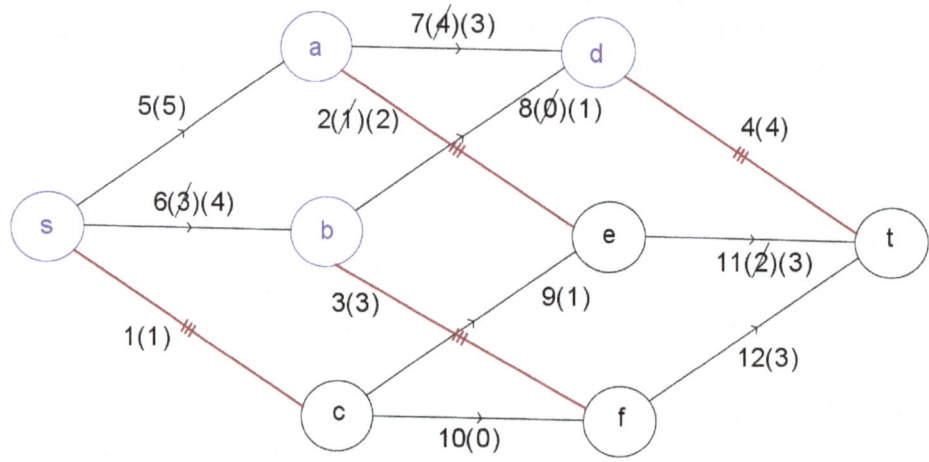

Figure 88: The maximal flow and minimal edge cut have capacity 10.

I.7.4 The Hungarian Algorithm

Algorithm 11 (The Hungarian algorithm). *Suppose we have the resources or workers $i = 1 \ldots n$ to which we want to assign the tasks or jobs $j = 1 \ldots n$ on a one-to-one basis. Suppose also we know the cost c_{ij} of assigning to resource i the task j. We assume the costs are nonnegative integers. We want to find an optimal assignment, one for which the total cost*

$$\sum_{i=1\ldots n, j=1\ldots n} c_{ij}$$

takes the minimum.

initialization step: For each $i = 1 \ldots n$, replace $c_{i,j}$ by $c_{i,j} - m_i$, where $m_i = \min\{c_{i,j} : 1 \leq j \leq n\}$.

In other words, for each row of the cost matrix, the minimum element in that row is subtracted from each element in the respective row.

initialization step: For each $j = 1 \ldots n$, replace $c_{i,j}$ by $c_{i,j} - n_j$ where $n_j = \min\{c_{i,j} : 1 \leq i \leq n\}$.

In other words, for each column of the cost matrix, the minimum element in that column is subtracted from each element in the column.

main step 1: Draw the minimum number of (horizontal respectively vertical) lines through the rows and columns to cover all zeros in the reduced matrix.

If the minimum number turns out to be n, an optimal solution is available. Otherwise go to main step 2.

main step 2: *Find the minimum uncovered element c_{min}. Subtract c_{min} from all uncovered elements, and add c_{min} to all twice covered elements. Return to main step 1.*

The algorithm stops when in main step 1, an optimal solution has been found.

Remark 23. For each step, the reduced cost matrix has the same set of optimal solutions as the original cost matrix.

Remark 24. For each step, the reduced cost matrix $d_{i,j}$ has a lower total cost as the original cost matrix $c_{i,j}$. Hence the algorithm stops after finitely many steps.

Reason. This is clear for the initialization step. Suppose that in main step 1, we have covered all zeros by covering p rows with union R and q columns with union C. The reduced cost matrix has lowered the total sum (virtual cost) by

$$\sum_{i=1\ldots n, j=1\ldots n}[d_{i,j}-c_{i,j}] = \left[\sum_{(i,j)\in R\cap C} + \sum_{(i,j)\in R\setminus C} + \sum_{(i,j)\in C\setminus R} + \sum_{(i,j)\notin R\cup C}\right][d_{i,j}-c_{i,j}]$$

$$= \sum_{(i,j)\in R\cap C} c_{min} + 0 + 0 + \sum_{(i,j)\notin R\cup C}(-c_{min}) = pq\cdot m - (n-p)(n-q)\cdot c_{min}$$

$$= n(p+q-n)\dot{c}_{min}$$

which is positive as long as $p+q<n$. Hence the algorithm necessarily stops after finitely many steps. □

Remark 25. We see that it is not necessary to determine the exact minimum vertex cover $\beta(G)$. It is enough to find a vertex cover with less than n horizontal/vertical lines. Already under that weaker assumption, one is allowed to go to the main step 2. In this relaxed mode, the algorithm still works and stops after finitely many steps.

Remark 26. Once $p+q=n$ occurs in main step 1, an optimal assignment can be found. This follows from the König-Egervary Theorem. Let G be the bipartite graph with the resources and tasks as black and white vertices, and edges between pairs of them where the reduced cost is zero. Note that this graph changes with each step of the algorithm. Any assignment is a matching of edges of this graph. Any covering of all zeros by covering p rows and q columns, is a $p+q$ vertex cover of the graph G.

By the König-Egervary Theorem 1, for any bipartite graph, maximal matching and minimal vertex cover have the same size. Hence maximal assignment and minimal row/column-covering of zeros have the same size. Especially, an assignment of n resources (workers) to n tasks (jobs) at zero reduced cost has been obtained if and only if the minimum number of (horizontal respectively vertical) lines needed to cover and zeros in the reduced matrix turned out to be n.

Remark 27. The assignment obtained at the stop of the algorithm is optimal. One can see this from the dual pair of optimization problems:

(I.7.1)
$$\text{Minimize} \sum_{i,j} x_{i,j} c_{i,j}$$
$$\text{under the constraints } x_{i,j} \geq 0$$
$$\text{and } \sum_i x_{i,j} = 1 \text{ for } 1 \leq j \leq n \text{ and } \sum_j x_{i,j} = 1 \text{ for } 1 \leq i \leq n$$

(I.7.2)
$$\text{Maximize} \sum_i u_i - \sum_j v_j$$
$$\text{with } u_i, v_j \text{ unrestricted}$$
$$\text{and the constraints } u_i - v_j \leq c_{i,j} \text{ for } 1 \leq i, j \leq n.$$

It is easy to check that for any pair of solutions of problems (I.7.1) and (I.7.2) indeed

(I.7.3)
$$\sum_i u_i - \sum_j v_j \leq \sum_{i,j} x_{i,j} c_{i,j}$$

Once a stopping assignment $(i,j) \in STOP$ has been found, the system of equations

$$v_j = 0 \text{ for all } j = 1 \ldots n$$
$$u_i - v_j = c_{i,j} \text{ for all } (i,j) \in STOP$$

has a solution. Too, we put

$$x_{i,j} = 1 \text{ for all } (i,j) \in STOP$$
$$x_{i,j} = 0 \text{ for all } (i,j) \notin STOP$$

and check that inequality (I.7.3) becomes an equality.

(I.7.4)
$$\sum_i u_i - \sum_j v_j = \sum_{(i,j) \in STOP} c_{i,j} = \sum_{i,j} x_{i,j} c_{i,j}$$

Hence the optimality of both solutions, $x_{i,j}$ for the primal (I.7.1), and u_i, v_j for the dual (I.7.2) is confirmed.

I.8 Electrical Networks

Ein bisschen Technik dann und wann,

Auch Grübler amusieren kann,

Drum kühnlich denk ich schon so weit,

Wir legen noch ein Ei zu zweit.

Albert Einstein about his patent issued on January 10, 1934:

'Device, especially for sound-reproducing equipment,

in which changes of an electrical current

generate movements of a magnetized body

by means of magnetostriction'

Given is a simple graph G, which we assume to be connected. We assign a voltage source E to one edge. To all edges are assigned electrical resistances R_i, for which Ohm's law is assumed to hold. It is physically meaningful to assign an inner resistance to the voltage source, too. The problem is to find the currents in all edges and the voltage potentials at the vertices.

Problem 130. *Calculate the currents and voltages and find the effective resistance for the electrical network 129.*

Algorithm 12 (Procedure for calculation of electrical networks).

first-depth tree: *With one pole of the battery as root, we construct a first-depth tree. The vertex of the graph which we reach by each new edge is successively numbered $1, 2, \ldots, n-1$. The edge gets the direction from parent to child, which is marked by one arrow. The arc $e_i = \overrightarrow{v_{i-1}v_i}$ has the number $i = 1, 2, \ldots, n-1$.*

The edges of the given graph not in the spanning tree are called back-edges. *They get a direction $\overrightarrow{v_j v_k}$ from the vertex v_j with the higher label $j > k$ to the lower labeled vertex v_k, and are marked by a double arrow. They get the numbers $j = n, n+1, \ldots m$. It is convenient to give the battery edge the number n.*

fundamental system of cycles: *There are $\gamma = m - n + 1$ back-edges. This number is called the* cycle rank *of the graph. For a planar graph, it turns out to be one less than the number of faces.*

Each back-edge $\overrightarrow{v_j v_k}$ closes one cycle of the network, since there is a unique path from v_j to v_k in the spanning tree. In case of a first-depth tree, this path leads directly from the ancestor v_k to the descendent v_j. Thus the arrows chosen above give the direction of a flow around the cycle.

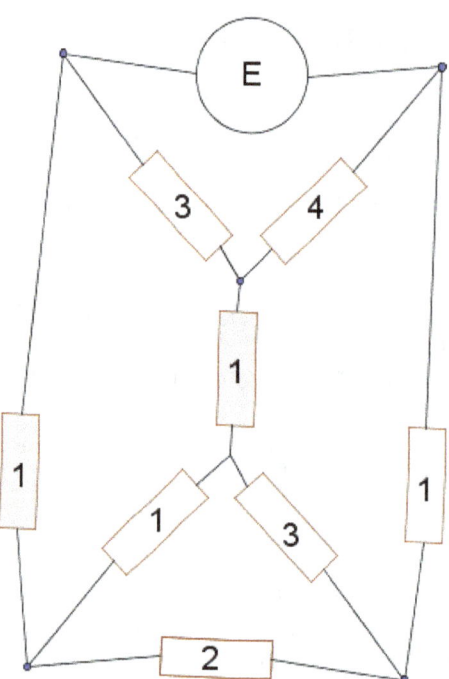

Figure 89: Calculate the currents and voltages.

flow matrix: The flow matrix F has $n-1$ rows labeled by the tree edges and g columns labeled by the back-edges. In any column j, the edges e_i which close a fundamental cycle with back-edge e_j get the matrix element $F_{ij} = 1$, the other matrix elements are zero.

Let $i_A \in \mathbb{R}^{n-1}$ be the vector for the currents in the tree edges and $i_B \in \mathbb{R}^g$ be the vector for the currents in the back-edges. In a tree, no conserved current can flow. Hence any current is a linear combination of flows in the fundamental cycles. Indeed we get

(I.8.1) $$i_A = F i_B$$

effective resistance: Let R_A be the $(n-1) \times (n-1)$ diagonal matrix giving the ohmic resistances of the tree edges, and R_B be the $g \times g$ diagonal matrix with the ohmic resistances of the back edges. It is important to be clear which inner resistance is assigned to the battery.

Let $E \in \mathbb{R}^g$ be the vector for the driving voltage of the battery. In case just one battery is present, it is convenient to put it in the first back-edge, in which case E is the battery voltage times the first vector of the standard basis.

The effective resistance turns out to be the $g \times g$ matrix

(I.8.2) $$R_\gamma = F^t R_A F + R_B$$

More details are given below. The superscript ^{t} indicates transposition.

current in the back-edges: The current in the back-edges satisfies

$$(\text{I.8.3}) \qquad R_\gamma i_B = E$$

Hence for given battery voltage E, we get a system of g linear equations with g unknowns. This system is non-degenerate under mild assumptions. For example, in the case that all resistances are nonnegative and the resistances in the tree edges are positive. We can solve the linear system and obtain

$$(\text{I.8.4}) \qquad i_B = R_\gamma^{-1} E$$

integer calculations: In textbook examples, it is very convenient stay with integer calculations. For this purpose, I choose the voltage

$$(\text{I.8.5}) \qquad E := \det(R_\gamma)$$

Of course, one can in the end scale to any other prescribed voltage.

current graph: To obtain the currents in the tree edges, we use equation (I.8.1). Finally, we draw the graph with the actual currents, the conservation of which should be checked at this point.

voltage graph: The voltages across the tree edges and back edges are obtained from Ohm's law to be $R_A i_A$ and $R_B i_B$, respectively. From the voltages across the tree edges, we get the electrical potentials of all vertices, as usual up to an integration constant. Let $-u \in \mathbb{R}^n$ be the vector [6], of the potentials for vertices $v_0, v_1, v_2, \ldots v_{n-1}$. With the numbering of vertices and tree edges chosen at the beginning we get

$$(\text{I.8.6}) \qquad u_i - u_{i-1} = (R_A)_{ii}(i_A)_i \quad \text{for all } i = 1, 2, \ldots, n-1$$

It is convenient to put $u_0 := 0$ by choice of the integration constant. Solving the equations above yields successively the potentials of all vertices

$$(\text{I.8.7}) \qquad u_0 = 0,$$
$$(\text{I.8.8}) \qquad u_i = u_{i-1} + (R_A)_{ii}(i_A)_i \quad \text{for all } i = 1, 2, \ldots, n-1$$

Finally, we draw the graph a second time with the actually calculated potentials at all vertices. One has to check whether one obtains at the second pole v_p of the battery the voltage chosen by equation (I.8.5).

effective resistance: Let $e_b = \overrightarrow{v_p v_0}$ be the back-edge for the battery. The voltage and the current across the battery yield the effective resistance

$$(\text{I.8.9}) \qquad R_{eff} = \frac{u_p - u_0}{i_B(b)}$$

For simple examples, we want to keep this number as an <u>exact fraction</u>.

---

[6]The minus sign results from the convention that the electrical field is <u>minus</u> the gradient of the potential—such that the current flows from the higher to the lower potential. This is the direction against the arrows.

coda: The resistance R_A and R_B, flow matrix F, effective resistance R_γ, currents i_A and i_B, and potentials should be gathered as in the table for the example.

Problem 131. *Calculate the currents and voltages and find the effective resistance for the electrical network on page 131.*

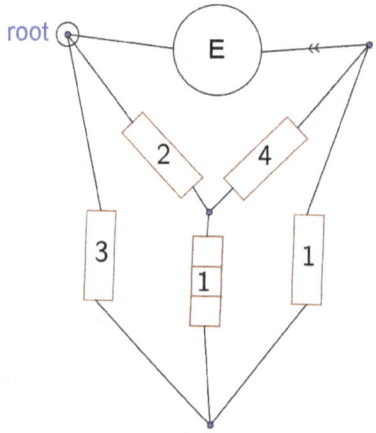

Figure 90: Calculate the currents and voltages.

Answer. I have used the first-depth tree and the labeling of vertices and edges as drawn in the figure on page 132. With this labeling the flow matrix is

$$F = \begin{bmatrix} 1 & 1 & 0 \\ 1 & 1 & 1 \\ 1 & 0 & 1 \end{bmatrix}$$

The effective resistance is

$$R_\gamma = F^t R_A F + R_B = \begin{bmatrix} 1 & 1 & 1 \\ 1 & 1 & 0 \\ 0 & 1 & 1 \end{bmatrix} \begin{bmatrix} 3 & 0 & 0 \\ 0 & 1 & 0 \\ 0 & 0 & 4 \end{bmatrix} \begin{bmatrix} 1 & 1 & 0 \\ 1 & 1 & 1 \\ 1 & 0 & 1 \end{bmatrix} + \begin{bmatrix} 0 & 0 & 0 \\ 0 & 2 & 0 \\ 0 & 0 & 1 \end{bmatrix} = \begin{bmatrix} 8 & 4 & 5 \\ 4 & 6 & 1 \\ 5 & 1 & 6 \end{bmatrix}$$

In order to stay with integer calculations, I put the voltage $E = \det R_\gamma = 74$. To obtain the currents in the back-edges, one has to solve the system $R_\gamma i_B = E e_4$, written out in components:

$$\begin{aligned} 8i_4 + 4i_5 + 5i_6 &= 74 \\ 4i_4 + 6i_5 + i_6 &= 0 \\ 5i_4 + i_5 + 6i_6 &= 0 \end{aligned}$$

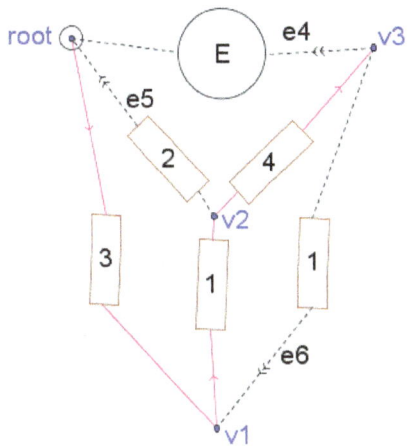

Figure 91: Labeling of the given network.

By Cramer's rule, we obtain for example the total current

$$i_4 = \frac{\begin{vmatrix} 74 & 4 & 5 \\ 0 & 6 & 1 \\ 0 & 1 & 6 \end{vmatrix}}{\begin{vmatrix} 8 & 4 & 5 \\ 4 & 6 & 1 \\ 5 & 1 & 6 \end{vmatrix}} = \frac{74 \begin{vmatrix} 6 & 1 \\ 1 & 6 \end{vmatrix}}{74} = 35$$

Hence the overall effective resistance is $R_{eff} = \frac{E}{i_4} = \frac{74}{35}$. The remaining currents and voltages are gathered in the table below and in the figure on page 133.

e_i	R_A	4	5	6				i_A	$u_i - u_{i-1}$	u_i
1	3	1	1	0				16	48	48
2	1	1	1	1				-10	-10	38
3	4	1	0	1				9	36	74
e_j	R_B	4	5	6				i_B	$i_B R_B$	
4	0				8	4	5	35	0	$E = 74$
5	2				4	6	1	-19	-38	
6	1				5	1	6	-26	-26	

Proposition 33. *Consider the special case that all resistances including the inner resistance of the battery are put to be equal to one. The effective resistance is*

(I.8.10) $$R_{eff} = \frac{\tau(G)}{\tau(G - e^b)}$$

where $\tau(G) = \det R_\gamma$ is the number of spanning trees of the given network G and $\tau(G - e^b)$ is the number of spanning trees for the network with the battery edge removed.

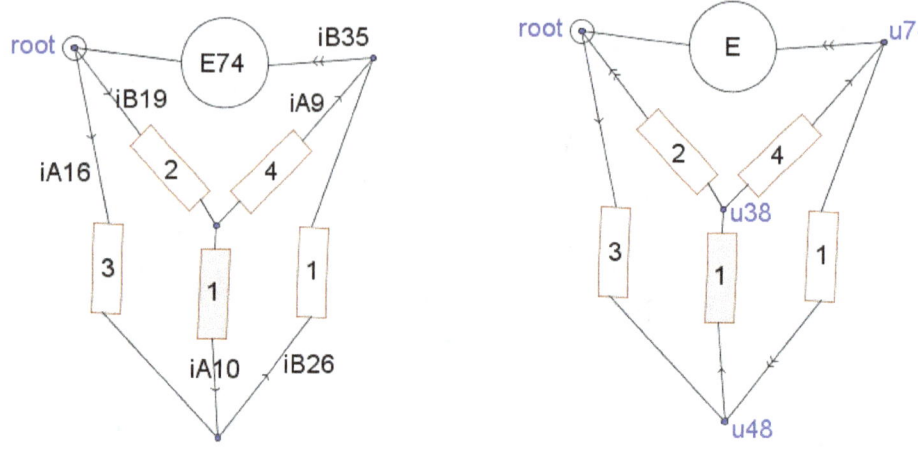

Figure 92: Currents and voltages, $R_{eff} = \frac{74}{35}$.

Reason. Let $e_b \in \mathbb{R}^\gamma$ be the standard unit vector for the edge with the battery. We put the voltage vector $E = (\det R_\gamma) e_b$ and solve the linear system

(I.8.3) $$R_\gamma i_B = E$$

by Cramer's rule. For the component i_b, which gives the total current, one obtains

$$i_b = \operatorname{adj}(R_\gamma)_{b,b}$$

This is the sub-determinant of $\det R_\gamma$ obtained by deletion of the b-th row and column. The Tree-matrix Theorem and Proposition 38 is used once for the graph G, then the graph $G - e^b$. One gets:

$$\tau(G) = \det R_\gamma = \det(I_\gamma + FF^t)$$
$$\tau(G - e^b) = \operatorname{adj}(R_\gamma)_{b,b} = \det(I_{\gamma-1} + F^b(F^b)^t)$$

where F^b is the flow matrix for the graph $G - e^b$. We get the effective resistance

$$R_{eff} = \frac{E}{i_b} = \frac{\det R_\gamma}{\operatorname{adj}(R_\gamma)_{b,b}} = \frac{\tau(G)}{\tau(G - e^b)}$$

□

(Program for the TI84). *At first, one has to obtain the first depth tree and the flow matrix by hand. Next we input the flow matrix as F. Then the program can be used. The program asks for the resistances of all edges, and in which edge B the battery is put.*

Unfortunately, in the program below, I needed to write L1 for L_1, L2 for L_2, L3 for L_3, and [C]-1 for $[C]^{-1}$. Please find out from the context.

```
PROGRAM:ELN
            Pause [F]
            dim([F]) -> L3
            L3(1)+1 -> N
            L3(2) -> G
            N-1+G -> M
            (N-1,N-1) -> dim([D])
            Fill(0,[D])
            M -> dim(L1)
            M -> dim(L2)
            For(I,1,N-1)
            Disp I
            Input "?RI ",R
            R -> [D](I,1)
            R -> L1(I)
            End
            [F]t[D][F] -> [C]
            For(J,N,M)
            Disp J
            Input "?RJ ",R
            R -> L1(J)
            J-N+1 -> K
            [C](K,K) + R -> [C](K,K)
            End
            Disp "RESISTENCE"
            Pause L1
            Pause[C]
            det([C]) -> D
            Disp "Det ",D
            (G,1) -> dim([E])
            Fill(0,[E])
            Input "?BATTERY",B
            D ->[E](B-N+1,1)
            [C]-1[E] -> [J]
            [F][J] -> [I]
            For(L,1,N-1)
            [I](L,1) -> L2(L)
            End
            For(L,N,M)
            [J](L-N+1,1) -> L2(L)
            End
            Disp "CURRENT"
```

```
Pause L2
L1*L2 ->L4
For(I,2,N-1)
L4(I-1)+L4(I) ->L4(I)
End
N-1->dim(L4)
Disp "VOLTAGE"
Pause L4
```

The output of the program consists of two lists and several matrices:

- The list of the currents is calculated as L_2.

- The list of he voltages is calculated as L_4.

- The matrix R_γ of effective resistances is calculated as C.

Solution of Problem 130 . See figures on page 135 and the following table.

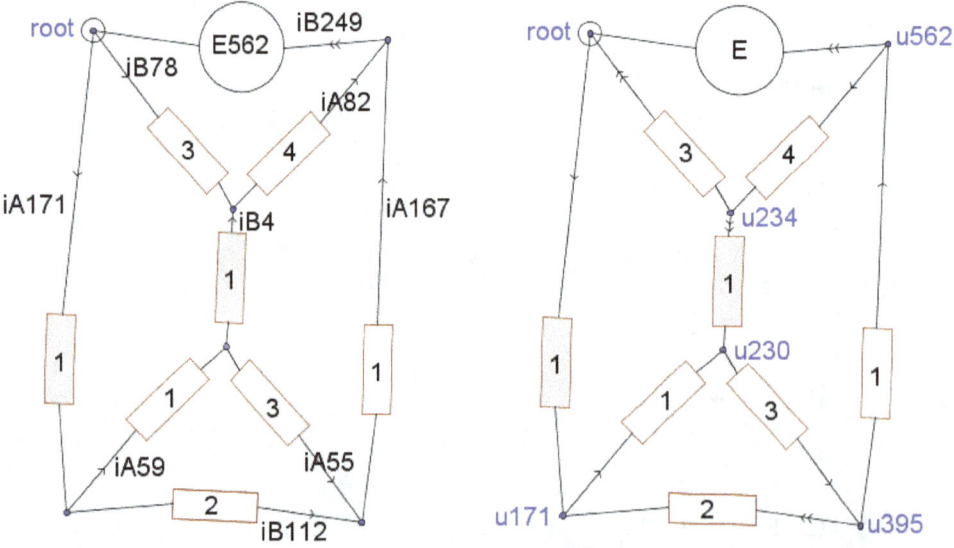

Figure 93: Currents and voltages.

e_i	R_A	6	7	8	9					i_A	$u_i - u_{i-1}$	u_i
1	1	0	1	1	0					171	171	171
2	1	1	1	1	0					59	59	230
3	3	1	1	1	1					55	165	395
4	1	0	1	1	1					167	167	562
5	4	0	0	1	1					-82	-324	234
e_j	R_B	6	7	8	9	6	7	8	9	i_B	$i_B R_B$	
6	2	4	4	4	3	6	4	4	3	-112	-224	
7	0		6	6	4	4	6	6	4	249	0	$E = 562$
8	3			10	8	4	6	13	8	-78	-234	
9	1				8	3	4	8	9	-4	-4	

$\square$

I.8.1 Justification of the electrical network calculation

The equations for the electrical voltages and currents can be derived from Kirchhoff's laws.

Kirchhoff's current law: The sum of the currents at each vertex is zero.

Kirchhoff's voltage law: The total voltage in each cycle, obtained by adding the voltages across the edges, is zero.

The current law follows from the conservation of electrical charge. The voltage law can be derived from the fact that electrical voltage is a potential of the electrical field strength. This is only valid as long as magnetic fields are weak, or changes are slow. The battery voltages have to be included in the voltage law. To set up the current and voltage equations, we need the signed incidence matrix.

Definition 45 (The signed incidence matrix of a directed graph). The *signed incidence matrix* for a loop-less directed graph with n vertices and m edges, is an $n \times m$-matrix M, with rows corresponding to the vertices, and columns corresponding to the arcs.
   The j-th column corresponds to the arc $e_j = \overrightarrow{v_i v_k}$ contains the two non-zero elements $M_{ij} = 1$ and $M_{kj} = -1$, since the arc e_j goes from vertex v_i to vertex v_k. $M_{sj} = 0$ for $s \neq i, k$. All other elements are zero.

   Let $i = (i_1, i_2, \ldots, i_m) \in \mathbb{R}^m$ be the vector of the currents in the edges $(e_1, e_2, \ldots, e_m)$ counted positively in the direction chosen for the edges. In terms of the signed incidence matrix, the current law gets the matrix equation

(I.8.11) $$Mi = 0$$

The i-th row of this vector equation states the conservation of current at vertex v_i, which tells that all currents coming out and into the vertex v_i sum up to zero.

   The flow of currents can be prescribed as a linear combination of flows around a basic set of *fundamental cycles*. The number of fundamental cycles is the *cycle rank* which is $\gamma = m - n + 1$.

For a planar graph, Euler's formula implies $\gamma = f - 1$. The cycle rank is one less than the number of faces because Euler's formula counts the unbounded face.

One back edge e_j is adjoined to the spanning tree to create the cycle C_j. Repeating this process for $j = n, n+1, \ldots, m$ produces a *fundamental system of γ cycles*. As has already been explained above, the information from the fundamental cycles is assembled into the flow matrix F.

Problem 132. *Here are good examples to do this procedure:*
(i) *The complete graph K_4.*
(ii) *The wheel W_4 with root on the four cycle.*
(iii) *The cube graph Q_3.*
(iv) *The prism $C_3 \times P_2$.*

For these graphs follows the steps we have explained up to now:

(a) *Make a drawing of the graph, determine the number of vertices n, the number of edges m, and the cycle rank γ.*

(b) *Choose a root, and draw a spanning tree in red. Number the edges and vertices accordingly. Color the back edges blue and give their orientation, too. Choose some numbering for the back edges.*

(c) *Draw each fundamental cycle $C_n, C_{n+1}, \ldots, C_m$ separately, and put in the orientation and numbering of its edges.*

(d) *Finally write down the flow matrix F.*

Lemma 21. *In a tree cannot flow a current by itself.*

Proof. Use induction on the size of the tree. The fact is clearly true for $n = 1$ or $n = 2$. Note that a tree has at least two end vertices. Kirchhoff law immediately implies current zero in them. By pulling out the ends of the tree, one produces a smaller tree. For this smaller tree, the current is zero by induction assumption. □

Lemma 22. *For a first-depth spanning tree, in each one of the fundamental cycles, the current can flow in the direction of the arcs. Hence the flow-matrix $F \geq 0$ is nonnegative.*

The partitioning of the edges into tree edges and back edges gives partitions of the current vector $i = (i_A, i_B)$, and the resistance matrix into matrices R_A and R_B. Furthermore, the signed incidence matrix is partitioned as
$$M = [A|B]$$

Lemma 23 (Relation of flow and incidence matrices).

(I.8.12) $$AF + B = 0$$

First proof. In a tree, no conserved current can flow. Hence any current is a *linear combination* of flows in the fundamental cycles and hence

(I.8.1) $$i_A = F i_B$$

The partition of the edges and equation (I.8.11) yields

$$Mi = A i_A + B i_B = (AF + B) i_B = 0$$

for any currents $i_B \in \mathbb{R}^\gamma$. Hence the assertion follows. □

Second proof. Take any vertex v_i and back edge e_j. The matrix element is

$$(AF+B)_{ij} = \sum_{e=1}^{n-1} A_{ie} F_{ej} + B_{ij}$$

The first sum counts how many tree edges of the fundamental cycle C_j go out of (counts as -1) or into (count $+1$) vertex v_i. The term B_{ij} count the single back edges possibly going into or out of vertex v_i. For every vertex of an oriented cycle, one edge goes out and one in. Hence the sum is zero at all vertices and $AF + B = 0$, as to be shown. □

Problem 133. *Calculate $AF + B$ explicitly for the graph K_4 as labeled in example (i) of Problem 132.*

We state the voltage law as matrix equation

$$RI = M^t u + E$$

Again we need to separate tree- and back edges and get

(I.8.13) $$R_A i_A = A^t u$$
(I.8.14) $$R_B i_B = B^t u + E$$

The driving voltage appears only for the back edges, as we have assume for simplicity. Together, equations (I.8.1), (I.8.13) and (I.8.14) are a system of $n + m$ equations, from which one has to determine the $n + m$ unknown currents and voltages. This is the huge system

(I.8.15) $$\begin{aligned} A i_A + B i_B &= 0 \\ -A^t u + R_A i_A &= 0 \\ -B^t u + R_B i_B &= E \end{aligned}$$

Proposition 34. *The system (I.8.15) can be reduced to the $\gamma \times \gamma$ system*

(I.8.3) $$R_\gamma i_B = E$$

for the current i_B in the back-edges. The effective resistance is

(I.8.2) $$R_\gamma = F^t R_A F + R_B$$

Proof. We take the linear combination F^t (I.8.13) + (I.8.14) and then use equation (I.8.1) to obtain
$$(F^t R_A F + R_B)i_B = F^t R_A i_A + i_B = (F^t A^t + B^t)u + E = E$$
With the effective resistance (I.8.2) we have obtained the $R_\gamma i_B = E$, as to be shown. □

Proposition 35. *The matrix R_γ is symmetric. It is positive definite in the case that all resistances $R_A \geq 0$ and $R_B \geq 0$ are nonnegative, and the subgraph with resistances zero does not have a cycle producing a short cut. The power consumed by the network is the sum of the powers consumed by all resistances*
$$P = i_B^t E = \sum_{e=1}^{m} R_e I_e^2$$

Proof. From the identity $(AB)^t = B^t A^t$, we see the matrix R_γ is symmetric. It is positive semi-definite because the quadratic form
$$i_B^t R_\gamma i_B = i_B^t F^t R_A F i_B + i_B^t R_B i_B = (F i_B)^t R_A (F i_B) + i_B^t R_B i_B$$
$$= i_A^t R_A i_A + i_B^t R_B i_B = \sum_{e=1}^{m} R_e i_e^2 \geq 0$$
is nonnegative for arbitrary currents $i_B \in \mathbb{R}^\gamma$. From basic physics and equation (I.8.3), the consumed power is
$$P = I_{source} E = i_B^t E = i_B^t R_\gamma i_B$$
which is the quadratic form above. □

Remark 28. With the counting of vertices and tree edges coordinated as explained, the matrix A has the elements
$$A_{i-1,i} = 1 \quad \text{for } i = 1, 2, \ldots n-1$$
$$A_{i,i} = -1 \quad \text{for } i = 1, 2, \ldots n-1$$
$$A_{i,j} = 0 \quad \text{otherwise}$$

We see that it is a $n \times (n-1)$ matrix of full rank $n-1$. Hence the homogeneous equation $Ax = 0$ has only the trivial solution $x = 0$. The adjoint homogeneous equation $y^t A = 0$ has a one-dimensional solution space spanned by $y^t = (1, 1, \ldots 1)$.

I.9 The Matrix-Tree Theorem

Theorem 10 (The Matrix-Tree Theorem). *Let D be the diagonal matrix of the degrees and A the adjacency matrix for a loop-less general graph G. All minors of $D - A$ are equal to the number $\tau(G)$ of spanning trees.*

Lemma 24 (Elementary properties of the signed incidence matrix).

(a) *For the vector $e_n \in \mathbb{R}^n$ with all entries equal to one, we get $e_n^t M = 0$. Hence $\operatorname{rank} M \leq n-1$.*

(b) *For the vector $e_m \in \mathbb{R}^m$ with all entries equal to one, the vector $M e_m$ gives the differences of the out-degrees minus in-degrees.*

(c) $MM^t = D - A$

(d) $e_n^t(D - A) = (D - A)e_n = 0$. *Hence $\operatorname{rank}(D - A) \leq n - 1$.*

Remark 29. In terms of the classical adjoint, one can state the Matrix-Tree Theorem as
$$\operatorname{adj}(D - A) = \tau(G)\, ee^t$$

For the proof the Matrix-Tree Theorem 10, we need the following two propositions from linear algebra:

Proposition 36. *The classical adjoint of a square matrix with rank one less than the rank maximal is a rank one matrix. The classical adjoint of a square matrix with rank two or more less than the maximal rank is zero.*

Let B be any $n \times n$ matrix with $\operatorname{rank} B \leq n - 1$ and assume that
$$l^t B = Br = 0 \quad \text{with } l^t \neq 0,\, r \neq 0$$

For a suitable constant β, we get the classical adjoint
$$\operatorname{adj} B = \beta\, l r^t$$

In the special case that $B = B^t$ and $\operatorname{rank} B = n - 1$, we may choose $l = r$. The constant is easily determined to yield
$$\operatorname{adj} B = (r^t r)^{-1}\, r r^t$$

Theorem 11 (Cauchy-Binet). *Let A be any $n \times m$ matrix, and B any $m \times n$ matrix. Their product has the determinant*

(I.9.1) $\qquad \det(AB) = \sum \{\det(A(S)B(S)) : S \subseteq \{1, 2, \ldots, m\} \text{ and } |S| = n\}$

where the sub-matrices $A(S)$ and $B(S)$ are obtained by the choice of the same subset S for their columns of A and rows of B. The sum is taken over all $\binom{m}{n}$ subsets of $\{1, 2, \ldots, m\}$ with n elements.

Part 1 of the proof the Matrix-Tree Theorem. Since the matrix $D - A$ is symmetric and has left- and right kernel e, Proposition 36 implies that all minors are equal. Hence the definition of a minor implies

(I.9.2)
$$\operatorname{adj}(D - A) = \rho\, ee^t$$
$$(\operatorname{adj}(D - A))_{i,k} = \rho \quad \text{for all } i, k = 1, 2, \ldots, n$$

We cannot yet get the constant ρ by this argument. But at least, we can say

Lemma 25. *If the graph G is disconnected, then the relation (I.9.2) holds with $\rho = 0$.*

Reason. The matrices D and A are block-diagonal, with one block for each component of graph G. Hence the kernel of $D - A$ has dimension at least the number of components of G. Hence Proposition (36) yields $\rho = 0$. □

In the next step, we consider the case that the graph G is a tree.

Lemma 26. *If the graph G is a tree, the relation (I.9.2) holds with $\rho = 1$.*

We use the same counting of vertices and tree edges as for the spanning tree of an electrical network. Similar to the set-up of electrical networks, we assign to the root the subscript 0. We get special form (28) for the signed incidence matrix M.

$$M_{i-1,i} = 1 \quad \text{for } i = 1, 2, \ldots n-1$$
$$M_{i,i} = -1 \quad \text{for } i = 1, 2, \ldots n-1$$
$$M_{i,j} = 0 \quad \text{otherwise}$$

The superscript $\sharp$ indicate a sub-matrix obtained by deletion of the row or column corresponding to the root vertex. We see that $M^\sharp$ is a triangular matrix with all diagonal elements equal to one, which implies $\det M^\sharp = 1$. Lemma 24 part (c) yields

(I.9.3) $$D^\sharp - A^\sharp = M^\sharp (M^\sharp)^t$$
(I.9.4) $$\rho = \det(D^\sharp - A^\sharp) = \det[M^\sharp (M^\sharp)^t]$$
(I.9.5) $$= \det M^\sharp \det(M^\sharp)^t = 1$$

□

Lemma 27. *For any subset $S \subseteq \{1, 2, \ldots, m\}$ of $n-1$ edges, the determinant $\det M^\sharp(S) = \pm 1$ if these edges span a tree. This happens for $\tau(G)$ choices of the subset S. Otherwise the determinant is zero.*

Reason. The subgraph containing $|S| = n - 1$ edges is a tree if and only if it is connected. By lemma 26, lemma 25 and equation (I.9.4), this happens if and only if $\rho = \det[M^\sharp(S) M^\sharp(S)^t] = 1$. □

Remark 30. The number of spanning trees of a graph with n vertices and m edges has the upper bound

$$\tau(G) \leq \binom{m}{n-1}$$

Part 2 of the proof the Matrix-Tree Theorem. Only the first two parts of equation (I.9.4) are still valid, since now $m > n - 1$. The Cauchy-Binet Theorem yields

$$\rho = \det[M^\sharp (M^\sharp)^t] = \sum \{\det(M^\sharp(S)(M^\sharp)^t(S)) \, : \, S \subseteq \{1, 2, \ldots, m\} \text{ and } |S| = n-1\}$$
$$= \sum \{1 \, : \, S \subseteq \{1, 2, \ldots, m\} \text{ are the edges of a spanning tree }\} = \tau(G)$$

□

Problem 134. *Use the Matrix-Tree Theorem to prove Cayley's Theorem 5 that the number of spanning trees of the complete graph K_n equals n^{n-2}.*

Answer. The adjacency matrix A for K_n has all non-diagonal elements 1, and the degrees of all n vertices is equal to $n-1$. Hence

$$D - A = \begin{bmatrix} n-1 & -1 & -1\ldots & -1 \\ -1 & n-1 & -1\ldots & -1 \\ \ldots & \ldots & \ldots & \ldots \\ -1 & -1 & -1\ldots & n-1 \end{bmatrix}$$

and the Matrix-Tree Theorem implies $\tau(K_n) = \det(D^\sharp - A^\sharp)$ where the subscript $^\sharp$ denotes a $(n-1) \times (n-1)$ sub-determinant. There are two convenient ways to calculate $\det(D^\sharp - A^\sharp)$, one can use either

- elementay row operations; or

- eigenvalues.

I explain first the use of elementary row operations. The sum of all $n-1$ rows turns out to have all entries 1. This vector is placed into the first row. Next we add the first row to the remaining rows $2, 3, \ldots n-1$. One obtains a block-diagonal matrix for which the determinant is $1 \cdot n^{n-2}$. We have obtained

$$\det(D^\sharp - A^\sharp) = \begin{vmatrix} n-1 & -1 & -1\ldots & -1 \\ -1 & n-1 & -1\ldots & -1 \\ \ldots & \ldots & \ldots & \ldots \\ -1 & -1 & -1\ldots & n-1 \end{vmatrix} = \begin{vmatrix} 1 & 1 & 1\ldots & 1 \\ -1 & n-1 & -1\ldots & -1 \\ \ldots & \ldots & \ldots & \ldots \\ -1 & -1 & -1\ldots & n-1 \end{vmatrix}$$

$$= \begin{vmatrix} 1 & 1 & 1\ldots & 1 \\ 0 & n & 0\ldots & 0 \\ \ldots & \ldots & \ldots & \ldots \\ 0 & 0 & 0\ldots & n \end{vmatrix} = n^{n-2}$$

for the number of spanning trees of K_n. For the calculation via eigenvalues, note that

$$D^\sharp - A^\sharp = nI_{n-1} - e_{n-1}e^t_{n-1} = nI - E$$

where I is the $(n-1) \times (n-1)$ unit matrix and E is the $(n-1) \times (n-1)$ matrix with all entries equal to one. The matrix E has the simple eigenvalue $n-1$ with eigenvector e_{n-1}, and the eigenvalue 0 with multiplicity $n-2$. Hence the eigenvalues of $nI - E$ are 1 with multiplicity one and n with multiplicity $n-2$. The determinant is the product of the eigenvalues and we get

$$\tau(K_n) = \det(D^\sharp - A^\sharp) = \det(nI - E) = n^{n-2}$$

which is the same result as above.

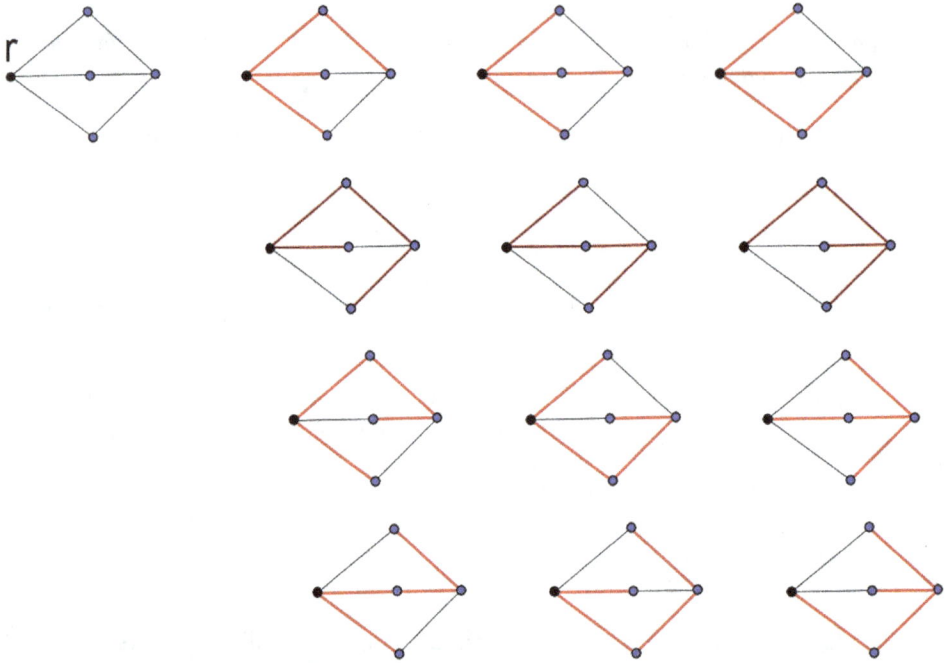

Figure 94: The graph $K_{2,3}$ and its twelve spanning trees.

Problem 135. *Draw the graph $K_{2,3}$ and separately all 12 spanning trees.*

Answer. The trees are drawn starting from the vertex r at right. They are organized according to whether the degree of r is three (three cases), two (six cases) or one (three cases).

Problem 136. *Use the Matrix-Tree Theorem to check that $K_{3,2}$ has 12 spanning trees.*

Answer.
$$D - A = \begin{bmatrix} 2 & 0 & 0 & -1 & -1 \\ 0 & 2 & 0 & -1 & -1 \\ 0 & 0 & 2 & -1 & -1 \\ -1 & -1 & -1 & 3 & 0 \\ -1 & -1 & -1 & 0 & 3 \end{bmatrix}$$

Hence the Matrix-Tree Theorem implies $\tau(K_{3,2}) = \det(D^\sharp - A^\sharp)$ where the subscript $^\sharp$ denotes a 4×4 sub-matrix. We use elementary row operations for this <u>sub-determinant</u> to get

$$\det(D^\sharp - A^\sharp) = \begin{vmatrix} 2 & 0 & -1 & -1 \\ 0 & 2 & -1 & -1 \\ -1 & -1 & 3 & 0 \\ -1 & -1 & 0 & 3 \end{vmatrix} = \begin{vmatrix} 2 & 0 & -1 & -1 \\ 0 & 2 & -1 & -1 \\ 0 & 0 & 1 & 1 \\ -1 & -1 & 0 & 3 \end{vmatrix} = \begin{vmatrix} 2 & 0 & 0 & 0 \\ 0 & 2 & 0 & 0 \\ 0 & 0 & 1 & 1 \\ -1 & -1 & 0 & 3 \end{vmatrix} = 12$$

for the number of spanning trees of $K_{3,2}$.

Problem 137. *Use the Matrix-Tree Theorem to prove that the complete bipartite graph $K_{a,b}$ has $a^{b-1}b^{a-1}$ spanning trees.*

Answer. The adjacency matrix A for $K_{a,b}$ naturally partitions into four blocks, with a and b row and columns. All elements in the two off-diagonal blocks are 1. One obtains

$$D - A = \begin{bmatrix} bI_a & -e_a e_b^t \\ -e_b e_a^t & aI_b \end{bmatrix} \text{ and } \tau(K_{a,b}) = \det(D^\sharp - A^\sharp) = \begin{vmatrix} bI_{a-1} & -e_{a-1}e_b^t \\ -e_b e_{a-1}^t & aI_b \end{vmatrix}$$

I use the elementary row operation to replace the $b+1$-th row (first row in the lower block) by the sum of all rows. The lower right block is split. Next I add this row to all rows in the upper block. One obtains a block-diagonal matrix for which the determinant is the product of the determinants of the two diagonal blocks.

$$\tau(K_{a,b}) = \begin{vmatrix} bI_{a-1} & -e_{a-1}, & -e_{a-1}e_{b-1}^t \\ 0 & 1, & e_{b-1}^t \\ -e_{b-1}e_{a-1}^t & 0, & aI_{b-1} \end{vmatrix} = \begin{vmatrix} bI_{a-1} & 0, & 0 \\ 0 & 1, & e_{b-1}^t \\ -e_{b-1}e_{a-1}^t & 0, & aI_{b-1} \end{vmatrix} = b^{a-1}a^{b-1}$$

for the number of spanning trees of $K_{a,b}$.

I.9.1 Once more electrical networks

Proposition 37. *For any $r \times s$ matrix F*

$$\det(I_r + FF^t) = \det(I_s + F^t F)$$

The matrix need not necessarily be square,—thus the two unit matrices I may correspond to different dimensions.

Proposition 38 (The resistance-determinant). *We consider a loop-less general graph as an electrical network with the resistances of all edges, including the battery edge put to one. The number of spanning trees of G is equal of the determinant of the effective resistance:*

$$\tau(G) = \det(I + F^t F) = \det(R_\gamma)$$

Proof. The partitioning of the edges into tree edges and back edges gives the partition of the signed incidence matrix

$$M = [M_A | M_B]$$

In order to avoid confusion with the adjacency matrix A, we have replaced $A \mapsto M_A, B \mapsto M_B$ in the notation in the section on electrical networks. With this new notation, equation (I.8.12) becomes $M_A F + M_B = 0$. The superscript $\sharp$ to a matrix denote a sub-matrix obtained by deletion of the row or column corresponding to the vertex chosen as the root. We get an identity for the flow matrix:

(I.9.6) $\qquad D^\sharp - A^\sharp = M^\sharp (M^\sharp)^t = M_A^\sharp (M_A^\sharp)^t + M_B^\sharp (M_B^\sharp)^t = M_A^\sharp (I + FF^t)(M_A^\sharp)^t$

The arrangement of the counting of vertices and tree edges results in the special form (28) for M_A. In the present notation

$$(M_A)_{i-1,i} = 1 \quad \text{for } i = 1, 2, \ldots n-1$$
$$(M_A)_{i,i} = -1 \quad \text{for } i = 1, 2, \ldots n-1$$
$$(M_A)_{i,j} = 0 \quad \text{otherwise}$$

Hence $M_A^\sharp$ is a triangular matrix with all diagonal elements equal to one, which implies $\det(M_A) = \det(M_A^\sharp) = 1$.

Now equation (I.9.6), Proposition 37 and the definition $R_\gamma = I + F^t F$ of the effective resistance yield

(I.9.7) $\quad \rho = (\operatorname{adj}(D-A))_{0,0} = \det(D^\sharp - A^\sharp)$

(I.9.8) $\quad\quad\quad\quad = \det(M_A^\sharp) \det(I + FF^t) \det(M_A^\sharp)^t = \det(I + FF^t)$

(I.9.9) $\quad\quad\quad\quad = \det(I + F^t F) = \det R_\gamma$

By the Matrix-tree Theorem this is the number of spanning trees of G, too. $\square$

I.10 Connectivity

Definition 46 (Vertex connectivity). The vertex connectivity κ of a graph which is not complete is the minimal number of vertices the removal of which disconnects the graph. The vertex connectivity of the complete graph K_n is $\kappa = n - 1$.

The vertex connectivity κ of a simple graph $G \neq K_n$ is the minimal number κ for which there exists a set of vertices $v_1, v_2, v \ldots, v_\kappa$ such that the induced subgraph $G \setminus \{v_1, v_2, v \ldots, v_\kappa\}$ is disconnected. Any graph $G \neq K_n$ with n vertices has connectivity $\kappa(G) \leq n - 2$.

Definition 47 (Edge connectivity). The edge connectivity λ of a graph is the minimal number of edges the removal of which disconnects the graph.

As usual, we denote the minimum degree by δ and the maximum degree by Δ.

Proposition 39 (Theorem of Whitney). *The vertex connectivity κ is less or equal the edge connectivity λ, which is less or equal the minimal degree δ.*

Proof. If the graph is complete $G = K_n$, we know that $\kappa = \lambda = \delta = n - 1$. Too, it is clear that $\lambda \leq \delta$.

We now assume that $G \neq K_n$, and let S be a minimum edge cut of size $|S| = \lambda$, removal of which disconnects the graph into components A and B. In other words $G - S = A \cup B$. We distinguish two cases:

case (a): The graph contains the complete bipartite graph $K_{A,B}$ as a subgraph.

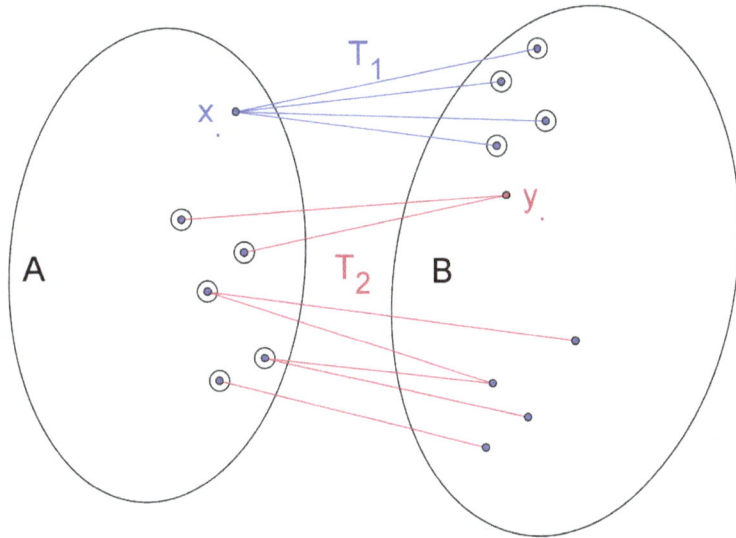

Figure 95: The vertex connectivity κ is less or equal to the edge connectivity λ.

In that case, $\lambda = |A| \cdot |B| \leq \delta \leq n - 1$. Hence $|A|(n - |A|) \leq n - 1$, which does only hold for $|A| = 1$ or $|A| = n - 1$. In other words, either A or B is a single vertex adjacent to all other vertices. Hence $\kappa = \lambda = \delta = n - 1$.

case (b): There exist two vertices $x \in A$ and $y \in B$ which are not adjacent.

In that case, we write the edge cut as a disjoint union $S = T_1 \cup T_2$. The part T_1 consists of the edges connecting vertex x to vertices in B. The part T_2 consists of the edges connecting vertices in $A - x$ to vertices in B. For the edges in T_1, we mark the end-vertex in B, and for the edges in T_2, we mark the end-vertex in A. The number of marked vertices is less or equal to $|S| = \lambda$. Removal of the marked vertices disconnects the graph. Hence $\kappa \leq \lambda$, as to be shown. □

Problem 138. *By the Theorem of Whitney, the vertex connectivity κ is less or equal the edge connectivity λ, which is less or equal the minimal degree δ.*

Determine vertex-connectivity κ, edge-connectivity λ and minimal degree δ for the graph in the figure on page 147.

Problem 139. *Suppose graph G has a bridge $e = ab$, and deleting the bridge leaves $G - e = A + B$ with two components A and B.*

In the <u>original</u> graph, there are an odd number of vertices of odd degrees among V_A, and an odd number of vertices of odd degrees among V_B. Explain why.

Answer. By the handshaking lemma, we know that in any graph, the number of odd vertices is even. Hence component A has an even number of odd vertices, and similarly component B.

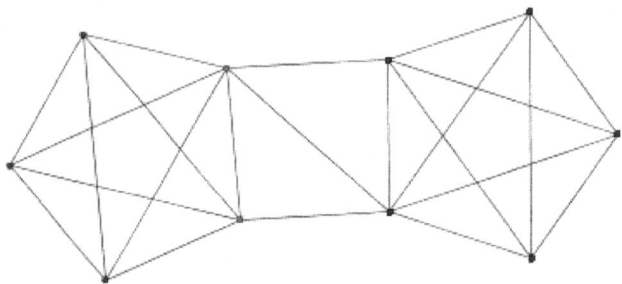

Figure 96: An example where κ, λ, δ are all three different.

After adjoining the bridge, the degree of vertex a is increased by one. Hence in the original graph, the number of vertices of odd degrees among V_A is one less or one more than the number of odd vertices of component A.

Hence in graph G, there are an odd number of vertices of odd degrees among V_A, and similarly for V_B.

Proposition 40. *For a 3-regular graph with more than two vertices, the vertex connectivity κ is equal to the edge connectivity λ.*

Hence a 3-regular graph with no bridge has no cut-vertex, neither.

Proof. By Whitney's Theorem 39, we know $\kappa \leq \lambda \leq 3$. Hence the proposition holds in the case that $\kappa = 3$. A graph with three vertices cannot be 3-regular. The case of a graph with two vertices and three edges needs to be excluded! [7]

We now assume that $\kappa = 1$ and the graph G has at least four vertices. Let v be a cut vertex cut of graph G. The remaining graph $G \setminus S = H + K$ is not a single vertex and hence it is disconnected. The vertex v has edges leading to both H and K, otherwise the graph G would be disconnected. Only one edge connects v to either component H or K. We cut this edge and confirm that $\lambda = 1$. From the contrapositive, we see a bridgeless 3-regular graph has no cut-vertex.

We now assume that $\kappa = 2$ and the graph G has at least four vertices. Let S be a minimal vertex cut of the given graph G. Hence $|S| = 2$ and $S = \{v, w\}$. The remaining graph $G \setminus S = H + K$ is not a single vertex and hence it is disconnected. Each of the vertices v and w has edges leading to both H and K, otherwise one checks that $\lambda = \kappa = 1$. We can now distinguish the following cases.

(i): Vertices v and w are not neighbours to each other. Only two edges connect v, w to one of the components H or K.

---

[7]Douglas West excellent book "Introduction to Graph Theory" forgets that difficulty,— one of its very few flaws.

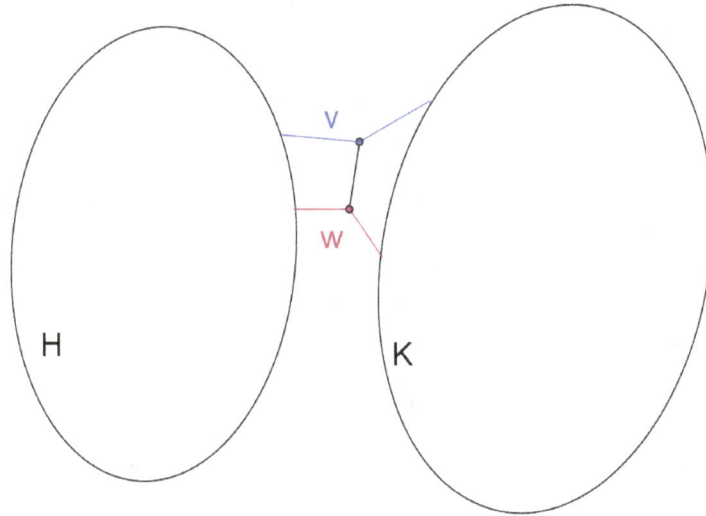

Figure 97: One possibility for a 3-regular graph with $\kappa = \lambda = 2$.

In this case, we cut these two edges and confirm that $\lambda = 2$.

- **(ii):** Vertices v and w are not neighbours to each other. Only one edge connects v to component H and only one edge connects w to component K.

  Again, we cut these two edges and confirm that $\lambda = 2$.

- **(iii): Vertices v and w are neighbours to each other.** The situation is drawn in the figure on page 148. One can cut two edges to either H or K and confirm that $\lambda = 2$.

- **(iv): Two edges connect vertices v and w.** One can cut one edge and would see that $\kappa = \lambda = 1$. Thus this case cannot occur.

□

I.10.1 Block-cutvertex decomposition

In analogy to the partition of the vertices into components, there exists a partition of the edges into *blocks*.

Definition 48 (Block). An induced subgraph $B \subseteq G$ is called a *block* if the two following conditions hold:

(1) either $B = K_2$ or $\kappa(B) \geq 2$.

(2) B is a maximal subgraph with property (1).

Proposition 41 (Block-cutvertex forest). *Any two different blocks of a graph are edge-disjoint. The number of cut-vertices is less than the number of blocks. The blocks $B_1, B_2, \ldots, B_h$ and cut-vertices $v_1, v_2, \ldots, v_k$ are the alternating vertices of the block-cutvertex forest. The edges of this forest connect any block B to any cut-vertex v contained in the block B.*
For any connected graph, the block-cutvertex forest is a tree.

Reason. We may assume the graph G is connected. We use the maximality of blocks as induced subgraphs which are either K_2 or 2-connected. Any two blocks can have at most one vertex in common. Any vertex $v \in B_1 \cap B_2$ common to two blocks is a cut-vertex. There cannot exist a cycles with edges in two dif and only if erent blocks. □

I.11 Menger's Theorem

Theorem 12 (Menger's Theorem in the edge form). *Given is a graph or digraph with source S and terminal T. The maximal number of edge-disjoint paths from source to terminal is equal to the minimal number of edges of an edge-cut that separates the source from the terminal.*

Constructive proof. Given is any set $\mathcal{P}$ of edge-disjoint paths from S to T.
   The goal of the algorithm now explained is to

(a) either find an additional edge-disjoint path—in case it exists—

(b) or to find a minimal edge cut—in case that no additional edge-disjoint path does exist. [8]

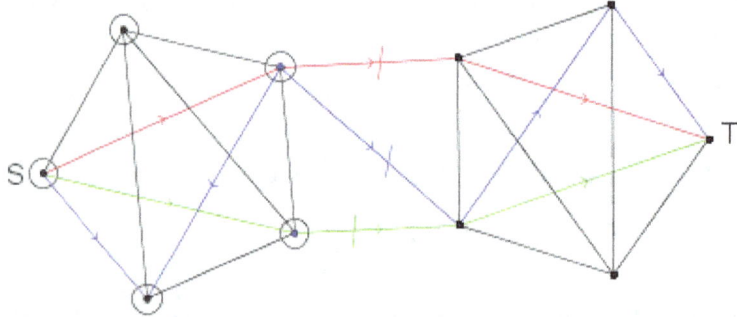

Figure 98: The minimal edge-cut is located between marked and unmarked vertices.

---

[8] In simple examples, it is easier to find at first a maximal number of edge-disjoint paths, and afterward to use the algorithm only to locate a minimal edge cut.

The edge-disjoint paths have to be directed from source to sink. To decide between possibilities (a) and (b), one marks the *vertices*, starting with the source S. A vertex adjacent to a marked vertex gets marked too, if it is either adjacent via an unused edge, or a used arc that is used for flow in the reversed direction.

If one arrives at marking the terminal, one has found an additional edge-disjoint path not in the set $\mathcal{P}$, and possibility (a) occurs.

If the terminal remains unmarked, then possibility (b) occurs, and one gets an edge cut consisting of all the edges between marked and unmarked vertices.

This edge-cut clearly is minimal, because it contains only as many edges as there are disjoint paths in the set $\mathcal{P}$. Hence we have confirmed that the maximal number of edge-disjoint paths from given source to sink is equal to the minimal number of edges of an edge-cut that separates source and sink. □

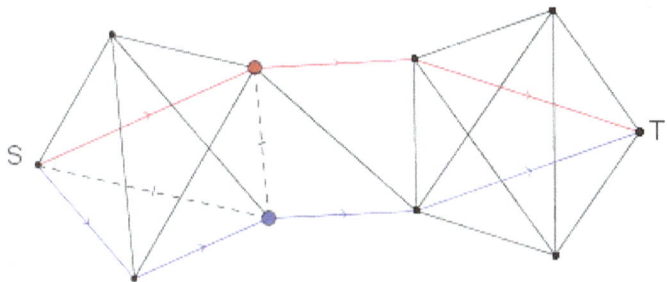

Figure 99: The minimal vertex-cut is located between marked and unmarked edges.

Theorem 13 (Menger's Theorem in the vertex form). *Given is a graph or digraph with source S and terminal T. The maximal number of vertex-disjoint paths from source to terminal is equal to the number of vertices of an minimal vertex-cut that separates the source from the terminal.*

Corollary 10. *In a graph without any cut-vertex, there exists a cycle through any two vertices.*

Independent proof the Corollary. Let x be any vertex, and take any second vertex y. Nonexistence of a cut vertex implies nonexistence of a bridge. Hence there exists a cycle C through vertex x—it is left to the reader to check this simple fact.

If $y \in C$, we are ready. Otherwise, we construct a cycle through vertex x that gets closer to vertex y than the cycle C. Let z be a vertex in C with minimal distance from y. Let P_1 and P_2 be the two disjoint paths from x to z making the cycle $C = P_1 \cup P_2$. Let P_0 be a shortest path from z to y. All vertices of $P_0 - z$ have smaller distance to y than z.

Because there exists no cut vertex, the graph $G - z$ is connected. Hence there exists a path Q from x to y in $G - z$. Draw a figure containing the items introduced so far.

Let $b \in Q$ be the vertex nearest to x lying in the path P_0, too. Let $a \in \overline{xb} \cap Q$ be the vertex lying in the cycle C, too, and farthest from x. We may assume that $a \in P_1$. Now a cycle through the vertices x and b is obtained by concatination the two disjoint paths $R := (P_1 \cap \overline{xa}) \cup (Q \cap \overline{ab})$ and $S := P_2 \cup (P_0 \cap \overline{zb})$. The reader can follow the new cycle $R \cup S$ in the figure.

The cycle $R \cup S$ contains vertex b, which is closer to y than z. By using this construction repetitively, we finally get a cycle through any two given vertices x and y. □

Indication of a constructive proof. Obviously, there exist one or several sets of vertex disjoint paths from source S to terminal T. Let $\mathcal{P}$ denote any (hopefully maximal) set of vertex disjoint paths from the given source to the given terminal.

An algorithm to get a minimal set of separating vertices located on $\mathcal{P}$ is a bid tricky. Again the vertex-disjoint paths $\mathcal{P}$ have to be directed from source to sink. A process of marking unused *edges* is used to find

(a) Either an additional vertex-disjoint path—in case it exists—

(b) or to find a minimal vertex cut in case that no additional vertex-disjoint path does exist.

One marks unused *edges*, starting with the unused edges adjacent to the source S. An adjacent unused edge gets marked until one hits a vertex v of a used path. Then one goes on marking unused edges temporarily, possibly hitting the same used path several times. *If one hits the initial segment Sv of the used path later*, say at vertex u, and then still is able to go on until one marks an edge adjacent to the sink, one has found an additional vertex disjoint path. We have arrived at case (a).

But if the coloring of unused edges has been started after a maximal set of vertex disjoint paths has been established, this cannot happen—and the first hit v becomes a vertex in the minimal vertex cut. The further edge coloring then restarts at the source or adjacent to edges colored before the hit at v. Finally one finds a minimal vertex cut and arrives at case (b). In this case, no additional vertex-disjoint path does exist. □

Problem 140 (An example for Menger's theorem in the edge form). *Work through the example given in the figure on page 187.*

(a) *Get the maximal number of edge disjoint paths from A to D. to find the edge connectivity $\lambda(A, D)$.*

(b) *Use vertex marking starting at the source to locate a minimal edge cut.*

Answer.

Problem 141 (An example for Menger's theorem in the vertex form). *Use the graph in the figure on page 187. once more*

Find the vertex connectivity $\kappa(A, D)$ and get a maximum set of vertex disjoint paths from A to D. Locate a minimal vertex cut.

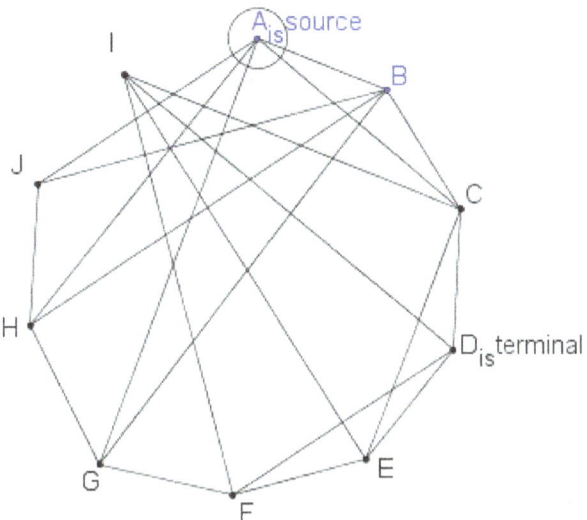

Figure 100: Find maximal number of edge-disjoint paths from A to D.

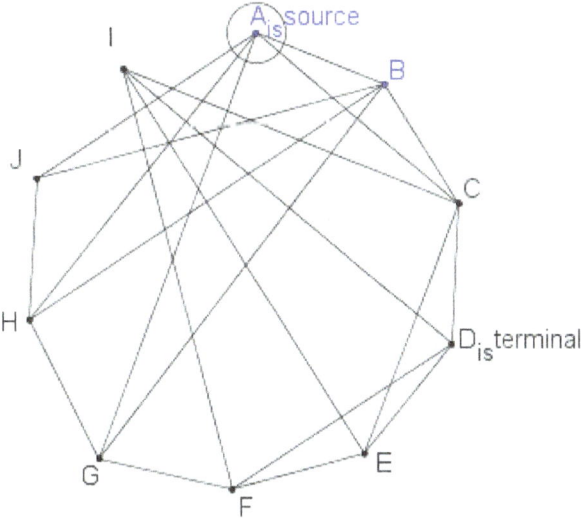

Figure 101: Find maximal number of vertex-disjoint paths from A to D.

Answer.

Proposition 42 (The bottleneck lemma). *Assume that a simple graph has edge connectivity strictly less its minimal degree $\lambda < \delta$, and the minimum edge cut S with $|S| = \lambda$ cuts the graph into the components A and B. Then these two components have both at least $\delta + 1$ vertices.*

Proof. We use the group handshaking lemma between vertices of A and B:

$$\sum_{\text{vertices } u \in A} \deg u = 2m(A) + \lambda$$

$$\sum_{\text{vertices } v \in B} \deg v = 2m(B) + \lambda$$

Since the degrees are at least the minimal degree, and the number of edges $m(A)$ is at most the edges of a complete graph of $n(A)$ vertices, we conclude

$$\delta\, n(A) \leq \sum_{\text{vertices } u \in A} \deg u = 2m(A) + \lambda < n(A)[n(A) - 1] + \delta$$

$$\delta\, n(B) \leq \sum_{\text{vertices } v \in B} \deg v = 2m(B) + \lambda < n(B)[n(B) - 1] + \delta$$

the first of which simplifies to $\delta[n(A) - 1] < n(A)[n(A) - 1]$. Since this is a proper inequality, we conclude at first $n(A) > 1$. Hence division by $n(A) - 1$ yields $\delta < n(A)$, as to be shown. □

I.12 Planar Graphs

I.12.1 The two handshaking lemmas and Euler's formula

Theorem 14 (Euler's formula). *For a planar connected graph or multigraph, the number n of vertices, number f of faces, and number m of edges satisfy*

$$n + f - m = 2$$

Note the outer (unbounded) face has to be counted, too.

Definition 49 (Length of a face). The minimal number of edges that one has to pass while surrounding a face, and covering the entire boundary of the face, is called the degree or the *length of the face*.

- If a face has a cut-vertex with a "hanging tree" attached, the tree's edges are counted double, since one has to pass them twice while surrounding the face.
- If a face is bounded by several components of a graph, one has to surround *all* these components.

Theorem 15. *For the counting of the vertices, edges and faces of a planar graph or multigraph with k components, we have three relations:*

The handshaking lemma: $\quad \sum \{\deg(v) \text{ of all vertices } v\} = 2m$

The dual handshaking lemma: $\sum \{\deg(f) \text{ of all faces } f\} = 2m$

Euler's formula: $$n + f - m = 1 + k$$

Lemma 28. (a) *Let G be a planar general graph, and suppose the interior of face F touches the edge $e = vw$ on both sides. Then the graph $G \setminus e$ has one more component than graph G. Thus the edge e is a bridge.*

(b) *If the edge e is a not bridge of the general planar graph G, there are lying two distinct faces on the two sides of edge e.*

(c) *For any acyclic graph G, there exists a planar representation with one face. Indeed, any planar representation has only one face.*

Proof (a). Let G be a planar general graph. Suppose that the interior of face F touches the edge $e = vw$ on both sides. Then there exists a closed Jordan curve C (or closed simple polygon) lying in the interior of this face, except one point of intersection $C \cap e \neq v, w$. The two parts of the graph in the interior and exterior domain of curve C are both non-empty. Hence the graph $G \setminus e$ has one more component than graph G. Thus the edge e is a bridge. □

Proof Euler's formula. We proceed by induction on the number of edges. For any null graph, the know that $m = 0$ and $n = k$. Moreover $f = 1$, since any two points of the plane can be connected by a simple polygon avoiding the vertices of the null graph. Hence Euler's formula holds for $m = 0$.

For the induction step, suppose Euler's formula holds for all graphs with less than m edges. Given is a general planar graph G with m edges. We distinguish the following two cases:

(a) **There exists an edge e that is not a bridge.** By the lemma 28 part (b), there are lying two distinct faces on the two sides of edge e. Hence the graph $G' = G \setminus e$ has $n' = n$ vertices, $k' = k$ components, $m' = m - 1$ edges, and $f' = f - 1$ faces. Hence

$$n + m - f = n' + m' - f' = 1 + k' = 1 + k$$

confirming Euler's formula.

(b) **All edges are bridges.** By the lemma 28 part (c), the planar representation has one face: $f = 1$. Again, we choose any edge e. There is lying the same face on the two sides of edge e. Hence the graph $G' = G \setminus e$ has $n' = n$ vertices, $m' = m - 1$ edges, and $f' = f = 1$ face. But by the lemma 28 part (a), the graph $G' = G \setminus e$ has $k' = k + 1$ components. Hence

$$n + m - f = n' + m' + 1 - f' = 2 + k' = 1 + k$$

confirming Euler's formula.

□

I.12.2 Euler's formula and Hamiltonian cycles

Proposition 43. *Suppose the loopless planar graph G has a cycle c. Let v' count the vertices in the interior domain of the cycle, and f'_l count the faces of length l lying in the interior domain. The length $\deg c$ of the cycle satisfies*

(I.12.1) $$\deg c = 2 - 2v' + \sum_{interior} (l-2) f'_l$$

Proof. Let G' be the graph consisting of the vertices and edges inside or on the boundary of the given cycle. Of course the graph G' has an unbounded face, to be included in the count for f'. For this graph, Euler's formula and the dual handshake lemma yield

$$2 = n' + f' - m' = [\deg c + v'] + \left[1 + \sum_{interior} f'_l\right] - \frac{1}{2}\left[\deg c + \sum_{interior} l f'_l\right]$$

$$= \frac{\deg c}{2} + v' + 1 - \sum_{interior} \frac{l-2}{2} f'_l$$

One has to carefully include the unbounded face in the counts for n', f' and $2m'$. Solving for $\deg c$ yields the equation (I.12.2). □

Corollary 11. *Suppose the loopless planar graph G has a cycle c. If the length $\deg c$ of the cycle is odd, the number of odd faces lying in the interior domain of cycle c is odd; and similarly, the number of odd faces lying in the exterior domain of cycle c is odd.*

If the length $\deg c$ of the cycle is even, the number of odd faces lying in the interior domain of cycle c is even; and similarly, the number of odd faces lying in the exterior domain of cycle c is even.

Proof. Taking equation (I.12.2) modulo 2, we obtain the equivalence

$$\deg c \equiv \sum_{interior\ and\ l\ odd} f'_l$$

$$\equiv \begin{cases} 0 & \text{if there exists an even number of odd faces in the interior of cycle } c; \\ 1 & \text{if there exists an odd number of odd faces in the interior of cycle } c. \end{cases}$$

The reasoning about the exterior of cycle c is similar. □

Problem 142. *Find out how the corollary 11 has to be modified for a graph with loops.*

Problem 143. *Check that equation (I.12.2) holds, too, for a planar graph with a bridge. Consider as example the triangular cycle from the figure on page 156. This may be hard to believe!*

Answer. For the triangle $\deg c = 3$, there are $v' = 4$ vertices in the interior, and faces of length 4 and 9 in the interior: $f'_4 = f'_9 = 1$. One checks

(I.12.2) $$3 = \deg c = 2 - 2\cdot 4 + (4-2)\cdot 1 + (9-2)\cdot 1 = 2 - 2v' + \sum_{interior}(l-2) f'_l$$

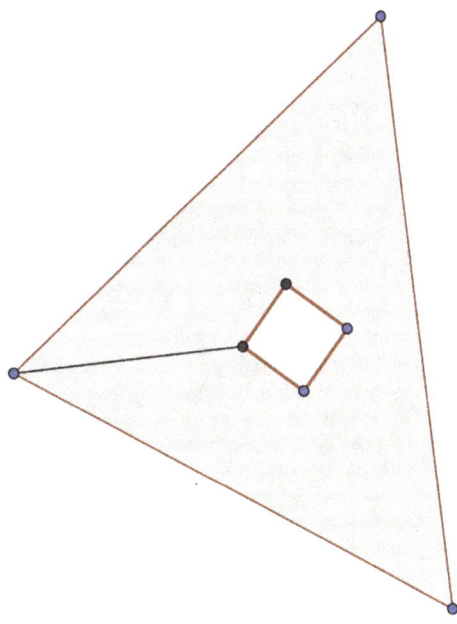

Figure 102: A planar graph with a bridge.

Corollary 12 (Grinberg 1968). *Suppose the loopless graph G is both planar and Hamiltonian. Let f'_l and f''_l count the faces of length l lying in the interior, respectively exterior domain, of the Hamiltonian cycle.*

(I.12.3) $$n - 2 = \sum_{interior} (l-2)f'_l = \sum_{exterior} (l-2)f''_l$$

Independent proof of the Corollary. It is enough to consider the interior domain $\mathcal{D}$ of the Hamiltonian cycle. We proceed by induction on the number m' of edges in $\mathcal{D}$. If there do not exist any such edges, then $f'_n = 1$ and $f'_l = 0$ for all $l < n$. Hence the claim (I.12.3) is true.

For the induction step, suppose claim (I.12.3) holds for all cases with less than m' edges in the interior domain. Consider a graph G with m' interior edges and take any edge e' among them. Since a Hamiltonian graph has no bridges, by the lemma 28 part (b), there are lying two distinct faces R and S on the two sides of edge e'. The graph $H = G \backslash e$ is planar and Hamiltonian. Graph H has still n vertices, and in the interior domain $\mathcal{D}$ lies a face $R \cup S$ of length $\deg(R) + \deg(S) - 2$, which is replacing faces R and S from graph G. Since $(r-2) + (s-2) = (r+s-2) - 2$, the sum on the right side of equation (I.12.3) and equal for the graphs G and H. By induction assumption, this equation holds for graph H and thus holds for graph G, too. □

Remark 31. Indeed, equation (I.12.3) is a generalization of Euler's formula. Summing over the cases for the interior and exterior domains, and using the dual handshake lemma, we get back Euler's formula:

$$2n - 4 = \underbrace{\sum (l-2)f'_l}_{\text{interior}} + \underbrace{\sum (l-2)f''_l}_{\text{exterior}} = \sum (l-2)f_l = 2m - 2f$$

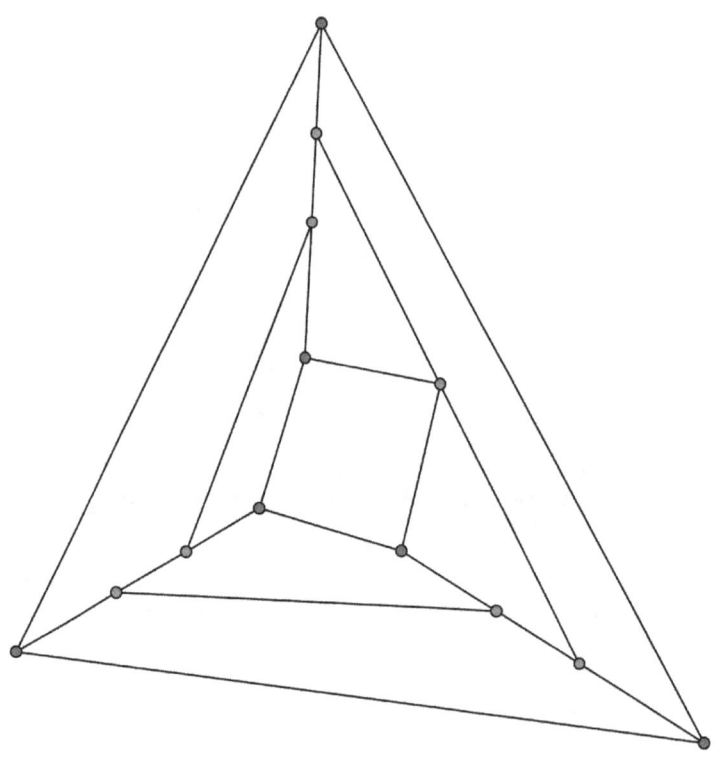

Figure 103: Find dif and only if erent types of Hamiltonian cycles.

Problem 144. *There exist different types of Hamiltonian cycles for the graph shown on page 157.*

(i) *Find the possible values of the vector (f'_3, f'_4, f'_5, f'_6) satisfying equation (I.12.3) and $f'_3 = 0$.*

(ii) *Explain why the solution with $f'_4 = 4$ does not correspond to a Hamiltonian cycle. Find the possible values of the vector (f'_3, f'_4, f'_5, f'_6)*

(iii) *Find Hamiltonian cycles corresponding to the two other solutions.*

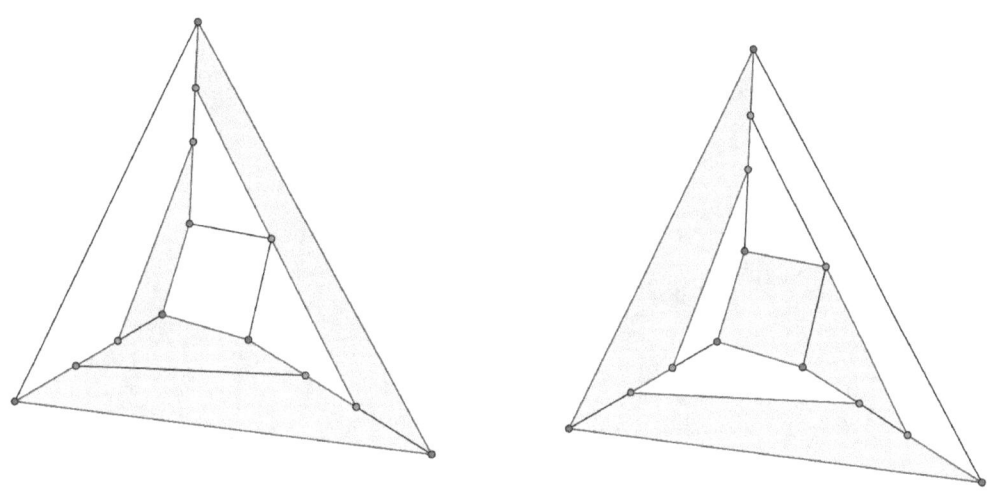

Figure 104: Different types of Hamiltonian cycles.

Answer. **(i)** There are three solutions (f'_3, f'_4, f'_5, f'_6) can be $(0, 2, 1, 1); (0, 4, 1, 0)$ or $(0, 1, 3, 0)$.

(ii) The case with $f'_4 = 4$ would have a vertex totally surrounded by three 4-cycles, which is impossible for a Hamiltonian cycle.

(iii) Example are given in the figure on page 158.

Problem 145. *The Grinberg graph, found ca. 1949, is shown in the figure on page 159. This is an example for three-regular planar graph that is not Hamiltonian.*

(i) *Determine the numbers f_5, f_8, f_9 of faces of the respective length.*

(ii) *Determine the number of vertices, edges and faces. Check the handshake lemma, dual handshake lemma, and check Euler's formula.*

(iii) *Check that equation (I.12.3) with $f'_9 = 0$ can never hold modula 3. Convince yourself that no Hamiltonian cycle exists.*

Answer. **(i)** $f_5 = 21$, $f_8 = 3$, $f_9 = 1$ for the Grinberg graph.

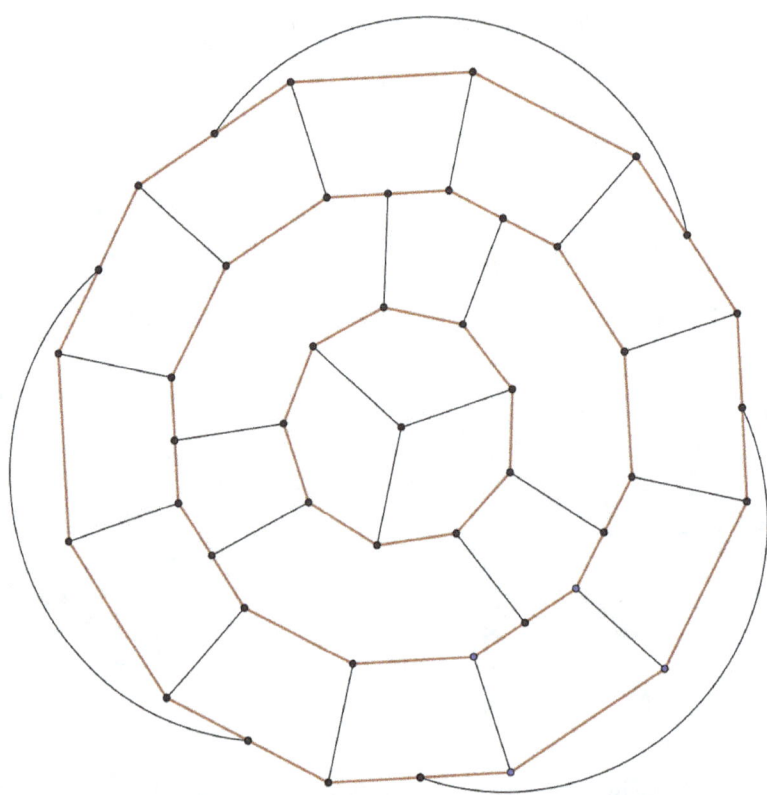

Figure 105: The Grinberg graph is not Hamiltonian.

(ii) Indeed, $2m = 3n = \sum l f_l = 5 \cdot 21 + 8 \cdot 3 + 9 = 138$. Hence $n = 46$, $m = 69$, $f = 25$ for the Grinberg graph. Euler's formula $n + f - m = 46 + 25 - 69 = 2$ holds.

(iii) If an Hamiltonian cycle would exist, equation (I.12.3) would tell

$$44 \stackrel{?}{=} [3 \cdot f'_3 + 6 \cdot f'_8]$$

were we have assumed $f'_9 = 0$, as is possible without loss of generality; by considering either interior or exterior domain of the H-cycle. Such an equation cannot be true since 44 is not divisible by 3. Hence no Hamiltonian cycle exists.

Problem 146. *Find three Hamiltonian cycles for the three copies of the graph in the figure on page 160:*

(a) *a cycle with 1 square and 5 hexagons in its interior domain;*

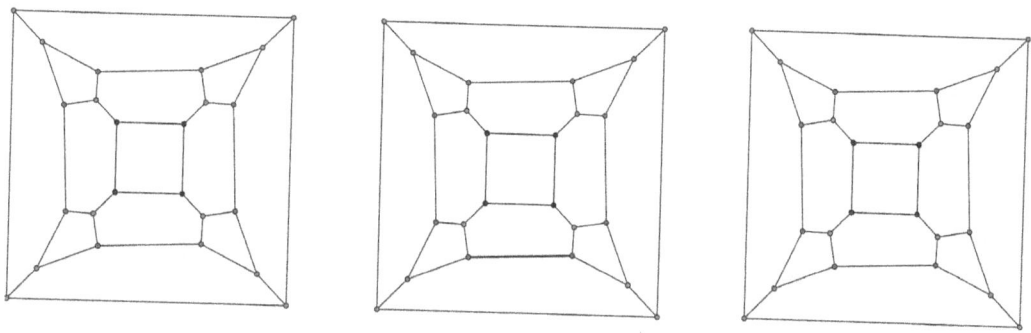

Figure 106: Find different types of Hamiltonian cycles.

(b) *a cycle with 5 squares and 3 hexagons in its interior domain;*

(c) *a cycle with 3 square and 4 hexagons in its interior domain.*

Answer.

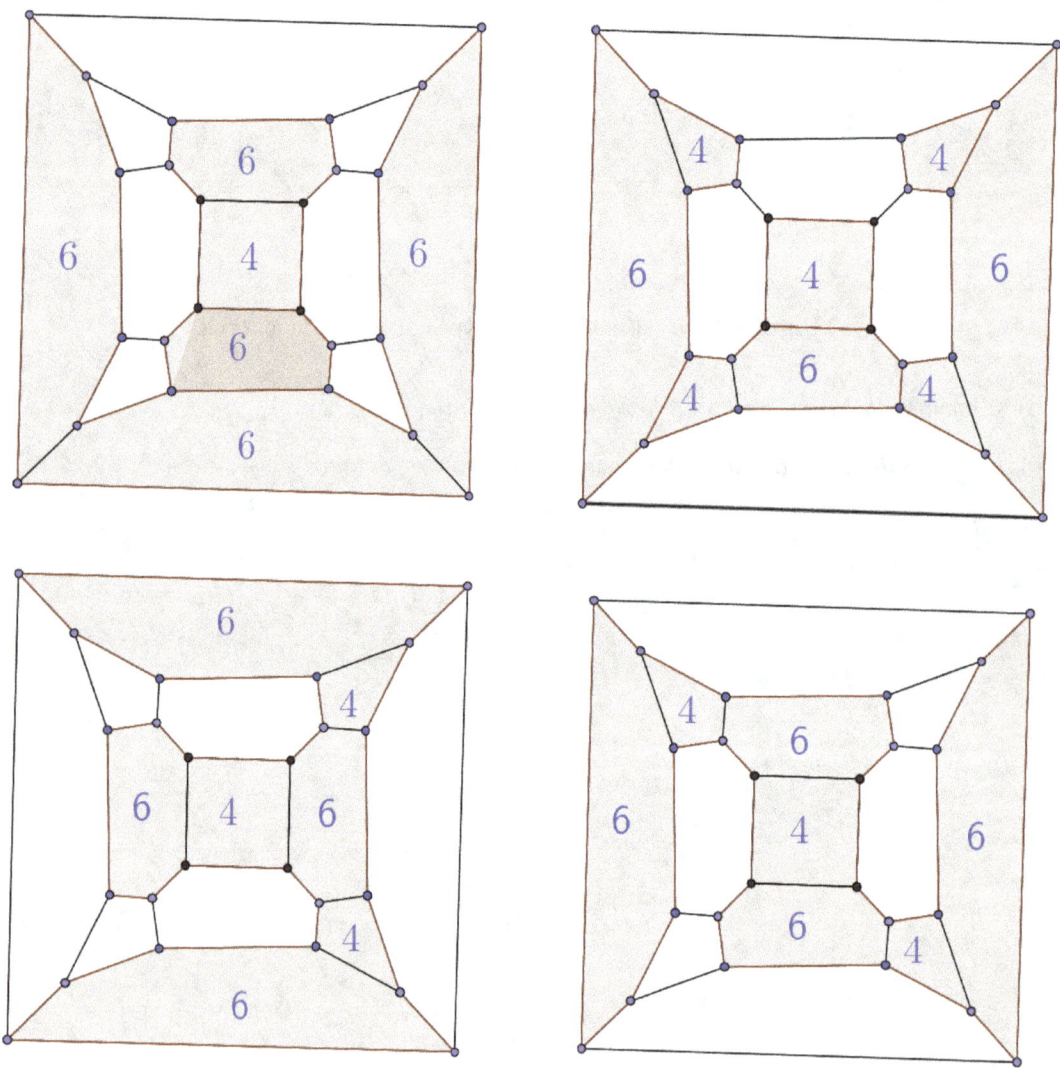

Figure 107: Different types of Hamiltonian cycles.

Algorithm 13 (Cycle game). *Given is a simple connected planar graph. The unbounded face is included in the usual way. Two players alternate their moves. A move occupies one (or several) unoccupied faces, say by writing the number of the move into them, in red for the first player, in blue for the second player. The goal of each player is to gain a connected domain, the boundary of which has length as long as possible.*

In the first and second move, each player just chooses one face. In the further moves, a player chooses to occupy one new face, adjacent to a face he has occupied in the moves before. Several new faces may be occupied only in the case of "serving", explained below.

It is forbidden to occupy an adjacent face in case a cycle of occupied faces would be produced, or especially if a vertex would be included into the interior of one's own domain. ("Cycle in the dual graph is forbidden.")

As first and last action in every move, it is mandatory to "serve" the other player. To "serve" means to occupy a face adjacent to the own already occupied fields, which the other player is prevented from occupying by the "no dual cycle" rule. In this situation, the player is occupying more than one field in a move. If possible, the player has to begin each move by serving, and go on serving. This action terminates his move. If no serving is possible, but a free move produces the possibility to serve, the player has to go on serving during the same move.

The game stops if one player has gained a domain which has a Hamiltonian cycle as boundary, or if one player can no longer move.

The winner is the player which has at that moment the domain with the longer boundary. If the boundary lengths for both players are equal, the player with the second last move is the winner.

Problem 147 (optional). *Determine the winner for the examples of the cycle game shown in the figure on page 163.*

Answer. (**game 1**) With the 11-th move red wins with a Hamiltonian cycle ($C = 24$), while blue has only gained a cycle of length 18.

(**game 2**) After the 8-th move, red can no longer move. Both red and blue have gained a cycle of length 22. Hence red is the winner.

(**game 3**) After the 8-th move, blue wins with a Hamiltonian cycle ($C = 24$), while red has only gained a cycle of length 16.

(**game 4**) After the 8-th move, blue wins with a Hamiltonian cycle ($C = 24$), while red has only gained a cycle of length 18.

Problem 148 (optional). *Play the cycle game for other graphs, for example the Grinberg graph, shown in the figure on page 159.*

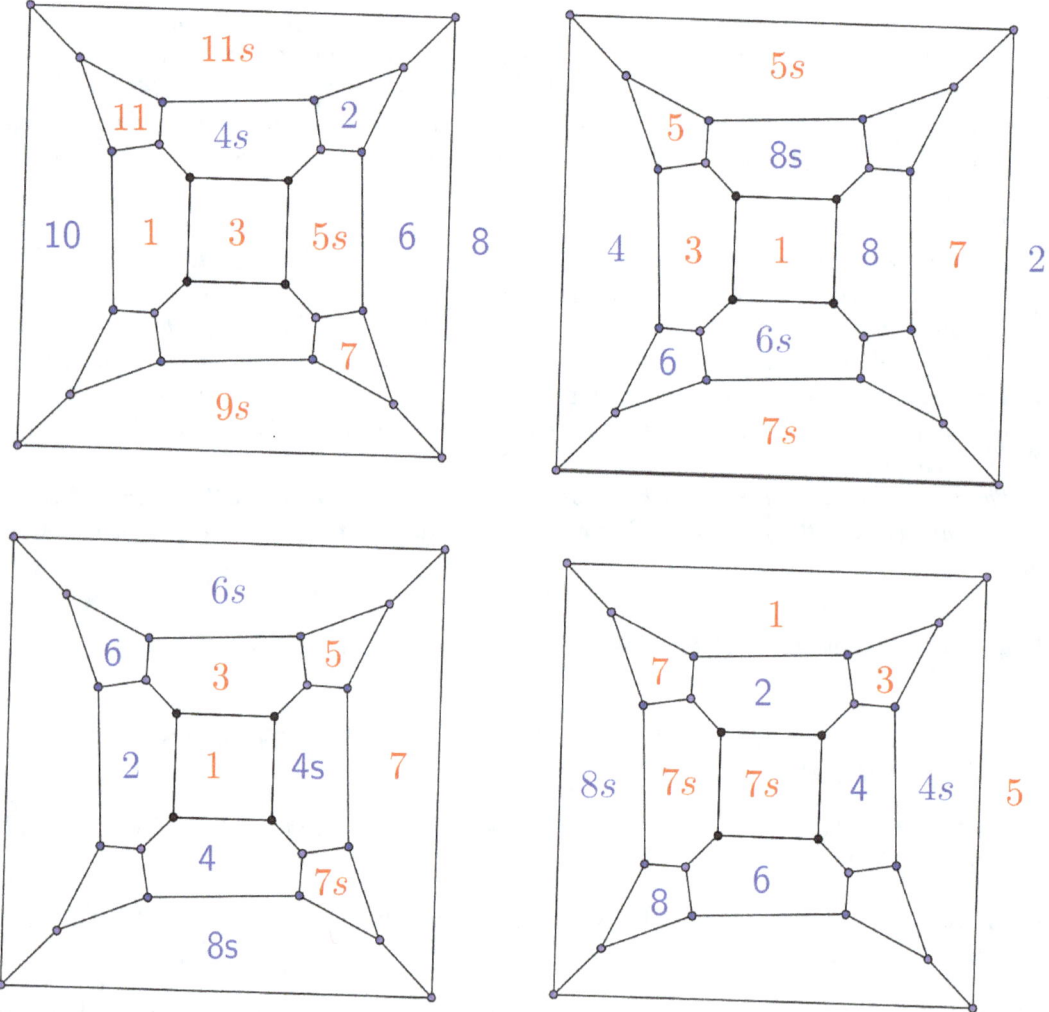

Figure 108: Determine the winners.

Lemma 29. *Let G be any general planar graph.*

(a) *If the general planar graph G is bridgeless, the interior of any face touches any edge only on one side. In other words, there are lying two distinct faces on the two sides of any edge.*

(b) *If the graph G is loopless, and has no cut-vertex, the boundary of any face consists of one or several disjoint cycles.*

(c) *If the graph G is connected, the boundary of any face is a closed trail.*

(d) *If the graph G is connected, loopless, and has no cut-vertex, the boundary of any face is a cycle.*

Proof parts (a) and (b). Part (a) repeats lemma 28 part (b).

To deal with part (b), we assume the graph G is loopless, and has no cut-vertex. A graph without cut-vertex has no bridge neither, and the minimal degree is $\delta \geq 2$. By part (a), there are lying two distinct faces on the two sides of each edge.

Take any face F and edge $e = vw$ on its boundary. Starting from vertices v and w, we follow the boundary ∂F and obtain a cycle contained in ∂F. For a disconnected graph, the boundary ∂F may consist of several such cycles. □

I.12.3 Book-keeping the lengths of faces

Proposition 44. *For a simple planar graph with k components, we assume that a cycle exists, and that all cycles have length at least $l \geq 3$. Then the number of edges and faces are at most*

(I.12.4)
$$m \leq \frac{l}{l-2}(n-k-1)$$
$$f \leq \frac{2}{l-2}(n-k-1)$$

Lemma 30. *Suppose the graph G is simple and planar. Let $l \geq 3$ be the minimal length of cycles, and assume a cycle of length l exists. In any plane representation, all faces contain a cycle as part of their boundary. Especially, all faces have length at least l.*

Proof. We distinguish the following two cases:

(a) For all faces F, at least one edge in its boundary ∂F occurs in some cycle, too.

(b) There exists a face F, and no edge in its boundary ∂F occurs in any cycle.

In case (a), all faces have some edge e of a cycle in their boundary, and hence have length at least l. Indeed, suppose edge $e = vw$ is part of a cycle, and lies in the boundary ∂F, too. The interior of face F cannot touch the edge e on both sides since it is not a bridge. Starting from vertices v and w, we follow the boundary ∂F and obtain a cycle contained in ∂F. Hence the length of the boundary ∂F is at least the length of the shortest cycle.

In case (b), we consider any component of the boundary ∂F of the exceptional face F, and let E be its set of edges. If all end-vertices of edges in E would have degree at least two, the return Lemma would imply existence of a cycle consisting of edges in E. This contradicts the assumption that no edge in boundary ∂F occurs in any cycle. Hence there exists a vertex of degree one, which is adjacent to an edge in E. Hence both sides of this edge are touched by ∂F. Recursively, we confirm that situation to occur for all edges in ∂F.

Moreover, there cannot be any component of the given graph which contains both edges in ∂F, as well as edges not in ∂F. Otherwise there would exist a vertex to which both types of edges are adjacent. One can see that this is impossible.

Hence we conclude that all edges of graph G are touched by the face F on <u>both</u> sides. For each component of boundary ∂F, there exists a closed curve coming very near to all the edges. Hence all edges of graph G are bridges, and the graph is acyclic. Thus case (b) can only occur for an acyclic graph, and is thus excluded by the assumption that a cycle exists made at the very beginning. □

Remark 32. In the common case (a), it can still happen that a cycle exists of length *smaller* than the minimal face length. An example is shown in figure on page 165. For this graph in the given plane representation, the minimal face length is 4, but a triangle exists.

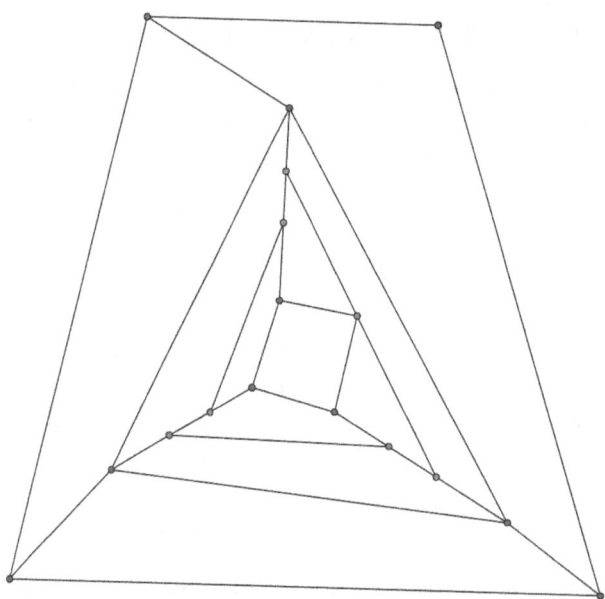

Figure 109: Minimal face length is 4, but a triangle exists nevertheless.

Remark 33. A sufficient assumption for existence of a cycle is that the minimal degree $\delta \geq 2$ is at least two.

Proof proposition 44. Take any planar representation of the given simple graph. Euler's formula implies $f = m - n + 1 + k$, where k is the number of components. Together with the dual handshaking lemma, we eliminate f:

$$l(m - n + 1 + k) = l \cdot f \leq \sum \{\deg(f) \text{ of all faces } f\} = 2m$$

$$(l-2)m \leq l(n-k-1) \quad \text{and hence} \quad m \leq \frac{l}{l-2}(n-k-1)$$

$$f \leq \frac{2m}{l} \leq \frac{2}{l-2}(n-k-1)$$

$\square$

Proposition 45. *Suppose a simple graph has only cycles of length at least $l \geq 3$, has k components, and has $n \geq k + l/2$ vertices. If the graph has a plane representation, then the number of its edges and faces is bounded above by*

(I.12.5)
$$m \leq \frac{l}{l-2}(n-k-1)$$
$$f \leq \frac{2}{l-2}(n-k-1)$$

Proof. In case the graph is acyclic, we know that $m = n - k$. If there exists a cycle, we can use proposition 44. In the (n,m)-plane, the two lines $m = n - k$ and $m = l(n-k-1)/(l-2)$ intersect at coordinates $n = k + l/2, m = l/2$. Indeed the assumption $n \geq k + l/2$ implies $n - k \leq l(n-k-1)/(l-2)$. Thus the claimed estimate for m holds, no matter whether the graph is acyclic, or a cycle exists. $\square$

Problem 149. *Use the estimate (I.12.5) to show that graph 2 from the figure on page 178 is non-planar, and one needs to delete at least two edges to obtain a planar subgraph.*

Definition 50 (triangulation). A planar simple graph is a called a *triangulation* if all its faces are triangles. It is called an *almost triangulation* if all its faces except the unbounded one are triangles.

Proposition 46. *Among simple planar graphs with $n \geq 3$ vertices the following three statements are equivalent:*

(i) *the graph is a triangulation;*

(ii) *the number of its edges is $m = 3n - 6$;*

(iii) *the number of edges is maximal among the simple planar graphs with the given vertices.*

Proposition 47. *For a simple, connected planar graph that is 3-regular, the number $f_3, f_4, f_5, f_6, f_7, f_8, \ldots$ of faces of length $3, 4, 5, 6, 7, 8 \ldots$ satisfy*

$$3f_3 + 2f_4 + f_5 = 12 + f_7 + 2f_8 + \ldots$$

Proof. As stated in Theorem 15, we get the three relations

(I.12.6) $$3n = 2m \qquad \text{(handshaking lemma)}$$
(I.12.7) $$3f_3 + 4f_4 + 5f_5 + 6f_6 + 7f_7 + 8f_8 + \ldots = 2m \qquad \text{(dual handshaking lemma)}$$
(I.12.8) $$f_3 + f_4 + f_5 + f_6 + f_7 + f_8 + \ldots = 2 + m - n \qquad \text{(Euler's formula)}$$

We multiply the third equation by 6 and subtract the second equation. In this way the number of edges m is eliminated and we obtain

$$3f_3 + 2f_4 + f_5 - f_7 - 2f_8 - \cdots = 12 + 6m - 6n - 2m = 12$$

as to be shown. $\square$

If we need only an inequality, we can relax the assumptions in Proposition 47.

Proposition 48. *Given a simple planar graph with minimal degree three. The number $f_3, f_4, f_5, f_6, f_7, f_8, \ldots$ of faces of length $3, 4, 5, 6, 7, 8 \ldots$ satisfy*

$$3f_3 + 2f_4 + f_5 \geq 12 + f_7 + 2f_8 + \ldots$$

Equality holds if and only if the graph is connected and three-regular. There always exists a face with length at most five.

Proof. Under the weaker assumptions, we obtain only inequalities:

$$3n \leq \sum \deg(v) = 2m \text{ (handshaking lemma)}$$
$$3f_3 + 4f_4 + 5f_5 + 6f_6 + 7f_7 + 8f_8 + \ldots = 2m \qquad \text{(dual handshaking lemma)}$$
$$f_3 + f_4 + f_5 + f_6 + f_7 + f_8 + \ldots = 1 + k + m - n \qquad \text{(Euler's formula)}$$

We multiply the third inequality by 6 and subtract the second equation to conclude

$$3f_3 + 2f_4 + f_5 - f_7 - 2f_8 - \cdots = 6(1 + k) + 6m - 6n - 2m \geq 12 + 4m - 6n \geq 12$$

as to be shown. $\square$

In the case of 4-regular and 5-regular graphs, we get the corresponding propositions:

Definition 51 (polyhedral graph). We call a simple graph *polyhedral* iff it is both planar and $\kappa \geq 3$, in other words 3-vertex connected. (see definition 46)

Problem 150. *Use Proposition 47 to show that a three-regular polyhedral graph all faces of which have either $4, 6$ or 8 sides has six more squares than octagons.*

Answer. We get immediately $2f_4 = 12 + 2f_8$.

Proposition 49. *Given a simple planar and bipartite graph with minimal degree three. The number $f_4, f_6, f_8, \ldots$ of faces of length $4, 6, 8 \ldots$ satisfy*

$$f_4 \geq 6 + f_8 + 2f_{10} + 3f_{12} + \ldots$$

Equality holds if and only if the graph is connected and three-regular. There always exist at least six faces with length four.

Proposition 50. *For a simple, connected planar graph that is r-regular, the number f_l of faces of length l satisfy*

$$\sum_{l \geq 3} [4 - (r-2)(l-2)] f_l = 4r$$

Actually, there are only the three cases $r = 3, 4, 5$:

$$\begin{aligned}
\text{3-regular graph}: & \quad 3f_3 + 2f_4 + f_5 = 12 + f_7 + 2f_8 + \ldots \\
\text{4-regular graph}: & \quad f_3 = 8 + f_5 + 2f_6 + 3f_7 + \ldots \\
\text{5-regular graph}: & \quad f_3 = 20 + 2f_4 + 5f_5 + 8f_6 + \ldots
\end{aligned}$$

Especially, we conclude that a 4-regular planar simple graph contains at least 8 triangular faces, and a 5-regular planar simple graph contains at least 20 triangular faces.

The case of a 4-regular graph. We get $4n = 2m$ from the handshaking lemma, and furthermore

$$3f_3 + 4f_4 + 5f_5 + 6f_6 + 7f_7 + 8f_8 + \ldots = 2m \qquad \text{(dual handshaking lemma)}$$

$$f_3 + f_4 + f_5 + f_6 + f_7 + f_8 + \ldots = 2 + m - n = 2 + \frac{m}{2} \qquad \text{(Euler's formula)}$$

We multiply the second equation by 4 and subtract the first equation. In this way the number of edges m is eliminated and we obtain

$$f_3 - f_5 - 2f_6 - 3f_7 - \cdots = 8$$

as to be shown. □

The case $r = 5$. The handshaking lemma yields $5n = 2m$. The dual handshaking lemma and Euler's formula yield:

(I) $\qquad 3f_3 + 4f_4 + 5f_5 + 6f_6 + 7f_7 + 8f_8 + \ldots = 2m$

(II) $\qquad f_3 + f_4 + f_5 + f_6 + f_7 + f_8 + \ldots = 2 + m - n = 2 + \dfrac{3m}{5}$

The linear combination $10 \cdot \text{(II)} - 3 \cdot \text{(I)}$ of these two equations does not contains m. Thus we have eliminated the number m of edges and obtain

$$f_3 - 2f_4 - 5f_5 - 8f_7 - 11f_8 - \cdots = 20$$

as to be shown. □

Remark 34. For any planar graph and natural numbers $l = 1, 2, 3, \ldots$, we define f_l to be the number of faces of length l. For any graph, it may be planar or not, we define c_l to be the number of cycles of length l.

Even for a planar graph, it may occur that $c_l \neq f_l$. For a polyhedral graph at least, we know that every face is a cycle, and hence $f_l \leq c_l$ for all l. But even for polyhedra, not every cycle needs to be a face. Hence it can happen that $c_l > f_l$.

Problem 151. *Use the proposition I.12.4 to show directly that the complete graph K_5 is not planar.*

Answer. In the case of the complete graph K_5, we have $n = 5$ vertices and $l = 3$ as minimal length of any cycle. Hence $\frac{l}{l-2}(n-2) = 9$. This is less than the number of edges $m = 10$. Thus the estimate in proposition I.12.4 is not true and hence the graph is not planar.

Problem 152. *Use the proposition I.12.4 to show directly that the complete bipartite $K_{3,3}$ is not planar.*

Answer. The complete bipartite graph $K_{3,3}$, has $n = 6$ vertices and $l = 4$ as minimal length of any cycle, since and cycles have even length.

Hence $\frac{l}{l-2}(n-2) = 8$. This is less than the number of edges $m = 9$. Thus the estimate in proposition I.12.4 is not true and hence the graph is not planar.

Problem 153. *Use the proposition I.12.4 to show directly that the Petersen graph is not planar.*

Answer. The Petersen graph has $n = 10$ vertices and $l = 5$ as minimal length of any cycle.

Hence $\frac{l}{l-2}(n-2) = \frac{40}{3}$. This is less than the number of edges $m = 15$. Thus the estimate in proposition I.12.4 is not true and hence the graph is not planar.

Proposition 51. *For a graph which is planar on a surface of genus g, has k components and is not acyclic,* [9] *and all cycles of which have length at least l, the number of edges and faces are at most*

$$m \leq \frac{l}{l-2}(n - 1 - k + 2g)$$
$$f \leq \frac{2}{l-2}(n - 1 - k + 2g)$$

Problem 154. *Use proposition 51 to get a lower bound for the genus of the Georges graph depicted in the figure on page 213, and the second Ellingham-Horton graph depicted in the figure on page 210.*

---

[9] a sufficient assumption is minimal degree $\delta \geq 2$ at least two

I.12.4   Other planarity considerations

In Proposition I.12.4, we have obtained the upper bound (I.12.5) for the number of edges of a planar graph. If this bound is violated, we conclude that the graph is not planar. (To be exact, we need to assume $m > \frac{l}{l-2}(n-2)$, and additionally that $m \geq n$ such that a cycle exists, and let l be the length of the minimal cycle.) On the other hand, there exists both planar and non-planar graphs with $m \leq \frac{l}{l-2}(n-2)$.

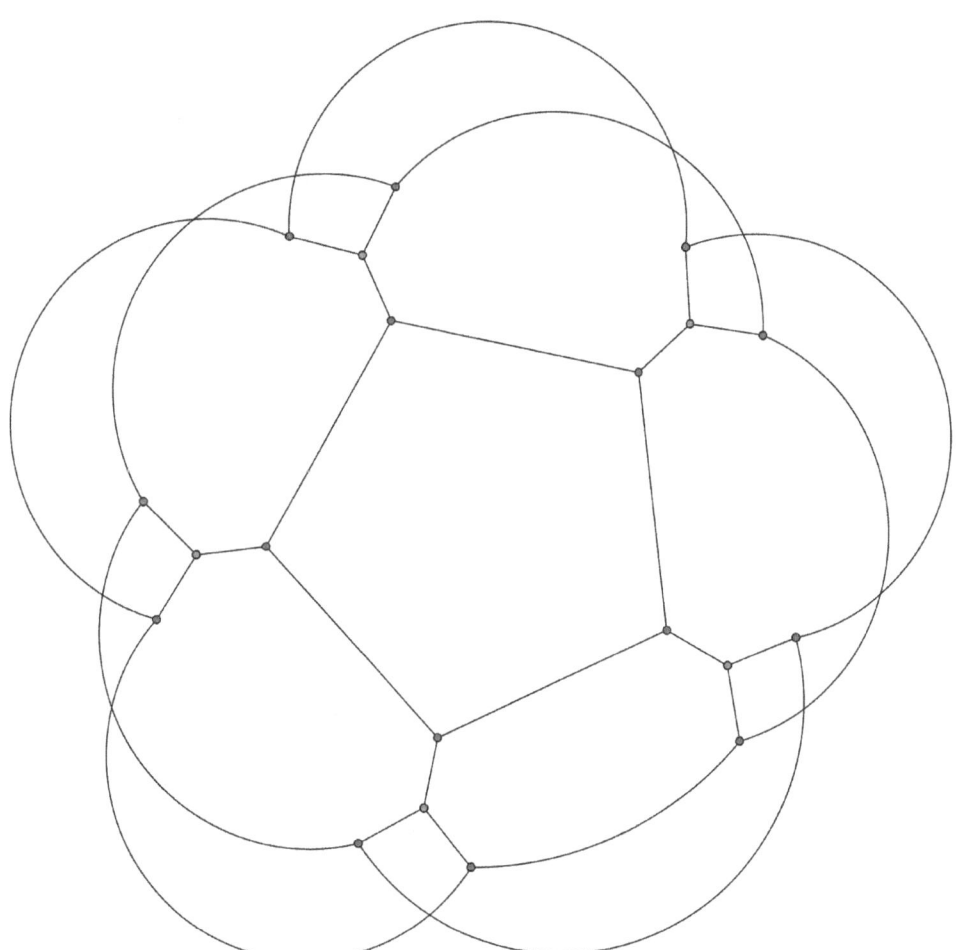

Figure 110:   A 5-cycle flower snark.

Problem 155. *In the figure on page 217, a 5-flower snark has been drawn. What are n, m and l for this graph. Does the upper bound (I.12.5) hold?*

Answer. $n = 20, m = 30$ and $l = 5$ are the numbers of vertices, edges, and the least cycle length, respectively. Hence $m = \frac{l(n-2)}{l-2}$ and the relation (I.12.5) holds as an equality. Based on this information, it is not possible to decide whether graph is planar or not.

Definition 52 (Subdivision). A *subdivision* of a graph G is a graph H which is obtained by putting one or more extra vertices onto the edges of the original graph G.

Definition 53. We say that graph G *contains a subdivision* of graph H; and write $G \triangleright H$ or $H \triangleleft G$; iff some subdivision of graph H is a subgraph of G.

Problem 156. *Show that the flower snark in the figure on page 217 contains (as a subgraph) a subdivision of the Petersen graph. Conclude that the flower snark is not planar.*

Answer. There is a 5-cycle connecting one of the three ends of each one of the five Y-subgraphs $K_{1,3}$. The other two end vertices are connected by a 10-cycle. We get a period doubling similarly as for a twisted Möbius band. We cut an edge at every second vertex of the 10-cycle and obtain a subdivided 5-cycle. Leaving as is the other edges and the five cycle, one gets a subdivision of the Petersen graph. Since the Petersen graph is not planar, we conclude that the snark is not planar neither.

Note that this reasoning does not work for the pseudo-flower-snark.

Problem 157. *Show that the Petersen graph contains $K_{3,3}$ as a subdivision. Since $K_{3,3}$ is not planar, we conclude that the Petersen is not planar.*

Answer. In the figure on page 173, the two groups of vertices of $K_{3,3}$ are denoted by a, b, c and x, y, z. We see that only two edges of Petersen graph have been deleted to obtain the subdivision of $K_{3,3}$.

Remark 35. For this subgraph S we get

$$13 = m < \frac{l(n-2)}{l-2} = \frac{5 \cdot 8}{3}$$

Once more, we see that the bound (I.12.5) holds, but the graph is not planar.

Problem 158. *Check that that the subgraph obtained from the Petersen graph by deletion of two stems is planar.*

I.12.5 Planarity Testing

Definition 54 (H-fragment, vertex of attachment). Let G be a connected, simple graph and $H \subset G$ be any subgraph. A *H-fragment* is

- either an edge of $G \setminus H$ with both end-vertices in the subgraph H;
- or a component of $G \setminus V(H)$, including any edges of $G \setminus E(H)$ together with their respective end-vertex in $V(H)$.

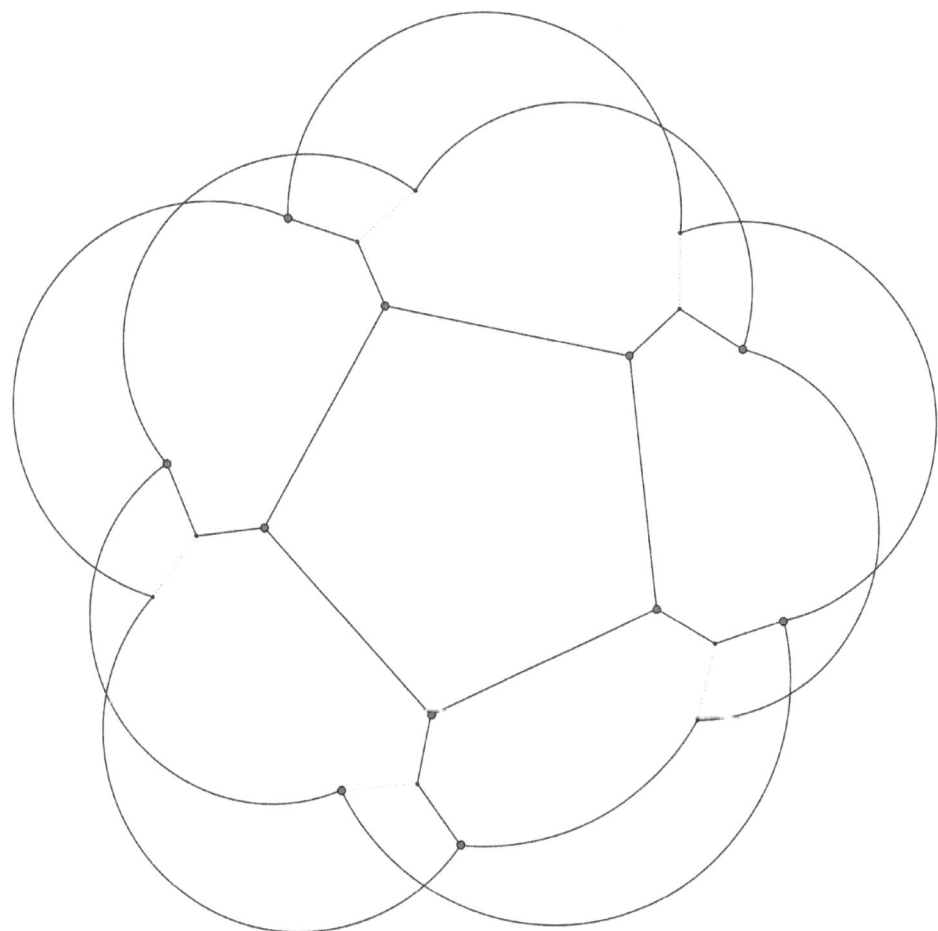

Figure 111: The five-fold flower snark contains a subdivision of the Petersen graph.

Let B be any H-fragment. The vertices of B lying in $V(H)$ are called *vertices of attachment*. Each fragment B has an *attachment set* $V(B) \cap V(H)$. It has to be tested into which faces the attachment set fits. For each fragment B, let $F(B)$ denote the set of faces F for which $V(B) \cap V(H) \subseteq \partial F$.

An example is given in the figure on page 174. Let H be the green 12-cycle. We get four fragments:

- the red edge eg, which has the vertices of attachment e and g;
- the purple arc with one "dangling" edge and the vertices of attachment e and h;

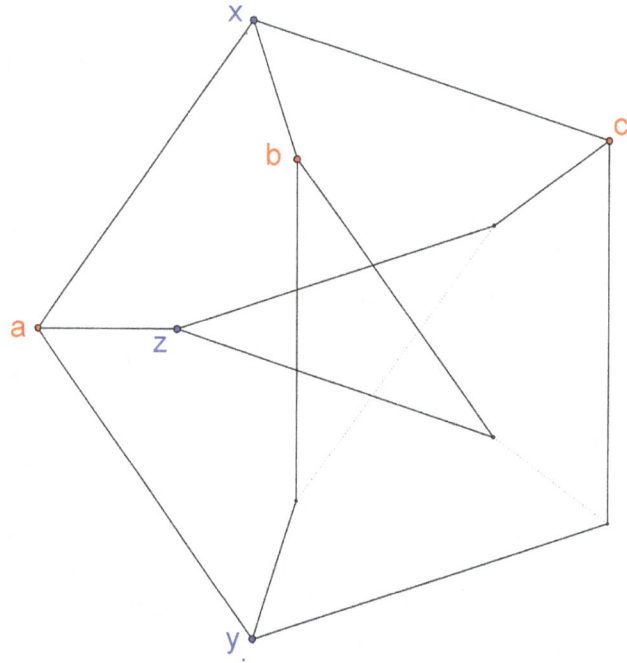

Figure 112: The Petersen graph contains a subdivision of $K_{3,3}$.

- the blue component, which has the vertices of attachment c and f;
- the black component, which has the vertices of attachment a, b and d.

Algorithm 14 (Easy planarity testing). *Given is a simple connected graph G. We may assume that no cut-vertex exists (The graph is a block). One grows a sequence $H_0, H_1, \ldots$ of nested subgraphs until either a plane representation of the entire graph G has been obtained, or it has been confirmed that the graph G is nonplanar.*

start: Let H_0 be any cycle in G, drawn as a planar representation. If G is acyclic, we know it is planar, and stop here.

step: while $H_j \neq G$: Determine the H_j fragments and their respective sets of vertices of attachment $V_1 \ldots V_s$.

For all attachment sets $V_1 \ldots V_s$, we whether there exists <u>at least</u> one face on the boundary of which the respective attachment set V_k lies.

- In case of answer no: $\exists H_j$-fragment B $F(B) = \emptyset$. The graph has been confirmed to be non-planar. We stop here.

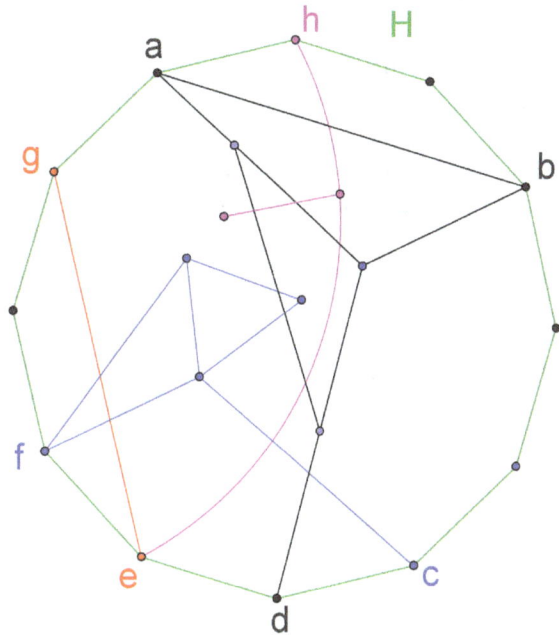

Figure 113: The cycle produces four fragments.

- *In case of answer yes, go on as follows:*

Check whether for some attachment set V_k, there exists a <u>unique</u> face F on the boundary of which the attachment lies. If yes, a forced move exists, <u>otherwise</u> no forced move exists.

a forced move exists *Written in symbolic logic:*
$\forall H_j$-*fragment* B $|F(B)| > 1 \land \exists H_j$-*fragment* B $|F(B)| = 1$. *Select in the corresponding fragment a path* P *between any two vertices of attachment* [10] *in* V_k. *Draw the path in the interior of the unique face* F. *Thus we obtain the larger subgraph* $H_{j+1} = H_j \cup P$.

no forced move exists *Written in symbolic logic:*
$\forall H_j$-*fragment* B $|F(B)| > 1$. *Choose any fragment, and any path* P *between any two of its vertices of attachment. Draw the path in the interior of any appropriate face. Thus we obtain the larger subgraph* $H_{j+1} = H_j \cup P$.

If $H_{j+1} = G$, *one has obtained a planar representation and the algorithm stops. Otherwise, the step is repeated.*

---

[10] If the graph is not a block, it will happen that some fragments have only one vertex of attachment. We may test planarity of such a fragment B separately, and continue the algorithm with the graph $G := G - E(B)$ and subgraph $H_j := H_j - E(B)$.

coda: *Even for the case the graph has already been confirmed to be non-planar, we may go on attaching as many pieces as possible. Thus it is possible to obtain a maximal planar subgraph H_s with all vertices of block G, and only a minimal number of edges are missing. (This is a good help for understanding one's result.)*

Remark 36. In the initial step H_0 is a cycle, which bounds just two faces. Hence a forced move cannot occur. One puts the first attachment inside or outside the cycle, as is more convenient.

Remark 37. In the case that the graph G has a cut-vertex, there exist some fragment with only a single vertex of attachment. Still one may go on attaching fragments.

Problem 159. *Use the algorithm for easy planarity testing to obtain a plane representation of the graph on the left side of the figure on page 175; or confirm the graph is not planar. Begin with the cycle $A, B, \ldots, H, I$. But after that you many different ways to go on. Mark the edges obtain in each step by numbers $1, 2, 3, 4, \ldots$. Thus all edges added in one step of the algorithm get the same number.*

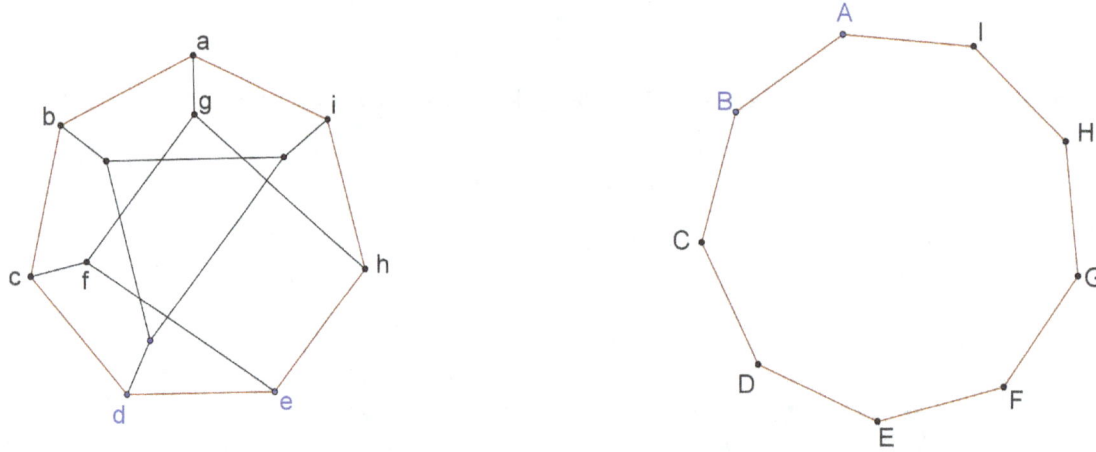

Figure 114: Example for the easy planarity testing.

Answer.

Problem 160. *Use the algorithm for easy planarity testing to obtain a plane representation of the graph on the left side of the figure on page 176; or confirm the graph is not planar. Begin with the cycle J, K, M, N, R, S. For the further steps you have many different ways to proceed. Mark the edges obtain in each step by numbers $1, 2, 3, 4, \ldots$. Thus all edges added in one step of the algorithm get the same number.*

Answer.

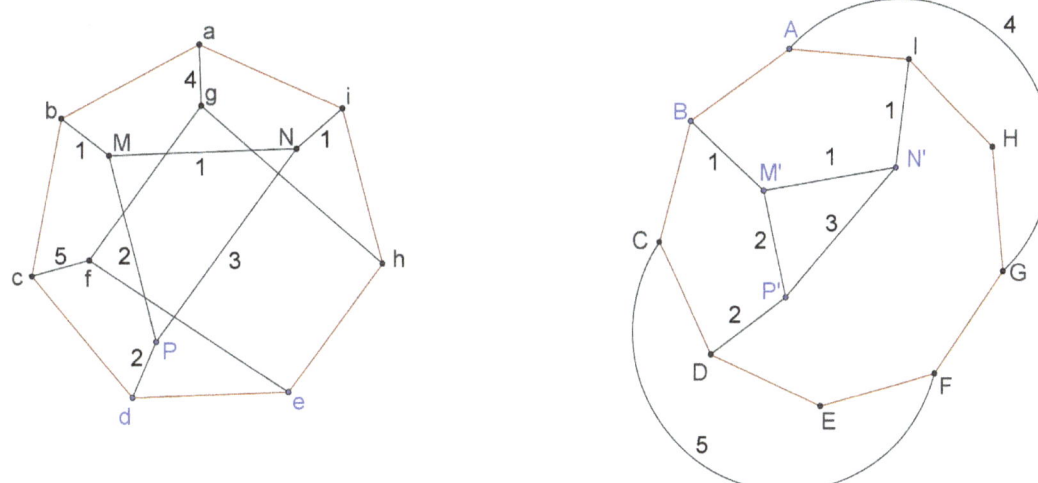

Figure 115: Example for the easy planarity testing.

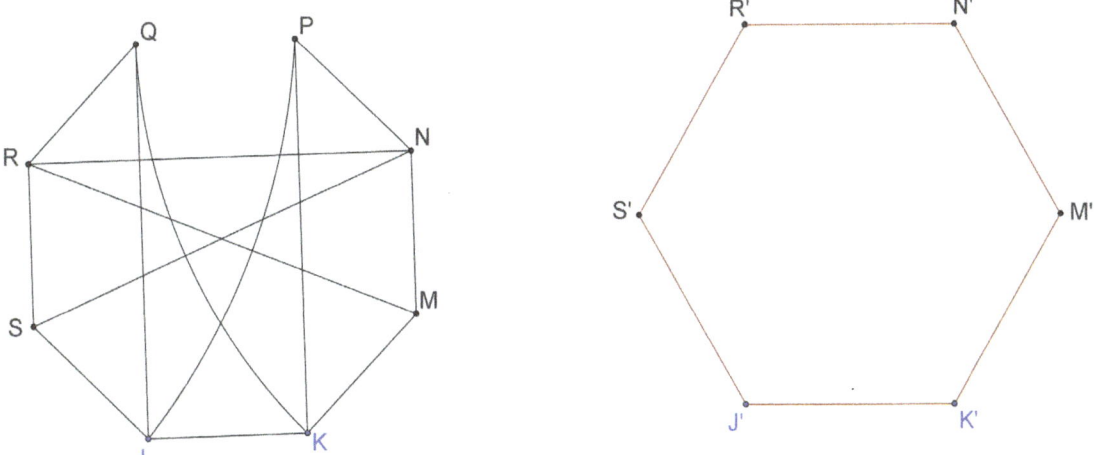

Figure 116: Another example for the easy planarity testing.

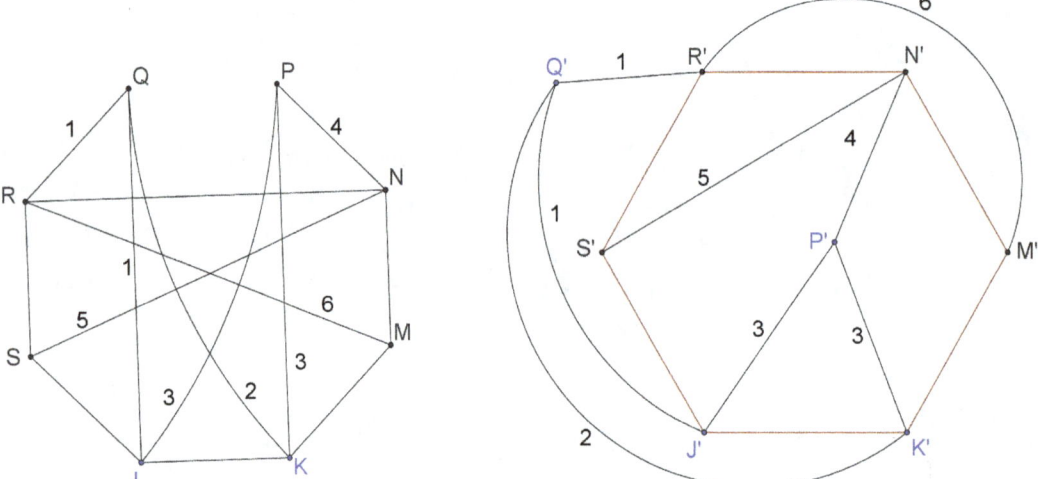

Figure 117: Another example for the easy planarity testing.

I.12.6 Some mixed Problems

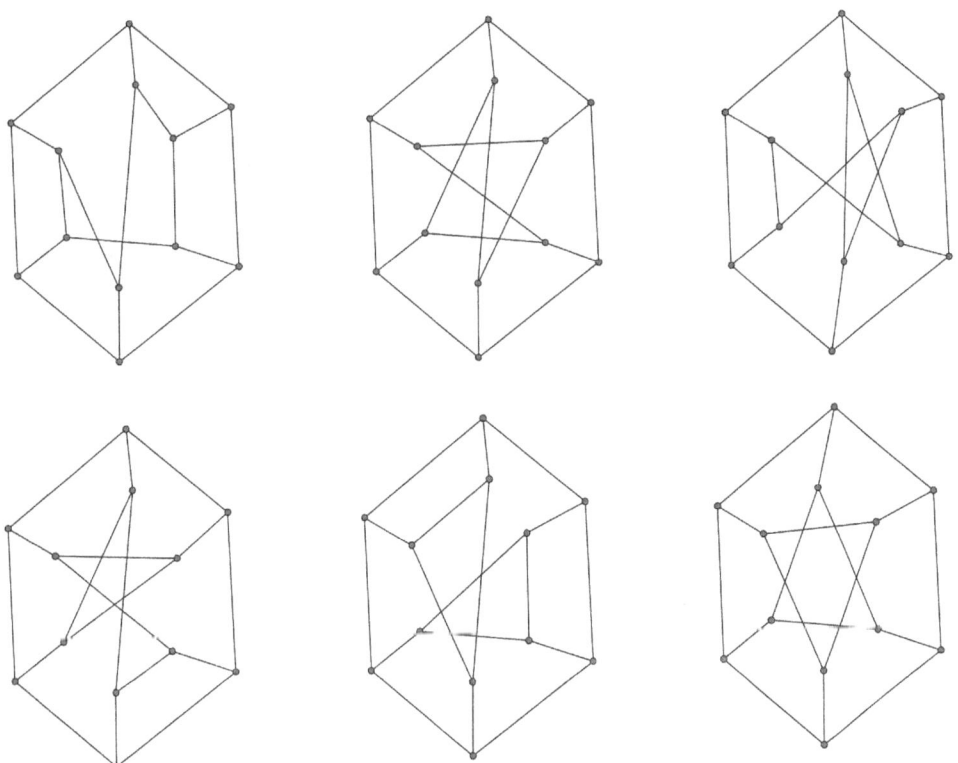

Figure 118: Six 3-regular graphs with $n = 12$ vertices.

Problem 161. *In the figure on page 178 are shown six 3-regular graphs with 12 vertices. We number them following the rows, as graph 1 through 3, and graph 4 to 6. Check whether they are all 3-connected. Decide, in any convenient order, the following questions.*

(i) *Which ones are planar, which are not.*

(ii) *For the non-planar examples, find a minimum set of edges, deletion of which leave a planar graph.*

(iii) *Decide which ones are Hamiltonian. Determine a cycle of maximum length C.*

(iv) *Either three-color the edges properly, or prove that this is impossible.*

Remark 38. The planarity test shows that graphs 1, 2, 3, 4 are nonplanar. For each one, at least two edges need to be deleted to get a planar subgraph. One sees rather easily that graphs 5 and 6 are planar.

For graph 2, the minimal cycle length is $l = 5$. Hence one can use the estimate (I.12.5) to show that graph 2 non-planar, and one needs to delete <u>at least</u> two edges to obtain a planar subgraph.

I found it easy to directly obtain a Hamiltonian cycle for graphs 1 and 2. In the other cases, I obtained at first a 3-coloring of the edges, and next an Hamiltonian cycle from two colors.

Problem 162. *Find five (possibly all) non-isomorphic connected simple graphs with $n = 12$ vertices, which are 3-regular and bipartite. Convince yourself that they are Hamiltonian.*

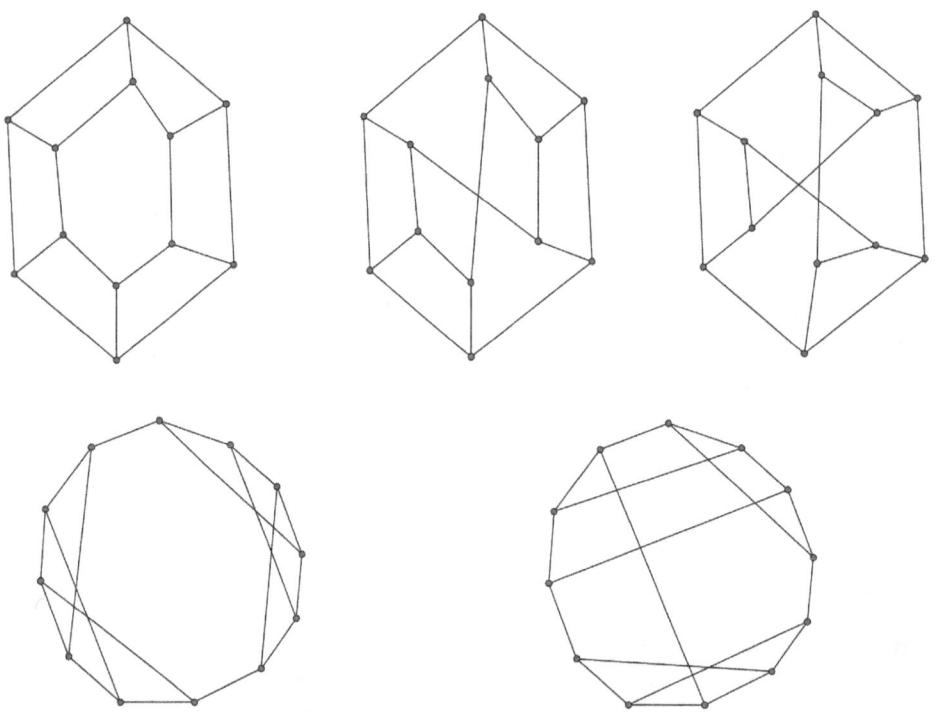

Figure 119: Five 3-regular bipartite graphs with $n = 12$ vertices.

Answer.

Problem 163. *During my attempt to find all non-isomorphic simple connected graphs with $n = 12$ vertices, which are 3-regular and bipartite, I have obtained the graphs G1 through G8*

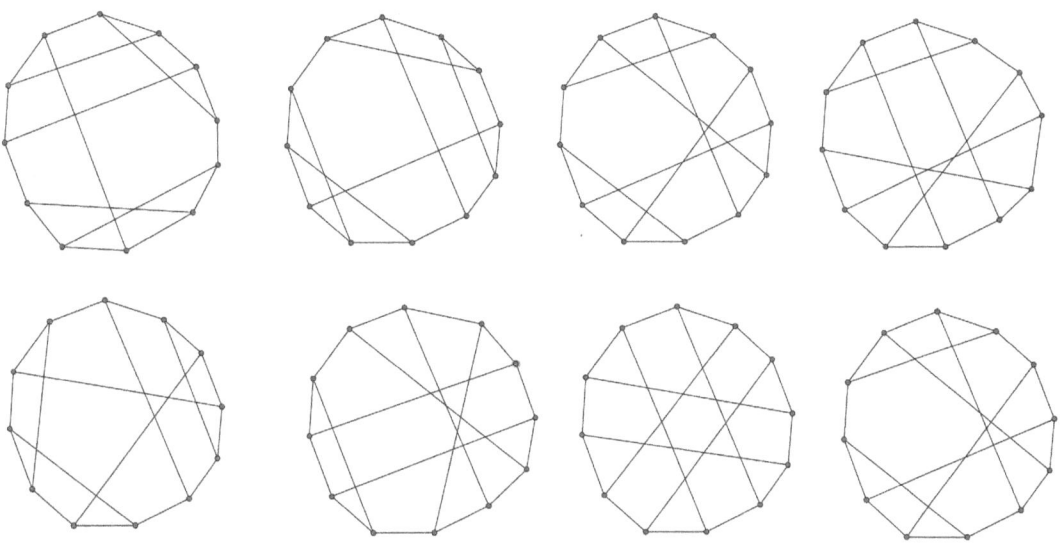

Figure 120: How many of these graphs are non-isomorphic?

shown in the figure on page 180. Find out how many are non-isomorphic. Number the vertices of graphs isomorphic to each other to show an isomorphism.

Answer. As a first step, I count the number c_4 of 4-cycles for each graph. Then I look for pairs of 4-cycles with a common edge. Finally, I check for which graphs there exist two vertex-disjoint 6-cycles. These steps help to find isomorphisms:

$$G1 \sim G2,\ G3 \sim G4,\ G3 \sim G5,$$
$$G4 \sim G6,\ G8 = G3$$

A set of all non-isomorphic examples is $G1, G3, G7$.

Problem 164. *Find all isomorphic pairs in the figure on page 182. Number the vertices of graphs isomorphic to each other to show an isomorphism. In problem 162, did we find all non-isomorphic connected simple graphs with $n = 12$ vertices, which are 3-regular and bipartite?*

Answer. As a first step, I count the number c_4 of 4-cycles for each graph. Then I look for pairs of 4-cycles with a common edge. Finally, I check for which graphs there exist two vertex-disjoint 6-cycles. These steps help to find isomorphisms:

$$G1 \sim G4,\ G3 \sim G6,\ G3 \sim G5,$$
$$G7 \sim G8,\ G5 \sim G10$$

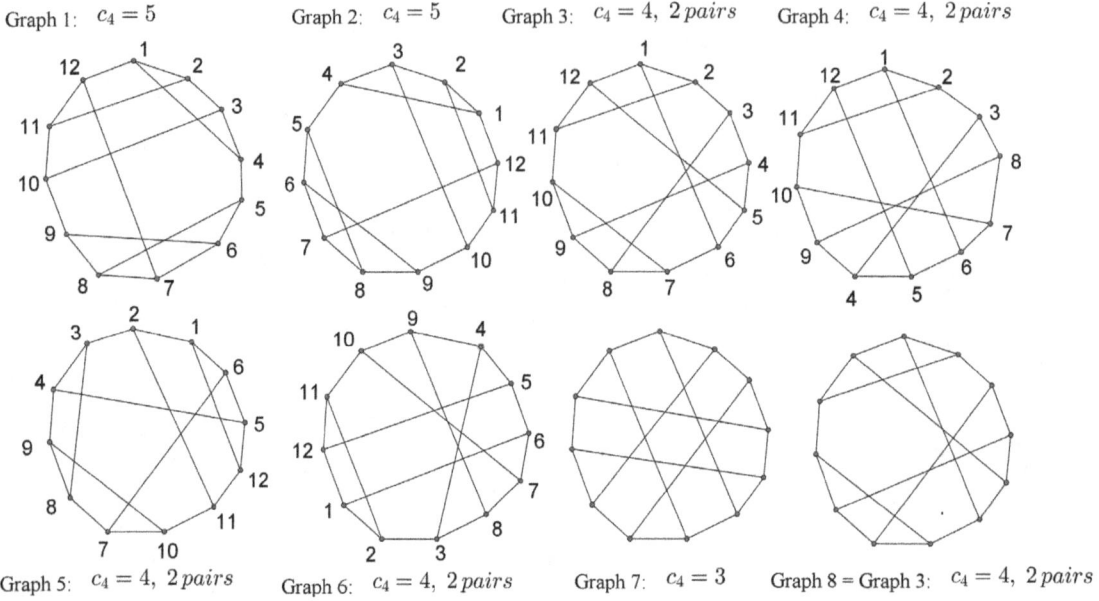

Figure 121: G1, G3, G7 are non-isomorphic.

A set of all non-isomorphic examples is $G1, G2, G3, G5, G8, G9$. In problem 162, we did not find all non-isomorphic connected simple graphs with $n = 12$ vertices, which are 3-regular and bipartite.

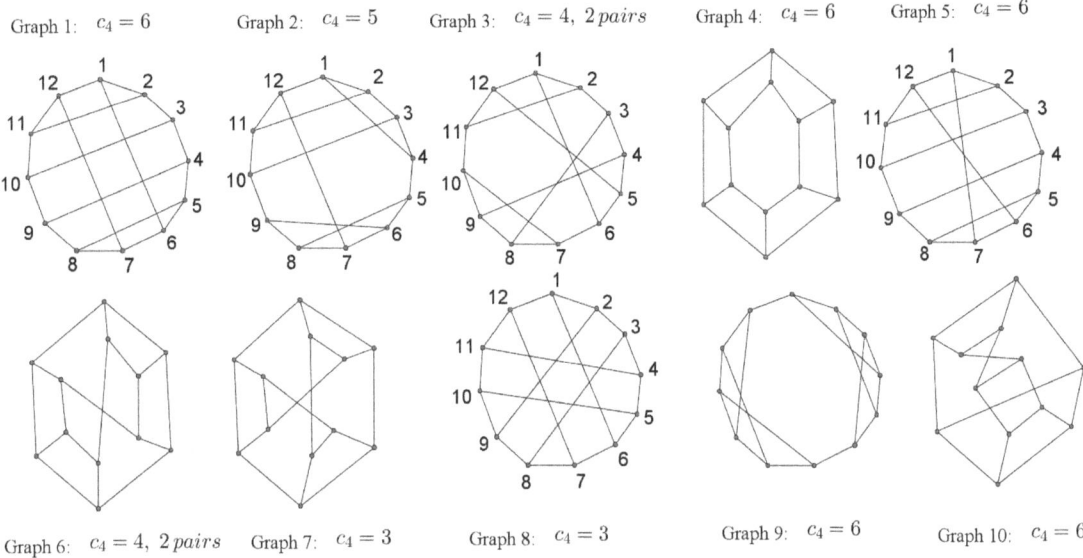

Figure 122: We try to find even more non-isomorphic examples.

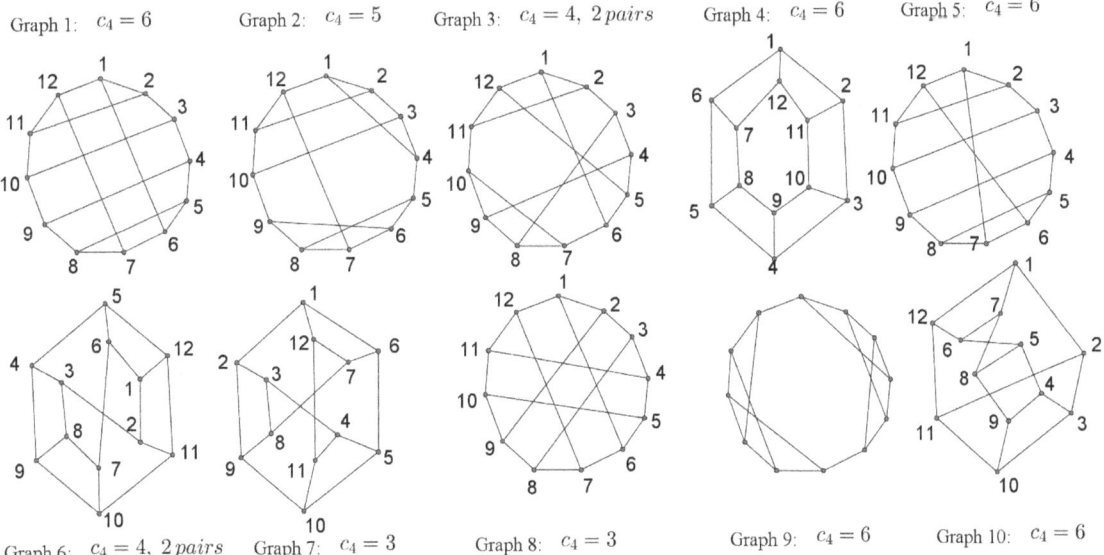

Figure 123: We have six non-isomorphic examples.

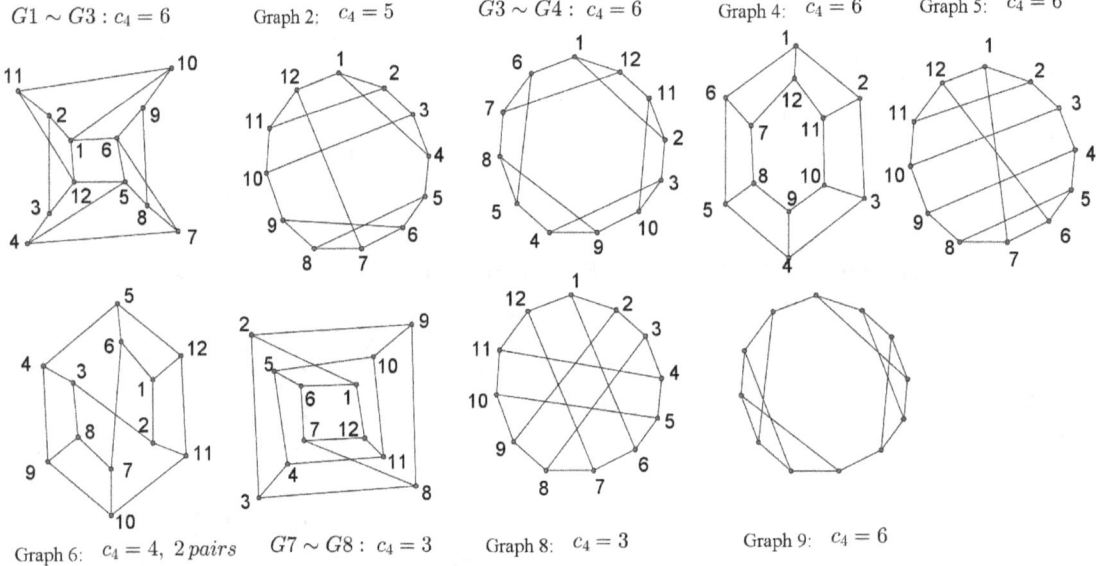

Figure 124: More surprising isomorphic drawings.

I.13 Coloring

I.13.1 Vertex coloring

Proposition 52 (An upper bound of the chromatic number obtained from the degree sequence). *The chromatic number χ of any simple graph with degree sequence $d_1 \geq d_2 \geq \cdots \geq d_n$ is at most*

(I.13.1) $$\chi \leq 1 + \max\{\min(d_i, i-1) : i = 1\ldots n\}$$

Problem 165. *Take as examples the degree sequences*

(a) $5, 4, 3, 3, 2, 1$

(b) $4, 4, 4, 3, 3$

(c) $4, 4, 4, 4, 4$

(d) $4, 3, 2, 2, 1$

(e) $5, 5, 4, 3, 3, 2$—*which is planar.*

(f) $5, 4, 4, 4, 4, 4, 3, 3, 3, 3, 3$—*same as Groetzsch.*

For each of these examples,

(i) *Calculate the right-hand side of formula (I.13.3).*

(ii) *Use the reduction algorithm to construct a graph with that sequence.*

(iii) *Find a minimal coloring.*

What kind of conjecture could you suggest?

Remark 39. Take for example the degree sequence (a): $5, 4, 3, 3, 2, 1$. The right hand side of the bound (I.13.3) is

$$1 + \max\min \begin{bmatrix} 5 & 4 & 3 & 3 & 2 & 1 \\ 0 & 1 & 2 & 3 & 4 & 5 \end{bmatrix} = 4$$

The reduction algorithm yields

(I.13.2)
$$\begin{array}{cccccc} 5 & 4 & 3 & 3 & 2 & 1 \\ 5-5 & 4-1 & 3-1 & 3-1 & 2-1 & 1-1= \\ & 3 & 2 & 2 & 1 & 0 \\ & 3-3 & 2-1 & 2-1 & 1-1 & 0= \\ & & 1 & 1 & 0 & 0 \end{array}$$

Hence the graph exists. Using some drawings, I can check that one needs 4 colors for a proper coloring.

Answer.

Proposition 53 (An upper bound of the chromatic number obtained from the degree sequence).
The chromatic number χ of any simple graph with degree sequence $d_1 \geq d_2 \geq \cdots \geq d_n$ is at most

(I.13.3) $$\chi \leq 1 + \max\{\min(d_i, i-1) : i = 1 \ldots n\}$$

Indication of reason. Starting with the vertex of highest degree, one colors the vertices greedily. Inductively, we check that having done the k-th vertex, one has used

(I.13.4) $$\chi_k := 1 + \max\{\min(d_i, i-1) : i = 1 \ldots k\}$$

colors. The vertex $k+1$ gets a new color if and only if $d_{k+1} \geq \chi_k$. Since $\chi_k \leq k$, and $\chi_{k+1} \leq 1 + \chi_k$, we see that

$$\begin{aligned}\chi_{k+1} &= 1 + \max\{\min(d_i, i-1) : i = 1 \ldots k+1\} \\ &= \max[\chi_k, \min(1 + d_{k+1}, k)] \\ &\geq \max[\chi_k, \min(1 + \chi_k, k)] = 1 + \chi_k \leq \chi_{k+1}\end{aligned}$$

where equality holds.

On the other hand, if $d_{k+1} < \chi_k$, the vertex $k+1$ does not need a new color. We need to check $\chi_{k+1} = \chi_k$.

$$\begin{aligned}\chi_{k+1} = 1 + \max\{\min(d_i, i-1) : i = 1 \ldots k+1\} &= \max[\chi_k, \min(1 + d_{k+1}, k)] \\ &\leq \max[\chi_k, \min(\chi_k, k)] = \chi_k\end{aligned}$$

$\square$

Theorem 16 (**Brook's Theorem**). *Let Δ denote the maximal degree. Any connected graph except an odd cycle or a complete graph, is colorable with Δ colors.*

Hence $\chi = \Delta + 1$ holds for a connected graph if and only if it is an odd cycle or a complete graph, and $\chi \leq \Delta$ for all other connected graphs.

Proof following Lovász 1975. We distinguish several cases, beginning with the easier ones.

Assume G is not regular. We choose any vertex v_n of less than maximal degree as root to grow a spanning tree of G, numbering the vertices in decreasing order. In a second step, the vertices are colored by greedy coloring in increasing order of this numbering—from the children back to the ancestors. Except for the root, each vertex has at most $\Delta - 1$ neighbors that are already colored, since its parent is colored only later. Hence a color is left to color v_i for all $i \leq n-1$. Since the root has degree $\deg(v_n) < \Delta$, there is a color left to finally color it, too.

The graph is regular and has cut-vertices. We color the vertices of one block of G at a time, as above. This is easy since a block cannot be regular. Afterwards, one needs to permute colors to adjust the coloring of the cut-vertices.

The graph is regular and has no cut-vertex.
To start the process, one needs a start-V.

Definition 55 (Start-V). Three vertices v_1, v_2 and v_n such that
$$G - \{v_1, v_2\} \text{ is connected}, \quad v_1 \sim v_n, \quad v_2 \sim v_n, \quad v_1 \not\sim v_2$$
I call a *start-V*

The lemma below shows how to obtain these three vertices.

The vertex v_n is chosen as root to grow a spanning tree in the graph $G - \{v_1, v_2\}$, again numbering the vertices in decreasing order.

The greedy coloring begins by giving v_1 and v_2 the same color. After that, the other vertices are colored by greedy coloring in increasing order—from the children back to the ancestors. A color is left to color vertices v_i for all $i \leq n-1$, since the parent is colored later. Since the root v_n has two neighbors v_1 and v_2 with the same color, there is a color left to finally color it, too.

□

Lemma 31. *Let G be an r-regular graph without cut-vertices, and $3 \leq r \leq n-2$. There exist three vertices v_1, v_2 and v_n such that $G - \{v_1, v_2\}$ is connected, and $v_1 \sim v_n$, $v_2 \sim v_n$ and $v_1 \not\sim v_2$.*

Proof. In case that $\kappa(G) \geq 3$, the proof is easy, and can be left to the reader. We now assume $\kappa(G) = 2$. We choose an arbitrary vertex x. There are two cases to be distinguished:

(a) $\kappa(G-x) \geq 2$

(b) $\kappa(G-x) = 1$

In the easier case (a), let $v_1 := x$. There exists a vertex v_2 at distance 2, not adjacent to v_1, since G is r-regular and $3 \leq r \leq n-2$, and not complete. Let v_n be the common neighbor of v_1 and v_2. Finally, $G - \{v_1, v_2\}$ is connected since $\kappa(G - v_1) \geq 2$ by assumption.

In case (b), let $v_n := x$. We use the block decomposition of $G - x$. We know there exist at least two end-blocks B_i for $i = 1, 2$. [11] By assumption, graph G has no cut-vertex, hence x has a neighbor b_i in every end-block B_i, different from the cut-vertex of B_i. Neighbors $b_1 \sim x$ and $b_2 \sim x$ in two such end-blocks are nonadjacent. The induced subgraph $B_i - b_i$ is connected, again by definition of a block. Hence $G - \{x, b_1, b_2\}$ is connected. Since $r \geq 3$, vertex x has a third neighbor besides b_1 and b_2. Hence $G - \{b_1, b_2\}$ is connected. We chose $v_i := b_i$ for $i = 1, 2$. □

Problem 166. *Find a graph which is regular with $r \geq 3$, has connectivity $\kappa \geq 2$, and $\kappa(G-x) = 1$ for all vertices x, or prove non-existence.*

Problem 167. *Following Lovász, 3-color the graph in figure ?? with v_1, v_2, v_{12} as given.*

---

[11] Since the block-cut-vertex tree has at least to end-vertices.

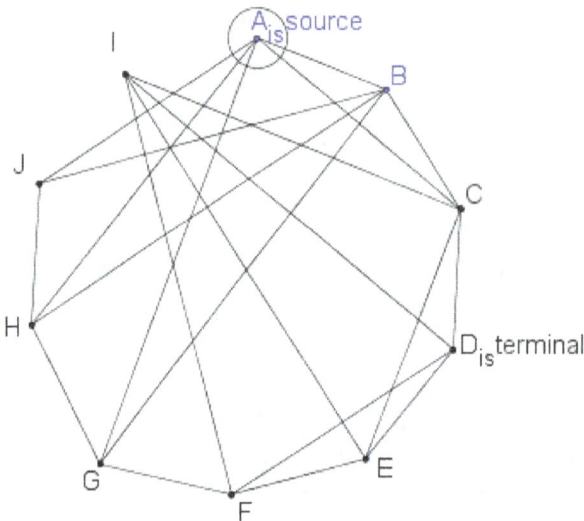

Figure 125: Find maximal number of vertex-disjoint paths from A to D.

Proposition 54 (Upper bound of the chromatic number from the cycle rank). *The chromatic number χ of any graph is at most two more than its cycle rank.*

(I.13.5) $$\chi \leq 2 + \gamma$$

Problem 168. *What is the cycle rank of a tree. Deduce from the bound that every tree or forest is 2-colorable.*

Give at least three other examples, where $\chi > 2$. Check whether the bound $\chi \leq \gamma + 2$. holds with equality or inequality. Is this a good bound or not?

Answer.

For a simple graph G with n vertices, m edges, and k components, recall that $\gamma(G) = m - n + k$ is the *cycle rank*. Indeed, $\gamma \geq 0$ for all graphs.

Proposition 55 (An upper bound of the chromatic number obtained from the cycle rank). *The chromatic number χ of any graph is at most two more than its cycle rank.*

(I.13.6) $$\chi \leq 2 + \gamma$$

Remark 40. For a tree or forest, $\gamma = 0$. Hence the bound (I.13.5) implies $\chi \leq 2$, which means that a tree or forest is 2-colorable. The bound is still strict for odd cycles. These are the only examples I have found where the bound is strict.

For the complete graphs K_n for $n \geq 4$ it is very far off the track.

For connected planar graphs, Euler's formula tells $n + f - m = 2$, where the number f of faces includes the unbounded one. Hence the cycle rank $\gamma = m - n + 1 = f - 1$ equals the number of bounded faces. The bound only tells that the chromatic number is less or equal the number of bounded faces plus two!

Proof. We use induction by n, the number of vertices. For $n \leq 2$, the claim (I.13.5) holds because $\gamma = 0$ and $\chi \leq 2$.

For the induction step, we assume bound (I.13.5) for all graphs G with less than n vertices and prove it for a graph G with n vertices. Let v be any vertex and $\widehat{G} = G \setminus v$. We distinguish the cases

(a) $\deg(v) = 0$ or 1

(b) $\deg(v) \geq 2$, and all neighbors of v lie in different components of $G \setminus v$

(c) $\deg(v) \geq 2$, but at least two neighbors of v lie in the same component of $G \setminus v$.

In case (a), no extra color is needed to color the new vertex, because two different colors are always available.
$$\chi = \widehat{\chi} \leq 2 + \widehat{m} - \widehat{n} + \widehat{k} = 2 + m - n + k$$
and hence the claim holds.

In case (b), the addition of the new vertex does connect together $\deg(v)$ different components of $G \setminus v$. Hence $k \geq k' - \deg(v) + 1$ and
$$\gamma = m - n + k = \widehat{m} + \deg(v) - \widehat{n} - 1 + k \geq \widehat{m} - \widehat{n} + \widehat{k} = \widehat{\gamma}$$

In other words, no new cycles are created.

Since all neighbors of the vertex v lie in different components of $G \setminus v$, one can recolor these components in a way that all neighbors of v get the same color. One needs no extra color for the new vertex. One gets $\gamma = \widehat{\gamma}$ and $\chi = \widehat{\chi}$. The induction assumption $\widehat{\chi} \leq 2 + \widehat{\gamma}$ implies the claim $\chi \leq 2 + \gamma$.

In case (c), one may need an extra color for the new vertex. Hence $\chi \leq 1 + \widehat{\chi}$.

But, since two neighbors of v lie in the same component of $\widehat{G} = G \setminus v$, the number of components of this graph is $\widehat{k} < k + \deg(v) - 1$, and hence $k > \widehat{k} - \deg(v) + 1$. There are created new cycles and
$$\gamma = m - n + k = \widehat{m} + \deg(v) - \widehat{n} - 1 + k > \widehat{m} - \widehat{n} + \widehat{k} = \widehat{\gamma}$$

The <u>strict</u> inequality $\gamma > \widehat{\gamma}$ and the induction assumption $\widehat{\chi} \leq 2 + \widehat{\gamma}$ imply the claim
$$\chi \leq 1 + \widehat{\chi} \leq 3 + \widehat{\gamma} \leq 2 + \gamma$$

□

Proposition 56 (Bounds by Nordhaus-Gaddum (1956)). *The chromatic numbers $\overline{\chi} = \chi(\overline{G})$ of a graph and its complement satisfy*

(a) $2\sqrt{n} \le \chi + \overline{\chi} \le n+1$

(b) $\dfrac{(n+1)^2}{4} \ge \chi \cdot \overline{\chi} \ge n$

(c) $2 \le \min[\chi, \overline{\chi}] \le \dfrac{1+\sqrt{1+4n}}{2}$

Lemma 32. *The chromatic numbers satisfy*

(a) $\chi + \overline{\chi} \le n+1$

(b) $\chi \cdot \overline{\chi} \ge n$

(c) *If* $\chi = 1$ *then* $\overline{\chi} = n$. *If* $\overline{\chi} = 1$ *then* $\chi = n$.

Proof item (a). We proceed by induction on n. The assertion is true for $n \le 2$. Assume it holds for all graphs with less that n vertices, and check the claim for any given graph G with n vertices. We choose a vertex v_n with degree $g = \deg(v_n)$.

By induction assumption $\chi(G \setminus \{v_n\}) + \chi(\overline{G} \setminus \{v_n\}) \le n$. Since the chromatic number $\chi(G)$ is at most one more than $\chi(G \setminus \{v_n\})$, and the chromatic number $\chi(\overline{G})$ is at most one more than $\chi(\overline{G} \setminus \{v_n\})$, the assertion is immediately clear except for the case that

- $\chi(G \setminus \{v_n\}) + \chi(\overline{G} \setminus \{v_n\}) = n$
- $\chi(G) = \chi(G \setminus \{v_n\}) + 1$

which we now assume. Since we needed an extra color for the vertex v_n of G, its degree is $g = \deg(v_n) \ge \chi(G \setminus \{v_n\})$. Hence the degree of v_n in the complement $\overline{G}$ satisfies

$$\deg_{\overline{G}}(v_n) = n - 1 - g \le n - 1 - \chi(G \setminus \{v_n\}) < \chi(\overline{G} \setminus \{v_n\})$$

and hence does not need an extra color. Hence

$$\chi(\overline{G}) = \chi(\overline{G} \setminus \{v_n\})$$
$$\chi(G) + \chi(\overline{G}) = \chi(G \setminus \{v_n\}) + 1 + \chi(\overline{G} \setminus \{v_n\}) = n+1$$

as to be shown. □

Proof item (b). The map from the vertices to the color pairs

$$v_i \mapsto (color_G(v_i), color_{\overline{G}}(v_i))$$

is injective. Indeed, any two different vertices $v_i \ne v_j$ are adjacent either in G or in $\overline{G}$. Vertices v_i and v_j have different colors in that one of the two graphs where they are adjacent. Counting implies $n \le \chi(G) \cdot \chi(\overline{G})$. □

Proposition 57. *For all chromatic pairs satisfying*

(a) $\chi + \overline{\chi} \leq n+1$

(b) $\chi \cdot \overline{\chi} \geq n$

there exist a graph and its complement having these chromatic numbers. Under the additional assumption

(d) $2 \leq \chi$ and $2 \leq \overline{\chi}$. If $\chi = 2$ then $\overline{\chi} \leq n-2$. If $\overline{\chi} = 2$ then $\chi \leq n-2$.

there exist a connected graph with connected complement having these chromatic numbers.

For example for $n = 6$, we get the possible color pairs

$$(1,6); (2,3), (2,4), (2,5)$$

and their reversals. For $n = 7$ the pairs

$$(1,7); (2,3), (2,4), (2,5), (2,6); (3,3), (3,4), (3,5)$$

and their reversals.

Lemma 33. *Let $n \geq 3$. The set of pairs (j, k) such that*

(a) $j + k \leq n+1$

(b) $j \cdot k \geq n$

(e) $2 \leq k \leq j$

is

$$S = \left\{ (j,k) : \lceil \tfrac{n}{k} \rceil \leq j \leq n-k+1 \text{ and } 2 \leq k < \frac{1 + \sqrt{1+4n}}{2} \right\}$$

The last restriction for k is equivalent to $2 \leq k \leq \lceil \tfrac{n}{k} \rceil$.

Construction of examples confirming Proposition 57. If $j = 2$, then $k = 2$ and $3 \leq n \leq 4$. These simple cases can be deal separately. We may now assume $j \geq 3$. Let (j, k) be any pair from the set S. Let

$$H = K_j + G_2 + \cdots + G_k$$

be the disjoint union of k complete graphs, the first of which has j vertices, the other ones have less or equal j vertices and are are ordered decreasingly. Since $n \leq kj$, we can adjust the orders of the G_i such that the sum H has order n. Since $3 \leq j$, we can choose two arbitrary vertices v, w and z of K_j.

To obtain the graph G from H, the vertex w is connected to an arbitrary vertex of G_2. The vertex v gets connected to arbitrary vertices in each one of the remaining graphs $G_3, G_4, \ldots G_k$. Let G be the graph obtained in this way. The graph G has chromatic number $\chi(G) = j$. The complement is k-partite and hence $\chi(\overline{G}) \leq k$. Too, since z is in $\overline{G}$ adjacent to all vertices of $\overline{G_i}$ for $i \geq 2$, the complement contains K_k as a subgraph and hence $\chi(\overline{G}) = k$.

Obviously, G is connected. The complement $\overline{G}$ is connected unless in the exceptional case $(j, k) = (n-1, 2)$. □

I.13.2 Planar and Eulerian graphs

Lemma 34. *A planar graph is 2 face-colorable if and only if all vertices have even degree.*

Reason. We begin by choosing color white for the unbounded face. Choose any start vertex. Going around it, we alternate to use black and white as color for the adjacent faces. One can go on until all faces are colored. Since all degrees are even no contradiction arises. □

Definition 56 (Poincaré Geometric dual). The geometric dual G^* is defined for a planar graph G <u>in a given planar representation</u>.

- In each face X of the graph G is chosen an arbitrary point, which becomes the corresponding vertex x of the dual graph G^*.

- To every edge e of the graph G corresponds an edge e^* of the dual graph G^*. Let the faces X and Y lie on the two sides of the edge e, and let the vertices x and y of the dual G^* represent the faces X and Y. Then the dual edge e^* has x and y as its endpoints.

Proposition 58. *For any planar graph G, the following statements are equivalent:*

(a) G *is Eulerian and has no isolated vertices;*

(b) G *is connected and all vertex degrees are even;*

(c) G *is connected and 2 face-colorable;*

Lemma 35. *A planar graph G is bipartite if and only if its dual G^* is Eulerian.*

Reason. The graph is bipartite if and only if all its cycles are even, which happens if and only if all its faces have even length [12]. This happens if and only if all vertices of its dual G^* are even. Since the dual is always connected, the last statement is equivalent to G^* being Eulerian. □

Proposition 59. *The following statements are equivalent for any graph:*

(a) G *is planar, three-regular and bipartite;*

(b) G *is planar, three-regular and 3 face-colorable;*

(c) G *is planar and three-regular and G^* is Eulerian.*

"(a) *implies* (b)": We color the vertices of the graph G black and white. We order the three given colors in a color list and use the following

> <u>coloring rule</u>: the order of colors for the faces surrounding any black vertex clockwise, or any white vertex counterclockwise follow the color list.

---

[12] A hanging tree adds an even number to the length of a face.

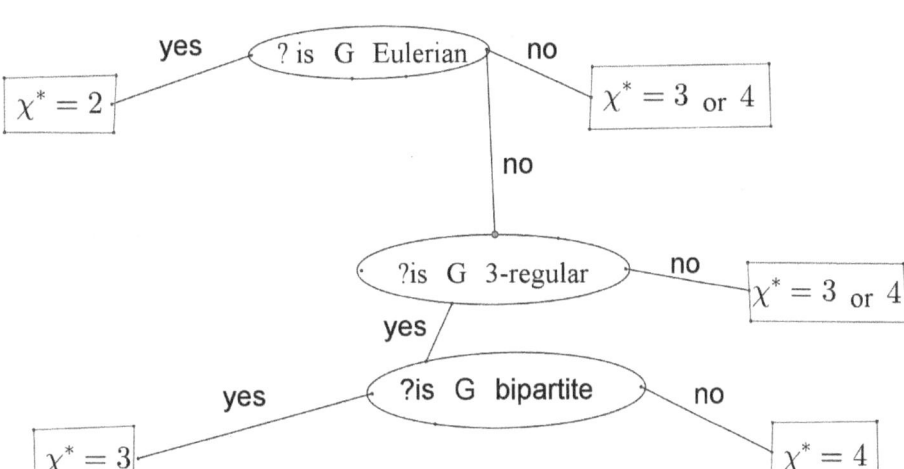

Figure 126: A guide to determine the face-chromatic number χ^*.

Since the Euclidean plane has an orientation such a rule exists. Next we construct a closed Eulerian trail for the dual G^*, starting at any vertex v^*. We color the faces of G starting at face $f = v^*$, and go on coloring neighboring faces following the order given by the Eulerian trail for the dual. Suppose face f has just been colored, and next we cross the edge $e = vw$ corresponding to the edge e^*, and arrive at face g. The color for g follows from the rule above, thus indeed depends on which of the vertices v and w is black and which is white. It can and indeed shall happen quite often that face g already has been colored in an earlier step. Since the color has been chosen according to the rule, no contradiction can arise. The process stops at the point the Eulerian trail of the dual has been exhausted. □

"(b) *implies* (a)": The order of the colors of the faces around a black vertex occur in clockwise order, but around a white vertex occur in counter clockwise order. Adjacent vertices have opposite sense of rotation. Hence we get a proper two coloring of the vertices. □

I.13.3 Planar, three-regular and bipartite graphs

Problem 169. *Convince yourself by means of Proposition 47 that for simple, connected planar, three-regular and bipartite graph the number $f_4, f_6, f_8, \ldots$ of faces of length $4, 6, 8 \ldots$ satisfy*

$$f_4 = 6 + f_8 + 2f_{10} + 3f_{12} + \ldots$$

Hence such a graph has at least six square faces.

Problem 170. *Look through the list of the Platonic and Archimedean polyhedra from Hartshorne's book[5] "Euclid and Beyond" and find out which ones are both three-regular and bipartite.*

Problem 171. *Draw a planar graph for at least four cases occurring in problem 170*

Problem 172. *Give a the proper three coloring for the faces of the graphs from problem 171.*

I.13.4 Edge coloring

Problem 173. *Give a the proper three coloring for the edges of the graphs from problem 171.*

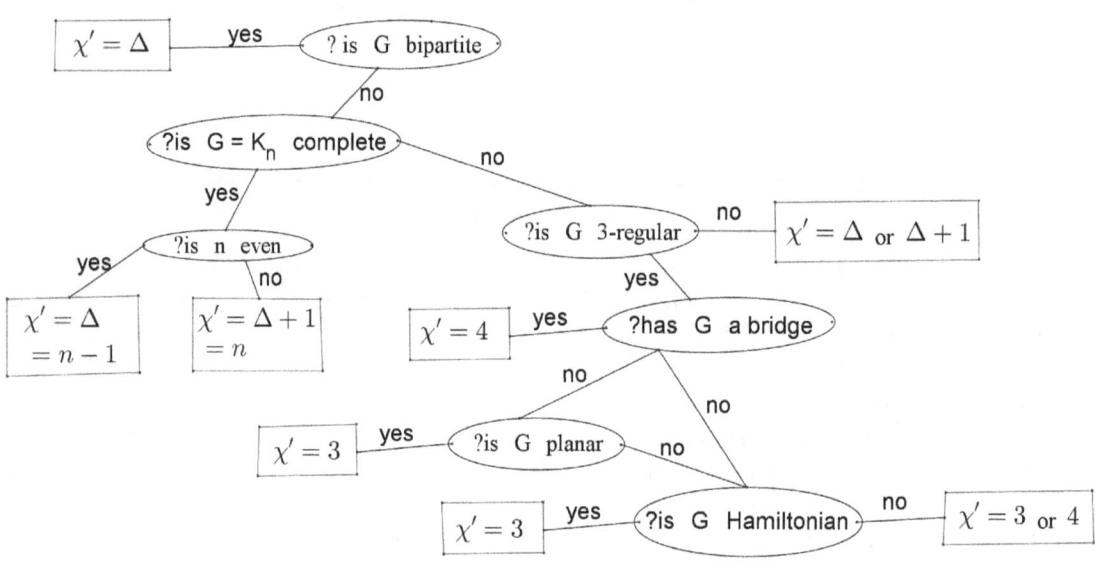

Figure 127: A guide to determine the edge-chromatic number χ'.

By $\chi'(G)$ we denote the minimal number of colors needed for a proper edge coloring of graph G. Let Δ denote the maximal degree.

Theorem 17 (Theorem of Vizing). *The minimal number of colors needed for a proper edge-coloring of a simple graph is either Δ or $\Delta + 1$.*

Theorem 18 (Theorem of König). *A bipartite simple graph can be properly edge-colored with $\chi'(G) = \Delta$ colors.*

Corollary 13. *A bipartite 3-regular graph is 3 edge-colorable.*

Proof the Theorem of König. The proof shall be done for the bipartite graphs which are subgraph of the complete bipartite graph $K_{p,q}$, and proceeds by induction on the number m of edges. Clearly the claim holds for $m = 0, 1, 2$. Assume that the claim is true for graphs with less than m edges. Take a graph $G \subseteq K_{p,q}$ with m edges and choose any edge $e = vw$. Imagine that the vertices of G have been colored back and white, and vertex v is black.

If the maximal degree for the graph $G - e$ is less than the maximal degree Δ for the graph G, we may color the edges of $G - e$ with $\Delta - 1$ colors and use an extra color for the edge e. Thus we have colored the edges of G with Δ colors as required.

Assume now the maximal degree for the graph $G - e$ and for the graph G are both equal to Δ. Using the induction assumption, we color the edges of $G - e$ with Δ colors. Since in the graph $G - e$ both vertices v and w have at most degree $\Delta - 1$, at these both vertices there is one color missing. Let α be the color missing at vertex v and β be the color missing at white vertex w, and let $H_{\alpha\beta}$ be the connected subgraph with all edges colored α or β which contains vertex w. [13]

In other words, the subgraph $H_{\alpha\beta}$ consists of all vertices x which can be reached from vertex w by a path consisting of edges colored with colors α and β. The two colors alternate along such a path, and the vertices alternate the sides of $K_{p,q}$. Hence either x is a black vertex and the last edge of the path adjacent to x has color α; or x is a white vertex and the last edge of the path adjacent to x has color β. In both cases we conclude $x \neq v$ since v is a black vertex and no edge adjacent to v has color α.

We conclude that the subgraph $H_{\alpha\beta}$ does not contain vertex v. We may interchange the colors α and β in this subgraph, and still get a proper vertex coloring of the entire graph $G - e$. Now the color α is missing at both vertex v and w, and thus we may use the color α for the edge $e = vw$ and thus complete the coloring of the edges of G with Δ colors. □

Proposition 60. *A 3-edge-colorable, 3-regular, connected graph is contractible to an Eulerian multigraph. Hence it cannot have a neither a bridge nor a cut-vertex.*

Especially, a bipartite 3-regular graph cannot have neither a bridge nor a cut-vertex.

Proof. Select any two of the three colors from a proper 3-edge coloring. The subgraph H with the same set of vertices as the original graph G, and the edges with these two colors is 2-regular. Hence it is the union of even cycles C_i for $i = 1 \ldots p$. These cycles are vertex-disjoint because of the proper 3-edge coloring.

For each cycle C_i, there are an even number of edges of the third color with exactly one end-vertex in C_i, but the other end-vertex in a different cycle. By contracting each cycle to one vertex, only the edges just mentioned survive. Hence we get a multigraph all vertices of which are even.

Such a multigraph is Eulerian and cannot have a bridge, as we have seen in Problem 63. By Proposition 40, we know a bridgeless 3-regular graph has no cut-vertex neither.

---

[13] One could call this subgraph a "König-chain".

By König's Theorem, the edges of a bipartite graph can be properly colored with Δ colors, where Δ is the maximal degree. Hence the edges of a bipartite 3-regular graph can be properly 3-colored. As in the first part, we conclude that neither a bridge nor a cut-vertex can exist. □

Definition 57 (Map). A simple, connected, planar and bridgeless graph is called a *map*.

Proposition 61 (Edge coloring of the complete graphs). *The minimal number of colors for a proper edge coloring of a complete graph is*

(I.13.7) $$\chi'(K_n) = \begin{cases} n & \text{for } n \geq 3 \text{ odd} \\ n-1 & \text{for } n \text{ even.} \end{cases}$$

which is always odd.

One can edge-color K_n with the given number of colors. To see this for the case of odd n, we draw K_n as a regular n-gon and its diagonals. We use the same color for one side and all diagonals parallel to it. There occur segments in n different directions, and hence n colors are needed. Note that at each vertex, one color is missing.

In the case of even n, we color at first the graph $K_{n-1} = K_n - w$ leaving out edges adjacent to vertex w. By the argument above, we need $n-1$ colors. We use the color missing at the vertex v of K_{n-1} to color the edge vw. Hence still $n-1$ colors suffice to color the all edges of K_n. □

Lemma 36. *For any graph $\chi' \geq \Delta \geq \frac{2m}{n}$. For a graph with an odd number n of vertices*

$$\chi' \geq \frac{2m}{n-1}$$

Reason. The first statement follows from the handshaking lemma. Assume now that n is odd. For any color, twice the number of edges using the same color can be at most $n-1$, since each edge occupies two vertices. Taking the sum over all colors yields $2m \leq \chi' \cdot (n-1)$ and hence $\chi' \geq \frac{2m}{n-1}$ as to be shown. □

Reason that the number of colors for K_n is minimal. Clearly $\chi' \geq \Delta = n-1$ holds for all n. Since $m = n(n-1)/2$ for the complete graph, the lemma yields $\chi' \geq n-1$ for n odd. □

Proposition 62. *A Δ-regular graph that is isomorphic to its complement has edge-chromatic number $\chi' = \Delta + 1$.*

Proof. By assumption the graph G is isomorphic to its complement $\overline{G}$. Hence $2\Delta = n-1$ and n needs to be odd. We may put the edge-colorings of G and $\overline{G}$ together to produce a proper edge coloring of the complete graph K_n. Hence proposition 61 yields

$$2\chi'(G) = \chi'(G) + \chi'(\overline{G}) \geq \chi'(K_n) = n \quad \text{and hence} \quad \chi'(G) \geq \frac{n+1}{2}$$

which implies the edge-chromatic number $\chi'(G) = \Delta + 1$ as to be shown. □

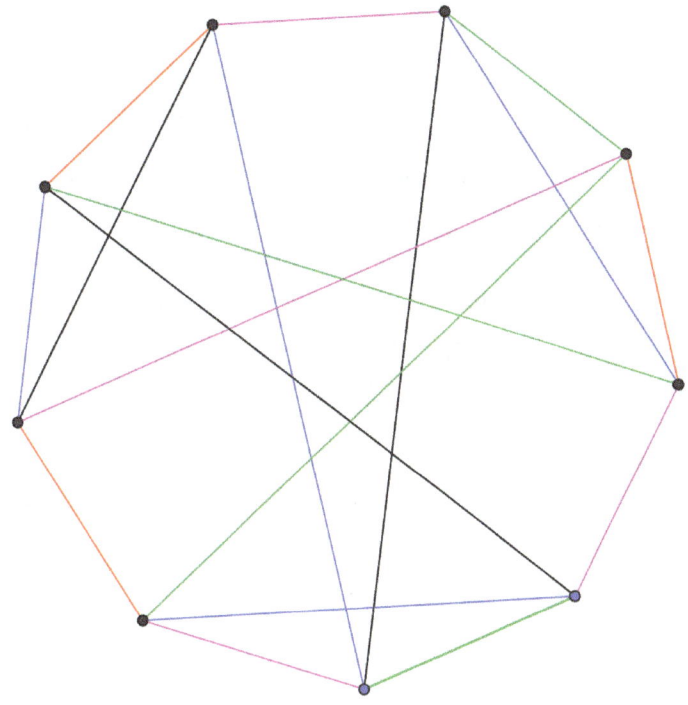

Figure 128: Five colors are needed for a proper edge coloring.

Proposition 63. *A graph with an odd number n of vertices and maximal degree Δ has edge-chromatic number $\chi' = \Delta + 1$ under any one of the following assumptions:*

(i) *the number of edges is $m \geq \dfrac{\Delta \cdot (n-1)}{2} + 1$;*

(ii) *the graph is Δ-regular;*

(iii) *it has maximal degree Δ, and is obtained from a Δ-regular graph by deletion of at most $(\Delta - 2)/2$ of its edges.*

Proof. The assumption (i) implies $2m > \Delta(n-1)$. By Lemma 36 this inequality implies $\chi' \neq \Delta$. Hence Vizing's Theorem implies $\chi' = \Delta + 1$. The assumption (iii) and the handshaking lemma imply $2m \geq \Delta n - (\Delta - 2) > \Delta(n-1)$ which yields the assumption made in item (i). The item (ii) is clearly a special case of item (iii). □

Proposition 64 (Edge coloring for near to complete graphs). *In the following cases, the minimal number of colors for a proper edge coloring of a graph G with n vertices is the same as* for the complete graph K_n:

(I.13.8) $\quad\quad \chi'(G) = \chi'(K_n) = \begin{cases} n & \text{for } n \geq 3 \text{ odd and } m \geq \frac{n^2-2n+3}{2}; \\ n-1 & \text{for } n \text{ even and } m \geq \frac{n^2-2n+2}{2}. \end{cases}$

Proof. Clearly $\chi'(G) \leq \chi'(K_n)$. We show that as many colors are needed for the edge-coloring of the graph G. Distinguish the cases

for $n \geq 3$ odd: Each color can be used for $(n-1)/2$ edges at most. If the number of edges is $m \geq (n-1)(n-1)/2 + 1$ one really needs n colors.

for n even: Each color can be used for $n/2$ edges at most. If the number of edges is $m \geq (n-2)n/2 + 1$ one really needs $n-1$ colors.

□

Problem 174. *Use the Lemma 36 to show that the graph H shown in the figure on page 197 is 5-edge-chromatic.*

Answer. Counting the vertices and edges yields $\chi' \geq \frac{2m}{n-1} = \frac{28}{6} > 4$. Hence by Vizing's theorem implies $\chi' = \Delta + 1 = 5$.

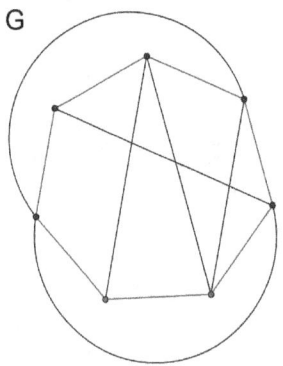
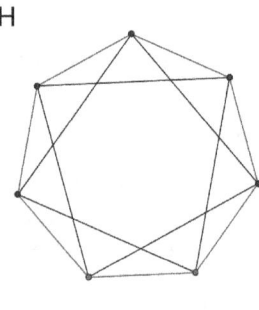

Figure 129: How many colors are needed for a proper edge coloring?

Problem 175. *Referring to edge coloring of graph H from the figure on page 197:*

(a) *What could the minimal number χ' for a proper edge coloring be by Vizing's Theorem.*

(b) *How many edges of this graph can get the same color.*

(c) *How many edges has the graph.*

(d) What is the minimal number χ' for a proper edge coloring.

(e) Do a proper edge coloring of the graph for the figure on page 197, with the minimal number of colors needed.

Answer. **(a)** The graph H is 4-regular, so Vizing's Theorem tells the minimal number χ' for a proper edge coloring is either $\delta = 4$ or $\delta + 1 = 5$.

(b) There are seven vertices. Hence at most 3 edges can get the same color.

(c) The graph H has 14 edges.

(d) But 4 colors, each for 3 edges, can color only 12 of the 14 edges. Hence one needs 5 colors for a proper edge coloring.

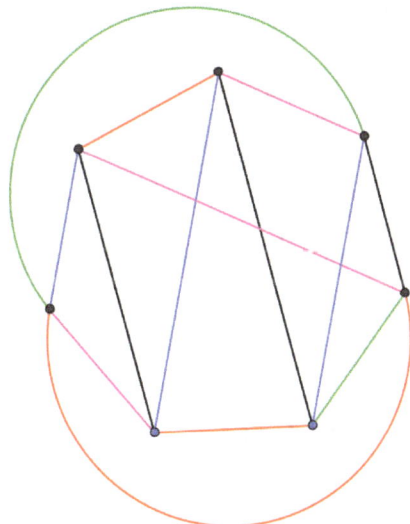

Figure 130: Five colors are needed for a proper edge coloring.

Proposition 65 (About regular bipartite graphs). *Assume that for the (simple or general) bipartite graph (A, B), all black vertices in A have the same degree Δ, and all white vertices in B have degree less or equal Δ. Under these assumptions:*

(a) *There are at least as many white as black vertices: $|B| \geq |A|$.*

(b) *$|A| = |B|$ holds if and only if the graph is regular.*

(c) *Any proper edge coloring with minimal number of colors uses the colors in equal numbers: always a set of $|A|$ edges gets the same color.*

(d) *The maximum matching of edges and the minimum vertex cover have the same size $\alpha' = \beta = |A|$.*

As a consequence, we have obtained a simpler proof of the König-Egervary Theorem for regular bipartite graphs.

Proof. We may assume $\Delta \geq 1$. By equation (I.1.2) from the handshake lemma 7 for bipartite graphs, we get the estimate

$$m = \sum_{v \in A} \deg_G(v) = |A| \cdot \Delta = \sum_{v \in B} \deg_G(v) \leq |B| \cdot \Delta$$

Hence $|A| \leq |B|$ confirming item (a). Moreover the assumption $|A| = |B|$ implies

$$m = \sum_{v \in A} \deg_G(v) = |A| \cdot \Delta = \sum_{v \in B} \deg_G(v) \leq |B| \cdot \Delta = m$$

where one gets everywhere equality. Hence the graph is Δ-regular, confirming item (b). Since each edge color marks an independent set, it can be used at most α' times. Hence we get $m \leq \alpha' \chi'$. By König's theorem the edge-chromatic number is $\chi' = \Delta$. Moreover Lemma 1 implies $\alpha' \leq \beta \leq |A|$. Hence

$$|A| \cdot \Delta = m \leq \alpha' \chi' = \alpha' \Delta \leq \beta \Delta \leq |A| \cdot \Delta = m$$

where one gets everywhere equality. Hence $\alpha' = \beta = |A|$ confirming item (d). Moreover $m = \alpha' \chi'$ and hence each color is used the same number α' of times, confirming item (c). □

I.14 More about 3-regular graphs

I.14.1 Tait's conjecture and counterexamples

Proposition 66 (Tait ca. 1880). *If a three-regular graph is Hamiltonian, it is 3 edge-colorable.*

Reason. The handshaking lemma implies that the number of vertices is even. Hence the the edges of the Hamiltonian cycle can be colored with two colors. One uses the third color for the remaining edges. □

Proposition 67. *The Petersen graph is not Hamiltonian and not even 3 edge-colorable.*

It is still true—and indeed equivalent to the Four Color Theorem—that every planar three regular graph is 3-edge colorable.

Problem 176. *Draw the dodecahedron graph and find a proper three-coloring of the edges.*
Explain the procedure you use. Explain how the edges of the dodecahedron can be partitioned into three disjoint sets of equal size such that the edges of each set are a perfect matching.

Answer. The dodecahedron is a three-regular Hamiltonian graph. At first one finds Hamiltonian cycle. This cycle has even length, and hence can be colored with two colors. The third color is used for the remaining edges not in the cycle.

In this way, the edges can be properly colored with three colors. Take any of the three colors. Two edges of this color are never adjacent to each other. But for any vertex v, there is exactly one edge of the color chosen adjacent to the vertex v. Hence the edges of the chosen color are a complete matching.

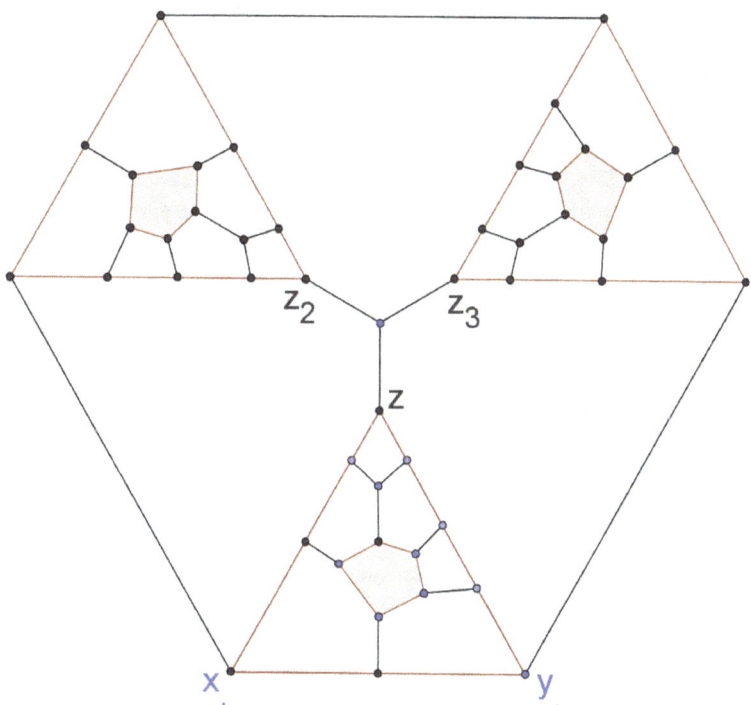

Figure 131: Tutte's counterexample to Tait's conjecture.

During his attempt to prove the Four Color Theorem, Tait wanted to generalize the procedure for four-face coloring the dodecahedron used in problem 176. Tait made around 1884 the following wrong conjecture:

"every 3-regular, polyhedral planar graph is Hamiltonian... —"

This statement is now known as "Tait's conjecture". Indeed, he justified his conjecture only by explaining that a bid of experimentation is enough to verify it. But Tait's conjecture turns out to be wrong. It took a long time to come up with counterexamples. It was disproven by W. T. Tutte (1946), who constructed a counterexample with $n = 46$ vertices. The smallest examples known has 38 vertices (Lederberg 1965), and was apparently also discovered by D. Barnette and J. Bosák around the same time.

Problem 145 above explains Ginberg's example with $n = 46$. The 46-Grinberg graph, found ca. 1949, is shown in the figure on page 159.

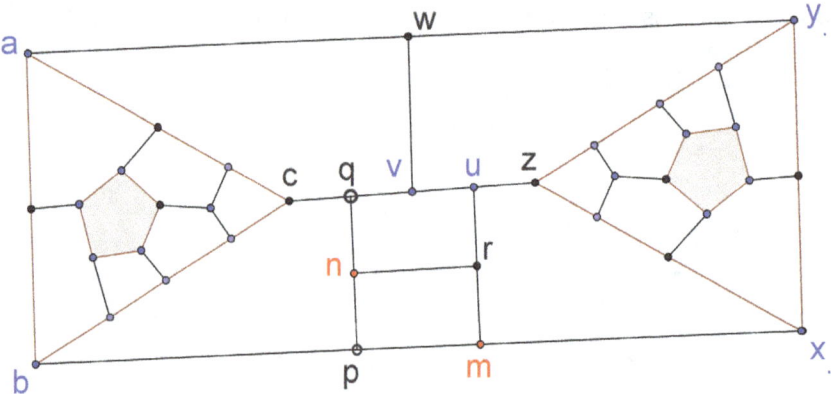

Figure 132: Lederberg's counterexample to Tait's conjecture.

Problem 177. *Check that a path though all vertices of a Tutte triangle can either enter at x and leave at z, or enter at y and leave at z. Such a path can never avoid leaving at z.*

Problem 178. *Give a reason why the Lederberg graph is not Hamiltonian.*

Answer. Consider a cycle $\mathcal{C}$ containing all vertices of both Tutte triangles. By the result of problem 177, any such cycle contains the edges cq and uz. Now we go through all possible cases.

- The cycle $\mathcal{C}$ leaves the Tutte triangles at vertices a and y, respectively. This cycle either misses vertex v or vertices n, m, p.

- The cycle $\mathcal{C}$ leaves the Tutte triangles at vertices b and y, respectively. This cycle misses vertex n.

- The cycle $\mathcal{C}$ leaves the Tutte triangles at vertices a and x, respectively. This cycle misses vertex r.

- The cycle $\mathcal{C}$ leaves the Tutte triangles at vertices b and x, respectively. This cycle misses vertex w.

We see that no Hamiltonian cycle exists. The longest cycle contains 37 of the 38 vertices. Hence the Lederberg graph is semi-Hamiltonian.

The longer list of such counterexamples is to be found on the website

http://mathworld.wolfram.com/TaitsHamiltonianGraphConjecture.html

and is depicted in the figure on page 202.

n	name	reference
38	Barnette-Bosák-Lederberg graph	Lederberg (1965), Thomassen (1981), Grünbaum (2003)
42	42-Faulkner-Younger graph	Faulkner and Younger (1974)
42	42-Grinberg graph	Faulkner and Younger (1974)
44	44-Faulkner-Younger graph	Faulkner and Younger (1974)
44	44-Grinberg graph	Sachs (1968), Berge (1973), Read and Wilson (1998, p. 274)
46	46-Grinberg graph	Bondy and Murty (1976, p. 162)
46	Tutte's graph	Tutte (1972), Bondy and Murty (1976, p. 161)
94	Thomassen graph	Thomassen (1981)
124	124-Grünbaum graph	Zamfirescu (1976)

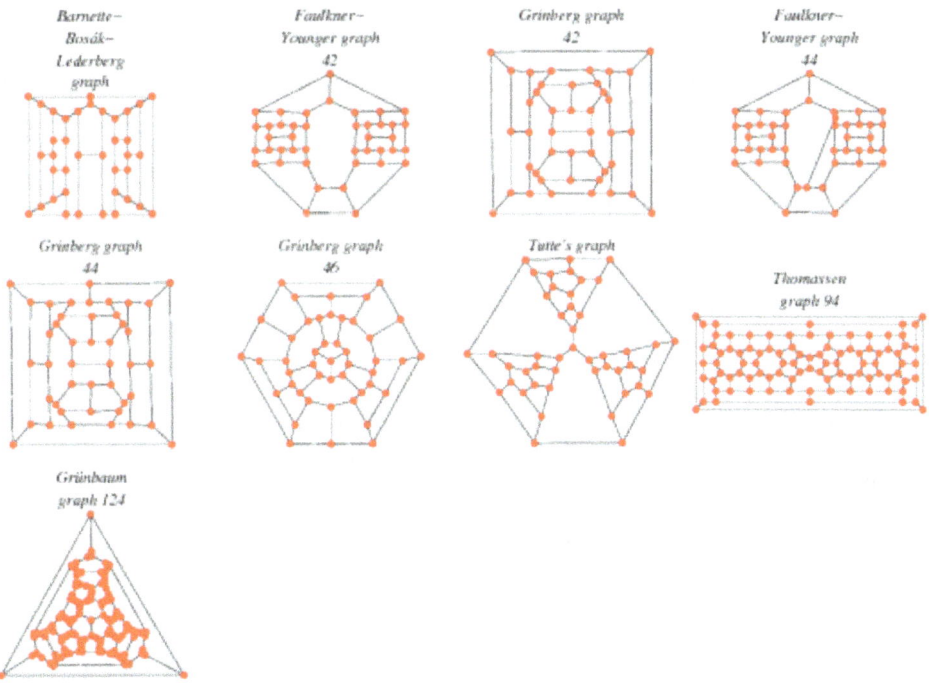

Figure 133: Examples refuting the Tait's conjecture.

As of 1983, it has been checked by computer that Tait's conjecture holds for graphs with $n \leq 33$ vertices. It remains a challenging computation problem to actually find the smallest 3-regular, 3-connected planar graph which fails to be Hamiltonian.

I.14.2 Face and edge coloring

For 3-regular graphs, there exists a one-to-one correspondence between proper face coloring with at most four colors, and proper 3-edge colorings. The correspondence is obtained by

Definition 58 (Tait's rule). Given is a 3-regular map, or a 3-regular planar bridgeless simple graph. We do any proper face coloring with at most four colors. The unbounded face gets a color, too. It is convenient to assign $(0,0)$ to the color of the unbounded (outside) face. Assign the other values $(0,1), (1,0), (1,1)$ to your colors, in any order. Too, assign the values $(0,1), (1,0), (1,1)$ to the edge colors. The colors are added in the same way as the elements in $\mathbb{Z}_2 \times \mathbb{Z}_2$.

The corresponding three coloring of the edges is obtained by *Tait's rule*: As one goes from one face across an edge to the opposite face, the edge color is the sum of the two colors from these faces lying on both sides of the edge. Conversely, from any given 3-coloring of the edges, together with the color for a single face, one obtains a unique face coloring.

It is helpful to put the four face colors on the faces of K_4—then assign the three different edge colors and four face colors.

In the following, I shift the point of view to the relation of face and edge coloring given from Tait's rule; and further to the *resulting two-colored cycles*.

Problem 179 (Lederberg's counterexample to Tait's conjecture). *Do a proper four coloring of the faces of Lederberg's map. This is relatively easy. Find the corresponding three coloring of the edges, following* Tait's rule.

Find the cycles which are colored with one pair of colors. Then look for a variety of different cycle lengths. Can you get a long two-colored cycle that exhausts at least one of the Tutte triangles, or more?

Remark 41. We know there does *not* exist a Hamiltonian cycle. But one finds two-colored cycles which miss just a few vertices. In some solutions these remaining four vertices are a second small cycle, in other solutions they lie far apart.

Problem 180. *Apply the approach of problem 179 to Tutte's counterexample.*

Answer.

Problem 181. *Finally, apply the approach of problem 179 to the Grinberg graph. Show your face coloring, edge coloring and survey of resulting two-color cycles for the Grinberg graph.*

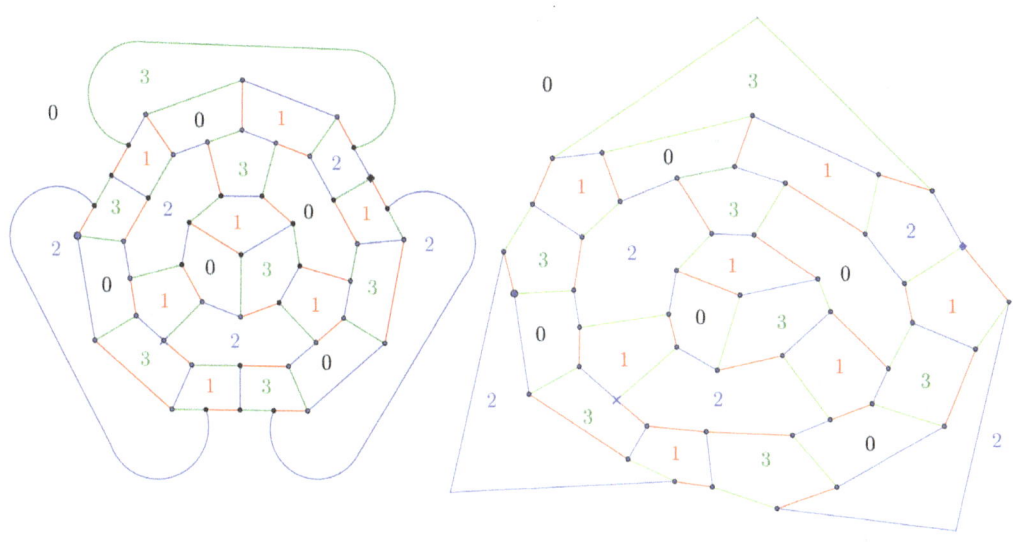

Figure 134: Face and edge coloring of the Grinberg graph.

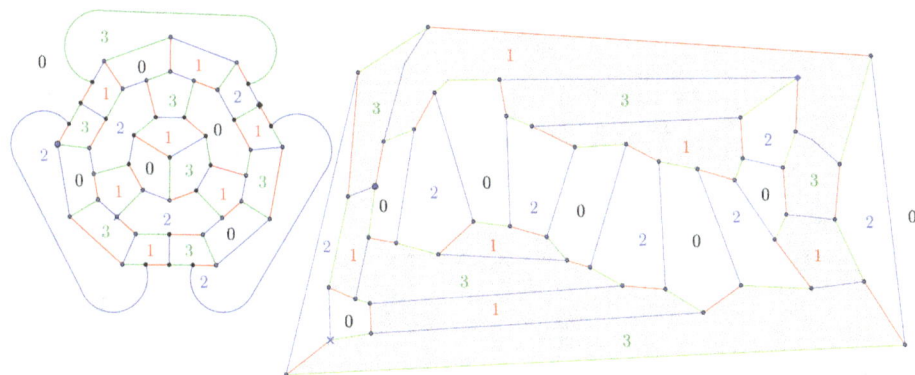

Figure 135: The red-green cycles from the edge coloring.

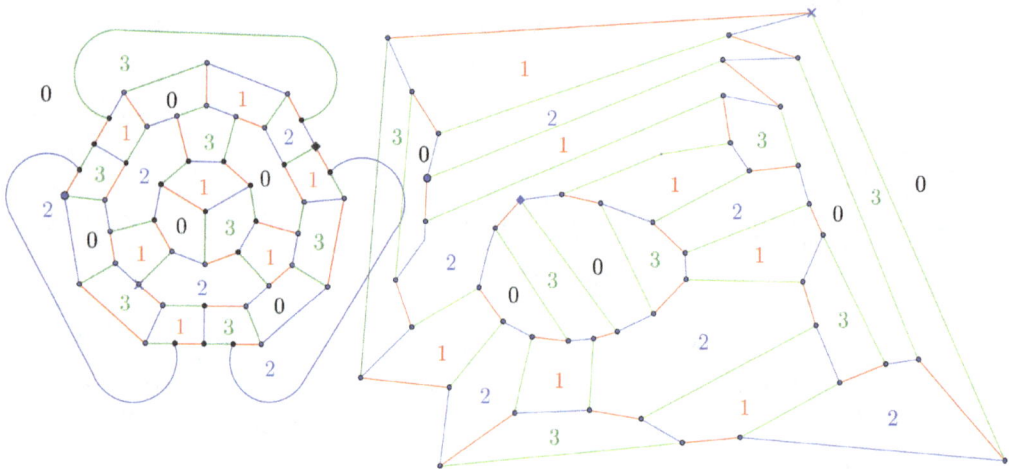

Figure 136: The red-blue cycles from the edge coloring.

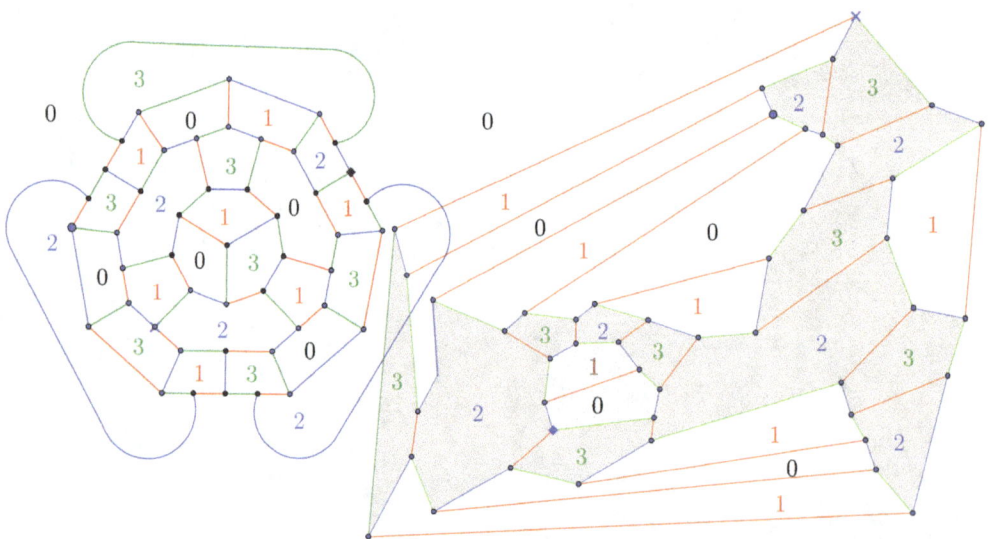

Figure 137: The blue-green cycles from the edge coloring.

I.14.3 Tutte's conjecture and counterexamples

We see from the results above that the two assumption "3-regular", "planar" are not enough to ensure that a polyhedral graph is Hamiltonian. However, none of these known counterexamples is bipartite. What about specializing to bipartite graphs? Tutte himself conjectured that

"every 3-regular, 3-connected bipartite graph is Hamiltonian... —"

Again, this conjecture was shown to be false by the discovery of counterexamples:

The Horton graph, discovered and named by Joseph Horton, and published by Bondy and Murty [1] in 1976. It provides a counterexample, with $n = 96$ vertices, to the Tutte conjecture that every cubic 3-connected bipartite graph may be Hamiltonian.

After the Horton graph, a number of smaller counterexamples to the Tutte conjecture were found. Among them are a 92 vertex graph by Horton published in 1982, a 78 vertex graph by Owens published in 1983, and the two Ellingham-Horton graphs (54 and 78 vertices). The first Ellingham-Horton graph was published by Ellingham in 1981 and was of order 78. At that time, it was the smallest know counterexample to the Tutte conjecture. The second one was published by Ellingham and Horton in 1983 and was of order 54. The Georges graph (1989) has $n = 50$ vertices. I have not found any smaller non-hamiltonian cubic 3-connected bipartite graph in the literature. [14]

n	name	reference
50	Georges graph	Georges (1989), Grünbaum (2006, 2009)
54	second Ellingham-Horton graph	Ellingham and Horton (1983)
78	first Ellingham-Horton graph	Ellingham (1981, 1982)
78	Owens graph	Owens (1983)
92	Horton 92-graph	Horton (1982)
96	Horton 96-graph	Bondy and Murty (1976)

Problem 182. *Give a reason why the second Ellingham Horton graph, —shown in the figure on page 210—, is not Hamiltonian.*

As a non-hamiltonian cubic graph with many long cycles, the Horton graph provides good benchmark for programs that search for Hamiltonian cycles.[8] More information is can be obtained from the websites

https://en.wikipedia.org/wiki/Horton_graph

http://mathworld.wolfram.com/TutteConjecture.html

---

[14] Wikipedia even falsely claims that the second Ellingham-Horton graph is the smallest counterexample.

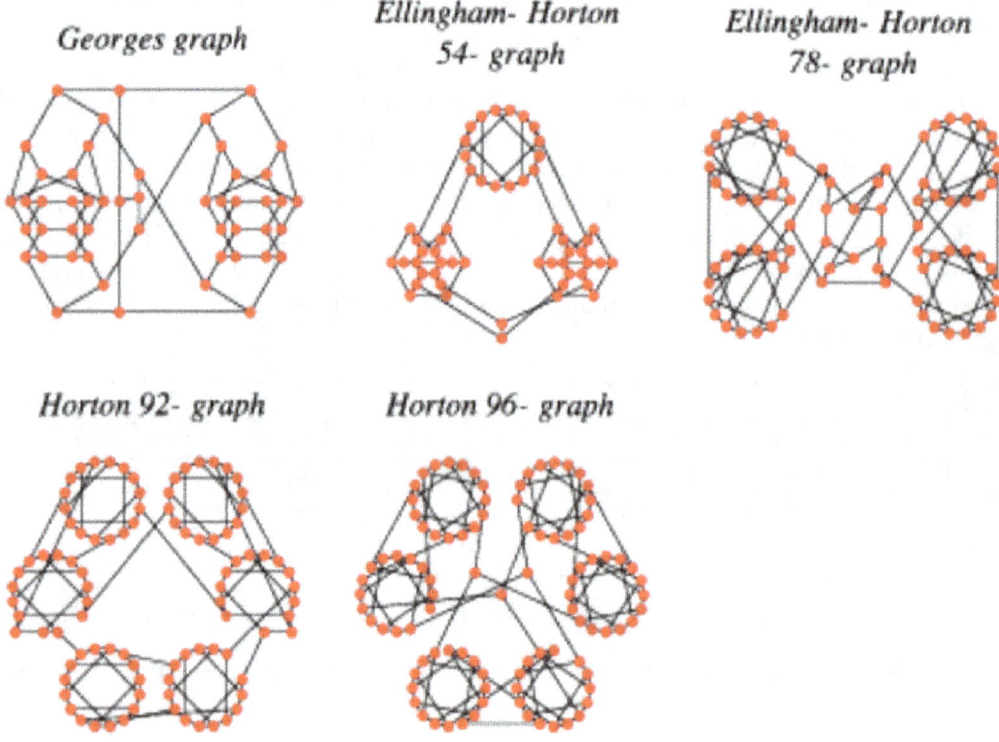

Figure 138: The know examples refuting Tutte conjecture.

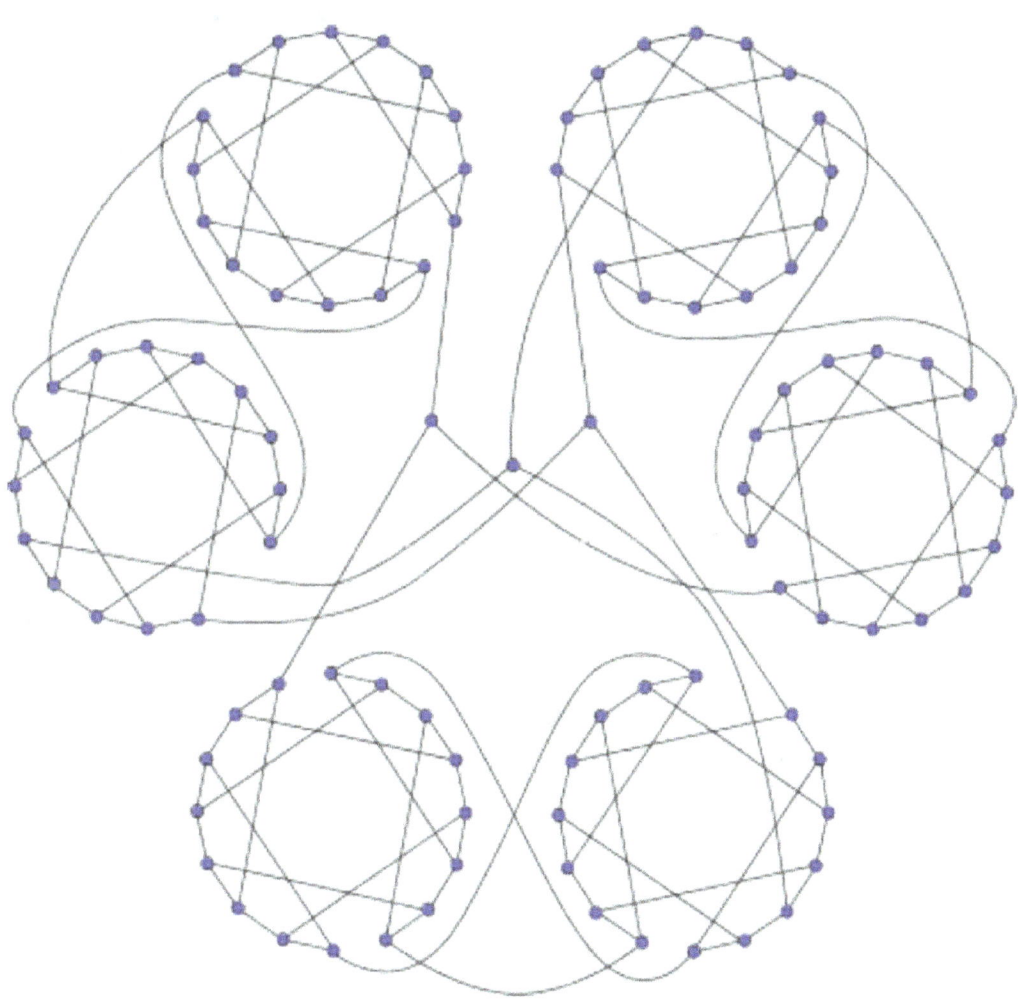

Figure 139: The Horton graph.

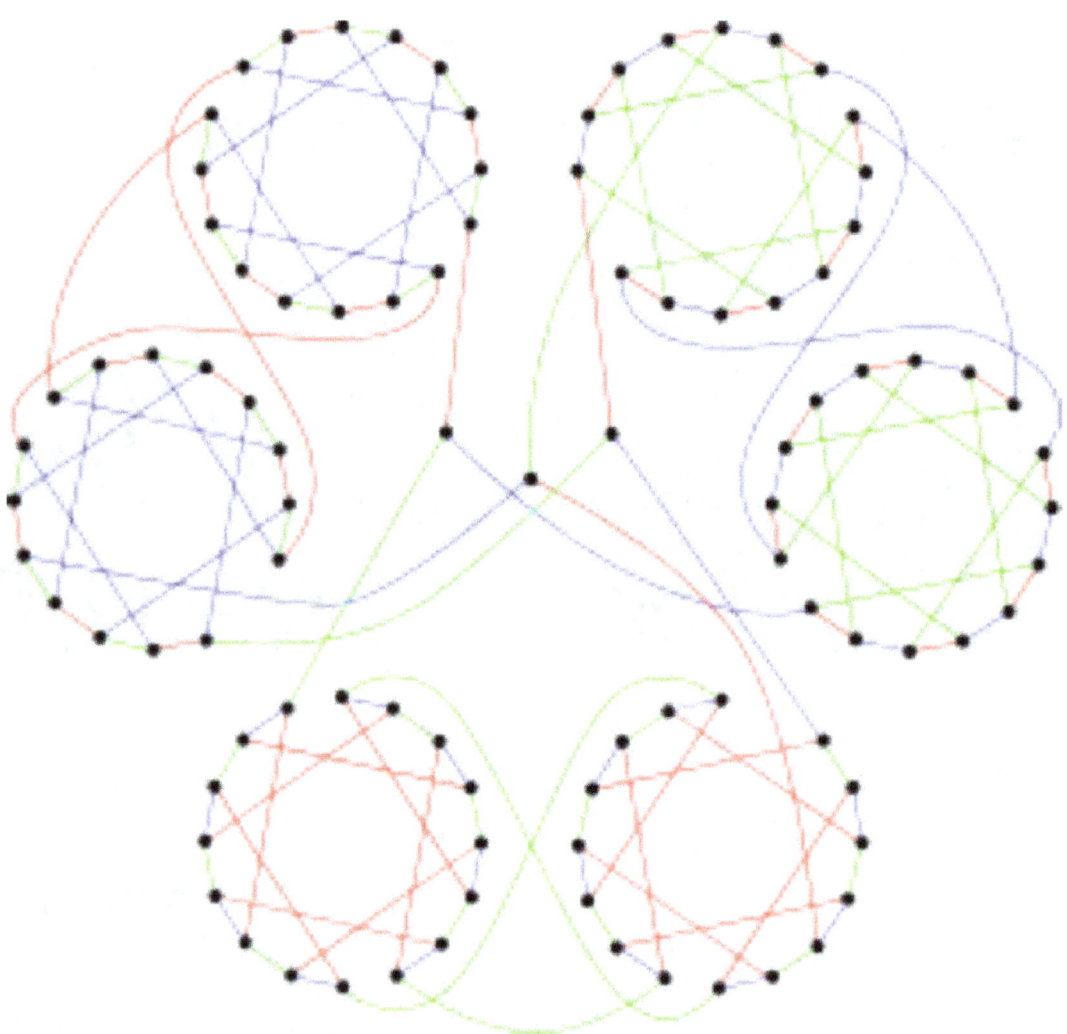

Figure 140: The Horton graph 3-edge colored.

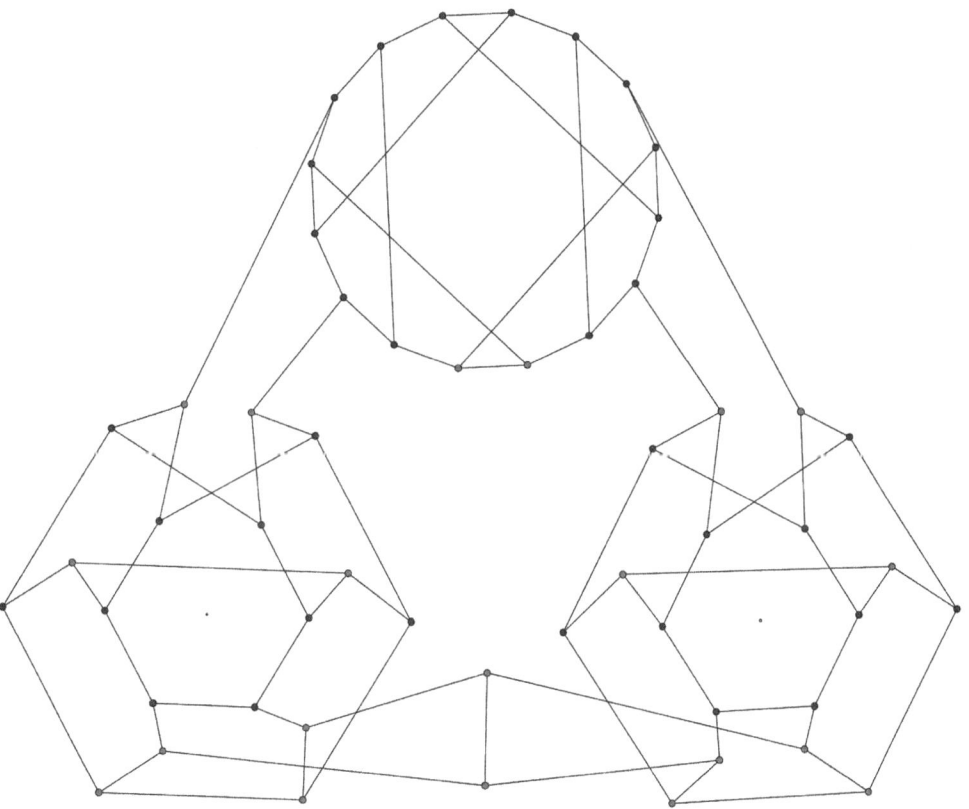

Figure 141: The second Ellingham-Horton graph.

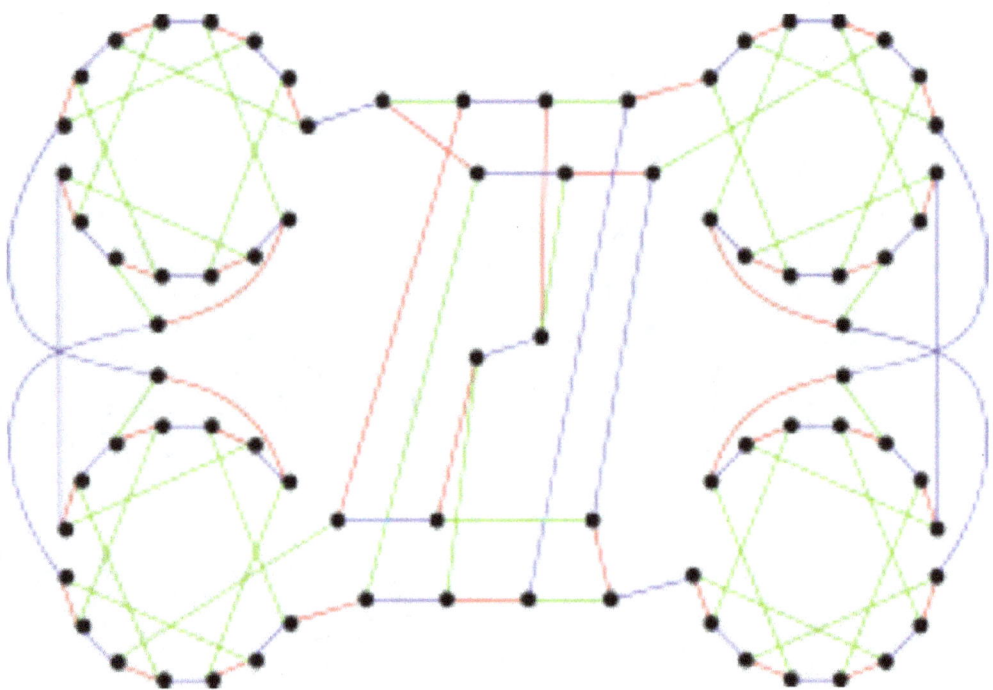

Figure 142: The first Ellingham-Horton graph 3-edge colored.

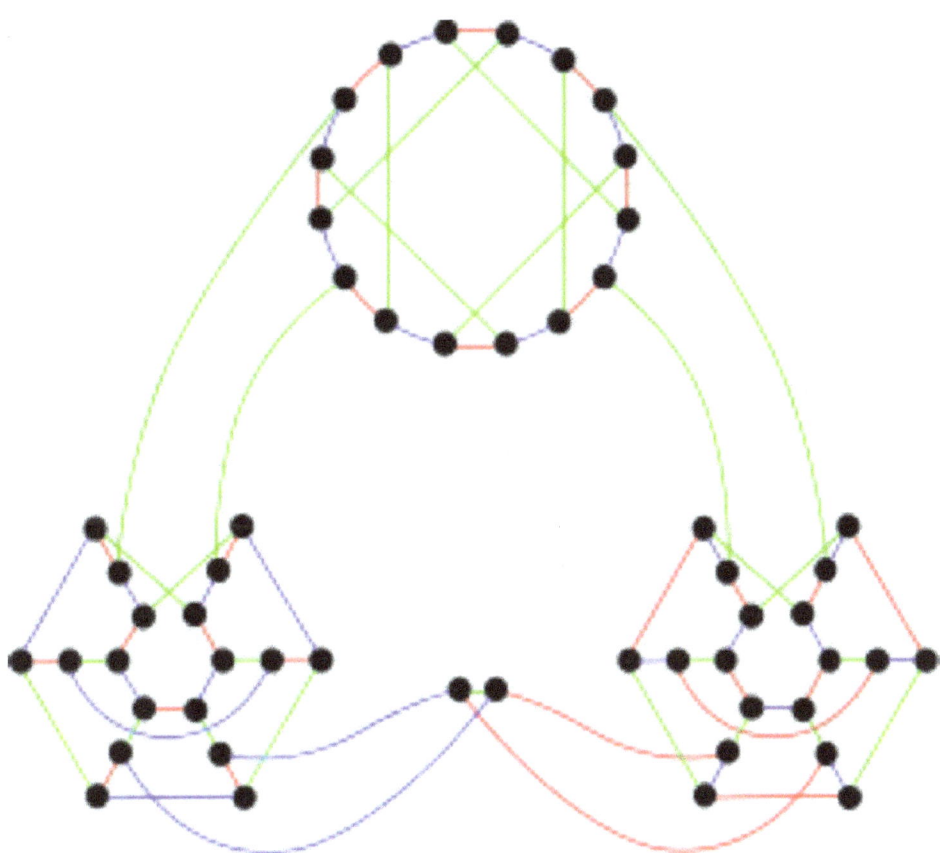

Figure 143: The second Ellingham-Horton graph 3-edge colored.

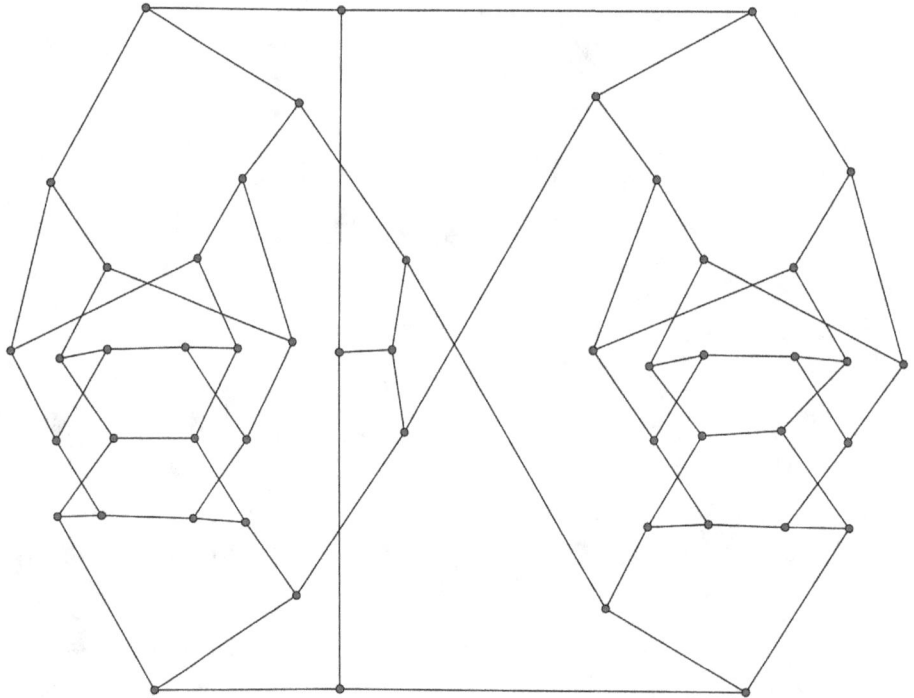

Figure 144: Georges graph.

I.14.4 Barnette's conjectures

We have thus seen that both Tait's and Tutte's conjectures have been disproved by counterexamples that are by themselves interesting. David W. Barnette (1969) proposed a weakened combination of Tait's and Tutte's conjectures, stating

> "every 3-regular, bipartite polyhedral graph is Hamiltonian... —"

or, equivalently, that every counterexample to Tait's conjecture is non-bipartite.

Barnette's conjecture is an unsolved problem in graph theory. The conjecture is named after David W. Barnette, a professor emeritus at the University of California, Davis. For some more information, see the website

https://en.wikipedia.org/wiki/Barnette

Equivalent forms

Kelmans (1994) showed that Barnette's conjecture is equivalent to a superficially stronger statement, that for every two edges e and f on the same face of a bipartite cubic polyhedron, there exists a Hamiltonian cycle that contains e but does not contain f. Clearly, if this statement is true, then every bipartite cubic polyhedron contains a Hamiltonian cycle: just choose e and f arbitrarily. In the other directions, Kelman showed that a counterexample could be transformed into a counterexample to the original Barnette conjecture.

Barnette's conjecture is also equivalent to the statement that the vertices of the dual of every cubic bipartite polyhedral graph can be partitioned into two subsets in such a way that every cycle of the dual passes through both subsets; that is, the dual can be covered by two induced forests. The cut induced by such a partition in the dual graph corresponds to a Hamiltonian cycle in the primal graph.

Partial results

Although the truth of Barnette's conjecture remains unknown, computational experiments have shown that there is no counterexample with fewer than 86 vertices. [2]

If Barnette's conjecture turns out to be false, then it can be shown to be NP-complete to test whether a bipartite cubic polyhedron is Hamiltonian. [3] If a planar graph is bipartite and cubic but only 2-connected, then it may be non-Hamiltonian, and it is NP-complete to test Hamiltonicity for these graphs.

Related problems

A related conjecture of Barnette states that every cubic polyhedral graph in which all faces have six or fewer edges is Hamiltonian. Computational experiments have shown that, if a counterexample exists, it would have to have more than 177 vertices.

I.14.5 Snarks

Definition 59 (Nontrivial edge cut). A *d-edge cut* for a connected graph G is a subset of its edges, removal of which separates the graph into two or more components. An edge cut is called *trivial* if one of these components consists of a single vertex. An edge cut is called *nontrivial* if each one of these components contains at least two vertices.

Definition 60. A *snark* is a 3-regular simple graph G with the following properties:

- the graph has connectivity $\kappa = 3$;
- the graph has only 3-edge-cuts that separate a single vertex;
- the graph contains no triangles or squares;
- the graph is 4-edge chromatic: $\chi' = 4$.

Problem 183. *Check that the Petersen graph is a snark.*

Problem 184. *The figure on page 216 shows the 5-pseudo flower snark. Find a proper 3-edge coloring. Conclude that the the 5-pseudo-snark is not a snark.* [15]
Use cycles formed from two of your three colors to look for a Hamiltonian cycle; alternatively, find a Hamiltonian cycle directly.

Problem 185. *The 5-flower snark is obtained from this graph by means of a single square-switch, of the type shown in formula (square-switch). The figure on page 217 shows the resulting 5-flower snark. Explain how the square-switch is applied. Check that the square-switch joins two 5-cycles into one 10-cycle. Check that the 5-flower snark is indeed a snark.*

Problem 186. *Find proper 3-edge colorings for the 6-pseudo-snark from the figure on page 218. Conclude that the the 6-pseudo-snark is not a snark.*
Use cycles formed from two of your three colors to look for a Hamiltonian cycle. Check all three color combinations in your example.

Answer.

Problem 187. *Find proper 3-edge colorings for the 6-cycle flower snark from the figure on page 219. Conclude that the 6-flower-snark is not a snark, but only a pseudo-snark.*
Use cycles formed from two of your three colors to look for a Hamiltonian cycle; or find a Hamiltonian cycle directly. Check all three color combinations in your example.

Answer.

---
[15] Not every toy dragon is a dragon.

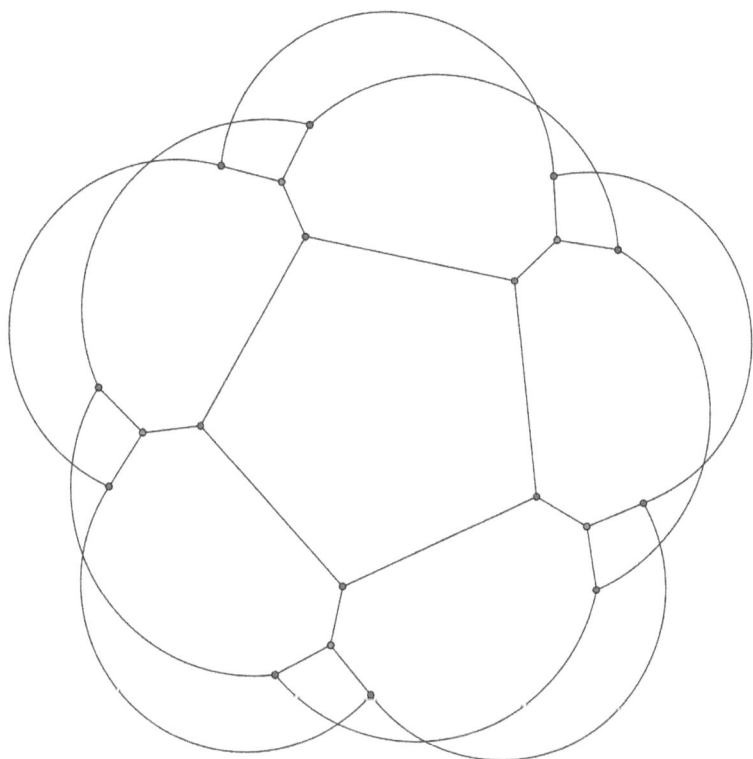

Figure 145: A 5-cycle pseudo-flower snark.

Proposition 68. *The n-pseudo-flower snarks are 3-edge colorable for all $n \geq 3$. Hence none of these graphs is a snark.*

Proof. The automorphism group $\text{Aut}(G)$ for the n-pseudo-flower snark G with $n \geq 3$ contains the direct product of the dihedral group D_n and the symmetric group S_3.

$$\text{Aut}(G) \supseteq D_n \times S_3$$

Here the action of the dihedral group is by rotations and reflections for the graph, which is to be drawn with its obvious n-fold symmetry. The action of the symmetric group is by simultaneous rotations and reflections of the n stars $K_{1,3}$.

We may color the edges of G in the following way: At first 3-color the central n-cycle in any proper way. Then one may 3-color the adjacent n edges properly. Next, we 3-color the edges of each one of the n stars $K_{1,3}$ such that the edges adjacent to its respective central vertex D get the colors 1, 2 and 3 surrounding vertex D counterclockwise. One can complete the 3-edge coloring to cover the edges of the remaining two n-cycles, indeed uniquely.

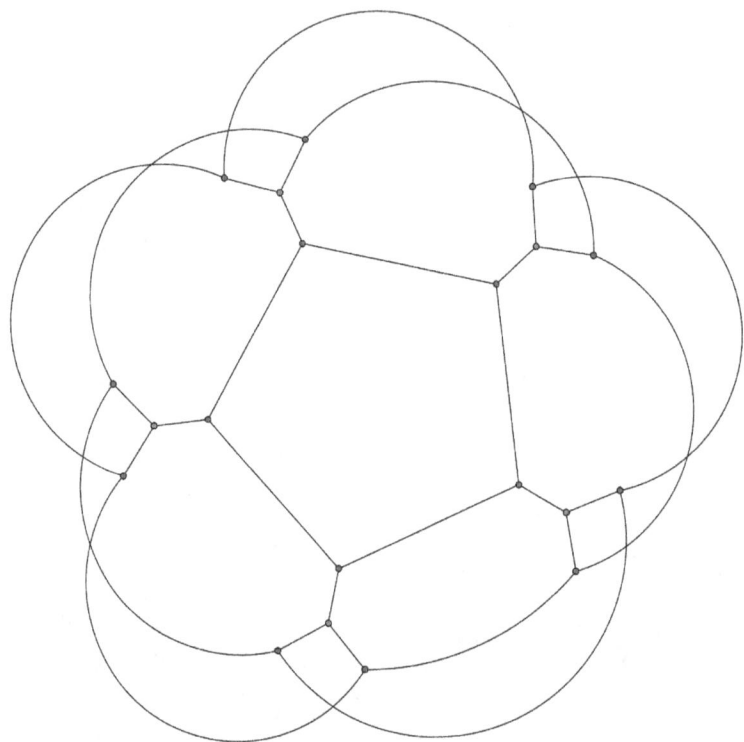

Figure 146: A 5-cycle flower snark.

For any permutation $\pi \in S_3$ let $C(\pi)$ denote the corresponding permutation of the three colors. Let $D(\pi) \in \text{Aut}(G)$ denote its action on the n-pseudo-snark G. By the process described above, one obtains a 3-edge coloring of the n-pseudo-snark G such that

$$C(\pi) = D(\pi) \quad \text{for all } \pi \in S_3$$

□

Problem 188. *Find proper 3-edge colorings for the 7-pseudo-snark, following the procedure from proposition 68.*

Answer.

Proposition 69. *The n-flower pseudo-snarks and the n-flower snarks are 3-edge colorable for all even $n \geq 4$. Hence none of these graphs is a snark.*

Proof. For even n, the n-flower pseudo-snark is bipartite. By the Theorem 18 of König, for a bipartite graph, the edge-chromatic number equals the maximal degree. Especially, the 3-regular bipartite graphs are 3-edge colorable.

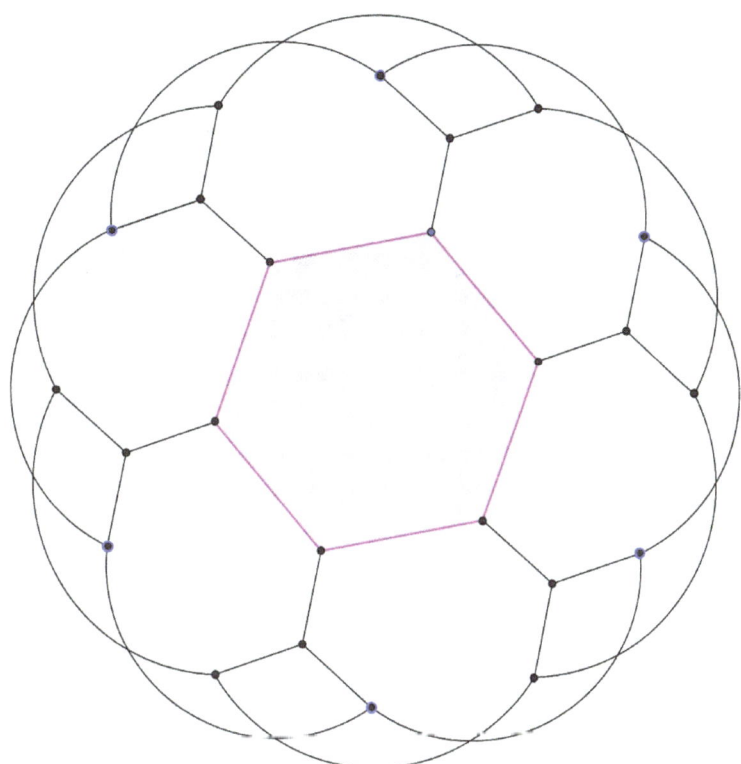

Figure 147: A 6-cycle pseudo-flower snark.

The n-flower snark is obtained from this n-flower pseudo-snark by means of a single square-switch, of the type shown in formula (square-switch). One may check that this square-switch leaves the graph to be bipartite. Thus the n-flower snarks are bipartite, and hence 3-edge colorable for all *even $n \geq 4$*. □

Remark 42. The proposition 68 begs the question: Which ones of the n-flower snarks are indeed snarks? My conjecture is that they are snarks is and only if $n \geq 5$ and n is odd.

Problem 189. *The square-switch which turns a n-pseudo flower-snark into the n-flower-snark $\mathcal{SN}_n$ links two n-cycles into one $2n$-cycle. The square-switch changes the automorphism group, too. Check whether*

$$\mathrm{Aut}(\mathcal{SN}_n) \supseteq D_n \times S_2$$

contains the direct product of the dihedral group D_n and the symmetric group S_2. Here the action of the dihedral group D_n is by rotations and reflections for the graph, which is to be drawn in a manner that the n-cycle at the center has its obvious n-fold symmetry. The action of the

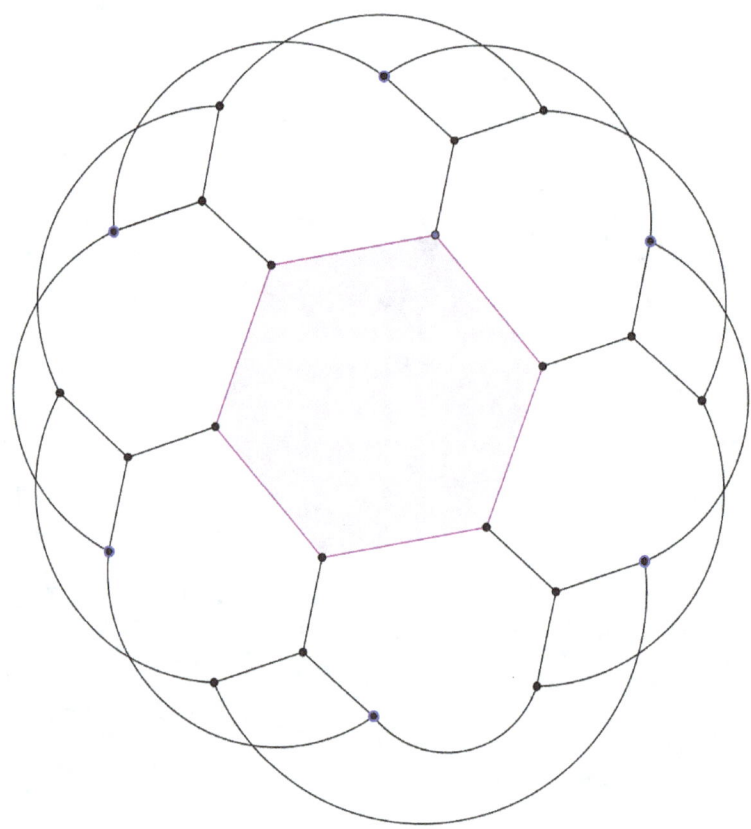

Figure 148: A 6-cycle flower snark.

symmetric group S_2 is by simultaneous switches of <u>only two</u> vertices in each one the n stars $K_{1,3}$. These vertices have to be from the long linked $\overline{2n\text{-cycle}}$.

Problem 190. *Find whether the 7-cycle flower snark has a proper 3-ege coloring.*

I use the figure on page 221. The colors for the stems emanating from the central 7-cycle, showed be tentatively colored in the three following ways:

$$1,2,3,3,3,3,3 \quad\quad 1,2,3,3,2,2,3 \quad\quad 1,2,2,2,3,3,3$$

Any other possibility may be reduced to these ones, using one or several symmetries. But any possible way to continue these 3-edge colorings finally leads to a conflict.

Problem 191. *Check that the first four graphs in the figure on page 222 are 3-edge colorable, and indeed Hamiltonian.*

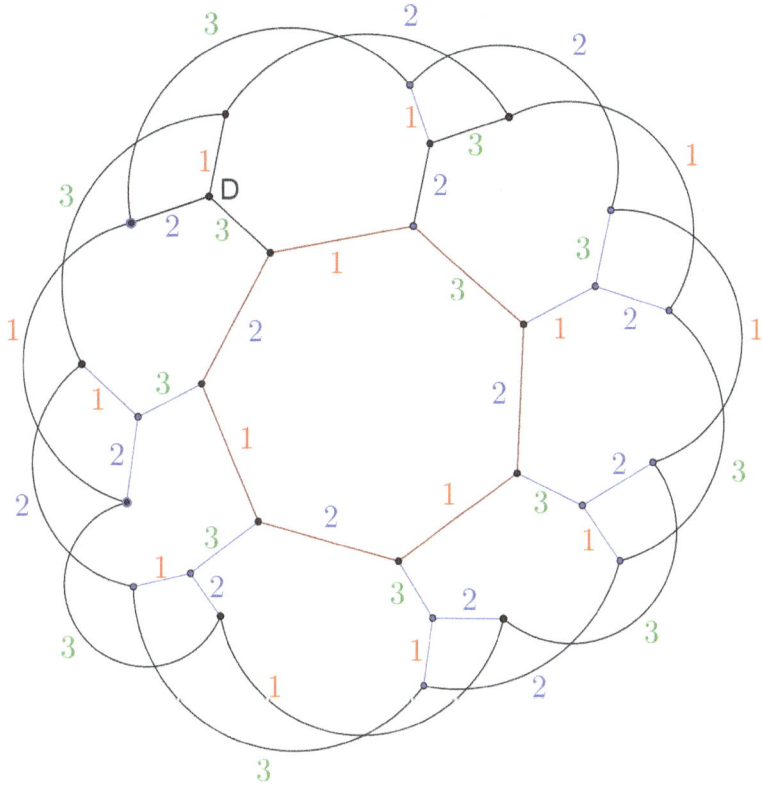

Figure 149: The regular 3-edge coloring which works for all n-pseudo-flower snarks.

Problem 192. *What about the two remaining graphs in the figure on page 222:*

(i) *Do they contain as a subgraph a subdivision of the Petersen graph? (Yes.)*

(ii) *Are they isomorphic to each other? (No, 6 respectively 5 five-cycles exist within each one.)*

(iii) *Are they 3-edge colorable? (Yes, both.)*

(iv) *Are the remaining two graphs snarks? (None is a snark.)*

(v) *Are the remaining two graphs Hamiltonian? (Yes, for both $1-2$ color cycle is Hamiltonian.)*

Answer.

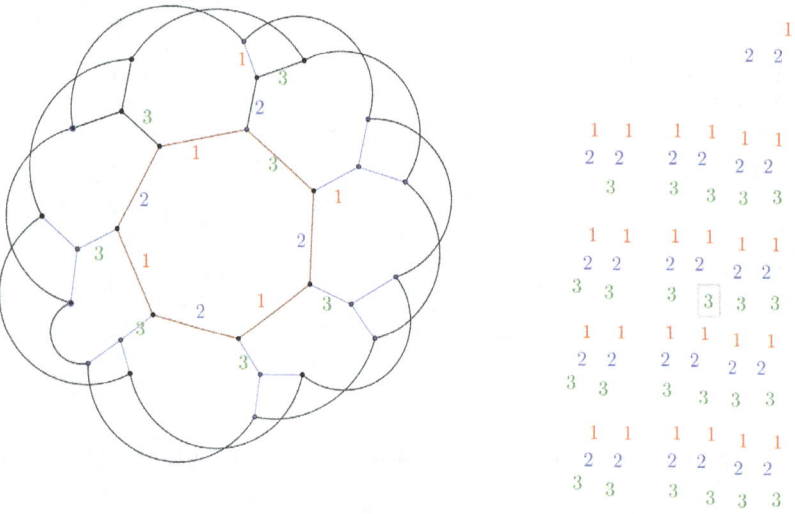

Figure 150: About the 7-cycle flower snark.

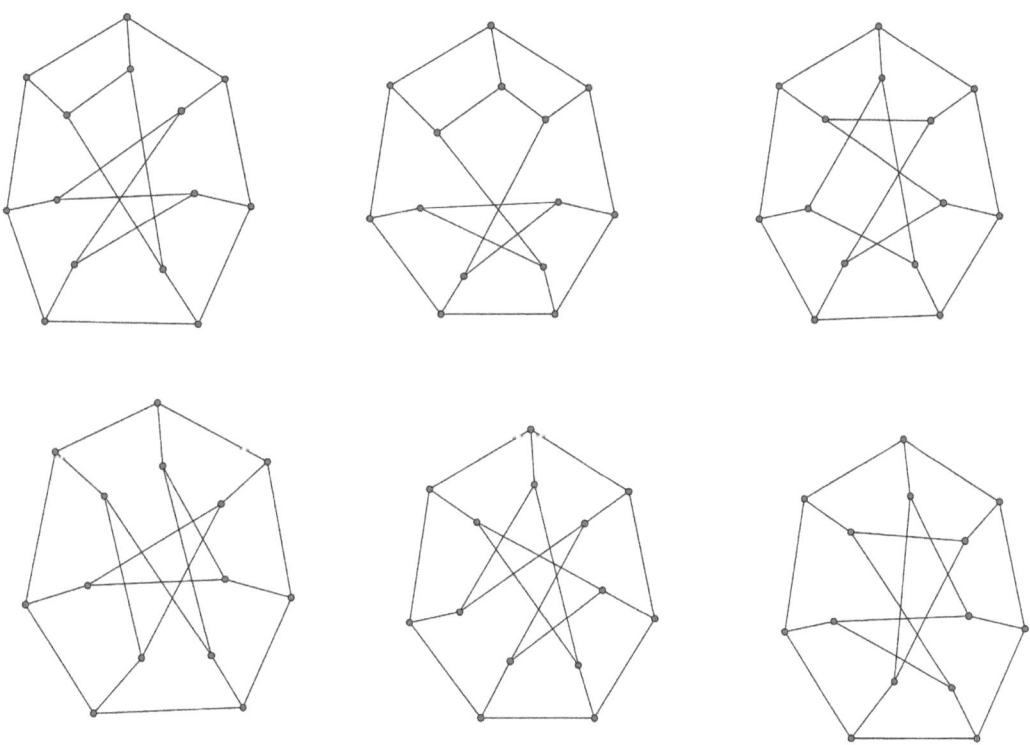

Figure 151: Which ones are snarks?

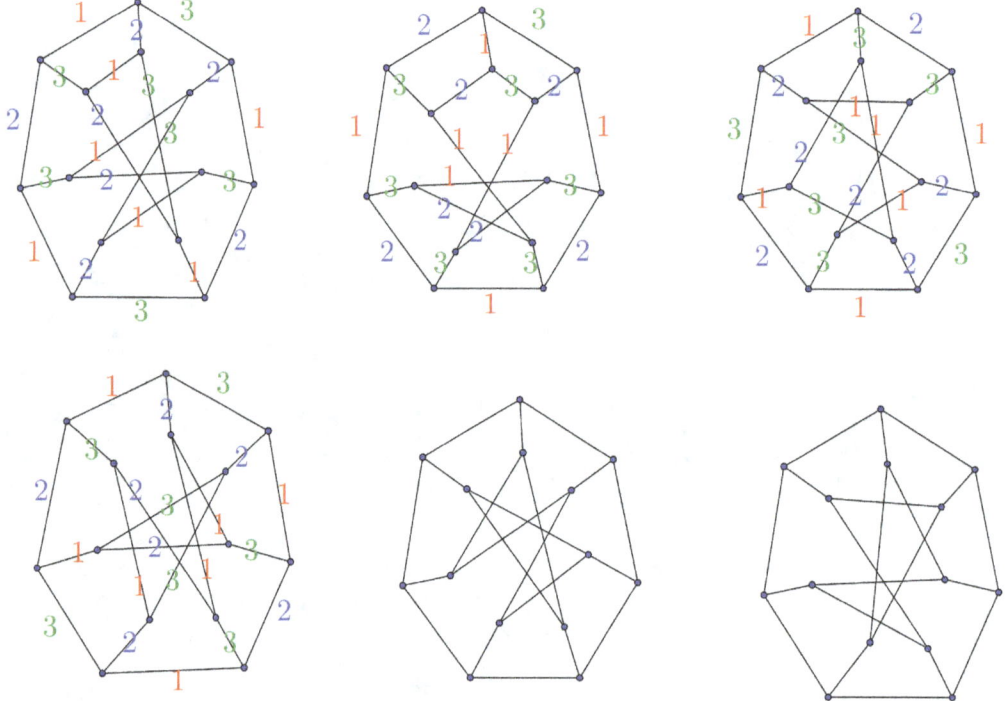

Figure 152: Which ones are snarks?

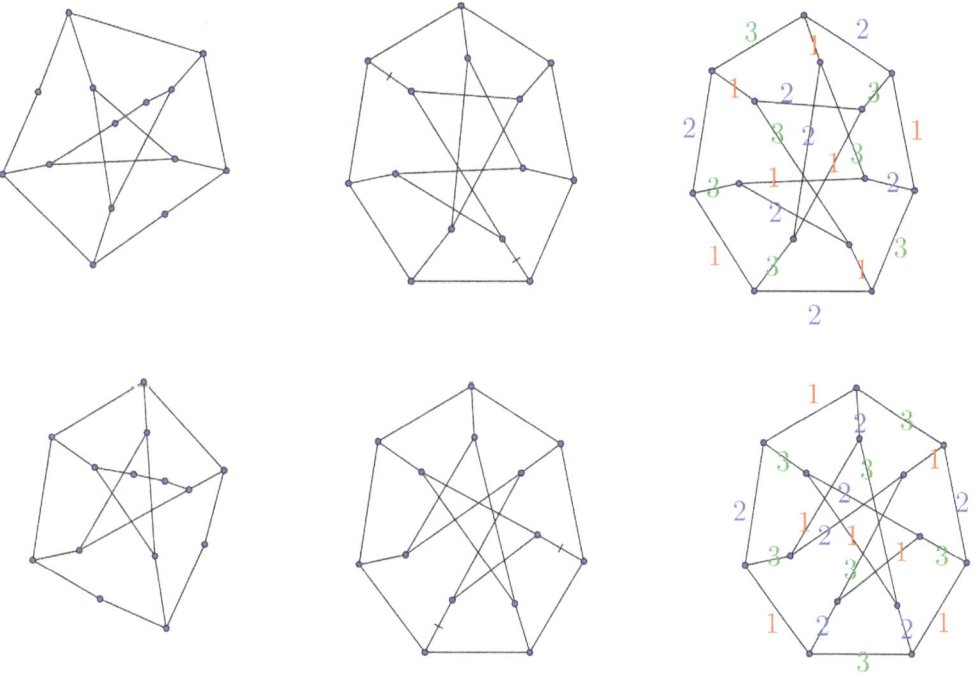

Figure 153: Which ones are snarks?

I.14.6 The landscape of 3-regular graphs

We have already defined for 3-regular graphs many interesting properties, and are discussing which relations exist among them. Each of these properties defines a subset of the class of all three-regular graphs. We depict these subsets schematically in a Venn diagram and put into the different regions of the diagram some example graphs. Such a Venn diagram I call a *landscape* of graphs. If we consider r properties and all 2^r fields are nonempty, we see there is non logical connection among the r properties. On the other hand, if we have a proof for a logical relations between the r properties, some of these 2^r regions is proved to be empty. In the context pursued below, we are especially interested in the three properties "planar", "bipartite" and "Hamiltonian".

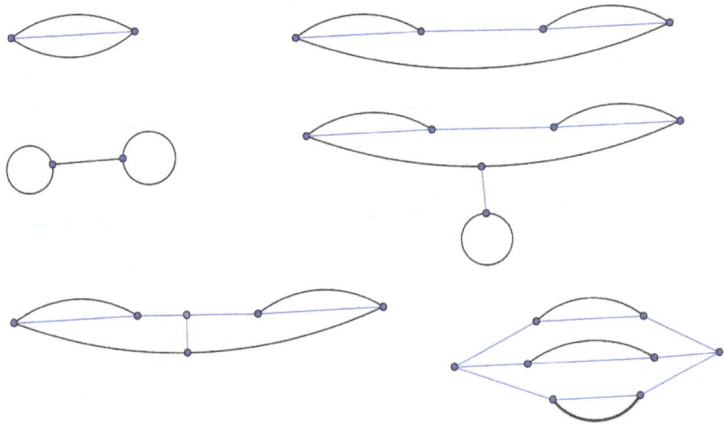

Figure 154: Some 3-regular graphs which are not simple.

Indeed there exist 3-regular graphs which are not simple. The figure on page 225 gives some examples. One may check that a 3-regular graph with a loop has a bridge, too; and a 3-regular graph with a multiple edge has vertex connectivity $\kappa \leq 2$. I intend to put apart these general graphs and restrict myself to simple graphs.

By Proposition 40, the vertex connectivity κ and the edge connectivity λ are equal for a 3-regular simple graph.

Problem 193. *Get an example for a 3-regular, 2-connected graph that is not 3-edge-colorable. My suggestion is to link two copies of the Petersen graph.*

There exists a surprisingly diverse collection of 3-regular simple graphs that are indeed 3-edge-colorable, as well as such graphs which are 4-edge chromatic. Among the 3-edge colorable graphs, there are all those which are either planar, bipartite or Hamiltonian. Indeed any one of these three properties implies $\chi' \leq 3$. This sweeping statement is obtained by combining the results from above:

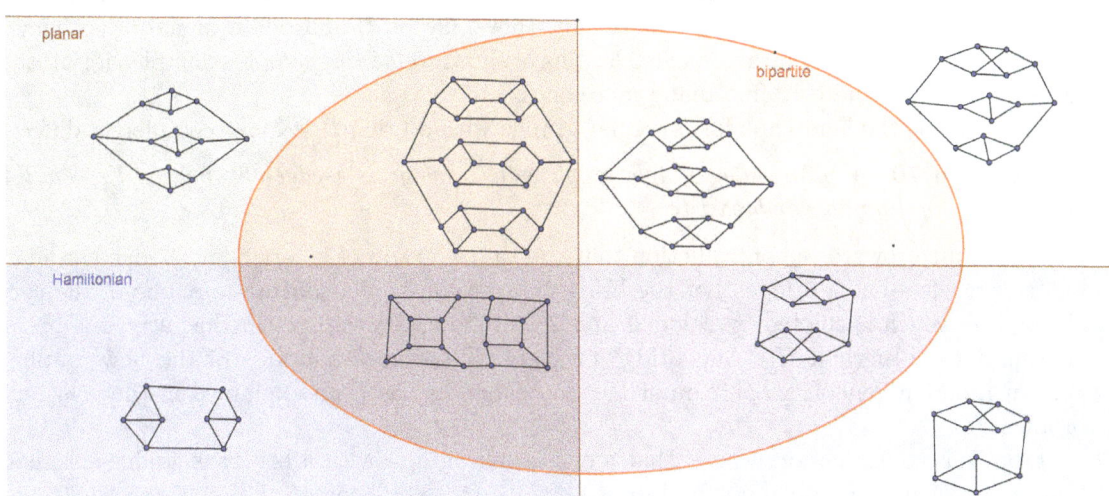

Figure 155: Landscape of 3-regular, 2-connected, 3-edge-colorable simple graphs.

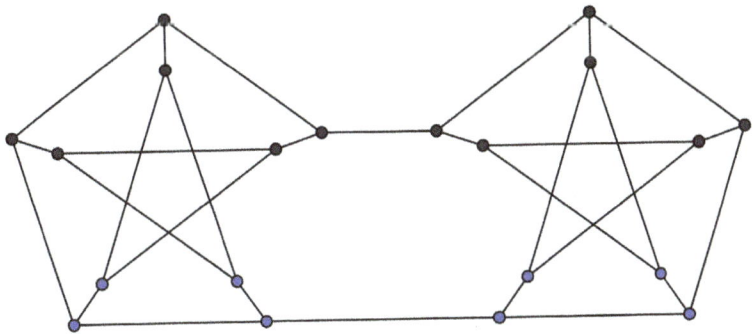

Figure 156: An example of a 3-regular, 2-connected, but 4-edge-chromatic graphs

- the four color theorem together with Tait's rule 58 imply that any bridgeless 3-regular graph is 3-edge colorable;

- Tait's proposition 66 tells any three-regular Hamiltonian graph is 3 edge-colorable;

- finally we apply the Theorem of König 18 to the 3-regular bipartite graphs, and conclude that these graphs are 3 edge-colorable.

Consequently, we get a landscape with eight cases for the 3-regular, 2-connected, and 3-edge-colorable graphs: they may be planar or not, they may be Hamiltonian or not, they may be bipartite or not. In the figure on page 226, I have shown relatively simple examples for all these cases. It is not too hard to find many more ones.

What about the landscape for 3-regular graphs with a bridge? It looks completely different.

Proposition 70. *Any 3-regular simple graph with a bridge is 4-edge-chromatic. Especially, it is neither Hamiltonian nor bipartite.*

Proof. Assume towards a contradiction that the simple graph G is 3-regular, 3-edge chromatic, but nevertheless has a bridge. Let the bridge have color 3. We contract any one of the cycles of graph G which is colored by colors 1 and 2 only, to a new vertex. In that way, one obtains an Eulerian multigraph H. Any bridge of graph G becomes a bridge of the new graph H. But an Eulerian general graph cannot have a bridge, as has been explained in the solution of problem 63.

From this contradiction, we see that any 3-regular graph with a bridge is 4-edge-chromatic. Especially, such a graph cannot be bipartite, since by the Theorem of König 18 any 3-regular bipartite graph is 3 edge-colorable. Neither can a graph with a bridge be Hamiltonian. □

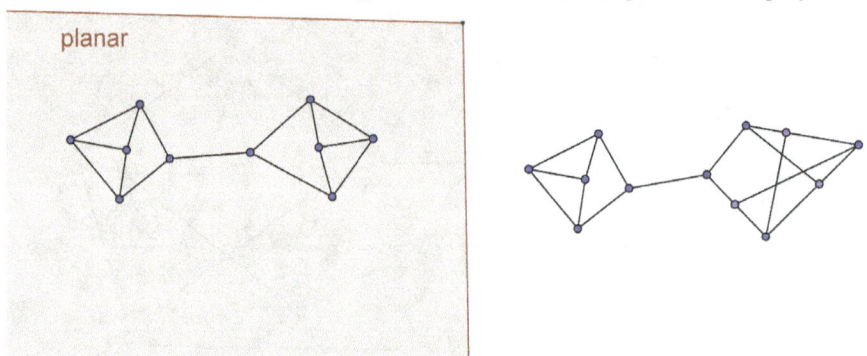

Figure 157: Landscape of 3-regular, 1-connected simple graphs.

Consequently the landscape for the 3-regular, 1-connected graphs gives me just two cases: these graphs may be either planar or not. In the figure on page 227, I have shown relatively simple examples for the two possible cases.

What about the vertex color number χ? Here a complete answer is easy and even independent from the connectivity: Clearly, $\chi = 2$ if and only if the graph is bipartite. By Brook's Theorem 16, the case $\chi = 4$ turns out to be very special: it occur just for one single case, the tetrahedron K_4. Otherwise, for all non bipartite cases we conclude $\chi = 3$.

What about their face color number χ^* for planar 3-regular graphs, with connectivity $\kappa = 2$ or $\kappa = 3$? By proposition ??, the bipartite ones have face color number $\chi^* = 3$. By proposition 59, for all non bipartite cases we get $\chi^* = 4$.

Problem 194. *Convince yourself that the 3-regular, 3-connected graphs are all simple.*

Answer. Disregarding the three-thick path, we have the following possibilities. Suppose a 3-regular, 3-connected has a loop at vertex u. There would exist an edge uv and $v \neq u$ has degree 3. If v has a loop, too, the graph has only two vertices and is hence not 3-connected. Otherwise, there exist further vertices besides u and v. Pulling out vertex v leaves two components. The vertex connectivity is $\kappa = 1$.

Suppose a 3-regular, 3-connected has two edges between vertices $v \neq u$ and no loop exists. There exist a further edge adjacent to u, another one adjacent to v and further vertices besides u and v. Pulling out vertex v leaves two components. The vertex connectivity is $\kappa = 1$.

We are now ready to attack the more interesting problem: to survey the landscape of the 3-regular, 3-connected simple graphs. At first we considered among them the 3-edge-colorable ones. I have agreed with definition 51 to call the planar and 3-connected graphs polyhedral. More important, by the Theorem of Steinitz, the polyhedral graphs correspond one to one to the three dimensional convex polyhedra. There is no easy proof of this nice theorem. At least, the special assertion that all 3-regular, 3-connected planar graphs are polyhedra is proved in Barnette's book [?]. The more easy converse shall also be proved in a further second part of these notes.

Using these insights, we may get among the Archimedean bodies and especially the prisms some nice examples to fill out more fields in our landscape on page 233. The odd prisms $P_2 \times C_{2n+1}$ with $n \geq 1$ give examples for 3-regular polyhedral graphs that are non-bipartite, planar and Hamiltonian. The even prisms $P_2 \times C_{2n}$ with $n \geq 2$ give examples for 3-regular polyhedral graphs that are bipartite, planar and Hamiltonian. See also problem 170.

It is harder to find examples for graphs which are 3-regular, 3-connected and 3-edge-colorable, but still neither Hamiltonian, nor bipartite, nor planar.

Problem 195. *Check if the graph in the figure on page 229 is neither planar, nor Hamiltonian, nor bipartite, but is indeed 3-edge colorable.*

Answer. By successively contracting adjacent vertices, each one of the three Tutte-triangles can be contracted to a single vertex. If the original graph G in the figure on page 229 would be planar, the contraction would be planar, too. But the contraction produces the complete bipartite graph $K_{3,3}$, which is known to be non-planar, as we have seen in problem 152. Hence the graph G is non-planar.

As we have seen in problem 177, a path though all vertices of a Tutte triangle has to leave or enter the triangle at vertex z_i. A Hamiltonian cycle for graph G would have to contain all three edges z_1A, z_2A, and z_3A,—which is impossible. Hence graph G is not Hamiltonian.

The graph G is not bipartite since many odd cycles exist. A proper 3-edge coloring of graph G is produced in the figure on page 230.

Problem 196. *Check that a path though all vertices of a Rotherberg triangle can either enter at x and leave at z, or enter at y and leave at z. Such a path can never avoid leaving at z.*

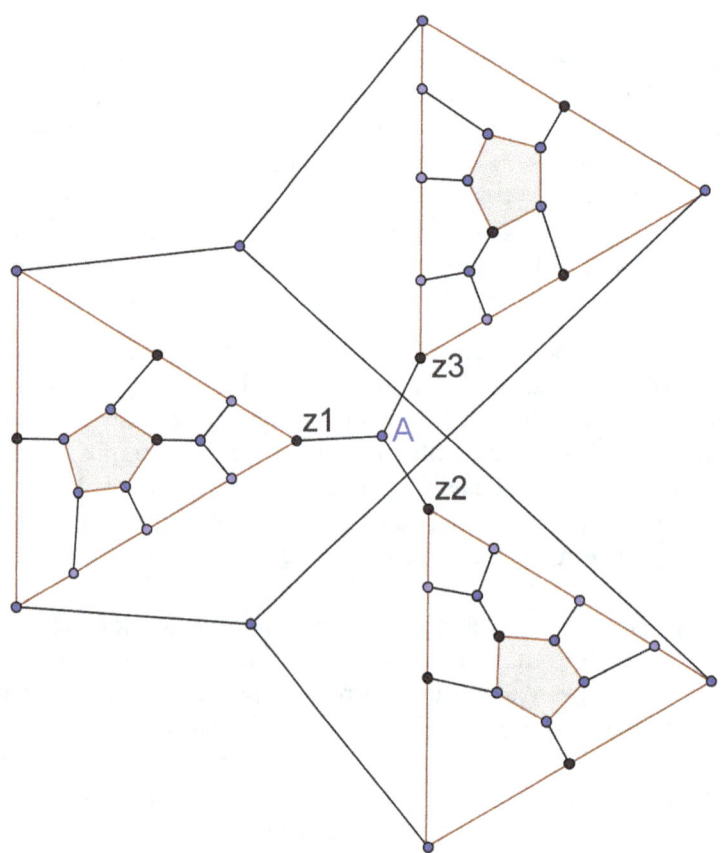

Figure 158: A 3-regular, 3-connected, 3-edge-colorable graphs which is neither Hamiltonian, nor bipartite, nor planar.

Answer. Consider a path entering the Rotherberg triangle at y and leaving at x. Such a path cannot visit all vertices if both the first and the last arc go towards and from z since then the vertex between x and y cannot be visited. The path could only possibly visit all vertices for the cases where the first and last arc are as shown in the figure on page 232, or a pattern obtained by an automorphism symmetry. Indeed, the Rotherberg triangle has an automorphism fixing vertex z and exchanging vertices x and y.

Hence it is enough to consider the cases drawn in the above mentioned figure. Going through all possible continuations of the beginning, and end part of the path, we find: A path entering the Rotherberg triangle at y and leaving at x can visit only 9 or 10, but not all 11 vertices. Consequently, a path visiting all 11 vertices and entering at x or y has to leave at z.

Problem 197. *Give a reason why the graph shown in the figure on page 231 is not Hamiltonian.*

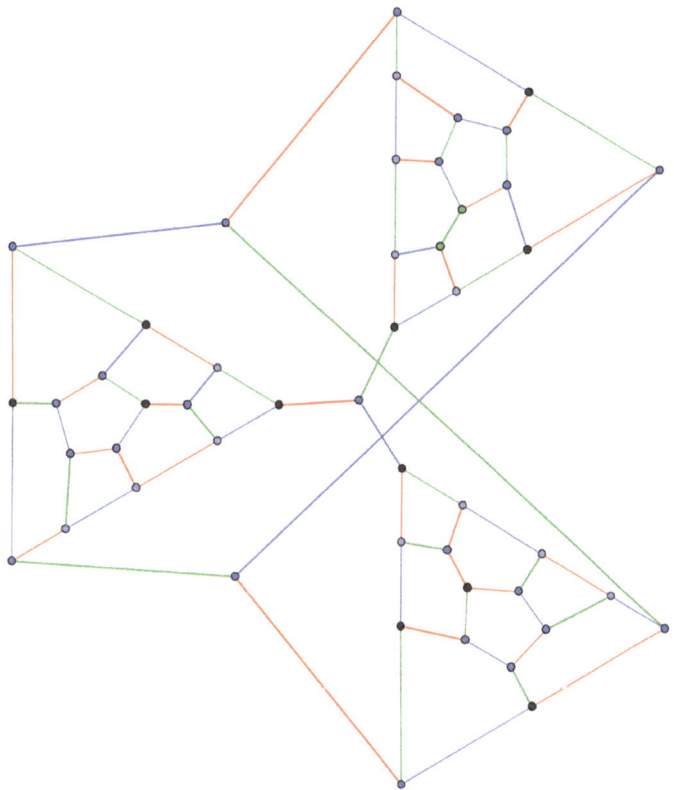

Figure 159: A 3-regular, 3-connected, 3-edge-colorable graph which is neither Hamiltonian, nor bipartite, nor planar.

Show the graph is semi-Hamiltonian.

In the figure on page 233, I have shown (relatively simple!) examples for the seven cases which are known to occur.

Problem 198. *Go through the entire script, and gather more examples in the landscape of the 3-regular, 3-connected, and 3-edge-colorable simple graphs.*

Now only a word about the 3-regular, 3-connected simple graphs which are 4-edge-chromatic. The most surprising ones are the *snarks*, see definition 60. Some are not, since they contain squares or even triangles.

Problem 199. *Check if the graph on the right side in the figure on page 234 is 4-edge chromatic, and moreover neither planar, nor Hamiltonian, nor bipartite.*

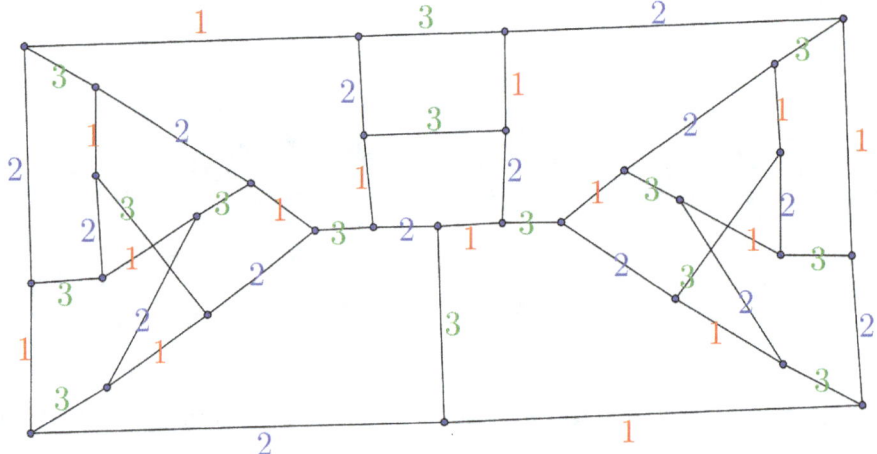

Figure 160: Rotherberg graph.

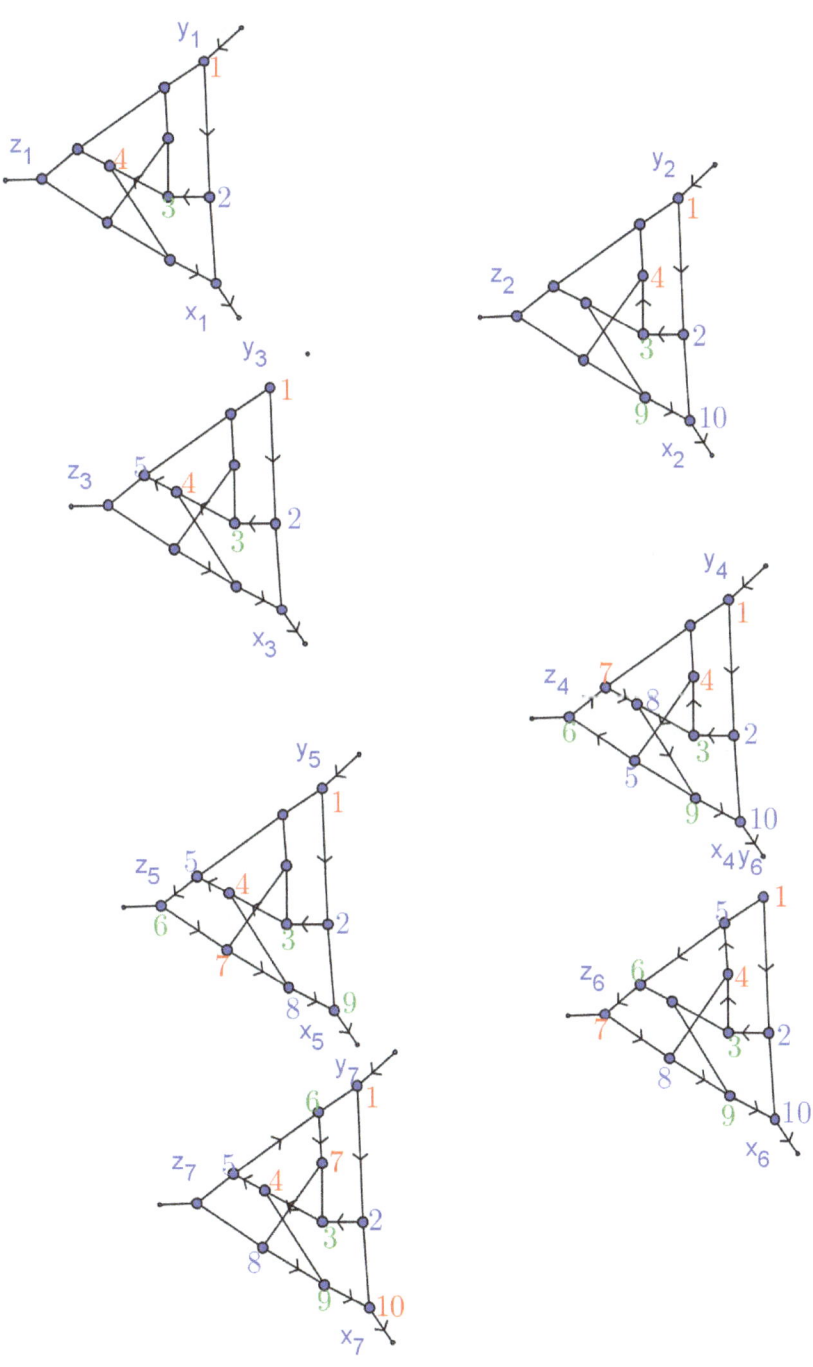

Figure 161: Paths in a Rotherberg triangle.

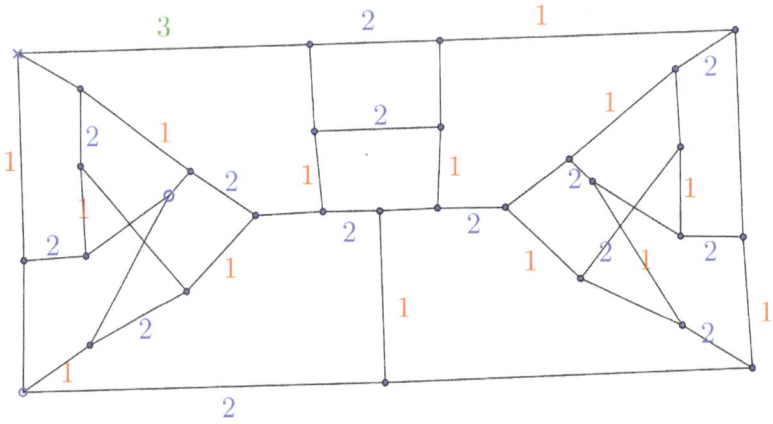

Figure 162: A cycle through 29 of the 30 vertices.

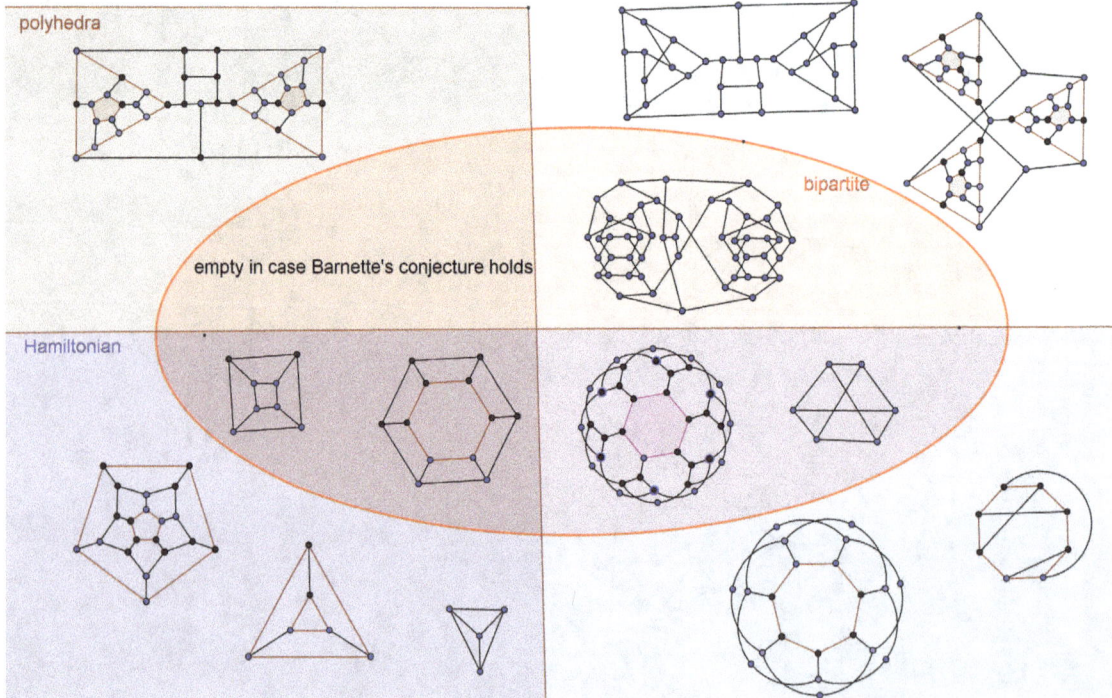

Figure 163: Landscape of 3-regular, 3-connected, 3-edge-colorable graphs.

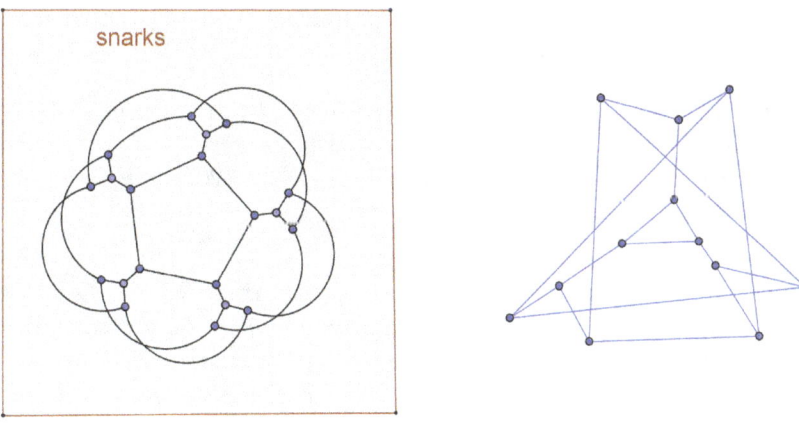

Figure 164: Landscape of 3-regular, 3-connected, 4-chromatic graphs.

I.14.7 Questions

The landscape of the 3-regular, 3-connected graphs puts up plenty of questions, some of which are of remarkable difficulty. It is natural to ask for the smallest graph in each field of the landscapes from the figures on page 233 and 234. For the Hamiltonian graphs, this is a rather easy question.

Problem 200. *Find the smallest 3-regular, 3-connected Hamiltonian graph that is*

(i) *planar and bipartite;*

(ii) *planar but not bipartite;*

(iii) *bipartite but nor planar;*

(iv) *neither bipartite nor planar.*

Non-Hamiltonian graphs, with additionel properties required, are hard to construct. The following two problems are supposed to stress this point.

Problem 201. *The Lederberg-graph is depicted in the figure on page 201. We have shown in problems 177 and 178 that it is not Hamiltonian. The "Lederturn graph" is obtained by rotating one of the two Tutte-triangles in the Lederberg graph by 120°, and reconnecting the triangle. Show that the Lederturn-graph* [16] *is Hamiltonian.*

Problem 202. *As mentioned below in the proof of proposition 72, the mate of any two snarks is again a snark, hence 4-edge chromatic and not Hamiltonian. The mating of two Petersen graphs is shown in the figure on page 242. Only the mate of two* snarks *is always again a snark. Show that the mate of the Petersen graph with the 5-flower pseudo-snark is Hamiltonian,— hence 3-edge colorable and* not *a snark.*

---

[16]That is my own nickname.

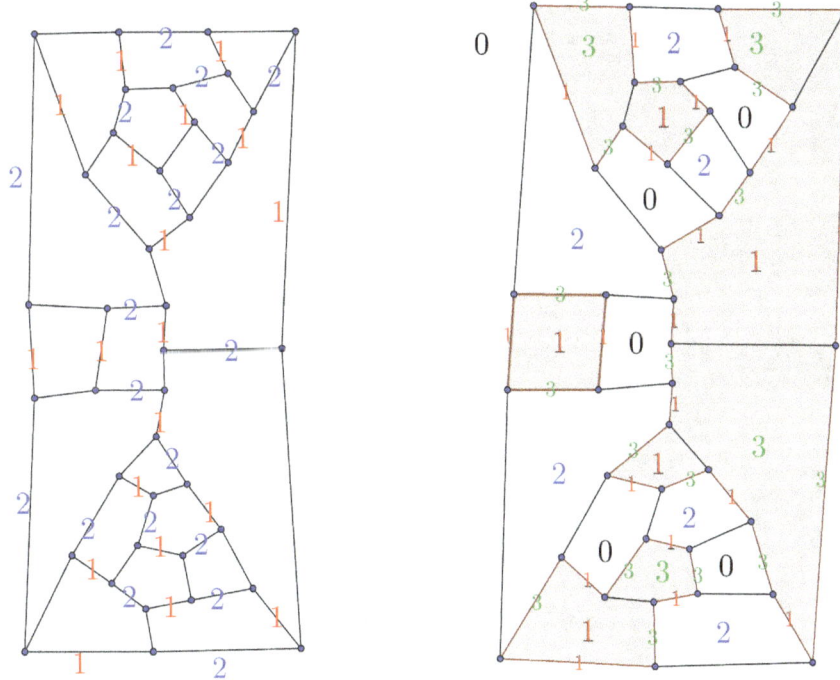

Figure 165: The Leder-turn graph is Hamiltonian.

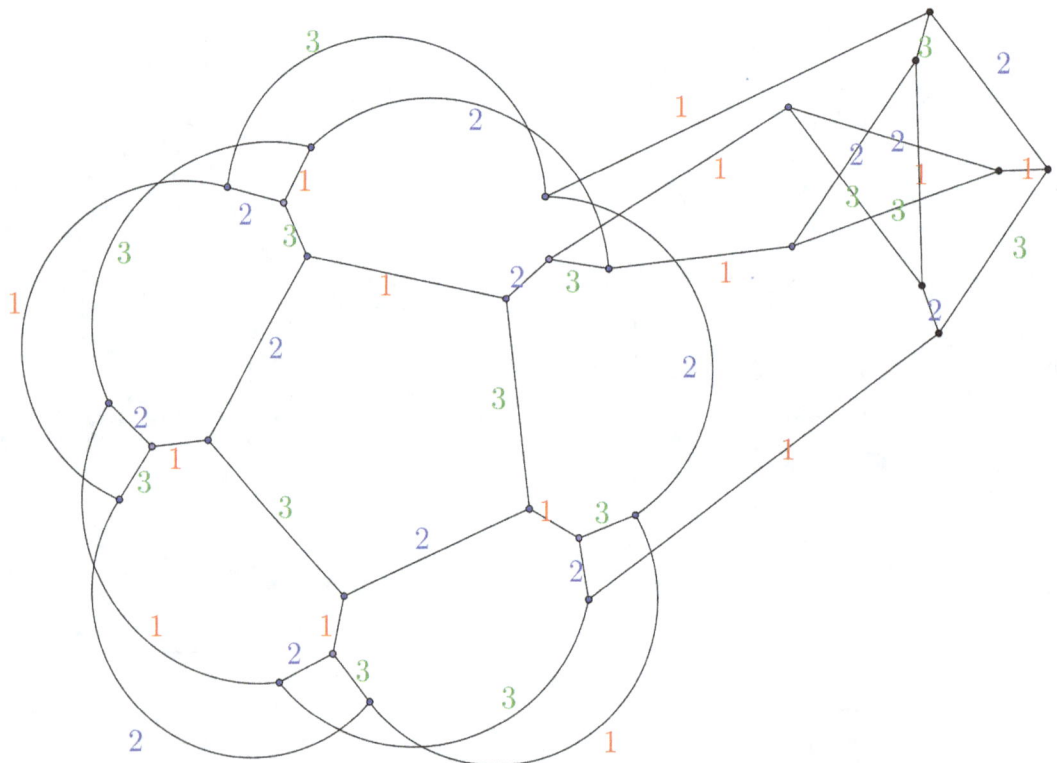

Figure 166: Mating the Petersen graph with a pseudo-snark does not produce a snark.

Thus the non-Hamiltonian case gives really tough questions. To somehow estimate how tough, the reader should look again at the figures above from page 222, and page 183. All these examples just do not solve the problems below.

Open problem 3. *Find the smallest 3-regular, 3-connected graph that is planar and bipartite, but not Hamiltonian. Such a graph exists if and only if Barnette's conjecture turns out to be false.*

Open problem 4. *Find the smallest 3-regular, 3-connected graph that is planar, but neither bipartite nor Hamiltonian. Such a graph exists,—and it could indeed be the Lederberg graph depicted in the figure on page 201.*

Open problem 5. *Find the smallest 3-regular, 3-connected graph that is bipartite, but neither planar nor Hamiltonian. Such a graph exists,—and it could indeed be the Georges graph depicted in the figure on page 213.*

Open problem 6. *Find the smallest 3-regular, 3-connected and 3-edge colorable graph that is not Hamiltonian. Such a graph exists. But I do not think that I have found that example. Nevertheless, it may be the Rotherberg graph,* [17] *already depicted in the figure on page 231.*

Open problem 7. *Find the smallest 3-regular, 3-connected and 3-edge colorable graph that has only 3-edge cuts separating a single vertex, and is not Hamiltonian. Such graphs exist. It may indeed be the 42-Faulkner-Younger graph and the 42-Grinberg graph, which are depicted in the figure on page 202.*

Open problem 8. *Find all snarks with 20 or less vertices. Are there more than just what we have seen? Remember the Petersen graph, its double mate as shown in the figure on page 242, and the 5-flower snark shown in the figure on page 217.*

I.15 An independent proof of the Four-Color Theorem

Every 3-regular bridgeless planar graph which is 3-edge colorable, can easily be 4-face colored, too, using via Tait's rule 58. Thus it is enough for a proof of the four color theorem, to show that every 3-regular bridgeless planar graph is 3-edge colorable; or equivalently to show the contrapositive:

> every 3-regular bridgeless that is not 3-edge colorable, is not planar.

Indeed, guessing and including the reason why such a graph is not planar, Tutte made around 1967 the following 3-edge coloring conjecture:

> every 3-regular bridgeless that is not 3-edge colorable, contains a subdivision of the Petersen graph.

---

[17] I chosen the nickname "Rotherberg graph" since my math highschool teacher always called me Rother, and the graph resembles the Lederberg graph.

Clearly, we know that the Petersen graph is not planar. This has been shown above, even in two different ways, by problems 153 and 157. The reader should recall the notion "subdivision" from definition 52; and the notion "graph G contains a subdivision of graph H" from definition 53. Any graph G which contains a subdivision of a non-planar graph H can neither be planar. Unlike Tutte's other conjectures, the conjecture above has meanwhile been proved!

Theorem 19 (Robertson, Sanders, Seymour, and Thomas 2001). *Every 3-regular bridgeless and 4-edge chromatic graph contains a subdivision of the Petersen graph.*

This statement is far reaching and hard to deduct! It has been proved, around 2001, in a series of five papers. Its computer assisted proof uses discharging methods. One reason the statement is so interesting, is the independent proof of the Four-Color Theorem following directly as a corollary of theorem 19.

Corollary 14 (A second way to the four color theorem). *Every 3-regular bridgeless 4-chromatic graph contains a subdivision of the Petersen graph. Every 3-regular bridgeless 4-chromatic graph is non-planar.*

From the contrapositive we see: Every 3-regular bridgeless planar graph is 3-edge colorable; and via Tait's rule 58 also 4-face colorable. Thus the four color theorem follows.

This section only tries to give the flavor of these ideas. Above all, I want to explain some results about snarks, which were popularized by Martin Gardener. By definition 60, a *snark* is a 3-regular but 4-edge chromatic simple graph G with some additional properties. As a corollary to the Main Theorem 19 from Robertson, Sanders, Seymour, and Thomas 2001, we see:

Corollary 15. *Every snark contains a subdivision of the Petersen graph.*

Remark 43. This Corollary is still a very hard result! It would have been easy only in the case that would exist only finitely many, and indeed very few snarks. Since they are so difficult to construct, this false impression was considered to be possible in former times. Indeed there exist infinitely many snarks, as is proved in proposition 72 below!

Proposition 71 (Finding the snark). *Every 3-regular bridgeless 4-chromatic graph G contains a subdivision of a snark.*

Lemma 37. *Suppose the 3-regular bridgeless 4-chromatic graph G has a triangle or square. Then graph G contains a subdivision of a proper subgraph H, written in symbols as $H \triangleleft G$. The graph H is 3-regular bridgeless and 4-chromatic.*

Proof. We begin with the case that the given graph G contains a triangle. Subgraph H is obtained by deletion of the marked edge and the two crossed vertices, in the left part from the figure on page 240. Now we consider the case that the given graph G contains no triangles, but a square. Subgraph H is obtained by deletion of the two marked edge and the four crossed vertices, in the right part from the figure on page 240.

For each two examples, a proper 3-edge coloring of graph H can easily extended to a proper 3-edge coloring of the original graph G. Thus $\chi'(H) = 3$ implies $\chi'(G) = 3$. Hence, by the contrapositive, $\chi'(G) = 4$ implies $\chi'(H) = 4$. □

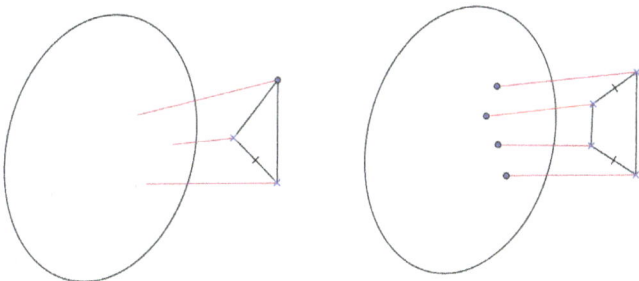

Figure 167: Subgraph H is obtained by deletion of the marked edges and crossed vertices.

Lemma 38. *Suppose the 3-regular bridgeless 4-chromatic graph G has a non-trivial 2-edge cut. Then graph G contains a subdivision of a proper subgraph H, which is also 3-regular bridgeless and 4-chromatic.*

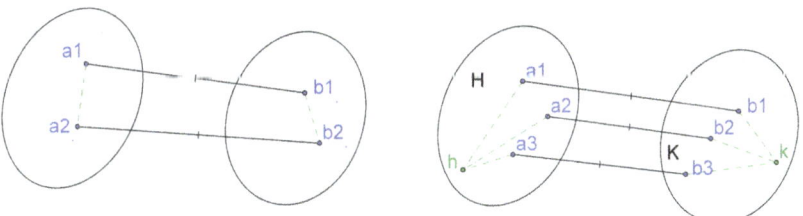

Figure 168: The cases of 2-edge and nontrivial 3-edge cut.

Proof. Suppose that the given graph G contains a 2-edge cut $\{e, f\}$. Let A and B the part of the graph G linked by these two edges e and f. The two edges have different end-vertices $a1, a2$ in A as well as $b1, b2$ in B. Otherwise a cut-vertex and a bridge would exist, which is ruled out. Thus one gets the situation as drawn in the left part from the figure on page 240.

Let H be the graph obtained from part A by joining vertices $a1$ and $a2$ by an extra edge. The graph H has a subdivision which is a subgraph of the original graph G. Indeed $H \triangleleft G$ holds since vertices $b1$ and $b2$ are linked by a path inside part B, and deletion of the vertices along this path leaves us with graph H.

Similarly, let K be the graph obtained from part B by joining vertices $b1$ and $b2$ by an extra edge. Again $K \triangleleft G$ holds since vertices $a1$ and $a2$ are linked by a path inside part A.

Suppose towards a contradiction that $\chi'(H) = \chi'(K) = 3$. For graphs H and K, we may choose two three colorings for which edges $a1a2$ and $b1b2$ get the same color. Now we can link the graphs H and K by edges $a1b1$ and $a2b2$, color them again with this same color, and obtain back the original graph, together with a proper 3-edge coloring. But this contradicts the assumption $\chi'(G) = 4$. Hence $\chi'(G) = 4$ implies that either $\chi'(H) = 4$ or $\chi'(K) = 4$.

Thus the graph G contains a subdivision of a proper subgraph, actually either H or K, which is also 3-regular bridgeless and 4-chromatic. $\square$

Lemma 39. *Suppose the 3-regular, 3-connected 4-chromatic graph G contains no triangles, but has a non-trivial 3-edge cut. Then graph G contains a subdivision of a proper subgraph H, which is also 3-regular bridgeless and 4-chromatic.*

Proof. Suppose that the given graph G contains a *non-trivial* 3-edge cut $\{e, f, g\}$. Let A and B the part of the graph G linked by these three edges. All three edges have different end-vertices $a1, a2, a3$ in A as well as $b1, b2, b3$ in B, for otherwise a 2-edge cut would exist, which is ruled out. Thus one gets the situation as drawn in the right part from the figure on page 240.

Let H be the graph obtained from part A by joining vertices $a1, a2$ and $a3$ by three extra edges to a new vertex h. The graph H has a subdivision which are subgraph of the original graph G. Indeed $H \triangleleft G$ holds since vertices $b1, b2$ and $b3$ are linked by two paths inside part B. Deletion of the vertices along these paths, with the exception of the branching point h, leaves us with graph H.

Similarly, let K be the graph obtained from part B by joining vertices $b1, b2$ and $b3$ by three extra edges to a new vertex $h..$ Again $K \triangleleft G$ holds since vertices $a1, a2$ and $a3$ are linked by two paths inside part A.

Suppose towards a contradiction that $\chi'(H) = \chi'(K) = 3$. For graphs H and K, we may choose two three colorings for which edges $a1h$ and $b1k$ get the same color, edges $a2h$ and $b2k$ get the same color, and edges $a3h$ and $b3k$ get the same color. Now we can delete vertices h and k, link the remaining graphs by edges $a1b1, a2b2$ and $a3b3$. The colors match, and we obtain back the original graph, with a proper 3-edge coloring. But this contradicts the assumption $\chi'(G) = 4$. Hence $\chi'(G) = 4$ implies that either $\chi'(H) = 4$ or $\chi'(K) = 4$.

Since the 3-edge cut is non-trivial we get indeed *proper* subgraphs H and K. Thus the graph G contains a subdivision of a proper subgraph, actually either H or K, which is also 3-regular bridgeless and 4-chromatic. $\square$

Problem 203. *The reader should check that $G \triangleright H$ and $H \triangleright K$ imply $G \triangleright K$.*

In other words, if graph G contains a subdivision of graph H, and graph H contains a subdivision of graph K, then graph G contains a subdivision of graph K.

Proof of proposition 71. In case the graph G is not itself a snark, at least one of the item from definition 60 fails. Either

- the graph has connectivity $\kappa = 2$; or
- the graph a nontrivial 3-edge-cut; or
- the graph contains a triangle or square.

By the lemmas 37, 38, 39 above, in each of these cases, the graph G contains a subdivision of a smaller 3-regular bridgeless 4-chromatic graph H. Since the graph is assumed to be finite, there can only be a finite chain

$$G \triangleright H \triangleright K \triangleright \cdots$$

Thus by repetition of the process, we arrive at a minimal H, which does not contains any subdivision of a proper subgraph. Hence the minimal graph H is a snark. □

Having found the snark is only the easy part. That was not clear from the beginning, since for a long time, only very few snarks where known. But it has indeed been proved

Proposition 72. *There are infinitely many snarks.*

This proposition is again a spoiler. How can one know that all snarks are non-planar? I have to rely on the specialists to have verified the big theorem 19. Moreover, the proof is still computer assisted and uses discharging methods; like the original proof of the four color theorem.

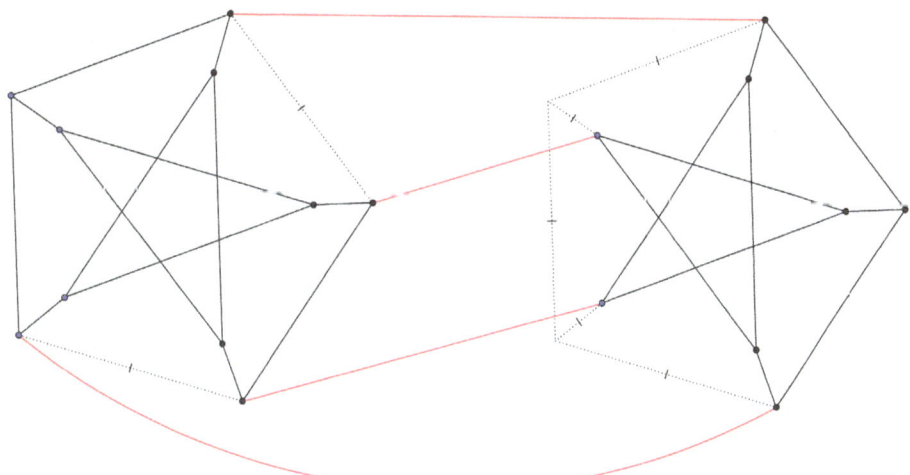

Figure 169: Mating of two Petersen graphs.

Proof of proposition 72. Any two snarks can produce a new snark by mating. The process is shown, for two Petersen graphs in the figure on page 242. Beginning with two Petersen graphs, and repeating the process, produces an infinite sequence of snarks. □

Bibliography

[1] J. A. Bondy and U. S. R. Murty, *Graph Theory with Applications*, North Holland, New York, 1976.

[2] Geir Agnarson and Raymond Greenlaw, *Graph Theory, Modeling, Applications and Algorithms*, Pearson and Prentice Hall, Upper saddle river, NJ 07458, 2007.

[3] Joan M. Aldous and Robin J. Wilson, *Graphs and Applications*, Springer, 2000.

[4] David Barnette, *Map Coloring, Polyhedra, and the Four-Color Problem*, The Mathematical Association of America, 1983.

[5] Robin Hartshorne, *Geometry: Euclid and Beyond*, second ed., Springer, 2002.

[6] Kenneth H. Rosen, *Handbook of Discrete and Combinatorical Mathematics*, CRC Press LLC, 2000.

[7] Douglas B. West, *Introduction to Graph Theory*, second ed., Prentice Hall, Upper saddle river, NJ 07458, 2001.

[8] Robin Wilson, *Four Colors Suffice*, Princeton University Press, 2002.

Index

adjacency matrix, **92**
adjacent, **5**
algorithm
    cycle game, 162
    degree sequence, 44
    Dijstra's, 119
    electrical network, 131
    Fleury's, 65
    Ford-Fulkerson, 123
    Hungarian, 126
    Kruskal's, 113
    planarity test, 175
    Prüfer, 105
    Prime's, 112
    travelling salesman
        nearest neighbor, 114
        sorted edges, 116
antiautomorphism, 18
automorphism group, **26**

bipartite graph, **30**
bottleneck lemma, 152
braced frames, 107
Brook's Theorem, 185

Cartesian product, **38**, 67
Cauchy-Binet Theorem, 140
Cayley's Theorem, 37, **105**
Chvátal's Theorem, 89
circuit, **12**
clique, **17**
component, **15**
connected, 17
connectivity
    edge, 145
    vertex, 145
cube, **39**
    four-dimensional, 56
cycle, **12**
    Hamiltonian, 67
    planar, 156
cycle rank, **100**, 187
cycles
    splitting into, 54

degree, **10**
    maximal, 10, 145
    minimal, 10, 145
degree sequence, **43**
dihedral group, 20
Dirac's Theorem, 83
dodecahedron, 200

edge, **5**
    number of, 100
edge coloring, 193
    bipartite graph, 193
    complete graph, 195
electrical networks, 128, 144
Euler's formula, 153

face, 153
    length, **153**, 164, 166
flowersnark, 171
Four-Color Theorem, 238

geometric dual, 191
graph, **5**
    acyclic, 99
    bipartite
        regular, 199

complete
    edge coloring, 195
complete bipartite graph, 8
complete graph, 8
connected, 14
cyclegraph, 8
demi-Hamiltonian, 70
Eulerian, 53, 99
general, 5
Grindberg, 158
Hamiltonian, 67, 99
join, 33
labelled, 36
non-Eulerian, 53
non-Hamiltonian, 67
nonplanar
    K_5, 169
    $K_{3,3}$, 169
    Petersen, 169
nullgraph, 8
octahedron, 95
pathgraph, 8
Petersen, 95
    semi-Hamiltonian, 68
planar, 153
polyhedral, 167
semi-Eulerian, 53
semi-Hamiltonian, 67
simple, 5
unlabelled, 36
graph, simple
    complement, 17
Groetzsch graph, 20

handshaking lemma, **10**, 32, 94
    dual, 154
homomorphism, 26

icosahedron
    Hamiltonian, 67
incidence matrix, **92**
independence, **17**
instant insanity, **48**

isomorphism, **18**, 180

König's Theorem, 193
König-Egervary Theorem, **35**, 126, 199
Kirchhoff's current law, 136
Kirchhoff's voltage law, 136

Lederberg graph, 201
Lederberg's graph, 203
line graph, **94**

map, 195
matching, **33**
Matrix-Tree Theorem, 139
maximal flow, 124
Menger's Theorem, 35, 62, **149**
    edge-form, 149
    vertex-form, 150
minimal edge-cut, 124

octahedron, **41**
Ore's Theorem, 83

partial order, 103
path, **12**
    Hamiltonian, 67
Petersen graph, 20, 215
    non-Hamiltonian, 199
    not 3-edge colorable, 199
pseudo-rhomb-cuboctahedron, 28
Pulling-out Theorem, 73

return lemma, 54

snark, 215
spanning tree, 105, **109**
    first-breadth, 109
    first-depth, 109
    number of, 141
subdivision, **171**
subgraph
    induced
        block, 148
subgraph, induced, **17**

Tait's (false) conjecture, 200
Tait's proposition, 199
Tait's rule, 203
trail, **12**
    Eulerian, 53
travelling salesman problem, 114
    lower bound, 116
tree, **99**
    labelled, 36, 105
    leaves, 101
    rooted, **103**
        ordered, 104
    unlabelled, 36
triangles
    nonexistence, 47
triangulation, 166
Tutte's counterexample, 200
Tutte's Petersen-conjecture, 239

vertex, **5**
vertex coloring, **184**
vertex cover, **33**
Vizing's Theorem, 193

walk, **12**
Whitney's Theorem, 145

www.ingramcontent.com/pod-product-compliance
Lightning Source LLC
Chambersburg PA
CBHW081344070526
44578CB00005B/719